A WORLD IN FLAMES

A World in Flames

A Short History of the Second World War in Europe and Asia, 1939–1945

Martin Kitchen

LONGMAN
London and New York

Longman Group UK Limited,
Longman House, Burnt Mill, Harlow,
Essex CM20 2JE, England
and Associated Companies throughout the world.

Published in the United States of America
by Longman Inc., New York

First published 1990

British Library Cataloguing in Publication Data
Kitchen, Martin, *1936–*
A world in flames : A short history of the Second World War in Europe and Asia, 1939–1945
1. World War Two
I. Title
940.53

ISBN 0–582–03408–6 CSD
ISBN 0–582–03407–8 PPR

Library of Congress Cataloging in Publication Data
Kitchen, Martin.
A world in flames : a short history of the Second World War in Europe and Asia. 1939–1945 / Martin Kitchen.
p. cm.
Includes bibliographical references.
ISBN 0–582–03408–6. — ISBN 0–582–03407–8 (pbk.)
1. World War, 1939–1945—Europe. 2. World War, 1939–1945—Asia.
I. Title. II. Title: World War 2.
D743.K53 1990
940.53—dc20 90–5531
CIP

Produced by Longman Singapore (Pte) Ltd
Printed in Singapore

We shall not capitulate – no never!
We may be destroyed, but if we are, we shall
drag a world with us – a world in flames.

Adolf Hitler at Nuremburg, 1939

Contents

List of Maps

Acknowledgements

The original impetus for writing this book was provided by the Distance Education Department of Simon Fraser University, who asked me to write a course on the Second World War centred around a series of television films. This proved to be a challenging and rewarding experience. I am particularly grateful to Colin Yerbury for the help he gave me in this project.

Beate Giuffre gave me skilful and dedicated assistance in tracking down the more obscure literature on the war, particularly in foreign languages, and I am greatly in her debt. I have plundered the works and picked the brains of so many fellow historians that it would be impossible to list them all. The bibliography, which lists only works in English, is too modest a tribute.

Dedications are so often a pathetic attempt to make amends for adultery, neglect or betrayal. I am in the enviable position of being able unblushingly to place this book in the hands of one for whose generosity, support and understanding it is pitifully inadequate recompense.

To Bettina

Introduction

The European war which began on 1 September 1939 was Hitler's war. Historians will continue to argue about the social, economic and political forces which prompted him to take a series of calculated risks which led to full-scale war. They will debate the ideological roots of Nazi Germany's bid for world power, and examine the decision making process in the Third Reich. Students will no doubt continue to write endless essays on whether Hitler had a blueprint for conquest or was essentially an improviser, impetuously reacting to events. It is unlikely that any of these issues will ever be finally settled, for history is a continuing dialogue between the present and the past, but it is unthinkable that Hitler will disappear from the picture. Only a purblind ideologue can envision him as the disembodied point of intersection of mysterious economic forces, or as the spirit of world history in jackboots. Nazi Germany is unthinkable without Hitler, as is Nazi Germany's war. That the invasion of Poland led to the most destructive and extensive war in history was due to Hitler's decisions to attack in the West in 1940 and then to invade the Soviet Union in 1941. He did not get quite the war he wanted, nor could he fight it on terms of his own choosing, but it was still his war.

It may be objected that such an argument is crudely personalistic and shifts the blame for all the evil done in the name of the German people on to one man. By being presented as a superhuman demon, Hitler becomes a convenient scapegoat. In fact, Hitler could never have done what he did had he not articulated so many of the desires and longings of his followers. He did not descend from the skies, nor was he the product of some arcane historical accident. His foreign policy, in spite of its excesses, its breathtaking changes of course and its daring gambles, was at least in part within the traditions of German foreign policy since Bismarck and was conducted, with a few notable exceptions, with the approval of the diplomatic and military elites as well as the vast majority of the German people. There were objections to his rapprochement with Poland in 1933, many feared that the remilitarization of the Rhineland in 1936 was far too risky a gamble, and there were similar misgivings over the invasion of Austria and the Sudeten crisis of 1938 which led to the Munich conference. There was, however, precious little opposition to the general direction of his policy, merely to his precipitous style.

Such objections from on high clearly show that Hitler was fully in command of Germany's foreign policy, a fact that even the sternest of structuralist historians is unable to deny. A dictator, however powerful, is forced to operate within a given social setting, is constrained by economic forces, and has to rely on the active support of his underlings. Hitler was no exception. He made history, but not in circumstances of his own choice.

Hitler's gamble that he could move into the Rhineland without France or Britain reacting was a triumphant success. The Stresa front of Britain, France and Italy had collapsed when the British and French gave singularly lukewarm support to the League of Nations sanctions against Italy for its invasion of Ethiopia. The French would not act without the full support of the British. The British would not act until there had been full consultation. The talks between Britain, France and Belgium were inconclusive. The political right wing in Britain and France felt that Hitler was perfectly justified in looking after his own back yard and accepted his argument that the Franco-Soviet pact, which was ratified by the French Chamber of Deputies on 27 February 1936, was a violation of the treaty of Locarno which guaranteed the Franco-German status quo.

Hitler skilfully exploited this widespread sympathy for his anti-Soviet stance, which had made it seem that he had marched into the Rhineland in order to stand up to the threat of world communism. In July he agreed to support Franco against the Spanish Popular Front Government, determined that Spain should not become part of a Franco-Soviet bloc aimed at Germany. Also in July he signed the anti-Comintern pact with Japan. Meanwhile, the system of collective security began to collapse. Poland and Czechoslovakia, both of whom had expressed their willingness to support France should

Hitler march into the Rhineland, were disgusted at the supine attitude of the French Government. Belgium, fearing that the Franco-Soviet pact was needlessly provocative to the Germans, announced its neutrality. This left France wide open to attack as there was no money available to extend the heavily fortified Maginot Line, which ran from Switzerland to the Belgian border, as far as the Channel. In both Britain and France the military were violently opposed to serious talks with the Russians, so that the Franco-Soviet pact greatly weakened the Western pact, which was rapidly disintegrating.

The Spanish Civil War, with its ideological frenzy and its appalling brutalities, had a profound effect on world opinion. For the right, the activities of the Soviet secret police, coupled with the blood-letting in the Moscow show trials, was further proof of the evils of communism. The left felt that the struggle against fascism would be won or lost in Spain. When it was lost, the gloomy comrades fatalistically resigned themselves to the inevitable triumph of fascism, comforting themselves with the thought that some corrupt bourgeois states would be crushed in the process, and that after a brief if unpleasant interlude the Red Dawn would finally break. Some of the more spectacular horrors of the war, skilfully exploited by master propagandists on the left, provided a hideous reminder of the likely consequences of a European war. The Basque town of Guernica had been flattened by German bombers and it was widely believed that Paris and London would meet a similar fate. The Spanish Civil War thus provided compelling arguments for those who wanted to appease the dictators, and further weakened the case of those who still argued for collective security.

In May of 1937 Neville Chamberlain became British Prime Minister. He laboured under the unfortunate illusion that Hitler and Mussolini were reasonable men with whom it was possible to negotiate in good faith. There were a number of reasons why he believed that war had to be avoided at all costs. He felt that money was better spent on social welfare than on armaments, for otherwise the Labour Party was liable to win the next election. He detested the Soviet Union and all that it stood for, and regarded the French as unreliable and spineless. He knew that he could not count on any support from the United States in its present isolationist mood. The service chiefs warned him that Britain was in no position to fight a war against Germany, Italy and Japan, and he was treated to horrific accounts from the military experts of the likely effects of a bomber offensive against London.

In France the Popular Front Government was sent packing and the new administrations of Chautemps and Daladier, wishing to make their peace with the propertied classes, set about appeasing the fascists both at home and abroad. In Moscow the show trials reached absurd new heights as Stalin set about slaughtering his Officer Corps, thus further lessening both his desirability and his effectiveness as an ally against Nazi Germany. Hitler looked around at the steady disintegration of the forces opposed to his schemes, and decided to push ahead.

On 5 November 1937 he called a meeting of the service chiefs, the War Minister, von Blomberg, and the Foreign Minister, von Neurath. The protocol of the meeting was kept by Colonel Hossbach, whose memorandum was written from memory but there is no serious reason to doubt its accuracy. In the course of a long and rambling tirade, Hitler insisted that 'living space' (*Lebensraum*) would have to be found for the German people by 1943–45 or the German economy would collapse, the Nazi movement run out of steam and the armed forces become obsolete. He argued that Britain and France had already 'tacitly written off the Czechs and were reconciled to the fact that this question would be cleared up by Germany in due course'. Hitler also believed that Austria could be annexed without intervention from the powers.

The German High Command immediately set about revision of 'Operation Green', the plan for the invasion of Czechoslovakia. As soon as Germany was prepared, Czechoslovakia was to be attacked 'so that the solution of the German problem of living space can be carried to a victorious conclusion even if one or other of the great powers intervene against us'. Hitler still hoped that this would be possible without a war, even though Chamberlain was not prepared to give him a completely free hand in the east. The Lord President, Lord Halifax, assured Hitler that the British Government had full understanding of Hitler's revisionist ambitions in Austria, Czechoslovakia and Danzig, but when he suggested that it would then be possible to reach a general European peace settlement Hitler declined to discuss the matter any further. Back in London the Foreign Secretary, Eden, urged the French to persuade the Czechs to 'demonstrate their good will' towards Nazi Germany, and the Prime Minister suggested that Britain might well be unable to support the French guarantee to Czechoslovakia were Germany to go to war in support of its claim to the Sudetenland.

In the course of 1937 Hitler made some important personnel changes, removing a number of leading figures who were critical of the irresponsible daring of Hitler's policies. Schacht, who felt that the forced armaments programme after 1936 and the desire to achieve autarky at almost any price were a disastrous mistake, was replaced as Minister of Economic Affairs. The War Minister and the Chief of General Staff, Blomberg and Fritsch, were dismissed and Hitler appointed himself Minister of War. The subservient Keitel was made chief of the Armed Forces' High Command (OKW) and Brauchitsch was appointed chief of the Army High Command (OKH). The conservative nationalist Foreign Minister, von Neurath, was replaced by the frightful Ribbentrop whose diplomatic skills as ambassador to Britain had earned him the nickname of 'von Brickendrop'. Hitler now had personal command over the armed forces and had a completely free hand in foreign policy. There was no further serious discussion at the top of major policy issues or about how Hitler's decisions were to be implemented.

The invasion of Austria was a typical example of the new approach. The Austrian Chancellor, Schuschnigg, was invited to Hitler's mountain retreat at the Obersalzberg in Bavaria on 12 February 1938 where he was treated to an astonishing harangue from the Führer, who was surrounded by his generals for greater effect. Schuschnigg was given three days to sign an agreement which would allow a number of Nazis to enter his Government, one of whom was to be given the key Ministry of the Interior. Schuschnigg gave way under such massive pressure, but on 9 March he announced that there would be a plebiscite in Austria to decide whether the people wished for 'a free, German, independent, social, Christian and united Austria'. Hitler flew into a terrible rage when he heard of Schuschnigg's move, and ordered the army to prepare for an invasion. Schuschnigg then agreed to abandon the idea of a plebiscite but the Austrian Nazi Minister of the Interior, Seyss-Inquart, was ordered by Goering to insist on replacing Schuschnigg as Chancellor. Schuschnigg appealed to France and Britain for help, but the British were anxious not to provoke Hitler, the ambassador, Henderson, implying that his Government had no objections in principle to an *Anschluss*. The French would do nothing without British support. Schuschnigg saw no alternative but to resign, thus leaving the problem to the unfortunate President, Miklas. The President at first refused to appoint Seyss-Inquart, and when he relented it was too late. Hitler had already ordered the invasion of Austria, which began in the early morning of 12 March 1938. It was a cheap and bloodless victory. Hitler returned to Vienna to address an adulatory crowd on the Heldenplatz. In a plebiscite, 99 per cent of those voting favoured the reduction of Austria to a mere German province with the unattractive name of 'Ostmark'.

The annexation of Austria further weakened Czechoslovakia by exposing its southern flank to German attack. The Sudeten German Nazis, prodded by their extremist leader Konrad Henlein, clamoured for the return of their native land to the German Reich. The Czech Government decided to begin talks, but they were labouring under two serious illusions: first that the Germans genuinely wanted to settle the problem, and second, that the British and French would help them out if things went seriously wrong.

Confident that the British and the French would do nothing, Hitler ordered provocative troop movements along the Czech border on 19 May. The Czechs responded by begining to mobilize their army, and the British and French Governments issued uncharacteristically firm statements. This merely provoked Hitler to inform his top military, state and party officials on 28 May that he intended to smash Czechoslovakia before attacking in the west. Two days later further changes were made to 'Operation Green' which expressed Hitler's 'unalterable intention to smash Czechoslovakia by military action in the near future'. Meanwhile the French Government hastily began to retreat, warning the Czechs to stop their mobilization and telling the British that they had no intention of supporting the Czechs, in spite of their treaty obligations, if they were 'unreasonable'. The British sent Lord Runciman, the Liberal leader, to report on the situation of the German minorities. Runciman greatly enjoyed the hospitality of Sudeten German landowners, but otherwise found Czechoslovakia an 'accursed country'. Predictably he reported that 'Czechoslovakian rule in the Sudeten areas for the last twenty years has been marked by tactlessness, intolerance and discrimination'. His conclusion was that the Sudetenland should be handed over to Germany.

At the begining of September the British Government persuaded the Czechs to accept Henlein's proposal for a Sudeten German parliament. Henlein was horrified at this suggestion, fearing that it would bring the crisis to an end. In the Reich, Hitler worked up his audience at the Nuremberg party rally into a frenzy of indignation over the grim lot of their racial comrades in the Sudetenland. On 13 September Chamberlain, without consulting the French, announced that he would visit Hitler in his mountain retreat and discuss the Czech situation.

Hitler submitted to the Prime Minister a long list of Czech atrocities against the hapless Germans and announced that he was prepared to launch a world war to bring these unfortunates back into the fatherland. Chamberlain agreed in principle that the Sudetenland should be returned to the Reich, but urged Hitler to desist from the use of force. Back in London, Chamberlain received Daladier who was concerned that Hitler was intent not merely on seizing the Sudetenland but on destroying the whole of Czechoslovakia. He therefore proposed a joint guarantee of rump Czechoslovakia which Chamberlain, who had always argued that Hitler was a man who kept his word, had no alternative but to accept.

On the following day, 19 September 1938, the British and French Governments urged the Czechs to hand over the Sudetenland to Germany. President Benes initially rejected this suggestion, but gave way when told that the British and French would not support him if he refused.

Chamberlain visited Hitler again on 22 September at Bad Godesberg, only to be told that his proposed solution to the Sudeten German problem was unacceptable and that Hitler wanted immediately to occupy the Sudetenland, to hold plebiscites in as yet undefined areas and to meet the territorial demands against Czechoslovakia of both Hungary and Poland. Hitler ended by assuring his guest that this was his last territorial demand, adding, somewhat ominously, 'in Europe'.

Chamberlain still believed Hitler, but in Whitehall there was a growing feeling that he had gone too far. The Foreign Secretary, Halifax, persuaded Chamberlain not to cave in completely to Hitler's demands and the Prime Minister agreed to send his closest adviser, Sir Horace Wilson, to see Hitler. Hitler told Sir Horace that any further talk was pointless and that he would destroy Czechoslovakia if necessary. In a second meeting, Chamberlain's envoy first threatened Hitler that Britain and France would be prepared to fight to defend Czechoslovakia, and then spoiled any effect this might have had by assuring the Führer that the British Government would use every means at its disposal to 'try and make those Czechos sensible'. In such a spirit, Chamberlain informed Benes on 27 September that there was nothing Britain and France could do to help him. The same evening he told the nation on BBC radio that the British Empire was not prepared to go to war over a 'quarrel in a far-away country between people of whom we know nothing'. In the middle of a long and dreary report to the House of Commons on these exchanges, the Prime Minister was handed a note saying that Hitler had agreed to host a four-power conference at Munich to discuss the Czech crisis. The House was wildly enthusiastic when

Chamberlain told them that he intended to go to Munich. There were those, prominent among them Churchill, Eden and Amery, who did not join in the general jubilation, but only one lone Scottish Communist, Willy Gallagher, spoke up against Chamberlain's decision to continue to appease Hitler.

The Munich agreement gave Hitler almost everything he wanted. He was to be allowed to occupy the Sudetenland, and Polish and Hungarian claims against Czechoslovakia were to be respected. Britain and France gave a feeble guarantee to the remains of Czechoslovakia, but Chamberlain, again without consulting the French, signed an agreement with Hitler that their two countries would never again go to war, thus rendering the guarantee virtually worthless. Benes, who had never been consulted by his supposed allies, was without outside help and feared civil war at home. He thus had no alternative but to accept the Munich ultimatum and to resign on 4 October 1938.

In both Britain and France the Munich agreement was rapturously received. It was believed that war had been avoided and that Chamberlain had indeed secured not only 'peace with honour' but 'peace for our time'. Public opinion began to change somewhat when the appalling anti-Jewish violence on 9 November 1938 in the cruelly inappropriately named 'Night of Broken Glass' (*Reichskristallnacht*) and Hitler's boastful speeches about the feebleness of Chamberlain and Daladier and the victory of force over pusillanimity at Munich revealed the true face of National Socialism. At the end of January 1939 Hitler told the Reichstag that the 'final solution' of the Jewish problem was the 'radical, racial, ideological objective of the coming war'. To his henchmen he made repeated references to an imminent war to secure a vast European Empire for the German people. All of this passed virtually unnoticed in London and Paris, and in spite of the mounting pressure on Czechoslovakia, Chamberlain proclaimed that Europe was 'settling down to a period of tranquillity'.

President Hacha of Czechoslovakia did what he could to keep his country together and to preserve the last vestiges of a democratic order. He arrested the separatist Slovakian Premier, Monsignor Tiso, a man who dutifully addressed Hitler as '*mein Führer*'. Released from jail, Tiso rushed to Berlin where he was ordered to appeal to Hitler for protection, and a declaration of Slovak independence was dictated to him by the German authorities. This document was accepted by the Slovak Diet on 14 March. Hacha immediately went to Berlin and was received by Hitler at 1.15 a.m. on 15 March. He was viciously attacked by Hitler, who announced that he intended to invade Czechoslovakia at 6 a.m. The wretched President collapsed, and having been revived with an injection he signed a document entrusting the future of his hapless country to Hitler. Abandoned by Britain and France, the Czechs offered no resistance and thus on 15 March the Germans established the 'Protectorate of Bohemia and Moravia' and soon reduced Slovakia to vassal status with a treaty which set up a 'protective relationship' with the Reich. There were few illusions in either case as to what 'protection' by Nazi Germany involved.

The invasion of Czechoslovakia resulted in a slight stiffening of the attitudes of the British and French Governments. Chamberlain gave a somewhat petulant speech in Birmingham and both nations withdrew their ambassadors for consultation. Hitler took no notice of any of this. He demanded Memel from the Lithuanians, who promptly gave way. These German successes encouraged Mussolini to push ahead with his plans to invade Albania in an inglorious campaign mounted on Good Friday, 7 April.

There was now mounting evidence that Romania was next on Hitler's list and considerable concern in London and Paris that he was out to seize the Romanian oilfields. The Polish Foreign Minister, Beck, did not want to become involved in a four-power declaration, which might include the Soviet Union, designed to preserve the sovereignty of all European states, a move aimed at discouraging Hitler from moving against Romania. He therefore suggested a secret Anglo-Polish agreement. On 31 March 1939 Chamberlain told the House of Commons that Britain and France would lend Poland 'all support in their power' if its independence was threatened. Four days later Beck arrived in London and secured an extension of the interim guarantee to Poland by playing down the threat from Germany.

There were misgivings in London and Paris about a pact with Poland. The British felt, quite rightly, that Beck was less than frank and prone to duplicity. The French disliked the way Poland had fallen upon Czechoslovakia after Munich, and some were disgusted by fresh outbursts of a virulent anti-Semitism which had so often disfigured Polish life. Most of all, the French were concerned that if the guarantee were to go into effect it was they, not the British, who would be called upon to do most of the fighting. The French fascist Marcel Déat asked the famous question: 'Why die for Danzig?' Many felt that there was no particular reason why they should. Both Chamberlain and Daladier hoped that the guarantee to Poland would force Hitler to be more moderate in his demands, and the same argument was used when extending the guarantee to Romania and Greece in April.

The Anglo-French guarantees to Poland and Romania greatly strengthened the position of the Soviet Union, which could now wait and see whether the western powers or Germany would make the better offer. The British Government never took the Soviet approaches seriously, although stalwart anti-appeasers like Churchill felt that they should be accepted. They disliked and distrusted the Soviets and were overly concerned about the susceptibilities of Poland and Romania, both of which wanted nothing to do with communists. A major stumbling block was the Soviets' insistence that some states would have to be guaranteed whether they wanted to be or not, and that states which became the objects of aggression, either direct or indirect, would have to be helped even if they did not ask for such assistance. Halifax thought that this would permit the Soviets to endulge in 'naked, immoral interference' in the affairs of their unfortunate neighbours. Military talks did not begin until 12 August and promptly stalled when Marshal Voroshilov asked the key question: would the Poles and Romanians allow Soviet troops on their territory in order to uphold the guarantees? Britain and France tried to get the Poles to agree, but Beck replied that this would amount to yet another partition of Poland, and added: 'With the Germans we risk losing our liberty. With the Russians we lose our soul.' On 21 August the military talks were adjourned. That evening it was announced that the German Foreign Minister, Ribbentrop, was to visit Moscow. Two days later the Soviets signed a pact with the Nazis.

Unofficial talks between Germany and the Soviet Union had been going on throughout the summer. The Germans became increasingly concerned that Britain and France would reach an agreement with the Soviets, and the Soviets were angered that the western powers would not let them have their way in the Baltic and doubted that they were interested in serious negotiations. The Germans, on the other hand, were prepared to give them everything they wanted in the Baltic, Poland and Bessarabia.

The day before the pact was signed Hitler told his generals that with Germany allied with the Soviet Union, Britain and France would never dare give assistance to Poland. The same day Chamberlain urged Germany and Poland to reach an agreement over Danzig. Shortly afterwards Daladier offered to mediate between Germany and Poland. The next day, Hitler ordered the invasion of

Poland to begin on 26 August. Prompted by British and French offers to negotiate, Hitler postponed the invasion of Poland, hoping to achieve another Munich. But by 28 August when Hitler received the British ambassador, Henderson, he had lost all interest in negotiation. His reply to the British offer was so insulting that even Henderson, an arch-appeaser and anti-Semite, lost his temper. On 31 August Mussolini proposed a conference, this second 'Munich' to be held on 5 September, but it was too late. At 4.45 a.m. German troops crossed the borders of Poland.

On 2 September the British Government agreed to issue an ultimatum that would expire at midnight, but Chamberlain and Halifax still hoped that there would be a conference. In the Commons later that day the Prime Minister said he would welcome a conference if the Germans agreed to withdraw their forces. The House was outraged by this statement, for he had not insisted on an actual withdrawal of German troops. When Greenwood rose to speak on behalf of the Labour Party, Amery called out from the Conservative ranks, 'Speak for England, Arthur!'

At number 10 Downing Street Chamberlain was told by his Cabinet colleagues that the time for prevarication was over. 'This means war,' he gloomily declared. To heighten the drama there was a sudden thunderclap. Henderson was promptly instructed to deliver the British ultimatum at 9 a.m., to expire at 11 a.m. The French once again followed behind. Their ultimatum expired at 5 p.m. Thus on 3 September Britain and France were at war although there was little fighting until May of the following year. While the German *Blitzkrieg* was triumphant in the east, the western Allies endured the boredom of the '*Sitzkrieg*', or 'phoney war'.

CHAPTER ONE

From the Outbreak of the War to the Fall of France (September 1939–July 1940)

The German High Command's (OKH) operational orders for the attack on Poland, codenamed 'Plan White', were finalized on 15 June 1939. Although Hitler was confident that Britain and France posed no serious threat, mistakenly believing that their attitude had not changed since Munich and that they would continue to prevaricate and appease, the Wehrmacht was less optimistic. For this reason the plan called for a swift campaign so that troops could be withdrawn to make up for the deficiencies of the 'West Wall', a defensive system which had not yet been completed and which was only lightly manned. A rapid campaign would also make it possible to crush the Polish army before it had time to complete its mobilization and before it could be fully deployed to the west of the Vistula and the Narew.

The plan called for a two-pronged attack centred on Warsaw: Army Group North swooping down from Pomerania and East Prussia, and Army Group South advancing from Silesia and Galicia. Only a handful of troops were ordered to take Danzig. The major problem for the planners was that Army Group North had both to secure the Polish Corridor and to advance towards Warsaw. Forces had also to be ready to encircle Polish units able to escape this massive pincer movement by moving to the east of the capital. For this purpose, tanks were ideal.

To give the political leadership maximum freedom of action, mobilization had to be swift and secret and thus could not include industry and the civilian population. Hitler ordered a 'mobilization without a public announcement' to take effect on 28 August, by which time the army had been increased by three million men. A series of manoeuvres and exercises was carried out from the end of

June, designed to set the stage for an attack on Poland without arousing undue suspicion. The mobilization and deployment of troops was carried out with exceptional skill and in the minutest detail, and although the Poles were well aware of the concentration of troops along their frontiers, they were caught by surprise when the war began on 1 September.

The German occupation of Czechoslovakia on 15 March 1939 and the establishment of the Protectorate of Bohemia and Moravia placed Poland in a perilous situation, but the Polish general staff underestimated the danger of an outflanking movement far to the east. They did not think that the Germans would be able to deploy large forces in the south, but they incorrectly assumed that there was no serious threat of a significant outflanking movement from the troops stationed in East Prussia. The Poles had to fight as far west as possible to protect their industrial base, and a retreat behind the Vistula was unthinkable given the state of relations between Poland and the Soviet Union. The Nazi–Soviet pact had been signed immediately after the rejection of the Soviet proposal that their troops should be allowed on to Polish territory to meet the threat from Germany. Outflanked, hopelessly outnumbered and unable to retreat, the Poles could only hope to hang on as long as possible in anticipation of an offensive by the French and the British. The Franco–Polish military pact of 19 May 1939 gave the Poles the guarantee that the French would mount a full-scale attack on Germany within fifteen days after the beginning of hostilities, and although there was considerable debate about the precise nature of France's obligations under the treaty, the Poles were convinced that they would be given effective support in the event of a German attack.

Faced with mounting political pressure from Germany, the Poles began the mobilization of their armed forces on 23 March, but they were hampered not only by serious economic difficulties at home but also by Britain and France, who feared that full-scale military preparations would serve only to provide the Germans with an excellent excuse to begin a preventive war. It was suggested that in such an eventuality the German version of events would be widely accepted and that Poland would be left politically isolated. In the course of the summer the Poles became convinced that Hitler had no intention of fighting a war of nerves, but had a full-scale invasion in mind. After Ribbentrop's visit to Moscow on 22 August, no shadow of a doubt remained. Back in Warsaw the Foreign Minister, Beck, clung to the illusion that a peaceful solution was still a possibility, but on 28 August the Polish general staff requested that the President order a general mobilization. The order was countermanded the following day when the British and French Governments called for restraint, pending a reply from Berlin to suggestions made by the British Government for a negotiated settlement. The result was uncertainty and confusion which had disastrous consequences, particularly on the transportation system which became seriously overloaded with troops moving hither and thither. By the time the German invasion began, only one-third of the Polish troops were fully prepared for battle.

Poland was in an impossible strategic position and confronted an army which was superior in every respect, and its position was further weakened by the hesitations over mobilization, by placing the bulk of the army too close to the frontier, by inadequate communications and by an underestimation of the capacity of the Germans for rapid and powerful offensive thrusts. With a Soviet offensive in the east and the reluctance of the British and the French either to honour their obligations or to provide any real assistance, the fate of Poland was sealed.

There was little enthusiasm in Germany for this new war and the Government felt obliged to describe it as a mere 'police action' when it became obvious that there was going to be no repetition of the heady days of August 1914. Hitler gave a speech in the Reichstag justifying the attack on Poland and assuring Britain and France of his peaceful intentions towards them. This offer was ignored, and the British and French Governments declared war on Germany on 3 September.

The German army command was determined to bring the Polish campaign to a swift conclusion because they were anxious to move troops west as soon as possible to meet the threat from France. They thus eagerly seized the opportunity to encircle the Polish forces west of the Vistula. The pincer movement on Warsaw closed rapidly, and the outer pincer was completed on 12 September when Guderian's Panzers reached Brest Litovsk. Although the Poles tenaciously defended the Westerplatte, the strip of land protecting the entrance to Danzig harbour, and mounted a counter-offensive across the river Bzura which forced General Blaskowitz's 8th Army to divert troops away from the advance on Warsaw, by 18 September the Poles were encircled and 120,000 prisoners had been taken. The Luftwaffe's attacks on columns of soldiers caused widespread panic. Road transport and railways were disrupted by aerial attacks, making it impossible for the Poles to strengthen their position east of Warsaw.

Meanwhile, on 17 September the Soviets crossed the Polish frontier, having signed an armistice with the Japanese two days earlier which had ended the fighting in Manchuria, and the war entered a new phase.

The German Government had been urging the Soviets to move, hoping either that this would dissuade the western Allies from taking any action, or that they would declare war on the Soviet Union. Stalin acted cautiously until he felt confident enough to announce that since there was no longer a Polish Government, the neutrality treaty between the two states was null and void and the Soviet Union felt obliged to assist White Russians and Ukrainians who were no longer protected by a viable government. At the same time the Soviets, although remaining closely allied to Nazi Germany, announced that they remained strictly neutral.

The Soviet invasion obliged the Germans to pull some of their troops back from the east. The Soviets were naturally suspicious of the Germans, but on 28 September Molotov and Ribbentrop signed the German–Soviet Boundary and Friendship Treaty which cynically guaranteed the Polish people 'a peaceful life in keeping with their national character'. Lithuania was recognised as being within the Soviet sphere of influence, in return for which the Soviets made concessions which allowed the Germans to move the demarcation line further east. In a joint declaration made in Moscow on the same day, the British and French were called upon to end the war, the continuation of which was said to be entirely their responsibility.

The final assault on Warsaw began on 25 September with an aerial bombardment by 1200 planes in which many civilians were killed along with some of the German front-line troops. By 28 September Warsaw was in German hands, and within a few days the campaign in Poland was over. The Poles fought bravely against overwhelming odds, but the Polish Commander-in-Chief, Marshal Smigly-Rydz, by stubbornly refusing to give up any territory, denied the army any freedom of movement, thus allowing the German *Blitzkrieg* specialists to fight a series of battles of encirclement with a speed and precision which demonstrated their mastery of this new form of warfare.

Hitler had no clear idea what he intended to do with Poland, and Stalin's objectives were equally uncertain, but when the western powers rejected his peace offer of 6 October, and when the Soviets made it perfectly clear that they intended to annex those areas which they had occupied, he opted for a policy of ruthless exploitation and repression. A new province of Wartheland was created out of West Prussia, Danzig and Posen. In East Prussia and Silesia the frontiers were extended to include substantial chunks of Polish territory. The remainder of German-occupied Poland formed the 'General Government', the precise legal status of which was never fully clarified. The General Governor, Hans Frank, lived in splendour in the royal palace in Cracow and was virtually independent from the Ministries in Berlin, but from the outset he found himself in an awkward dilemma. On the one hand he was called upon to treat Poland as a mere reservoir for manpower and raw materials, while on the other he wanted to use his new office to strengthen his own position within the hierarchy of the Third Reich, and that could be done only if Poland flourished.

The same dilemma faced the German occupation authorities. The military wanted the rational exploitation of Polish resources. Hitler and the SS wanted to destroy any traces of opposition to their policies, regardless of international law. The Wehrmacht made a few half-hearted protests against the atrocities committed by the SS, but to no effect. Only the stubborn resistance of the Polish people to the policies of 'depolonization' and 'germanization' (*Volkstumspolitik*) forced Himmler and Heydrich to listen to the cautioning words of Goering and Frank and to order a certain degree of restraint in the winter of 1939. All this was relative and temporary. In early 1940 the SS built a concentration camp at Auschwitz where Polish prisoners were treated as slave labour and executed at will.

The ferocity of German occupation policy in Poland was a direct result of Nazi racial and geopolitical ideology, but it was intensified by the Poles' own mistreatment of Polish citizens of German origin both before and during the war. Before the war such Germans had been harried and persecuted by the Poles, denied their right to cultural expression, accused of espionage and sabotage and forced into exile. When the war began, the situation worsened until on 3 September some 1000 Germans were cold-bloodedly murdered at Bromberg (Bydgoszcz) in eastern Poland on 'Bloody Sunday' by Polish troops who falsely claimed that they had been shot at. An estimated 13,000 Poles of German origin lost their lives in similar circumstances.

With the defeat of Poland these ethnic Germans were determined to get their revenge and saw themselves as the new ruling class, the Poles as their mute vassals. They were never able fully to realize this hope, because the SS, who were the real power in the land, had little sympathy for their ambitions and did not regard them as real

Germans. However, when Himmler was given yet another title as 'Reichs Commissar for the Strengthening of the German Race' and began his extensive programme of confiscation, deportation and resettlement, their lust for revenge was at least partially satisfied. More than 200,000 German settlers arrived in General Government territory from the areas bordering Poland, particularly from those now occupied by the Soviets, in search of a new and secure life under the protection of their compatriots.

The authorities in the Reich demanded that one million Polish workers should be sent to Germany, mainly for agricultural work. Frank hoped that this could be achieved on a voluntary basis, but the proposed wage levels were so low that the programme met with little success. By September 1940 only one-third of the quota was filled. For all the brutality and capriciousness of the German occupation authorities, they were unable to function without a certain degree of co-operation from the Poles, who were thus given an opportunity to organize a skeleton resistance movement.

The Polish Government fled to Romania on 17 September, where they were arrested owing to German pressure. A Government-in-exile was formed in France by representatives of the opposition parties under General Sikorski, and was immediately recognized by the British, French and Americans. An army of 84,000 men was formed, made up of soldiers who had managed to escape and Polish workers living in France. A total of 17,000 of these men were able to make their way to England after the fall of France along with the Sikorski Government. Although the Government-in-exile lacked a mandate and had few contacts in Poland, it did have a certain authority over the Polish underground army which by 1940 numbered over 100,000 men. The ferocious measures taken by the German and Soviet occupation authorities against any signs of civilian unrest served merely to strengthen the Poles' determination to resist, and Poland was one of the very few European countries in which there was virtually no collaboration with the Germans, with the obvious exception of Poles of German origin.

Soviet-occupied Poland was divided up between the Ukrainian and the White Russian Soviet Republics, and Vilna returned to Lithuania, only to be swallowed up by the Soviet Empire in the following year. Landowners were disappropriated, industry nationalized, and one and a half million Poles were deported to the Soviet Union of whom only 700,000 survived. Some 15,000 Polish officers were taken prisoner, most of whom were murdered by Soviet troops at Katyn, an atrocity which for many years was conveniently attributed by the Soviets to the Germans. On 31 October Molotov gave a speech to the Supreme Soviet in which he expressed his satisfaction at the disappearance of Poland, 'that monster child of the Treaty of Versailles', and he went on to say that it was 'nonsensical and criminal' for Britain and France to continue the war against Germany since 'Germany now stands for peace'. In the same speech Molotov demanded frontier rectifications with Finland in order to improve the defences of Leningrad.

Negotiations over an exchange of territory between Finland and the Soviet Union began in Moscow on 12 October 1939, but it soon became apparent that the Finns were not prepared to make the concessions demanded of them, and the talks reached a deadlock. Finland tried to win German support but the German Government, in spite of its need for Finnish copper and nickel, remained true to their Soviet ally. The Soviets began to deploy troops along the Finnish border and there was a series of frontier incidents which were probably engineered by the Soviets. On 29 November the Soviets broke off diplomatic relations with Finland, and on the following day Soviet troops invaded Finnish territory.

Hitler's support for the Soviet Union was economically and politically costly. It was extremely unpopular at home, and Goebbels's propaganda machine was unable to change the popular perception of the 'Winter War'. Germany lost vital imports of raw materials from Finland, and the Soviets were unable to meet their quotas under the terms of the German–Soviet economic agreement. German support for the Soviet Union was also extremely unpopular in the Scandinavian countries, which improved the political position of Britain and France in the region. The Italians had been sending arms to Finland and were also annoyed by the German stance. Most troublesome of all was the possibility that Britain and France might actively support Finland and cut off supplies of Swedish iron ore designated for the Reich. For this reason Hitler ordered preparations for a pre-emptive strike against Scandinavia.

In spite of the overwhelming superiority of the Soviet forces in terms of both manpower and matériel, the Finns managed to put up a stubborn resistance against the invaders throughout the winter, and their brave struggle had an electrifying effect on public opinion in Britain and France. Here was a heroic people defending their homeland against the bolshevik bully-boys. The British and French Governments began lengthy discussions of the possibility of an intervention in the war, to the point of considering a declaration of war on the Soviet Union. The prospect was not without its attractions. The Soviet Union was a close ally of Nazi Germany and was sending large amounts of supplies that were vital to the German war effort. If these could be stopped, Germany would be seriously weakened. Furthermore, aid for Finland could go only through Norway and Sweden, and such an action would make it possible to cut off supplies of iron ore to Germany.

However attractive these prospects seemed at first, there were a number of problems which proved to be insurmountable. The idea that Soviet oil supplies could be cut off by a raid on the Caucasus oilfields at Baku, Batum and Groznyi by bombers stationed in the Middle East was dismissed by the Chiefs of Staff as hopelessly unrealistic. Troops could not be sent to Finland without the permission of the Norwegian and Swedish Governments, and this was not forthcoming. Both feared reprisals from the Soviet Union and Germany, and neither the British nor the French were prepared to risk putting too much pressure on the Scandinavian countries for fear of reaction from other neutrals and because Britain particularly was in desperate need of Swedish ore. Lastly, and most important of all, it was feared that any aid sent to Finland would be wasted, since military experts agreed that with the spring thaw the Finns would have to abandon the struggle.

On 13 March 1940 the Soviet Union and Finland signed a peace treaty. Soviet gains were modest, but they greatly strengthened the defence of Leningrad. Stalin was anxious that the war should remain localized and was prepared to drop the marionette Government of the Finnish Communist leader, Kuusinen, which had been formed in Moscow. Hitler had every reason to be pleased. The trade agreement with the Soviets of February 1940 guaranteed him the supplies he needed for the next phase of the war, and he could move his troops to the west confident of Soviet benevolence. One far-reaching consequence of the Finnish war was not yet apparent. Hitler shared the view, held by military experts throughout the world, that the poor performance of the Soviet troops in the early stages of the war was an indication that the Red Army need not be taken seriously. This proved to be a fatal mistake.

German plans for operations in Scandinavia were stepped up after an incident in February 1940 in which the British Royal Navy attacked the *Altmark*, a German ship which was carrying British prisoners-of-war but which was in Norwegian territorial waters. Planning for an invasion of Norway ('Operation *Weserbüng*' in fact began in January 1940), Hitler needed some excuse to act. The

OKW was frustrated by the fact that a British landing in Norway seemed less likely after the end of the Finnish war. At the end of March Hitler decided to move, claiming that British actions against German shipping along the Norwegian coast made it imperative to occupy Norway in order to secure the flow of iron ore to the Reich. It was not until 4 April that the Germans learned that the British were also planning a landing in Norway. The race for Scandinavia had begun.

The British had been planning an attack on Narvik, but with the end of the Finnish war the expeditionary forces were disbanded in spite of protests from Churchill and the Chiefs of Staff. At that time the British had no idea that the Germans also had plans for an invasion of Scandinavia. On 25 March the new French Premier, Reynaud, proposed to the British Government that a landing should be made in Narvik and that the Caucasus oilfields should be bombed. The French were confident that Hitler would not dare to attack France in 1940 and an attack on the Soviet Union would be extremely popular in anti-communist circles. They were not concerned with the effects of these actions on the neutral countries. As the French Foreign Ministry put it: 'We should not let ourselves be bound . . . by some juridic scruples which our enemies have since thrown to the winds.'

Chamberlain's Cabinet rejected the French proposals, arguing that they were not directed specifically against Germany and that they were likely to have an adverse effect on neutral opinion. They proposed going ahead with 'Operation Royal Marine', the mining of the Rhine to disrupt river traffic, but this in turn was rejected by the French on the grounds that it would provoke the Germans to retaliate. At the meeting of the Supreme War Council on 28 March Chamberlain and Reynaud reached a compromise. At the beginning of April the Norwegian coast would be mined and 'Royal Marine' would be mounted, but there would be no attack on the Soviet Union.

Churchill and Admiral Darlan, Commander of the French Navy, agreed that an expeditionary force should be prepared to land in Norway, arguing that the mining of Norwegian territorial waters would probably lead to a German invasion and the Allies should strike the first blow. Then Daladier, the former Premier who was now Minister of Defence, torpedoed 'Royal Marine' with the familiar arguments. Chamberlain's response was 'no mines – no Narvik'. Churchill went to Paris to pursuade Daladier to accept 'Royal Marine', but to no effect. Eventually the British Government agreed to go for Narvik without the Rhine mines, and on 8 April mines were laid around Narvik. By this time the naval deployment for the German invasion of Norway had already begun.

In the early-morning hours of 9 April 1940 German troops landed at Trondheim, Narvik, Bergen and Kristiansand. Stavanger was taken by paratroops. German troops entered Oslo the following day, the operation having run into a number of difficulties. The cruiser *Blücher*, one of the finest ships in the German navy, had been sunk and the battleship *Lützow* seriously damaged. With the exception of Oslo the landings were swift, economical and met with little serious resistance, but the major problem was bringing the escort vessels back to Germany through waters dominated by the Royal Navy. The German plan had been simple to the point of folly. Warships had sailed directly into Norwegian ports and assault troops disembarked directly from them. The gamble had paid off, but a heavy price was paid on the return journey. The Royal Navy sank much of the German naval force at Narvik. The *Hipper* was rammed, although not seriously damaged, by HMS *Glowworm* in a suicide attack in which most of the crew was lost; the captain won a posthumous VC. The *Königsberg* was damaged by Norwegian coastal batteries and then sunk by the Fleet Air Arm, to become the first major warship to be sunk by air attack. A number of escort vessels, tankers and transport ships were also sunk.

The attack on Denmark, 'Weser Exercise South', was an even greater success, in large part because the attack on Copenhagen did not run into such difficulties as were experienced in Oslo. Landings were made at a number of strategic points on 9 April, and in the early morning of the following day the King ordered the cessation of hostilities.

The British Government decided to land troops at Narvik in an attempt to wrest it from the Germans, and Churchill proposed 'Operation Hammer', an attack on Trondheim supported by flanking movements based on Namsos and Andalsnes. Admiral Pound (affectionately known as 'Don't-do-it Dudley') vetoed a frontal attack on Trondheim, but the two flanking operations went ahead. British and French troops landed between 14 and 17 April.

Although Hitler became extremely anxious about the Allied landings in Norway, and even suggested for the first and only time in his career that German troops should consider escaping to be interned in Sweden, the Allied operation was seriously mismanaged. Planners had failed to notice that the French cruiser *Ville d'Alger* was too big to enter the harbour at Namsos. The RAF used obsolete

Gloucester Gladiators whose crews were not equipped with oxygen, and one squadron lost all but one plane. The expeditionary force was virtually without air cover, insufficiently supplied and poorly led. But the Germans seemed to be in a perilous situation at Narvik. Major General Dietl was hopelessly outnumbered, and bad weather robbed him of vital air support. Allied troops entered Narvik on 28 May but were withdrawn on 8 June because of events in France. Two days later Norway capitulated.

The campaign in Scandinavia was a serious setback for the Allies and a remarkable German victory, but in the long run its effects were more harmful for Germany than for the Allies. Naval losses were about equal, but the Germans with their smaller navy were left with only three cruisers and four destroyers able to go to sea. Hitler had begun to show the first signs of his proclivity for interfering with the details of military operations which was later to prove so disastrous. The success of the operation strengthened his gambler's instinct and his obsession with surprise attacks, with which he could win campaigns, but not a war.

On 27 September 1939 Hitler told the service chiefs that he intended to attack in the west. He announced that Germany could not stand idly by while its enemies grew stronger, and pointed out that the Ruhr was Germany's Achilles' heel which had to be protected against an Allied attack. He proposed that France should be invaded before Christmas. This speech was designed in part to stifle the OKH which, much to his annoyance, had serious reservations about an offensive in the west. He had not yet made up his mind whether to attack, for he still hoped that Britain and France might be persuaded to accept the German occupation of Poland. Failing that, he hoped that the massive German and Soviet propaganda campaign blaming the Allies for the continuation of the war might have an effect both on the neutral states and on Allied morale. When Chamberlain rejected his peace offer of 6 October, Hitler immediately prepared a memorandum for Halder and Brauchitsch calling for an offensive in the west.

The arguments were familiar. Time was working for the Allies. Holland and Belgium had to be secured as bases for a bomber offensive against England. The Soviet Union was an untrustworthy partner. The United States was becoming increasingly hostile towards Germany. The Ruhr was dangerously vulnerable. Hitler ordered operational plans for an attack in the north-east as soon as sufficient armour and motorized vehicles were ready and when weather permitted.

The army leaders did not share Hitler's low opinion of the French and had great respect for the Royal Navy and the RAF. They had also learnt in Norway that the British were tough soldiers, even though their leaders lacked imagination and dash. The generals insisted that it would take a long time to make good the losses in matériel suffered in the Polish campaign. They stressed the enormous economic and manpower reserves of the British Empire, which would place Germany in a hopelessly inferior position in a protracted war. They still hoped that a political solution was possible, and suggested that they should react only in the event of an attack on the Ruhr. But now they were given orders to plan an operation which they opposed for professional reasons. There were some murmurings of discontent and even some discussion of a coup against Hitler, but planning went ahead for 'Situation Yellow'.

In the following months there were lengthy discussions of various alternative plans for an attack in the west, which were carried out in a heated and mistrustful atmosphere culminating in Brauchitsch handing in his resignation, which Hitler refused. Meanwhile, von Manstein, the Chief of Staff of Army Group A, worked feverishly on a plan which developed an idea which Hitler had proposed independently, although Manstein had no knowledge of this coincidence. This plan called for an attack along a line running south of Namur, Arras and Boulogne, from the Ardennes to the Channel, which would divide the Allied forces and encircle those in north-eastern France and Belgium. In a second phase this 'sickle' would be reversed and the forces in western France would in turn be encircled.

At first the OKH, hoping that an offensive in the west could still be avoided, was not even prepared to discuss Manstein's plan. It was not until December that the OKH tried out a number of proposals, including Manstein's, in a series of war games, but they would not forward these ingenious suggestions to Hitler. It was only when Brauchitsch and Halder gave up all hope of stopping Hitler that they began to look seriously at Manstein's plan. On 17 February Hitler's adjutant, Lieutenant-Colonel Schmundt, arranged a meeting between Hitler and Manstein. Hitler was impressed and the result was a plan developed by the OKH based on ideas put forward by Hitler and Manstein.

The French stuck to their doctrine of strategic defence and felt that the Germans were unlikely to attack before 1941. At the same time the *Deuxième Bureau* greatly overestimated the strength of the German forces in the west and maintained that their West Wall could not be breached without more planes and heavy artillery. The French troops were poorly trained and demoralized by months of inactivity behind the Maginot Line, the heavily fortified positions along the German border from Switzerland to Belgium which were believed to be impregnable. The disastrous outcome of the Norwegian expedition and the failure to give effective help to Finland further discredited the army and led directly to the fall of the Daladier Government in March 1940. The new Premier, Reynaud, wanted to get rid of the Commander-in-Chief, Gamelin, whom he dismissed as a 'lethargic philosopher'. Gamelin was ready to go, but was persuaded to stay in office by Daladier, now Minister of Defence, and by the President, Lebrun.

The situation in Britain was very different. On 10 May 1940 Winston Churchill was appointed Prime Minister. Unlike Reynaud who no longer had a majority in the Chamber, Churchill enjoyed the full support of all parties and his policy was unequivocal: 'to wage war, by sea, land and air, with all our might and with all the strength that God can give us; to wage war against a monstrous tyranny, never surpassed in the dark, lamentable catalogue of human crime'. But Britain was still far from ready to implement this policy and for the moment could do little more than take comfort in such rhetoric and hope that a naval blockade would eventually wear down the Germans. Relations with France were somewhat strained, as national interests stood in the way of a common strategy.

In October the British sent an expeditionary force (BEF) to France where it was stationed along the Belgian border. By May 1940 the British commander, Lord Gort, had some half a million troops under his command, most of which were poorly trained and inadequately equipped.

The Allies assumed that the Germans would attack in north-eastern France, but an effective defensive strategy was impossible as the Belgians remained neutral and refused to allow Allied troops to deploy in Belgian territory. Hitler's persistent fears that talks to alter this would be successful proved to be unfounded. There remained only the hope that the Belgians would be able to hold up the Germans long enough to allow British and French troops to move up to the Antwerp-Dyle-Namur line, which divided Belgium in half from north to south, and thus defend the industrial region of north-eastern France. The entire plan was based on the assumption that the Germans would attack through Belgium and Holland and that the Ardennes, which lay between this defensive line and the Maginot Line, were impassable, even though the Belgians suggested that the

Germans might attack through the Ardennes. This was a serious mistake which placed the Allies in an impossible strategic position. The spearhead of the German attack, Army Group A, was to advance through the Ardennes and head for the Channel, thus cutting off all the Allied forces in Belgium.

Both Belgium and Holland imagined that they could stay out of the war, even though all indications were to the contrary. On 1 January 1940 a German plane was forced to land in fog at Malines, between Brussels and Antwerp, and in it were found details of the German invasion plans. Colonel Oster of the Foreign Intelligence section of the OKW passed on information to the Dutch about Germany's intentions. But the Dutch refused to co-ordinate their strategy with the Belgians and also, like the unfortunate Poles, imagined that they would be able to hold up a German attack until the Allies came to their rescue.

The Allied forces were numerically approximately equal to the Germans and they had a superiority in artillery and tanks. The Germans had overwhelming superiority in the air, and the Allies had a chronic shortage of anti-aircraft and anti-tank guns. The French communications system was also woefully deficient, which was to cause endless problems once the fighting started.

The invasion of the Low Countries began on 10 May. In spite of lengthy and detailed preparations by the Germans, a number of daring special operations failed miserably. Although the Belgian fort at Eben Emael, which defended the Albert canal, was seized by paratroopers, other surprise attacks were less successful. The Germans suffered heavy losses in their assault on The Hague and the Dutch were able to destroy a number of important bridges before they could be secured by German commandos. The greatest success was the close co-operation between the army and the Luftwaffe which was to play such an important part in the outcome of the campaign.

Meanwhile, the Allies moved slowly up to the Dyle line. French troops positioned near Breda were subjected to heavy aerial bombardment. Feeling too weak to attack, they retreated towards Antwerp. This enabled the Germans to push forward towards Rotterdam and encircle the Dutch troops in 'Fortress Holland'. Negotiations for the capitulation of Rotterdam were under way when German bombers took off to attack the city. Orders recalling the planes were never received, and the city was flattened in a totally unnecessary attack in which more than 800 civilians were killed. The Dutch Commander-in-Chief, General Winkelmann, anxious to avoid any further bombing raids on Dutch cities and convinced that the situation was now hopeless, decided to sign an armistice on 15 May.

Army Group A had been advancing rapidly through the Ardennes. On 13 May German tanks crossed the Meuse near Dinant in spite of determined efforts by the French to dislodge them from their bridgeheads. On the same day, Guderian's tanks crossed the Meuse near Sedan after heavy and costly fighting. The way was now open for the deployment of German troops to the west of the Allies' strongest defensive position. The OKH strengthened the forces between Dinant and Sedan with armour and motorized infantry taken from Army Group B to the north, and ordered a rapid advance towards Arras and the Channel coast which would trap the Allied troops in Belgium.

As late as 13 May Gamelin, who remained as Commander-in-Chief in spite of Reynaud's justified reservations, still believed that the German attack would be concentrated in the north. By the time German intentions were apparent, it was too late to withdraw troops from the Maginot Line to attack the southern flank of the German advance. When Churchill asked General Gamelin where and when he intended to attack the flanks of the bulge, he listed the reasons why he was unable to act – 'inferiority of numbers, inferiority of equipment, inferiority of method' – and then shrugged his shoulders in resignation. The weakness of the Allied position was not clear to Hitler, Rundstedt or the commander of 16th Army, General Busch, all of whom feared that too rapid an advance would leave the left flank dangerously exposed to counter-attack.

As the situation deteriorated, tensions between London and Paris increased. Reynaud asked Churchill to send as many aircraft as possible to mainland Europe to counter the devastating effects of German air supremacy, but Churchill refused. He wanted to send all the aid he could, but he was determined not to weaken Britain's defences, particularly at a time when the fall of France seemed imminent. In Paris the burning of Government archives had already begun.

The British army tried to hold up the German advance between Arras and Valenciennes while the French 7th Army attacked on the flank, but the Germans were able to overcome this threat with concentrated aerial attacks and established bridgeheads across the Somme. On 21 May two British battalions broke through Hoth's flank to the south of Arras. The Germans greatly overestimated the danger posed by the 'Arras crisis' and Rundstedt ordered Kleist to halt his advance towards Calais and Dunkirk. But the French were unable to exploit the situation and the German advance continued.

Meanwhile, on 20 May General Gamelin was replaced by Weygand in the hope that his reputation at least would act as a boost to French morale. The day before this change took effect Gamelin suggested that the French army might be evacuated overseas, but the navy insisted that such an operation was impossible. The British began to plan a retreat across the Channel. This was an essential precaution, but when it became known it had a disastrous effect on Allied unity and further demoralized the troops. Gamelin's plan for an offensive on the Somme was adopted by his successor as the 'Weygand Plan', but it was the fruit of wishful thinking. The Allied troops were fighting a purely defensive campaign and lacked the strength even for a break-out towards the south-west. On 24 May the British abandoned Arras and two days later Lord Gort received the order to retreat across the Channel. Weygand was not informed of British intentions until 28 May, by which time 'Operation Dynamo' had already begun. He felt betrayed by the British who had kept him in the dark, and he had little time to order his troops to abandon the bridgehead and escape with the British. For this reason, relatively few French soldiers were able to cross the Channel.

The hopelessness of the situation and the deterioration of relations between the Allies provided further ammunition for those Frenchmen who were arguing in favour of an armistice. They were led by Pétain, the eighty-four-year-old hero of Verdun, who had been recalled as ambassador to Spain to enter the Government. He argued that British assistance had been so minimal that the agreement made on 28 March 1940 that there should be no separate peace should now be considered null and void. Reynaud despaired at the defeatist attitude of many leading generals, but found their arguments increasingly difficult to counter.

Hitler was unaware that the Allies were in such desperate straits. He was still obsessed with the exposed southern flank, where de Gaulle's armour had made a gallant counter-attack. He ordered the tanks to halt and wait for infantry support. This move was supported by Guderian, commanding the 19th Corps, who reported to his divisional commander, Kleist, that half his tanks were out of action, his men were tired and he would not be able to stand up to a counter-attack in force. Rundstedt, the commander of their Army Group A, also believed that the final phase of the operation on the Channel coast should be left to the infantry and the armour spared in preparation for the advance westwards. The OKH, contrary to the advice of the Chief of the General Staff, Halder, therefore ordered Army Group A to halt and gave Army Group B the task of destroying the Allies at the port of Dunkirk, where they were preparing to evacuate across the Channel. Units from Army Group A were sent to strengthen the southern flank. Goering, anxious that his Luftwaffe should have the honour of delivering the *coup de grâce*, persuaded Hitler that he could finish the job.

Once it became clear that the British were leaving the Continent, Hitler ordered Kleist's armour to move forward, but only far enough so that Dunkirk was within range of the artillery. The Luftwaffe had only limited success. Most bombers took off from bases in Germany and thus could not be given support by short-range fighters. Radar warnings allowed the RAF to send fighters based in southern England across the Channel, and they were able to inflict considerable damage on the bombers which were also harassed by concentrated anti-aircraft fire. The Luftwaffe was further hindered by bad weather and could not operate at night. Many of the bombs became buried in the sand on the beaches and had only limited effect. On 3 June the Luftwaffe stopped attacking Dunkirk and concentrated on raids on industrial targets around Paris. Marseille and the Rhône valley were also bombed.

Under the brilliant leadership of Admiral Ramsay, 'Operation Dynamo' was an organizational triumph. A total of 370,000 men, of whom 139,000 were French, were shipped across the Channel in the 'nine days' wonder'. A shattering defeat was thus turned into something approaching a victory, and the 'spirit of Dunkirk' soon became part of popular mythology and was reduced to the status of an overworked cliché.

Hitler's motives remain something of a mystery. Rundstedt claimed after the war that Hitler deliberately allowed the British to escape, in the hope of reaching a political agreement. On 17 May he told a group of officers of his intention to divide up the world with the British. All the British had to do was to accept German domination of mainland Europe and they could maintain their naval supremacy and their Empire. On 21 May Halder was told that the German Government hoped to reach an agreement with Britain on the division of the world. Again, on 2 June, Hitler told a group of officers that he hoped Britain would accept a 'reasonable peace' which would leave him free to pursue his 'really great task' of crushing the Soviet Union. The British Empire, he insisted, had a vital role to play on behalf of the white race which not even Germany could fulfil.

There seems little reason to doubt that Hitler's hesitations at the time of Dunkirk were due to military rather than political considerations, but there is ample evidence that he hoped that some arrangement with Britain was possible. Such ideas were seen as absurd and dangerous by the anti-British clique led by Ribbentrop and Admiral Raeder, but both men had already lost most of their influence. Hitler's hopes were based on a misreading of the political situation in Britain, but they were by no means absurd. There could be no doubt of Churchill's determination to continue the war at any cost and his refusal to negotiate with a detested enemy, but not all his colleagues shared this view. In a letter to Roosevelt calling for military assistance, Churchill used the veiled threat that his Government might not survive the pressure from those who hoped for an arrangement with the enemy. R.A. Butler, Under-Secretary of State to the Foreign Minister, Lord Halifax, was the most active member of this group and had the support of his Minister.

In Switzerland Max zu Hohenlohe-Langenburg, who shared the more moderate views of Goering, discussed the possibility of a negotiated settlement with the British plenipotentiary, Sir David Kelly. Similar discussion took place in Spain, with Butler's blessing, between the British ambassador, Sir Samuel Hoare, an old enemy of Churchill's, and the Germans. Butler also tried to involve the Swedish Government as an intermediary, but without success. Sumner Welles visited Europe to sound out the possibility of a settlement and was warmly supported by Butler, as well as the National Peace Council whose efforts were endorsed by such well-known figures as the writer George Bernard Shaw, the socialist economist G.D.H. Cole and the actor John Gielgud. But Hitler felt that his two trump cards were Lloyd George and the Duke of Windsor who was busy hobnobbing with Nazi dignitaries in Lisbon. This again was pure fantasy. Lloyd George had lost all political influence, and the ridiculous idea of a coup engineered by the SA, Hitler's Brown Shirts, to return the Duke of Windsor to the throne was never attempted.

The necessary precondition for any negotiations was the fall of Churchill, and by July Hitler realized that this was most unlikely. The Prime Minister's dogged determination and inspiring oratory transformed the country in 1940. It was a superb achievement which silenced his critics and united the nation at a time when all seemed lost. In his speech to the Reichstag on 19 July Hitler renewed his peace offer to Britain and warned that if this were not accepted he would flatten the country with his Luftwaffe. His intention was to undermine Churchill's position, but once again he failed.

Negotiations continued in Washington between the British ambassador, Lord Lothian, and German diplomats. Lothian was also in close contact with the pro-German American ambassador in London, Joseph Kennedy. Goering put forward a peace plan in which Germany would be satisfied if its demands against Poland and Czechoslovakia made in October 1939 were accepted, and would be prepared to relinquish all conquests in the west and the north. Halifax found these proposals interesting, but there were no further negotiations as the battle of Britain was at its most intense and Hitler, not surprisingly, felt that the time for negotiations was hardly propitious. Proposals by the King of Sweden and by the Holy See were equally unsuccessful, and on 22 July Halifax, prompted by Churchill, gave a talk on the BBC which rejected Hitler's offer. Hitler now decided to bomb the British into submission.

The British army had escaped at Dunkirk but they had lost the bulk of their equipment along with 68,000 men. The remaining troops in north-eastern France were quickly mopped up, and the Germans were now in possession of this vital industrial centre. For the Belgians the situation was hopeless, and on 28 May the army capitulated.

With the successful completion of the sickle movement, the Germans were in a position of overwhelming superiority. The French army was outnumbered two to one and their reserves of manpower were virtually exhausted. Brauchitsch told Hitler that the campaign was already won. All that remained to be done was to smash the hastily improvised French line of defence along the Somme, Oise and Aisne. The OKH proposed a swift sweep to the west of Paris in the manner of the original Schlieffen plan, the invasion plan implemented in August 1914 which many strategists still believed to be the infallible recipe for success if only it was properly carried out. Hitler, however, ordered a drive to the south-east which would trap the bulk of the French army behind the Maginot Line.

The French army, in spite of the profound pessimism of most of its leaders, put up a spirited defence on the Weygand Line, but the Germans soon broke through and the way was open for the final phase of the campaign. On 10 June Weygand told Reynaud that the army could not hold on much longer. Reynaud proposed a retreat to a defensive stronghold in Brittany, but this was a military impossibility. Weygand and Pétain insisted that an armistice was unavoidable, but Reynaud was determined to continue the struggle as long as possible. Churchill realized that France was lost, but hoped that at least the French fleet could be saved and that France could continue the war from its colonial territories. He tried desperately to involve the United States in the war in the hope that this would strengthen Reynaud's position, but Roosevelt was not prepared to give the Allies the assurance they required.

On 16 June de Gaulle had luncheon with Churchill at the Carlton Club, during the course of which he proposed a political union between their two countries. Churchill endorsed the idea, hoping that this would keep the French in the war and at least save the French fleet from falling into German hands. In fact, the proposal had the opposite effect. Those who favoured an armistice saw it as evidence that the British position was desperate and that Churchill was merely clutching at straws. Reynaud realized that with Paris in German hands since 14 June, an armistice was unavoidable. He resigned on 16 June and was replaced by Pétain, who refused point-blank even to consider the proposal that the Government should move to north Africa, and asked for an armistice. Negotiations began on 21 June, pointedly in the same railway coach in the forest of Compiègne in which the Germans had been forced to capitulate in 1918. The armistice was signed the following day.

Hitler decided that a French Government with which he could negotiate a peace should be allowed to remain in office. He wanted to avoid the high costs of the occupation of the whole of France, and feared that if the German terms were too severe the French would form a Government overseas which would offer at least moral support to the British. A French base in north Africa might oblige Hitler to disperse his forces at a time when he was beginning to think of his great campaign against bolshevik Russia. Above all, he was determined that the French fleet should not fall into British hands. The OKW did not share these political concerns and called for the occupation of all of France, but Hitler was fearful that the French would continue the fight elsewhere if he did not negotiate. On 17 June he told Mussolini that he had to avoid at all costs a 'situation in which the French Government might reject the German proposals, then flee abroad to London to continue the war from there, quite apart from the unpleasant responsibility which the occupying powers would have to assume, among others, in the administrative sphere'.

His concerns were unfounded. Virtually no one in the French Government had any desire to continue the war. Reynaud had been injured in a motoring accident and he had in any case lost much of his fighting spirit. Georges Mandel in Morocco and de Gaulle in London felt hopelessly isolated. The army had lost all desire to continue the struggle. Even before the armistice was signed, a number of officers who wanted to stand up to the Germans were shot by their own men. There was a widespread conviction that Britain would soon be defeated and that any prolongation of the war was therefore senseless. Germany had won the war and, as Pétain suggested to Hitler, those who 'tried to make a new start' expected better terms in the final peace. They did not know what the Germans had in mind. On 9 July Goebbels told representatives of the German press that France was to become a 'large Switzerland' suitable for tourism and for the manufacture of 'certain fashionable items'.

With Bordeaux in German hands the Government moved to Vichy, north-west of Lyon. This solidly bourgeois spa offered ample hotel accommodation and, unlike so many of the other major centres in southern France, it was not the fiefdom of a prominent political figure. The move was seen as temporary, since it was believed that the Germans would respect the guarantee in the armistice that the Government would soon return to Paris. From the outset the Government was determined to seize the opportunity afforded by the collapse of the Third Republic to make a real break with the past. Its object was not to carry on as best one could under trying circumstances, but to create a new state. Most Frenchmen longed for a return to normal life and for this reason supported the decision of the Government to remain in France and save at least part of the country from occupation, but many were fed up with the old state of affairs and welcomed the end of the Republic. France was now divided between the notionally independent Vichy in the south and occupied France, including Paris and Bordeaux, which was controlled by the German army.

The Vichy constitution, contrary to post-war apologetic legend, was not the result of the sinister machinations of evil men like Laval, nor was it a coup engineered by fascistic defeatists. It was a widely approved attempt to begin the process of national revival and purification after years of frivolous materialism, undemocratic chicanery and moral depravity. The Parliament was still that of the Popular Front of 1936, and it voted 569 to 80 to give Pétain full authority for all legislative and executive acts, with the exception of declaring war, without reference to Parliament. The majority of the 80 who voted against these measures demurred only in as much as they wanted Pétain to consult the National Assembly when drafting a new constitution. They were not the stalwart defenders of the

Republic and the fathers of the resistance of later mythology. In 1940 the resistance was virtually non-existent and there was almost no support for de Gaulle's quixotic stance. The left saw him as too reactionary, the right as a traitor. De Gaulle was alone in London, surrounded by a handful of relatively insignificant malcontents without any ties to broader political movements. He had a few supporters in French Equatorial Africa and in the Pacific islands, but few Frenchmen were prepared to run the risks of arrest, exile and obloquy to support a country which had raided the French fleet at Mers-el-Kebir in Algeria at the cost of 1200 French lives and which was determined to prolong a war which could not be won in pursuit of its own selfish interests. It was only with the first glimmers of the possibility of an eventual German defeat that the Gaullist movement began to gather significant support.

Hitler was prepared to allow a rump régime in France which was treated as an independent state, but this situation was unique. Every other nation conquered by the Germans was brought directly or indirectly under German civil or military control. Much to their annoyance, the Wehrmacht were pushed aside and Hitler appointed Seyss-Inquart, a prominent and fanatical Austrian Nazi, to take charge of a civilian administration in Holland. For the time being Hitler was prepared to treat Holland, Belgium and northern Luxembourg as separate political and economic entities pending a peace treaty, but he soon changed his mind.

In Belgium the situation was complicated by Nazi politico-racial considerations. Hitler was at first uncertain whether to allow the country to remain as a monarchy in close association with Germany, or to create a Flemish Administrative District (*Gau*) which would be incorporated into the Reich. For the time being Belgium remained under military rule, and north-eastern France was also placed under the military commander in Brussels rather than Paris, so that the eventual annexation of this industrially important area could be facilitated. The Flemish were given special privileges and advantages, a clear indication of Hitler's intention to redraw the map of Europe along 'racial' lines.

In the course of the summer Alsace-Lorraine and Luxembourg were incorporated into the Reich, and only those refugees who could prove that they were of German 'stock' (*Volkstum*) were allowed to return to their homes. Refugees were also refused permission to return to their homes along the German border, and their property was administered by the inappropriately named 'Association of Eastern Lands' (*Ostland Gesellschaft*).

Various proposals for an eventual western frontier were discussed in Berlin during the summer, and although no final decision was made it was generally agreed that it should extend as far as Amiens and the mouth of the Somme. Exotic schemes for an independent Brittany and for the restoration of a Burgundian state were eventually dropped as impracticable. More pressing seemed to be the creation of the basis for a German-dominated European economy along the principles of 'extensive area economics' (*Grossraumwirtschaft*). Behind all the ideological verbiage produced by the 'Society for European Economic Planning and *Grossraumwirtschaft*' and the endless propaganda about European unity lay the determination to exploit the occupied areas for the benefit of the German war economy. Details were worked out by the Ministry of Economics and the appropriate military and party bodies were established at Goering's behest. The aim was to create a unified economy from the Pyrenees to the Urals and from northern Scandinavia to Albania, but it was agreed that the final details would have to await the eventual outcome of the war. A great deal of detailed planning was also devoted to schemes for a vast overseas empire, but although it provided employment for a horde of bureaucrats who engaged in endless struggles for power over their imaginary satrapies, Hitler was hardly interested and all this effort was generally regarded as somewhat premature.

In Norway the leader of a minuscule fascist party, the *Nasjonal Samling*, Vidkun Quisling, formed a Government as soon as the King and his administration left Oslo. The Germans decided to make use of Quisling, largely because they could find no one else whom they deemed suitable for the role. The King, however, refused to appoint him Prime Minister. To overcome this confusion Hitler appointed Josef Terboven as Reich Commissar for Norway. Terboven was answerable directly to Hitler and his authority ran parallel to that of the military and the SS. His task was to build a pro-Nazi Government in Norway and to turn Trondheim, in Hitler's words, into a German Singapore, 'the most beautiful German city' and the 'northernmost cultural centre of the Greater German Reich'.

Quisling seemed to be the only man suitable to play this role, but he only had 1500 party members in 1940. The vast majority of Norwegians regarded him as a contemptible stooge who had ordered the arrest of the King and his Ministers, and his name was to become a synonym for treachery. Terboven also detested Quisling and wanted to build a Government which had wider support. He therefore sent Quisling to Germany and began negotiations with leading Norwegian politicians for the formation of a new Government. The negotiations were successful, largely because the politicians wanted to avoid either a Quisling Government or direct German rule. After the fall of France there seemed to be no other alternative. Hitler, prompted by Rosenberg and Raeder, decided that Quisling should return to Norway to head the administration. The Norwegians refused to accept a Quisling Government and negotiations between Terboven and Parliament soon broke down. Terboven then appointed a Council of State with thirteen members, of whom nine belonged to the *Nasjonal Samling*.

Terboven failed to form a credible Government, and was faced at every turn by determined patriotic resistance to his policies. All Norwegian judges resigned in protest at German violations of established legal practice. An attempt to bring sports and athletics clubs into one association under German control resulted in a strike by both players and fans. But economically he was successful. The Norwegian economy henceforth was forced to serve German interests and provided valuable raw materials, particularly aluminium.

In Denmark the situation was quite different. King Christian X refused to go into exile and formed a national Government so as to be in the strongest possible position to deal with the Germans. The German chargé d'affaires in Denmark, von Renthe-Fink, was given plenipotentiary powers but the Danish Government remained in office and he initially acted in a largely supervisory capacity. His long-term aim, however, was to create a pro-German Government in which the democratic parties were no longer represented. This proved to be impossible. The Danish fascists, the DNSAP, were an even more pathetic bunch than Quisling's party, and the Government was able to resist Renthe-Fink's attempts to include them in a new administration. He managed to secure the dismissal of a few ministers whom he particularly disliked, and to force the Government to disavow some of Denmark's diplomatic representatives abroad. Until 1943, when their country was placed under martial law, the Danes showed great courage and resourcefulness in defending what was left of their independence, and no country has a more honourable record of refusal to bow to the Nazi tyranny.

In the summer of 1940 Hitler was master of Europe and it was generally believed that it would be only a matter of weeks before Britain would be forced to sue for peace. With the Soviet Union still allied to Nazi Germany and busy churning out virulent propaganda against the war-mongering British, the only possible hope for Britain was that the United States would become involved in the war.

At the outset of hostilities President Roosevelt was determined to keep the United States out of the war, but at the same time he wanted to do everything possible to help Britain and France without violating the Neutrality Act of 1935 which enforced an arms embargo and the limitation of trade with belligerent countries. Without amendments to the Act no effective assistance to the Allies was possible, and Roosevelt therefore called for major changes in the Neutrality Act. There was widespread fear both in Congress and among the public that such a step would greatly increase the risk of American involvement in the war. The President had to tread very carefully, making frequent and profuse declarations of his determination to keep the United States out of the war while at the same time pressing for the repeal of embargo provisions forbidding the export of 'uncompleted instruments of war' so as to allow the sale of all types of goods on a 'cash-and-carry' basis.

In spite of constant prodding from the American ambassador in London, Joseph Kennedy, who wanted the United States to mediate a peace after the defeat of Poland, Roosevelt was interested only in overthrowing Hitler and his 'regime of force and aggression'. He added that he thought Kennedy 'a pain in the neck'.

Restrained by Congress and by the fear that he might strengthen the ties between Moscow and Berlin, Roosevelt was unable to grant the Finnish request for a sixty million dollar loan, and there were insufficient quantities of surplus arms that could be sent to help the Finns in the Winter War. Roosevelt was deeply concerned about public reactions to events in Europe. In a letter to a prominent newspaper editor, William Allan White, he wrote that 'my problem is to get the American people to think of possible consequences without scaring the American people into thinking that they are going to be dragged into this war'. Elsewhere he complained that 'the country as a whole does not have any deep sense of world crisis'. Nor did Congress, who were 'a bunch of Uriah Heeps . . . who do not realize that what is going on in Europe will inevitably affect this country'.

During the 'phoney war' from September 1939 to May 1940 when there was no fighting in the west, Britain and France, hampered by the Neutrality Act and the closing of American money markets, placed relatively few orders in the United States. The Allies agreed to the American suggestion that they should establish a Purchasing Commission in the United States as part of an attempt to circumvent the Neutrality Act, which was not repealed until November 1941. By early 1940 there was a marked increase in the sale of arms, particularly planes, although the Secretary of War, Woodring, and the service chiefs complained that they were being deprived of weapons which they badly needed themselves.

Receiving very pessimistic appraisals from the London and Paris embassies, Roosevelt attempted to stop a German attack on the west by negotiation. At the begining of 1940 he sent James D. Mooney of General Motors, who had good contacts in Germany, to sound the waters. He invited forty-six neutral nations to discuss the situation. Most important of all, he sent Sumner Welles to Berlin, Rome, Paris and London in February and March on a mission which at least might persuade Mussolini to stay out of the war and possibly give the Allies a breathing space to strengthen their position. Roosevelt was careful to disguise his real intentions, for fear that these initiatives might provide the isolationists with further ammunition to use against him and sow discord between Paris and London. None of these efforts came to anything, however, and Welles returned home at the end of March 1940 convinced that negotiations were impossible.

The Allied defeat in Norway was a matter of great concern to the American Government. Roosevelt feared that Britain would soon be defeated unless the Americans played a more active role. Twice he warned Mussolini that should Italy decide to enter the war the United States might be obliged to intervene, but the Italian dictator ignored these warnings. On 16 May 1940 the President made an impassioned plea to Congress to increase aircraft production to 50,000 planes per year and to give the highest priority to the despatch of aircraft to Britain and France, which he saw as essential to national defence. General Arnold pointed out that this was hopelessly unrealistic. The United States had only 52 heavy bombers and 160 pursuit planes. The most that could be spared would be enough to keep the Allies going for only three days at their current rate of losses, and would seriously hamper pilot training at home. With the British army bottled up at Dunkirk, these essential aircraft would be simply poured down the drain.

Roosevelt was thus unable to meet the urgent requests from Reynaud and Churchill for massive assistance. The service chiefs insisted that nothing could be spared without seriously weakening America's defences. Public opinion was still strongly against anything that smacked of intervention, and Roosevelt could not afford to do anything that would spoil his chances of re-election. The

Senate Foreign Relations Committee overwhelmingly rejected a Bill allowing the Government to sell new ships and planes to the Allies.

After Dunkirk, and with the German army marching on Paris, there was a remarkable swing in American public opinion in favour of sending all possible aid to the Allies. When France collapsed there was some feeling that, since Britain would probably soon be defeated, there was little point in sending more aid. Nevertheless, two-thirds of the American public still favoured assistance for Britain. The President was determined to do everything possible to help, and to strengthen his hand he appointed Henry Stimson Secretary of War and Frank Knox Secretary of the Navy. Although both men were Republicans they were staunch upholders of the Allied cause and had long called for colossal increases in defence spending.

In June and July the Americans were placed in an exceedingly difficult position. How were they to respond to Churchill's persistent clamourings for war matériel, especially destroyers? The military was firmly opposed to sending any supplies which might endanger America's own defences, and the President agreed that matériel should be sent to Britain only if it could be shown that it would substantially increase British chances of survival. If Britain were to fall, it would all land in Germany's lap and might eventually be used against the United States. Substantial American aid therefore depended on their assessment of whether or not it would make a decisive difference. The Battle of Britain was soon to convince the American Government that the fates of Britain and the United States were inextricably entwined.

CHAPTER TWO

The Battle of Britain and the Balkan Campaign

(July 1940–June 1941)

After the fall of France, Hitler still hoped that the British Government would be prepared to negotiate a settlement which would leave him master of Europe but with the British Empire intact. If the British were unwilling to treat with the Germans, then they could be forced to the negotiating table by a bomber offensive and an intensified war at sea which would cut off essential supplies. Only if everything else failed would it be necessary to invade, but this was considered a last resort. An invasion across the Channel would be an exceptionally risky enterprise and if it were to fail it would result in a disastrous loss of German prestige. Even if it were successful, the British Government would probably move to Canada and continue the war from overseas.

OKW agreed with this analysis and called the invasion plan an 'act of desperation' which should be considered only if all other possibilities were exhausted. Britain posed no immediate threat to Germany, and planning could go ahead for the invasion of the Soviet Union, an operation which, it was felt, might be welcomed by anti-communist circles in Britain. Hitler believed that Britain refused his peace offers only in the hope that Germany and the Soviet Union would eventually go to war. The defeat of the Soviet Union would leave the British no other alternative but to sue for peace. Thus, his short-term aim of peace talks with Britain and his long-term aim of smashing bolshevik Russia and creating a *Lebensraum* in the east could be achieved in one final and decisive campaign.

At the beginning of July Hitler ordered his military planners to work out the details of an invasion of England, codenamed 'Sea-lion'. He was careful to point out that an invasion was possible only if the Germans achieved air supremacy over England, and underlined the fact that an invasion would probably not be necessary. He gave 'Sea-lion' a very low priority and the planners hoped that a successful air offensive would render it superfluous. He added that if it was not possible to complete preparations for the invasion by the end of September, other plans would have to be made. Among these was the invasion of the Soviet Union. The German navy had the strongest reservations. Landing craft were not available and nor was there sufficient time to make up this deficiency before the autumn, when bad weather would make a cross-Channel landing impossible. Admiral Raeder also pointed out that the Channel would have to be cleared of mines and that, as the Führer had insisted, without air supremacy an invasion would be doomed to failure.

In Jodl's memorandum of 30 June, in which he discussed the future course of the war, he argued that the most important immediate task was the destruction of the RAF. This would secure Germany against bombing raids and enable the Luftwaffe to destroy the industrial centres of southern England. If this was coupled with 'terror raids', carefully disguised as reprisals, civilian morale would break and the British Government would be forced to sue for peace. An invasion was possible only as a 'death blow' to a country tottering on the brink of collapse after a successful air offensive.

Confusion and doubts over the invasion plans made the task of the Luftwaffe particularly difficult, since they were never quite certain what was expected of them and they had no experience of operating without the support of ground forces. The objectives of Goering's plan for the air offensive, codenamed 'Eagle', were the destruction of the RAF and attacks against the Royal Navy. Ports on the south coast which would be needed in the event of an invasion were not to be bombed, but those in the west where American supplies were unloaded were to be attacked. Goering also placed particular emphasis on the need to put the radar stations out of action. The Luftwaffe were confident of success. They felt that they were superior in every way to the RAF and they seriously underestimated the productivity of the British aircraft industry. It was assumed that the British could produce only 180–200 fighters per month, when in fact they were producing an average of 470. The strength of Britain's ground defences was also seriously misjudged. Believing that the task which faced them was so easy, the Luftwaffe made insufficient preparations for their offensive and their planning was vague and sloppy.

Although Air Chief Marshal Sir Hugh Dowding had done everything possible to preserve Fighter Command for what he believed to be its essential role – the defence of the home country against a 'knock-out blow' – he had suffered heavy losses in France not only of planes but, more importantly, of experienced pilots. He did everything possible to make up for these deficiencies in the breathing space the Germans allowed him, but he knew that he could beat the Germans only by a dangerously narrow margin. The key to success lay in the magnificent communications system he had built up, which was based on the swift analysis of information gleaned from the radar stations around England's south and east coasts.

Dowding knew that timing was essential if the German bombers were to be stopped. Fighters had only enough fuel to remain in the air for about an hour, and their ammunition was used up in a matter of seconds. 'Scrambling' too early could well prove disastrous, but adequate warning had to be given to allow the fighters to gain sufficient height for a successful attack. Fifty-two radar stations from Pembrokeshire to the Shetlands could pick up incoming planes from a distance of about 75 miles and could make reasonably accurate estimates of their numbers and altitude. As soon as the planes reached the coast, they were followed by the Royal Observer Corps. This information was relayed to the four Fighter Command Groups and to the Fighter Command Headquarters at Bentley Priory. Beginning in February 1940, additional information was provided by 'Y Service' which monitored radio traffic between German aircraft. This was analysed by 'Station X' at Bletchley Park, which was also responsible for cracking the German 'Enigma' codes. Dowding was provided with 'Ultra' information by means of a teleprinter link with Bletchley Park, but it is not clear how useful this intelligence was to Fighter Command during the Battle of Britain.

Information from Bentley Priory was relayed selectively to the four Groups. There it was further refined and forwarded to the sectors, and from the sectors to the squadrons. The sector Operations Rooms were the decisive final link in the chain, where the controllers made the critical operational decisions to despatch the squadrons and had full executive authority over them until they came into direct contact with the enemy. The controllers were usually squadron leaders with flying experience, many of whom had been in combat.

Fighter Command suffered heavy losses in the air war over the Channel (*Kanalkampf*), and by 19 July statisticians warned Dowding that his fighters would all be destroyed within six weeks if losses continued to climb at the same rate. Even if the aircraft were quickly replaced, skilled pilots needed months of training. But the Germans also had to face some unpleasant facts. Their bombers, the Dornier 17 ('flying pencil') and the more heavily armoured Heinkel 111, were very vulnerable to fighter attack and therefore needed close escorts of Messerschmitt 109s. Since the Me 109s had only thirty minutes' flying time over Britain, the range of the bombers was severely restricted. The Junkers 87B (*Stuka*) which had proved so terrifying in Poland and in the western campaign was painfully slow and was thus an easy target for modern fighters. Even in its screaming dive it was extremely vulnerable to anti-aircraft fire. The Spitfire proved to be the match of the Me 109 in everything but high-altitude flying, but the *Kanalkampf* had shown that German pilots were better trained and their tactics were superior. The RAF, however, was quick to learn from the Luftwaffe and used their methods against them to devastating effect.

Although 'Ultra' decrypts gave the British ample warning of the German attack, their radar stations along the south coast suffered severe damage on 12 August. On the following day Fighter Command's ground installations were badly hit and a number of aircraft still on the ground were destroyed. 'Ultra' provided precise information of the Luftwaffe's intentions on 15 August and the Germans were to suffer severe losses, although nothing like as great as those claimed by the RAF. In the following days the Luftwaffe kept up the attack, concentrating on Fighter Command's airfields and causing serious damage, but they were still being outshot by the RAF.

In these critical days Dowding showed his true genius. He realized that his prime task was to protect his airfields and his communications network, and that therefore it was essential to shoot down bombers before they released their payloads, rather than concentrating on their fighter escorts. Many of his pilots resented this unglamorous approach. They wanted to achieve the highest score of hits by going for the Me 109s which were forced to fly in close protective formations around the bombers and therefore had restricted manoeuvrability. Goering was out to get the fighters; Dowding was determined not to give him the opportunity. Air Vice-Marshal Keith Park, commanding 11 Group in south-east England, fully supported Dowding. On 19 August he ordered that the main objective was to engage enemy bombers, not to engage in fighter-to-fighter combat.

The opposition to Dowding's strategy was led by Air Vice-Marshal Sir Trafford Leigh-Mallory, commander of 12 Group in the

Midlands, vociferously seconded by a swashbuckling squadron-leader, Douglas Bader, commander of No. 242 Squadron at Coltishall. They rejected Dowding's penny-pinching tactics and developed their 'Big Wing' theory whereby three to five squadrons would rendezvous, climb to 20,000 feet while the enemy were crossing the Channel, and sweep down upon them 'up-sun', cannons ablaze.

The tactics of the Duxford Wing, named after the rendezvous point of the Big Wing, made a nonsense of Dowding's strategy. The task of 12 Group was to guard the industrial centres of the Midlands and to form a strategic reserve. This was a tedious and frustrating role for pilots anxious for action and obsessed with the numbers game. Bader rejected Dowding's fundamental premise and agreed with those, such as the Deputy Chief of Air Staff, Air Vice-Marshal Sholto Douglas, who stated that 'it does not matter where the enemy is shot down, as long as he is shot down in large numbers'. Leigh-Mallory and Bader were insubordinate, spending as much time fighting Dowding and Park as they did fighting Germans, and their strategy was wrong. But the aloof Dowding must also take some of the blame for not being fully informed of what was going on and for not settling an increasingly acrimonious squabble.

By the end of August, Fighter Command had suffered crippling losses of aircraft and severe damage to ground installations. But the Luftwaffe was also frustrated by its failure to draw the fighters into their 'meat-grinder'. On the night of 24 August they made a fateful mistake by sending a hundred aircraft on a bombing raid on London. It remains a mystery why the Germans decided to make this change in their strategy, but it altered the whole course of the Battle of Britain. The following night, in spite of the misgivings of the Air Staff and although the damage in London was minimal, Bomber Command sent a retaliatory raid of 81 bombers to Berlin. Hitler was furious and Goering, who had announced that he would eat his hat if a single bomb fell on the German capital, was equally displeased. Hitler now ordered a further raid on London for the afternoon of 7 September. 'Ultra' provided adequate warning and London's Civil Defence was placed on full alert.

The raid, aimed at the London docks and generating plants, was a triumphant success for the Germans. Flying at unusually high altitude and employing new fighter escort tactics, they eluded Park's fighters and suffered relatively few losses. But the diversion of the attacks away from Fighter Command's bases gave the RAF a welcome respite. London was a more distant target than the air bases in southern England and therefore gave Fighter Command more time to prepare to meet the attackers. It also further reduced the limited flying time of the Me 109s.

Although Liverpool had been bombed on the night of 28 August and on three subsequent nights, the main objective of the Luftwaffe was now London. The Luftwaffe Staff (*Luftwaffenführungsstab*) estimated that massive attacks on London's industrial and working-class neighbourhoods, combined with raids on Coventry and Sheffield, would cripple Britain's war industry, demoralize the workforce and strengthen the conviction of those industrialists, politicians and military leaders who they believed wished to depose Churchill and end a senseless war. In this new situation Hitler wanted to use the threat of an invasion as a psychological weapon to undermine British morale and to encourage the Luftwaffe, even though he no longer thought that 'Sea-lion' was likely to be launched in 1940, if at all. The Chief of Staff of the Luftwaffe, Jeschonnek, requested permission to bomb residential areas in order to cause panic among the civilian population, but Hitler expressly forbade such action, probably because he feared that Bomber Command would pay him back in kind. The Führer was somewhat more fastidious in this matter than the German Foreign Office, who argued that since the British claimed that the Luftwaffe was aiming at civilian targets they might as well go ahead and bomb them. The 'England Committee' of the Foreign Office argued that concentrated attacks on working-class districts would cause such consternation that the Labour Party would force the Government to end the war.

Although the Luftwaffe was generally optimistic that a bomber offensive against Britain's industrial centres, particularly against the aircraft factories, would be successful, there were those who took a less optimistic view. General Hoffmann von Waldau, Chief of the Luftwaffe's Operations Division, told Halder on 7 October that they had completely underestimated the strength of Fighter Command. The Germans had lost 350 of their 950 fighters and 500 of their 1100 bombers. He estimated that it would take until the spring for the Luftwaffe to make up for these losses and that to 'get' the British they needed four times the number of planes. This being the case, the Luftwaffe would be in no state to fight a war against both Britain and the Soviet Union. The Enemy Information Bureau in Berlin also justifiably warned that the Luftwaffe tended to exaggerate the effects of their raids.

The Luftwaffe now concentrated on industrial targets in the

Midlands. Goering's staff convinced themselves that the industrial magnates of the Midlands were Churchill's strongest supporters and when they saw their capital investments reduced to rubble they would call for peace. According to the Political Division of the *Luftwaffenführungsstab* the Midlands was the homeland of 'the truly conservative, stubborn and obstinate Englishmen who are the intellectual and moral foundation of Britain's resistance and endurance'.

The RAF had won the daytime battle by a hair's breadth but had no effective defence against night bombers. Dowding once again came up with the answer with airborne radar (AI), but it was fraught with problems. Radar could be used only in a two-seater fighter, but the only planes available for this role were the obsolete and slow Boulton Paul Defiants and Blenheims. The superb Bristol Beaufighter had still to overcome some technical difficulties before it became operational. Much against his will, Dowding was forced to allocate three Hurricane squadrons for night operations for which they were unsuited – even with pilots stuffed full of carrots, that miraculous vegetable said to improve night vision. Meanwhile the British public, battered by endless bombardment by night against which there seemed to be no defence and denied the encouragingly inflated tallies of German aircraft shot down, clamoured for action. But contrary to the Germans' expectations, morale, although never as high as myth would have it, did not crack; indeed, the determination to seek revenge for the 23,000 who died in the Blitz between July and December 1940 strengthened Britain's will to resist. Damage to industrial centres such as Coventry was quickly repaired and the factories back to normal production within a few days.

Bad weather in the winter of 1940 reduced the number of raids, and the Luftwaffe failed to achieve its strategic objectives. On 18 December Hitler issued Directive 21 for an attack on the Soviet Union before the defeat of Britain. Contrary to all expectations Britain had survived, thus offering hope to the occupied countries and an inspiring example of tenacity in adversity to the Americans. Hitler had at last suffered a reverse, however minor. Dowding, the principal architect of this success, was shabbily treated. On 13 November he was informed that he was about to be replaced. Three days later he was given twenty-four hours to clear his desk. At the end of September he was awarded the GCB, and he was made a baronet in May 1943. 'Stuffy' Dowding had no dash and no flair, and thus no appeal for Churchill. The Prime Minister did not feel that so much was owed to the leader of the few. Most of the Air Staff thought his strategy mistaken and favoured the 'Big Wing', but subsequent war games designed to show the superiority of the Leigh-Mallory approach proved that it would have been disastrous. Park was also pushed aside and given the command of a Training Group. He was, however, to have a distinguished though deeply frustrating career later in the war in the Mediterranean and Burma. The fighter pilots of the Battle of Britain are justly immortalized in one of Churchill's best known sayings, but it is sobering to remember that although 537 of these brave men were killed in the course of the battle, Bomber Command were later to lose more in a single night over Germany.

Having failed to create the necessary preconditions for an invasion of England, the German military proposed an indirect strategy. Jodl suggested that Germany should support the Italians in Libya and seize the Suez Canal, and also co-operate with Spain to take Gibraltar. He also saw the Arabs as potential allies against Britain. The German Navy came to similar conclusions and argued that Gibraltar and Suez were the keys to naval supremacy in the Mediterranean. The oil supplies of the Middle East would then be in the hands of the Axis and the way to India open. Co-operation with Spain would also make it possible to seize the French colonies in Africa and use them as bases for the domination of the Atlantic. The Balkans would be secure from British intervention. Hitler was particularly interested in securing the Azores, the Cape Verde Islands and the Canaries, intending to use the Azores as a base for long-range bombers to attack America. Neither Hitler nor OKH was particularly keen on sending troops to north Africa; the most that was considered in the winter of 1940 was a Panzer brigade. They hoped that Luftwaffe support would be enough to keep the Italians going.

Mussolini, who declared war on 10 June 1940, proclaiming from the balcony of the Palazzo Venezia that 'a people of 45 million souls is not truly free unless it has free access to the oceans', was desperately looking for a victory. At first he thought of invading Yugoslavia from his base in Albania, but Hitler vetoed this proposal for fear that it would lead to British intervention in the Balkans. If the British were to establish airfields in the Balkans they would then be in an excellent position to bomb the Romanian oilfields and thus cut off the supplies needed for his offensive against the Soviet Union. The Italians were annoyed by this negative German attitude, but in the middle of August 1940 Mussolini ordered studies for an invasion of Greece. This strategy was equally unwelcome to the Germans, who found themselves dragged into the war in the Balkans at a very awkward time in order to save their ally from a disastrous loss of prestige.

Franco prudently waited for the fall of France before he proposed entering the war at Germany's side. In return he wanted arms and matériel, Gibraltar and the French colonies in north and west Africa. He did not wait for German approval to seize the international sector of Tangier. Hitler saw Franco as a valuable ally against Britain and ordered an operational study of an attack on Gibraltar, codenamed 'Felix'. But Franco was already beginning to have second thoughts. He was suspicious of Hitler's annexationist intentions and realized that Britain was far from beaten. These suspicions were amply founded. Hitler described the proposals for an anti-British continental bloc from Madrid to Tokyo, a favourite idea of Ribbentrop's, as a 'gigantic swindle'. It was designed as a purely temporary measure until Germany was in the position to conquer *Lebensraum* in the east and bases in the Mediterranean and Atlantic, including Gibraltar.

Hitler met Franco on 23 October at Hendaye, but the talks led nowhere. Hitler was concerned that if he were to agree openly to Franco's seizure of the French colonies, this would weaken the Vichy Government and strengthen de Gaulle. Franco saw no advantage in making a pact with Hitler in return for which he was offered nothing but vague promises. He was also under considerable economic pressure from the United States not to get any closer to the Axis powers, and he depended on Canadian wheat for which the Germans were unable to provide any alternative. On 7 December Franco told Admiral Canaris that he was not interested in pursuing the matter and any further consideration of operation 'Felix' had to be abandoned. Henceforth relations between Germany and Spain were distinctly cool and were scarcely improved when Spanish volunteers in the 'Blue Legion' arrived on the eastern front. In his political testament Hitler dismissed Franco's regime as a group of 'plutocratic exploiters led by the nose by the priests', but at the time Franco's cautiousness could not be so easily dismissed and was deeply disturbing.

Although Germany had won a brilliant victory in the west, the *Blitzkrieg* strategy had failed. Britain had not been forced to the negotiating table and had won a breathing space to recover militarily and politically from the defeat in France. This placed the Germans in a strategically weak position in that they were now driven to fight a protracted war in which the chances of ultimate success were extremely remote.

In the second half of 1940 Hitler concentrated on the Mediterranean. He hoped to drive Britain out of the area and at the same time protect his southern flank in anticipation of an attack on the Soviet Union. He hoped that Spain and Italy would do the job for him with discreet help from Germany, and that the Vichy regime would be favourably disposed towards this policy. But Hitler also knew that the differences between Italy, Spain and Vichy were fundamental and that the propaganda needed to disguise this fact would be exceedingly unlikely to prove convincing. Hitler hoped that the Three-Power Pact of 27 September 1940 between Germany, Italy and Japan would help to overcome some of his immediate strategic concerns by putting further pressure on Britain to negotiate, and by isolating the United States. In fact it had the opposite effect, bringing Washington and London closer together. It also annoyed the Soviets who, convinced that Hitler wanted to reach an understanding with Britain, felt that the tripartite agreement had distinctly anti-Soviet overtones. German reaction to the Soviet–Finnish war, the guarantee to Romania and the mounting backlog of shipments to the Soviet Union promised in the trade agreement fuelled these suspicions.

Hitler was not particularly concerned about these developments and told Mussolini in the course of their discussions on the Brenner in early October that Stalin was being reasonable and that the Soviet Union was militarily so weak that there was no cause for concern. He claimed that British hopes for support from the Soviet Union and from the United States, which was the only reason for their refusal to negotiate in spite of their 'militarily hopeless situation', were unfounded. The United States, in Hitler's view, had reacted in a 'very cowardly' manner to the Three-Power Pact.

Mussolini showed little enthusiasm for Hitler's idea of an anti-British continental bloc because he feared that an agreement between Germany, Vichy and Spain would be at Italy's expense. After meeting Franco at Hendaye, Hitler went to Montoire for talks with Pétain. While in France he was informed of Mussolini's attack on Greece, but although he was later to describe the campaign as 'idiotic' he avoided discussing it with Mussolini during their meeting in Florence.

Hitler's trip to France and Italy solved none of the outstanding problems. That 'Jesuit pig' Franco made it abundantly clear that he intended to keep out of the war, and the Vichy regime was prepared to offer only limited collaboration. His Mediterranean strategy was now dictated by the Italians, whose military incompetence was such that there was no hope of fighting a war by proxy. He was now faced with the problem of whether to attack the Soviet Union immediately and thus risk a war on two fronts, or to seek an accommodation with Britain and then move east. There was no uncertainty in his mind about the long-term aim: *Lebensraum* in the east and a German-dominated Europe.

In the summer of 1940 the Germans paid particular attention to the Balkans. The region was important for a number of reasons. Germany was more dependent than ever on supplies from the Balkans since the Royal Navy had cut off vital provisions from overseas. Particularly important were petroleum and wheat from Romania. Politically it was essential to stop the British from establishing better relations with the Balkan states and to reduce Soviet influence in the area so as to secure a launching-pad for the attack on the Soviet Union. The Germans had every reason to preserve the status quo in the Balkans but this proved impossible, not only because of the rivalries between the different states, but also because of Italian ambitions which were to cause the Germans endless problems.

The Romanians had every reason to be concerned by the Molotov–Ribbentrop pact, although they were unaware of the secret protocol which gave Bessarabia to the Soviet Union. The Anglo-French guarantee offered them little comfort, and they prudently remained neutral during the Polish campaign. With Poland in German hands the Romanians did everything possible to appease the Germans. The King granted a general amnesty to members of the Iron Guard (the Romanian fascist movement) who had been exiled and imprisoned for their complicity in the murder of Minister President Calinescu. A new commercial treaty was negotiated with the Reich whereby the Romanians received 100 million marks' worth of plunder from Poland, mainly armaments, and Germany received all the petroleum products it requested. After the fall of France the Romanians lost Bessarabia and the northern Bukovina to the Soviet Union, and tried desperately to persuade the Germans to stop the Hungarians from taking Transylvania and the Bulgarians from seizing the southern Bukovina.

Hitler, having decided on 31 July to attack the Soviet Union in the spring of 1941, was prepared to guarantee the Carpathian frontier with the USSR. A division which included the SS *Leibstandarte Adolf Hitler* and the infantry regiment *Grossdeutschland* was kept on the alert lest the Soviets should be tempted to take advantage of Romania's difficulties with Hungary to attack. Hitler was not, however, prepared to support Romania against Bulgaria. The Hungarian territorial demands were strongly supported by Mussolini, and at the end of August the Germans acted as arbitrators in the dispute. The result annoyed both sides, and even the Iron Guard and the Hungarian Arrow Cross were alienated from their German sponsors. Henceforth the SS organized the German minorities in Romania and Hungary, using them as pressure groups for German interests, and the indigenous fascist movements were dropped in favour of more traditional conservative politicians.

The Romanians, knowing that they could expect no help from Britain, decided that their only option was to co-operate with the Germans. They therefore began to persecute the Jews, and asked for a military mission. The arbitration of the Romanian–Hungarian dispute triggered off a severe domestic political crisis and the Iron Guard attempted a coup. King Carol appointed the strongly pro-German General Ion Antonescu as Minister President with exceptional powers. Antonescu promptly forced the King to abdicate and his son ascended the throne as Michael I. A German military mission was promptly sent to Romania, along with a large number of instructors whose task was to prepare the Romanian army for an offensive war against the Soviet Union. Further troops were sent to Romania, ostensibly to protect the country against attack by a 'third power' and to guard the oil-wells against British saboteurs. In fact the British oil engineers had been unable to carry out any sabotage actions, as they had been given twenty-four hours to leave the country. On 23 November Romania joined the Three-Power Pact, Antonescu having told Hitler and Ribbentrop that Carol II's regime was controlled by the 'sinister powers of bolshevism and Jewry' and that he looked forward to 'drawing his sword alongside the Axis powers to fight for the victory of civilization'.

Relations between Germany and Hungary followed a similar pattern. Hungary as a revisionist power realized that its ambitions could be fulfilled only with a victory for the Axis. The leader of the Arrow Cross, Szalasi, was released from prison. German troops were allowed to travel through Hungary. Further anti-Semitic legislation was passed which intensified the discrimination against Jews begun by Kalman Daranyi in February 1938. In October 1940 a trade treaty was signed which met all Germany's demands. After the failure of Molotov's visit to Berlin in November, Hungary was permitted to join the Three-Power Pact and 146,000 Hungarian troops joined in the invasion of Yugoslavia where they behaved in an appallingly brutal manner, committing numerous atrocities against

Jews, Serbs and Germans. But the Hungarian leadership had serious reservations about this close association with Nazi Germany. Temperamentally both the Regent, Admiral Horthy, and the Minister President, Count Teleki, were closer to the conservative and aristocratic British than to fascist louts. It was impossible, however, to pursue revisionist aims alongside the Germans and at the same time hope to keep the lines open to London. Teleki committed suicide in April 1941, driven to desperation by the fear that Hungary was too closely tied to Germany in a war whose outcome was still far from certain. Horthy and the new Minister President, Bárdossy, shared some of these concerns but were not seriously troubled when Britain broke off diplomatic relations three days after Teleki's suicide.

Germany's relatively cautious policy in the Balkans was placed in serious jeopardy when Italy attacked Greece on 28 October 1940. German military experts estimated that the Italians would find it exceedingly difficult to defeat the Greeks. This raised the unwelcome possibility of British intervention in the Balkans, something which Hitler was determined to avoid. The German military estimated that the British would send at least three divisions to Greece. Indeed, Britain had given Greece a guarantee of support in April 1940 and Minister President Metaxas immediately requested assistance. Churchill was not in a position to offer much help, and many of his military advisors argued that troops destined for Greece could be better used in north Africa to defeat the Italians before the Germans arrived. Others argued that the Italians, the Achilles' heel of the Axis, could be defeated in Greece. But the political arguments for intervention in Greece were overwhelming. Britain could not afford to renege on an obligation to help, and to do so would create a most unfortunate impression in the United States. Aid to Greece, if successful, might encourage the Turks and Yugoslavs to join the struggle against the Axis powers where Anthony Eden's diplomatic efforts had failed. Churchill insisted that the fall of Greece would have a 'deadly effect' on Turkey. Eden was in the Middle East at the beginning of November and agreed with Wavell that sending troops to Greece from Egypt would 'imperil our whole position in the Middle East and jeopardize plans for offensive operations now being laid in more than one theatre'. Churchill persuaded the Chiefs of Staff that aid for Greece was essential, and Wavell was ordered to give 'the greatest possible material and moral support' to Greece 'at the earliest possible moment'.

Hitler was well aware of British efforts to win over the Turks and

Yugoslavs, and feared that the Soviets might be drawn into an anti-Axis Balkan pact which would endanger the south flank of his attack on the Soviet Union. News that the RAF was steadily building up reserves in Greece convinced Hitler that the British intended to bomb the Romanian oilfields, and he promptly forced the Bulgarian Government to allow the Germans to set up early-warning stations along the frontier with Greece. He further ordered plans for the occupation of Macedonia and Thrace, where air bases could be established to counter this threat to the Romanian oilfields. Hitler still hoped that it might be possible to exert diplomatic pressure on the Greek Government to persuade them to request the British to leave. Planning for 'Operation Marita' went ahead, so that should this initiative prove unsuccessful the Germans would invade Greece and the troops could then be used on the southern flank of the invasion of the Soviet Union.

In preparation for the invasion, the German garrison in Romania was strengthened and troops were sent to Bulgaria to establish the infrastructure for the deployment of the invasion forces. The Soviets were understandably alarmed by these developments and Hitler tried to reassure Stalin and Molotov that these measures were aimed exclusively against the British. This was hardly comforting to the Soviets, for even if that were the case it would still mean a drastic diminution of Soviet influence in the Balkans. The Yugoslavs refused to allow German troops to cross their territory, and therefore Hungary had to be used as a deployment area. At the same time, Hitler persuaded Horthy to patch up relations with Yugoslavia and not to press for frontier rectifications. The Hungarian Government, hoping for substantial gains from a German victory, co-operated fully. Pressure was also exerted on the Bulgarian Government to distance themselves from the Soviet Union, join the Three-Power Pact and permit the deployment of German troops for the attack on Greece. Bulgaria was also persuaded to sign a friendship and non-aggression treaty with Turkey. In the course of the month of March 1941, fourteen German divisions arrived in Bulgaria and were stationed along the Greek border.

The Greek Government tried to persuade the Germans to negotiate a peace on the basis of the status quo and assured Berlin that their only quarrel was with the Italians. The Germans, who had become so concerned with the possible threat to the 'soft underbelly', had guaranteed the Bulgarians access to the Aegean and could not tolerate that their Axis partner should suffer such a loss of face. Unable to negotiate with the Germans, the Greeks asked the British for at least nine divisions to meet the threat of an invasion. Wavell would consider sending only two to three divisions. For the Greeks this was enough to provoke the Germans, but not nearly enough to stop them. The situation was somewhat improved at the beginning of February 1941 when the British captured Benghazi, and although Wavell had serious doubts whether the British presence in Greece would make a decisive difference, he was prepared to run the risk.

'Operation Lustre', the movement of British troops to Greece, had hardly begun when Eden reported that the Greek commander, General Papagos, was becoming 'unaccommodating and defeatist', having lost confidence after the death of Metaxas at the end of January. The Greeks once again tried to negotiate with the Germans, but Hitler was now determined to occupy the whole of Greece and drive the British out of the Aegean. Churchill began to wonder whether Greece could be defended except in the unlikely event of Yugoslavia and Turkey entering the war, adding that the loss of Greece would be 'by no means a major catastrophe for us provided Turkey remains honestly neutral'.

In the course of his meeting with Hitler at the Berghof on 4 March 1941, Prince Paul of Yugoslavia made it plain that his sympathies lay with Greece and Britain, but Hitler warned that if he did not sign a treaty with the Axis powers there would be serious political consequences. Yugoslavia eventually gave way to the Germans, but managed to secure certain concessions. German troops would not march through Yugoslav territory, and there would be no call for military assistance from the Reich. Yugoslavia was promised Salonika once the campaign was successfully completed. On 21 March the Yugoslav Government agreed by a vote of sixteen to three to join the Three-Power Pact. Although public opinion was opposed to the treaty, the Government took the view that Yugoslavia was in no position to defend itself against a German attack. The treaty was signed in Vienna three days later.

By the end of March 1941 Germany had greatly strengthened its position in the Balkans. Greece was effectively isolated and, with the exception of Turkey which jealously guarded its neutrality, all the other countries in the region had joined the Three-Power Pact and had signed trade agreements which enabled Germany to secure adequate supplies of vital raw materials. Greece could be easily overrun and the British driven from continental Europe. The exposed southern flank of the attack on the Soviet Union would be secure from attack. Hitler had tried to use diplomatic pressure to secure his aims, and had then been prepared to occupy only parts of Greece, but as the time for the attack on the Soviet Union drew nearer he decided to act drastically and decisively to settle the Balkan question in one fell swoop.

In Yugoslavia, opposition to the signing of the Three-Power Pact was combined with Serbian resentment at the pro-Croatian policies of the Cvetkovic Government. Two days after the signing of the pact a group of Serbian officers mounted a coup and deposed the Regent (whom Churchill contemptuously called 'Prince Palsy') and Peter II became King, although he was still a minor. Simovic, the leader of the coup, headed the new Government which, although it did not renounce the Three-Power Pact, clearly distanced itself from Germany. Only a few hours after the putsch, Hitler decided to attack Yugoslavia. He was angry at the arrest of the signatories of the Three-Power Pact, suspected that the coup had been masterminded by the British, was greedy to exploit Yugoslavia's economic resources, and was smarting at this affront to the prestige of the Reich at which Churchill was crowing with exaggerated delight. Hoping to play off the Croats against the Serbs, Ribbentrop promised the Croatian politician Macek that Croatia would become independent, but Macek had no desire to see his country destroyed and accepted the position of Vice-President in Simovic's Government. Simovic tried to convince the Germans that he wished to remain on close terms and had no intention of rejecting the Three-Power Pact. He thus rejected British approaches for co-operation against Germany. Hitler was convinced that the Yugoslavs were playing for time and were preparing the ground for an anti-German Balkan alliance. On 6 April, Palm Sunday, German bombers attacked Belgrade in an operation which, with the recent coup in mind, was codenamed 'Retribution'. On the same day Piraeus, where British troops were disembarking, was also bombed. Churchill knew of the intended attack on Belgrade from 'Enigma' decrypts and duly warned the Yugoslav Government, but to no avail. Several thousand civilians died in the raid on Belgrade and the operational centres of the Government and the military were destroyed.

The Germans struck at Yugoslavia and Greece before even the outline of a defensive strategy could be worked out with the British. Churchill's dream of a Balkan front proved to be pure fantasy. With their overwhelming air power the Germans had little difficulty in overrunning the courageous but ill-equipped Yugoslav army. On 17 April Yugoslavia capitulated. The army acted with extreme brutality against the Serbs who, unlike the Croats, were believed to be strongly opposed to the Germans. The savage persecution of the Serbs strengthened their determination to resist, and thousands joined the infant partisan movement. In Greece the Germans had some difficulty in breaking through the Metaxas Line, but by 9 April they had taken Salonika. On 27 April they entered Athens in triumph.

The British evacuated some 43,000 of their 55,000 men in Greece to Crete, but they had only six Hurricanes, seventeen obsolete aircraft and painfully few anti-aircraft guns. Crete had long been a strategic goal of the Germans, for Hitler feared that it could be used by the British as a base for air strikes against the Romanian oilfields. 'Enigma' decrypts had revealed the full details of the German plan of attack, but the British forces in Crete were caught inadequately prepared by a brilliantly planned and executed airborne attack on 20 May. Once the Germans had captured the airfield at Maleme, the battle for Crete was lost. Churchill ordered that Crete had to be saved at whatever cost, but there was little that General Freyberg could do. Some 18,000 men were evacuated from Crete in a heroic action by the Royal Navy in which three cruisers, six destroyers and twenty-nine smaller ships were lost along with 2000 men. Admiral Cunningham had cast aside the advice of his more cautious staff and mounted the action with the remark: 'It takes the Navy three years to build a ship. It would take three hundred to rebuild a tradition.'

The Royal Navy's tradition might have been saved, but Britain had suffered a severe defeat. It had lost its last foothold in Europe and with it control of the Aegean and the Black Sea. The forces in north Africa had been seriously weakened at a critical stage of the desert war. General Freyberg was a gallant soldier, but the defence of Crete had been shambolic, providing rich material for Evelyn Waugh's acidic pen. But Hitler had also lost 6000 elite troops and more than 300 aircraft. He became cautious. General Student, who commanded the invasion forces, ordered his men to 'eradicate' the male population of any villages suspected of harbouring guerillas and saboteurs, and the villages were destroyed. He reported that: 'True to the oath that we have given to the Führer as supreme commander of the armed forces, we are ready for new tasks'. But the Germans were in no position to mount another operation against Malta, Cyprus or the Suez Canal. In this sense, Crete was not a total disaster.

The British were now in an awkward situation in the Middle

East. They were no longer in a position to launch air raids against the Romanian oilfields and they could inflict only indirect damage on the Germans in the desert. It could never be a decisive theatre, because even if they were able to draw a substantial number of German troops from Europe there would be no allied force large enough to mount an invasion of north-western France. On the other hand, an Axis victory in which Britain lost control of the Suez Canal and the Persian Gulf could well make it impossible for the Allies to continue the war. It was fortunate that Hitler was obsessed with attacking the Soviet Union and therefore did not bother unduly about the Middle East once he had secured his Balkan flank.

When Mussolini declared war on 10 June the prospects for a splendid victory in north Africa were excellent. The French forces in north Africa, Syria and French Somaliland were loyal to Vichy. The British forces were overwhelmingly outnumbered both on land and in the air. But Marshal Graziani's offensive from Cyrenaica was slow and hesitant and constantly harassed by a series of hit-and-run raids by General Creagh's 7th Armoured Division, soon to be nicknamed the 'Desert Rats'. Graziani waited for three months before beginning his offensive against Egypt on 13 September. He moved forward to Sidi Barrani where he established a poorly designed defensive position. Wavell decided to hit the Italians as hard as he could with the limited forces available. A brilliant plan was developed by Brigadier Dorman-Smith, General O'Connor's unorthodox, caustic and highly controversial Staff Officer. The 7th Armoured Brigade cut off the Italian lines of retreat by driving towards the sea at Buq-Buq, while the 7th Royal Tank Regiment and the 4th Indian Division attacked the widely dispersed Italian positions around Sidi Barrani. Some 40,000 prisoners were taken and the remainder of the Italian army fled across the Libyan border to Bardia, where they were soon encircled by the Desert Rats.

Although the Italians were on the run, Wavell and 'Jumbo' Wilson decided to move the 4th Indian Division to the Sudan. The Indians played a decisive role in the battle for the heights of Keren which led to the loss of Eritrea, but three valuable weeks were lost while the 6th Australian Division was brought up from Palestine to support the advance. (Australia, along with the other dominions, had declared war on Germany shortly after Britain; the first Australian troops were shipped to England at the end of November 1939.) The Australians, along with the 7th Royal Tank Regiment with their Matilda tanks against which the Italians had no defence, had little difficulty in taking Bardia. The Desert Rats moved on to Tobruk, which fell on 21 January. O'Connor's forces were weakened by the build-up of British forces in Greece and he was badly in need of reinforcements, but he decided to make a quick dash to the west of Benghazi to cut off the Italian retreat. The Desert Rats covered 170 miles in 36 hours across difficult terrain, establishing a record for armoured mobility and surprising the Italians at Beda Fomm where a mere 3000 men took 20,000 Italian prisoners.

In the course of the whole 'Operation Compass', 130,000 prisoners were taken along with 845 guns and 380 tanks at a cost of only 500 dead. O'Connor longed to press on to Tripoli, even though his troops were exhausted, supplies running short and transport inadequate to supply Tripoli once it was taken. This was not to be. Churchill ordered that since a major effort had to be made to save Greece, the advance had to be halted. On 12 February not O'Connor but Rommel arrived in Tripoli with the rudiments of his Afrika Korps. A new stage in the desert war had begun.

In east Africa the Italians were equally slow in going on the offensive and thus gave the British time to build up their forces. Churchill could not make up his mind what to do. First he told Wavell to let the Italians wither on the vine and then he urged him to go on the offensive, but Wavell insisted that he had to wait until the rainy season was over. Throughout the winter almost the only activity was by Orde Wingate, the highly unorthodox commander of Gideon Force which enabled the charismatic emperor of Ethiopia, Haile Selassie, to return to his kingdom. Italian Somaliland was then captured in a two-pronged attack launched in February. In Eritrea the British came up against excellent commanders such as General Carnimeo who were firmly entrenched in the mountainous region around Keren. It took fifty-three days to dislodge them, but once Keren fell the Duke of Aosta, an admirable soldier, was forced to surrender on 19 May. The remaining pockets of Italian resistance were wiped out in the following months. Some 250,000 prisoners were taken in east Africa and Mussolini's dream of an African empire was now in ruins.

In January Hitler decided that he would send an armoured force to defend Tripoli, not so much because he thought it was strategically important but rather because he feared that further Italian defeats could well lead to the fall of Mussolini and the end of the Axis. Lieutenant-General Erwin Rommel, the commander of 'Operation Sunflower', an egotistical, glory-seeking, tough and immensely courageous general, had no intention of sitting tight. 'Hitler's favourite general' decided to go on the offensive immediately, and caught the British troops off their guard, beginning a rout which seemed to be almost as disastrous as that inflicted on the Italians.

Britain had suffered a series of humiliating defeats in Europe, and the remarkable successes in Africa against the Italians had done nothing to weaken Germany's dominant position in Europe. The British Chiefs of Staff were not overly concerned, believing that a policy of attrition and harassment would bring final victory. Britain would avoid any decisive battles on the ground, build up the Navy and RAF, blockade Germany, bomb the country to smithereens and encourage the resistance movements in the occupied countries to rise up against their German masters. The vast German war machine would thus be immobilized by lack of matériel, the population would starve and the army would be incapable of holding down the enslaved nations of Europe. In September 1940 the Chiefs of Staff estimated that the regime would collapse by 1942 and that a mere thirty divisions could then return to mainland Europe to receive the instruments of surrender.

This strategy was based on a whole series of miscalculations and illusions. Germany's ruthless exploitation of the resources of occupied and Allied Europe was such that a blockade was incapable of inflicting any appreciable results. Britain was soon to be placed in a far more precarious position in the Battle of the Atlantic, beginning in 1941. It took years before Bomber Command was in a position to inflict any serious damage on German industry, and even then the results were disappointingly meagre in relation to the effort expended and the losses sustained. Hopes for patriotic revolts were based on the exaggerated reports of refugees and on the fanciful notions of international proletarian anti-fascist solidarity entertained by public-school socialists.

Hitler's racial and political obsession with the Soviet Union gave Britain a breathing space, but critical to its survival and eventual victory was the support of the United States. President Roosevelt was determined to do everything possible to help, but he was constrained by domestic political concerns, by legal restrictions and by considerations of national security. In the summer of 1940 it indeed seemed that Britain would have its neck 'wrung like a chicken' and that supplies would therefore simply go down the drain. In June Roosevelt had to agree with his military planners that matériel should be sent only 'if the situation should indicate that Great Britain displayed an ability to withstand German assault, and that the release of such equipment as we could . . . spare would exercise an important effect in enabling Great Britain to [illegible] until the first of the year'.

In June, Churchill asked Roosevelt for fifty to sixty destroyers to make up for the heavy losses sustained by the Royal Navy. The President hesitated, and it was not until the end of August that he agreed to exchange the destroyers for bases in Newfoundland and the Caribbean. He had similar reservations about calling for conscription, fearing that his Republican presidential opponent, Wendell Willkie, might make political capital out of a measure which could well prove to be widely unpopular. In late August, Willkie announced his support for conscription, and Congress soon passed a selective service law for men between the ages of twenty-one and thirty-five which gave the President the right to call up the National Guard for service in the Americas.

In the election campaign Willkie played on the fear that Roosevelt was leading the country into a war. Roosevelt, seeing the gap between him and his opponent narrowing, made constant professions of his determination to preserve the peace, but at the same time he agreed to a British request for enough equipment for ten divisions and a more than twofold increase in aircraft shipments. He countered criticisms of this decision by stressing that it was a profitable business, and that it would lead to economic expansion and help place the American armaments industry in a position that would make it capable of meeting any future emergency. Two days after the election, Roosevelt proposed that half of American armaments production should be sent to Britain, including B–17s (Flying Fortresses).

It soon became clear to the administration that the major problem was that Britain was in no position to pay for these vast orders, and it came as no surprise when the British ambassador, Lord Lothian, announced at a press conference on 23 November: 'Well, boys, Britain's broke; it's your money we want.' Although Roosevelt felt that the British had more convertible assets than they were willing to admit, he also realized that the legal requirement that arms could be sold only for cash was completely unrealistic.

On 8 December Churchill wrote to Roosevelt with an urgent request for economic, naval, political and diplomatic assistance. The President, who was on a vacation trip aboard the cruiser *Tuscaloosa* in the Caribbean, responded with the idea of 'lend-lease', the object of which, he told Morgenthau, was to 'say to England, we will give you the guns and ships that you need, provided that when the war is over you will return to us in kind the guns and ships that we have loaned to you'. At a press conference he told reporters that it was like lending a garden hose to a neighbour to put out a fire, adding: 'I don't say to him before that operation, "Neighbour, my garden hose cost me $15; you have to pay me $15 for it". . . . I don't want $15 – I want my garden hose back after the fire is over.' In a fireside chat broadcast to the nation, the President said it was time to reject the notion of 'business as usual' and announced that the United States would now become 'the great arsenal of democracy'.

These sentiments were overwhelmingly approved by the American public, and Roosevelt ordered the Treasury to draw up a lend-lease Bill. The resulting legislation authorized the President 'to sell, transfer title to, exchange, lease, lend or otherwise dispose of . . . any defense article . . . to any country whose defense the President deems vital to the defense of the United States'. He was also free to decide whether payment should be 'in kind or property, or any other direct or indirect benefit'.

With the British defeat in the Balkans and Rommel charging towards the Egyptian border, Churchill clamoured for closer American involvement in the war. A number of Roosevelt's closest advisors, including Stimson, Knox and Ickes, were in favour of transferring the main weight of the fleet from Hawaii to the Atlantic where it could undertake effective patrols and defend the Azores, the Cape Verde Islands and Dakar from Nazi aggression. Although Roosevelt had approved in principle the strategic concept of Admiral Harold R. Stark, the chief of naval operations, outlined in 'Plan Dog' of November 1940, whereby in the event of war the United States should adopt a purely defensive strategy in the Pacific and launch a strong offensive in the Atlantic, he feared that any reduction of American naval strength in the Pacific would serve to encourage the Japanese. But by the middle of May 1941, with Vichy offering Middle Eastern and African bases to the Germans and the Japanese prepared to discuss their differences with the Americans, Roosevelt ordered one-quarter of the Pacific fleet to be transferred to the Atlantic and he instructed Admiral Stark to draw up plans for the occupation of the Azores. This was not enough for those who said that a step forward was fine but the President should keep on walking, and it was clear that he was waiting for an incident that would give him the excuse to declare war.

Britain was losing the Battle of the Atlantic and the President warned the American people that it would be suicide to wait until the Germans were in their front yard; but with his eye constantly on public opinion polls he was unwilling to go beyond hair-raising warnings of the Nazi menace. Even the sinking of an American freighter by a German U-boat did not make him change course. On 22 June 1941 Hitler launched 'Operation Barbarossa' which diverted his attention away from the Atlantic and the Mediterranean and gave Roosevelt further reason to postpone any momentous decisions

CHAPTER THREE

The Attack on the Soviet Union

(June 1941–December 1941)

In the summer of 1940 Hitler was at the height of his powers. Almost all of Europe from the North Cape to the Bay of Biscay was in his hands. At home, those who had questioned the soundness of his strategy were silenced and his control over the state apparatus was absolute. With breathtaking rapidity he had reversed the events of November 1918 and given Germany unprecedented power and glory. He was bathed in the unquestioning adulation of a united people.

Only Britain remained defiant, but it was generally assumed that the Wehrmacht would soon be despatched across the Channel and the country overrun within six weeks. Neither Hitler nor the German Foreign Office shared this view. They assumed that the British would realize the hopelessness of their situation and would soon begin peace negotiations whereby Germany would be accepted as master of continental Europe and Britain would remain a great maritime power with its vast overseas empire intact. It was therefore perplexing when the British Government rejected out of hand Hitler's 'appeal to common sense' in his Reichstag speech of 19 July. Hitler correctly assumed that the British hoped for increased support from America, but was incorrect in suggesting that they might also be counting on a dramatic change of course by the Soviet Union. Sir Stafford Cripps arrived in Moscow as ambassador in May and was hopeful that Anglo-Soviet relations would improve, but this optimism was not shared by either the British Foreign Office or the Cabinet. The Soviet occupation of the Baltic states and the confiscation of all British assets led to a worsening of relations, and by August even Cripps was ready to pack his bags and go home.

The Soviet occupation of the Baltic states was also a matter of concern to the Germans, even though it came as no surprise since it was agreed upon in the Nazi–Soviet pact. Although Halder ordered the dissolution of 35 divisions in order to bring existing units up to strength or to release men needed to overcome the manpower shortage, he also ordered the 18th Army to the east to provide a credible offensive force. On 3 July 1940 Halder ordered plans to be drawn up for an offensive against the Soviet Union 'to force them to accept the leading role of Germany in Europe'. The Chief of the General Staff did not consider that the Soviet troops in the Baltic states, the Bukovina and Bessarabia posed a threat, but thought in terms of an offensive that would lead to the occupation of the Baltic states, White Russia and parts of the Ukraine and would forestall an understanding between 'the bear and the whale'. It was not until 21 June that Hitler instructed the Commander-in-Chief of the Army, Brauchitsch, to examine 'the Russian problem'. At the end of the month Jodl told his fellow officers that Hitler intended to launch a surprise attack on the Soviet Union to rid the world of the bolshevik menace.

When it became obvious that an invasion of England was not possible in 1940, the army leaders became concerned about the dangers of fighting a two-front war. They therefore suggested that the alliance with the Soviet Union should be maintained, that the British should be driven out of the Mediterranean and the Middle East, and that Germany's position in Europe should be strengthened. Once this was achieved Germany could face the prospect of a protracted war with Britain with every confidence. Hitler came to a totally different conclusion. The leaders of the army and navy were ordered to the Berghof on 31 July and were told that the Soviet Union would be attacked in the spring of 1941. Once Russia collapsed the British would lose their last and only hope, since the Americans would be solely concerned with Japan, whose strength would be immeasurably enhanced by the defeat of the Soviet Union. Brauchitsch and Halder accepted Hitler's arguments without demur and agreed that the problem of Britain and the United States could best be solved by the defeat of the Soviet Union.

Hitler was determined to keep the strategic initiative, meet the threat posed by the United States and find an alternative to 'Operation Sea-lion'. Unable to think in any terms other than victory or defeat, all or nothing, he had to act. The Soviet Union was the only great power which he could attack before Britain and the United States had time to adjust to the demands of global war. Behind all this were Hitler's ideological obsessions: the destruction of

'Jewish bolshevism', the conquest of 'living space' in the east, and the lasting triumph of a purified Germanic race. The decision of 31 July 1940 was thus dictated both by Hitler's calculated strategic assessment of Germany's global situation and by his passionate commitment to his fantasies of race and space. The imperatives of his political programme coincided with his assessment of the long-term military situation and set in motion a series of military, economic and political actions which, although not yet irreversible, were to develop their own dynamic and which were to have fateful consequences.

Germany's immediate political concern was to strengthen its position with regard to the states bordering on the Soviet Union. In order to meet the threat of a Soviet seizure of the Romanian oilfields, a mobile force was assembled in the neighbourhood of Vienna prepared for a swift dash into Romania. With the help of the Italian Government, Germany forced the Romanians and Hungarians to reach an agreement on the bitterly disputed question of Transylvania. That the Soviets were excluded from these negotiations was regarded in Moscow as a serious affront. In Norway a force was prepared to capture the Petsamo ore fields should the Russians have similar intentions. Intensive efforts were also made to improve relations with Finland as a prospective ally against the Soviet Union, whereas hitherto the German Government had supported the Soviets against Finland in accordance with the spirit of the Nazi–Soviet pact.

Within the Germany military there was little immediate sympathy for Hitler's pathological racial and social evolutionary obsessions or for his negative utopian vision of a brave new purely Germanic European world, and yet they were more than willing to do everything possible to realize this dream. This was the result of a deeply ingrained anti-communism within an Officer Corps traumatized by a lost war which they attributed to the stab in the back by Marxists and fellow travellers, socialist-inspired mutinies and soldiers' councils, and the general collapse of discipline and morale. The Officer Corps, with its long tradition of anti-Semitism, was ready to accept the belief that 'bolshevism', a term used with breathtaking abandon, was Jewish in inspiration. There was thus at least a partial identity between Hitler's world view and the ideological preconceptions of the Officer Corps, and there was no fundamental contradiction between them.

The navy was at first opposed to the idea of attacking the Soviet Union before Britain was defeated, but, sharing the army's anti-communism and reassured by Hitler that after the defeat of the

Soviet Union there would be a massive naval building programme in preparation for the final defeat of Britain and possibly the United States, they soon accepted the Führer's strategic arguments for 'Barbarossa'.

The navy's reservations about attacking the Soviet Union were also shared by Ribbentrop. The Foreign Minister, with his anti-British obsessions, thought in terms of a firm alliance between Berlin, Rome and Tokyo aimed at the destruction of Britain and the Empire. For such an undertaking the neutrality of the Soviet Union was essential. For the Japanese, however, the 'Anti-Comintern Pact' was, as the name implied, aimed against the Soviet Union rather than against Britain and they were understandably horrified at the news of the Nazi–Soviet pact. New opportunities were offered when the Japanese decided on expansion in the Pacific rather than a war against the Soviet Union, and Ribbentrop was determined to exploit them to improve relations with Japan. The result was the Three-Power Pact signed in Berlin on 27 September 1940, a ten-year military and economic alliance designed to establish the Berlin–Rome–Tokyo Axis. Hitler, although he could not accept Ribbentrop's overall concept nor his belief that foreign policy should be free from ideological considerations, was also interested in strengthening ties with Japan in order to warn off the Americans. In fact the pact had the opposite effect and the Americans reacted by redoubling their efforts to meet the threat from both Japan and Germany and to help the British in their lonely and desperate struggle.

Hitler and Ribbentrop also agreed on the need to bring Spain and Vichy France into a continental bloc. Hitler wanted security to the rear for his attack on the Soviet Union, Ribbentrop the completion of an anti-British coalition extending across Europe to Asia. Negotiations with Franco and Pétain failed to bring any concrete results, but Ribbentrop's efforts to bring the Soviet Union into the Three-Power Pact were welcomed in both Tokyo and Moscow. The Japanese, having decided on a Pacific strategy, were interested in improving relations with the Soviet Union. The Soviets wanted to stay out of a war which they believed was inevitable for as long as possible, so as to continue their efforts to improve their defensive position while sitting back and watching the capitalist states destroy themselves. German initiatives in Romania and Finland were troubling, and a clarification of the relations between the two countries seemed necessary. On 12 November Molotov arrived in Berlin for discussions with Hitler and Ribbentrop. He showed no interest in exotic plans for a multinational crusade against Britain, the more so since he spent part of his visit in an air-raid shelter avoiding RAF bombers. His sole concern was to strengthen the Soviet position in the border states and on the Straits. The Germans answered Molotov's demands by stressing the importance of Finland and Romania to their war industry. Nothing concrete was achieved during the visit except the clear indication that the Soviet Union was prepared to join the Three-Power Pact provided the conditions were right.

On 10 January 1941 a second Soviet–German economic agreement was signed and shortly afterwards Molotov again raised the question of the Soviet Union joining the pact. No response was given to this démarche, although Hitler insisted that for political reasons the terms of the economic agreement would have to be meticulously respected even at the cost of Germany's economic preparations for war. For Hitler this was all a smokescreen and he told his generals that whatever the outcome of talks with the Soviets, preparations for the invasion of the Soviet Union must continue. On 18 December 1940 Hitler signed Directive No. 21, 'Case Barbarossa', which stated that: 'The German armed forces must be prepared, even before the conclusion of the war against England, *to crush Soviet Russia in a rapid campaign*.' This would be achieved by the destruction of the bulk of the Red Army in the west by armoured spearheads and the erection of a defensive barrier against Asiatic Russia from the Volga to Archangel. The main weight of the offensive was to be directed north of the Pripet marshes towards Leningrad. The attack was then to continue towards Moscow. The army group operating south of the Pripet marshes was to seize Kiev and capture the Donets basin. Some officers doubted whether it would be possible to destroy the Red Army so far forward, others questioned the economic advantages of the campaign, and a few felt that the risk was too great, but there were far fewer reservations about 'Barbarossa' than there had been about the attack on France. The German ambassador in Moscow, Schulenburg, and the State Secretary in the Foreign Office, Weizsäcker, both opposed the proposal to attack the Soviet Union on the grounds that it was likely to prolong the war against Britain rather than shorten it, and argued that Germany benefited greatly from the economic agreement with the Soviet Union. Ribbentrop dismissed the reservations of his subordinates and proclaimed his full support for the anti-Soviet course, even though it was completely contrary to his previous convictions.

The Foreign Office had initially been opposed to the idea of going to Moscow cap in hand begging for raw materials and foodstuffs, and immediate shortages were overcome with the conquest of Poland and its ruthless exploitation. But the invasion of France had to be postponed until 1940, in part because Hitler, for domestic political reasons, did not want to create a full-scale war economy. He feared the long-term consequences of an exceptionally hard winter in 1939 and was painfully aware of the inadequacies of Germany's war industry, particularly in the field of munitions. He therefore decided to seek relief in an economic agreement with the Soviet Union. Stalin had his reasons for welcoming these overtures: the war in Finland revealed serious deficiencies in military equipment; the Soviets felt that it was still possible that the British might be tempted to join an anti-communist crusade led by Germany; and the threat in the east from Japan was still very real. On 11 February 1940 an economic agreement was reached whereby the Germans received goods which were absolutely essential to their armaments programme, principally grain, oil and phosphates, and the Russians took delivery of equally vital machine tools and munitions. This placed the Germans in an awkward position of dependency on Russian deliveries, a situation which the Soviets were quick to exploit. It was only after the successful completion of the campaign in the west that the Germans were able to negotiate from a position of relative strength and force the Soviets to make a number of concessions, especially over oil and coal deliveries.

Although the Germans were able to negotiate better terms, they were still dependent on the Soviet Union for vital supplies and this was irreconcilable with their notions of an autarkic *Grossraumwirtschaft*. By the summer of 1940 there was general agreement among the military leadership, the civil service, industry and business that the situation was unsatisfactory in that future deliveries of essential raw materials were uncertain and that this was obviously incompatible with Germany's determination to achieve the unquestioned economic, political and military domination of Europe. It was partly for this reason that in such circles Hitler's decision to invade the Soviet Union came as no surprise and was widely accepted as highly desirable.

Economic considerations played an important part in the early planning stages for 'Barbarossa'. Clearly it would be impossible to occupy the whole of the Soviet Union, and therefore it was agreed to concentrate on capturing the economic centres of Moscow, Leningrad and the Ukraine. Furthermore, it was argued that the Soviets would have to defend the industrial and agricultural districts in the west, without which they would be unable to supply their armies and continue the war. This offered the opportunity to destroy the enemy in a rapid series of encirclements close to the frontier, and warnings that space and climate were powerful factors which could well prove difficult to overcome were thus discounted. The military planners ignored the resources available in Siberia, overlooked the fact that the Soviets had already built a sizeable war industry east of the Urals, and did not consider the possibility that they might be able to hold up the German advance long enough to move industrial plants to safety behind the Urals. This was due in part to woefully inadequate intelligence and a refusal to believe that official Soviet statistics were anything but propaganda, but also to the belief that the entire Soviet system was hopelessly incompetent and fundamentally unstable. Warnings from the German embassy in Moscow that the economic advantages of an invasion would be minimal because the Soviets would destroy industrial plant and the Ukraine was unlikely to yield any more than during the First World War, when it had scarcely enough to feed the occupying troops, were ignored, as were reports that the Soviet system was far more stable than was believed in Berlin.

Halder thought purely in military terms and wanted a concentric attack on Moscow, but the Quartermaster-General, General Wagner, insisted that there would be sufficient fuel, supplies and munitions for only twenty days, in which time the army could advance a maximum of 500 kilometres. Hitler was obsessed by the economic goals, but their pursuit would lead to a diffusion of effort and was beyond the logistical capabilities available. There was no clear plan as to how the economic resources of the Soviet Union should best be exploited, and in a manner typical of the Third Reich there were endless organizations and committees with contradictory plans and uncertain areas of competence which addressed this problem. The military and the civilians also disagreed about the fundamental approach to the administration of the occupied territories. The military supported the idea of ruthless exploitation, using force where necessary. The civilians were more concerned to build up a healthy economy and were prepared to make political concessions to the occupied peoples in order to secure their support.

On 20 February 1941 the chief of the Military Economic and Armaments Office, General Thomas, presented Hitler with a memorandum on these questions. Ignoring all warnings and appeals for caution, Thomas insisted that if Soviet grain consumption were reduced by 10 per cent, enough grain would be available to overcome all shortages in 1941 and 1942. He claimed, with blissful disregard of cogent arguments to the contrary, that Germany would be in possession of 75 per cent of the Soviet armaments industry in the course of a swift campaign. Industrial installations behind the Urals could then be destroyed by bombers based in occupied Russia. He stressed the importance of the Caucasus oilfields and insisted that they should be seized as early as possible in the campaign so as to save them from destruction and also to open up the route to the east to secure adequate supplies of rubber, much of which had previously come to Germany via the Soviet Union. Thomas, who later made the preposterous claim to have done everything possible to dissuade Hitler from launching his disastrous attack on the Soviet Union, provided the Führer with exactly the arguments he needed. Hitler promptly ordered Goering and Thomas to make plans for the exploitation of occupied Russia, underlining that to maintain order and secure the maximum amount of booty all bolshevik leaders would have to be 'exterminated'. Thomas's organization was made independent from the OKH and named the Economic Staff East. Thus he became an immensely important and independent figure, responsible for all aspects of the war economy, with the idle and incompetent Goering as his nominal superior.

Hitler restricted the activities of the Wehrmacht to the operational area. Further to the rear, Himmler's *Einsatzgruppen* were to be responsible for policing actions, including the extermination of undesirables. Rosenberg was to appoint the Reich commissars and Goering, through General Thomas, was to be responsible for economic affairs. Typically the relative fields of responsibility and the chains of command were never firmly established, and rivalry between these various organizations was to lead to a chaotic situation. Similar problems existed in the private sector. With Germany determined to fight a war of plunder and extermination, representatives of industry queued up outside office doors with shopping lists of desirable objects of booty and attempted to influence military planning so as to attain their aims.

None of this elaborate planning would ever have been undertaken were it not for the conviction that the campaign would be brief and decisive. That this was held to be an axiomatic truth was based on a serious underestimation of the Red Army. Military observers noticed the glaring faults of the Soviet military displayed in the Winter War against Finland in 1939–40. The Officer Corps, having been decimated by Stalin in the purges of 1937 and 1938, was deemed to be seriously deficient and lacking in initiative, imagination and basic operational skills. There had been serious logistical breakdowns in the Finnish war; attacks in depth had led to unnecessarily high casualty rates, and liaison between different branches of the army was totally inadequate. Artillery support for the infantry had been incompetent; armour had been poorly deployed and its effectiveness overestimated.

Although the efforts to reform and modernize the Red Army were felt to be remarkable, it was still believed that it was not capable of launching counter attacks on the flanks of an advancing German army. The strength of the Red Army was that it was large and well armed, and the ordinary soldier was tough and ferociously disciplined. The Soviet soldier was felt to be at his best on the defensive, and he would fight to the death. Those who best knew the Red Army, including General von Tippelskirch of the general staff and the military attaché in Moscow, General Köstring, although mindful of its many shortcomings, warned that it would be foolish to overlook its many strengths or to imagine that the state was on the point of collapse. These warnings were ignored by the planners, who saw the Red Army as being made up of ignorant and racially inferior men, incapable of fighting a modern mobile war, a muscle-bound colossus that would be unable to respond to a skilfully planned and rapid attack.

The Germans were certainly not alone in their low estimation of the Soviet armed forces. In spite of the outstanding performance of the Red Army against the Japanese in Mongolia, almost all foreign observers were convinced that the Germans would defeat the Russians within two months. This was reflected in the size of the army that Germany pitched against the Soviet Union. They had invaded France with 142 divisions; they attacked the Soviet Union with only 150. Furthermore, the Germans had fewer artillery pieces, far fewer aircraft, and most of their armour was obsolete.

'Barbarossa' was not only a military operation but an ideological war. As one senior officer remarked, it was the task of the army to defeat the enemy and of the SS to fight the political struggle. In a series of discussions between the SS and the Wehrmacht it was agreed that in order to secure the occupied territories and to 'lay the foundations for the final destruction of bolshevism', it would be necessary to round up all the political leaders and all 'politically dangerous personalities' (Jews, emigrants, terrorists, political churchmen etc.). The SS *Einsatzgruppen*, designed to undertake this historic task, were assembled in May 1941 at Pretzsch on the Elbe. They were led by civil servants from the Gestapo, the criminal police or the Security Service (SD) who were chosen for their administrative talents, their ideological commitment, their ambition and their educational background. In June 1941 Heydrich gave the leaders of the *Einsatzgruppen* an order from Hitler that all communists, Jews and 'other radical elements' were to be executed. They would be assisted by anti-Jewish and anti-communist Poles, Lithuanians, Letts, Estonians, White Russians and Ukrainians who were to undertake these 'self-cleansing actions'. German troops were also encouraged to be as violent as they liked with the civilian population. The courts-martial were informed that soldiers who committed crimes against Soviet citizens need not be prosecuted on the grounds that 'the collapse in 1918, the German people's time of suffering, and National Socialism's struggle with the movement's countless blood sacrifices are all principally due to bolshevik influence and no German has forgotten that'. Soviet citizens suspected of hostile acts were not to be brought before a court but were to be either shot on the spot or released.

Objections from the army to such ideas were based not on any humanitarian considerations, nor on any concern for such a clear violation of the Hague conventions, but on the fear that a restriction of the jurisdiction of courts-martial could lead to a breakdown of military discipline. In order not to encourage an army of looters and rapists it was decided not to make these changes known, and superior officers were still able to take disciplinary action against their troops. This resulted inevitably in far milder punishment for serious offences. The fact that any German soldier could shoot any Soviet citizen whom he claimed to suspect of being a partisan without fear of punishment made it singularly difficult for the army to pursue a carefully considered political course.

The most notorious of measures taken in preparation for 'Barbarossa' was the 'Commissar Order' of 6 June 1941 which laid down that all political commissars should be shot. Halder felt this to be in accordance with the Führer's ideas and argued that the war was also 'a struggle between two world views'. Neither OKW nor OKH objected to such a flagrant breach of international law. Curiously it was Rosenberg who, thinking more in power political than in ideological terms, suggested that it might be unwise to murder all but the very top échelons of the political elite as they might well be useful in the future administration of the country. For the army the commissars were propagandists for a 'barbaric, Asiatic way of fighting' to whom the norms of international law need not apply. By August 1941 not only the commissars were shot but also the subordinate political officers at company level, the *politruk*. It was also frequently suggested that since the commissars were mostly Jews, their removal was doubly desirable.

On 19 May 1941 the OKH published its 'Guidelines for the Behaviour of the Troops in Russia' in which the aim of the war was said to be the elimination of the 'destructive world view' of bolshevism and its carriers. It was therefore essential to fight 'energetically and without consideration' against 'bolshevik agitators, partisans, saboteurs and Jews'. The Asiatic soldiers in the Red Army were said to be especially 'impenetrable, unpredictable, devious and insensitive'. It is noticeable that once again the army accepted Hitler's notion of the symbiotic relationship between bolsheviks and Jews, a theme which was taken up in an edition of 'Information for the Troops' in early June.

> Anyone who has looked in the face of a red commissar knows what a bolshevik is. No theoretical discussion is needed. It would be an insult to animals if one were to describe the faces of these mainly Jewish torturers as bestial. They are the human embodiment of an infernal and insane hatred of everything honourable in mankind. In the form of the commissar we witness the revolt of the subhuman against pure blood.

Hitler, the 'instrument of providence', was the saviour of Europe from the horrors of Jewish bolshevism.

The war was presented as a preventive strike against Jewish bolshevism which formed part of an unholy alliance of Jews, democrats and reactionaries which encircled Germany. The racial and ideological aspects of the war were fully acknowledged by the army leadership, and it would be grossly wrong to believe that the horrors of the German occupation were due solely to *Einsatzgruppen* of the SS. The army played the major role in this 'war of world views' directed against Jewish bolshevism. The murder of the bolshevik elite and of the Jews, and the decimation of the peoples of the Soviet Union were the necessary preconditions for the creation of Hitler's negative utopia, his 'new order' with a racially purified and enslaved state that would be economically exploited for the benefit of his supermen. The army approved these aims and devoted all its energies to this many-faceted war of destruction against the Soviet Union. Subsequent efforts to present the generals either as mere technicians with no interest in ideological issues, or as weak-willed fellow travellers who grudgingly obeyed the Führer, are totally unconvincing and cannot be reconciled with the historical record. It is unfortunate that this version had been widely believed, particularly by those who have allowed their natural and justifiable revulsion towards the Stalinist state to colour their view of the men who nearly caused its destruction. The German army crossed the borders of the Soviet Union on 22 June 1941, not to fight a preventive war against a military power it conceived as a threat, but to fight an ideologically motivated war for specific strategic, economic and politico-racial ends. The army was to a considerable extent in agreement with Hitler's ghastly vision of the future.

The Soviet Union was a prize worth winning. It accounted for 10 per cent of the world's industrial production, was the second greatest oil-producing nation in the world, and led the world in the production of synthetic rubber and the extraction of manganese ore. The achievements of the forced industrialization programme were astonishing, but in key sectors progress had been impaired by unrealistic planning goals and dislocated by the effects of the purges. About 10 per cent of the adult population were in concentration camps, among whom were many managers, scientists, technicians and skilled workers. Those who had escaped the purges lived in constant terror of being branded as wreckers, and thus eschewed any innovations. There were therefore only disappointingly modest increases in iron and steel production between 1938 and 1941.

These problems were inevitably reflected in the armaments industry. Although budgetary allocations for defence increased dramatically, reaching a projected 13.1 per cent by 1941, production was hopelessly behind schedule and retooling had scarcely begun by the outbreak of the war. Excellent modern weapons such as the KV and T–34 tanks, Yak–1, MiG 3 and LaGG–3 fighters, the Yak–2 'stormovik' fighter-bomber and the Pe–2 bomber were in desperately short supply and were being produced on too small a scale. Purges had seriously affected the Officer Corps. At the outset of the war with Germany only 7 per cent of officers had received any higher military education and 37 per cent had not even completed their secondary education. About 75 per cent of commanding officers and commissars had less than one year's experience in their current posts. The situation was not improved by the fact that the head of the Defence Commissariat, Marshal Voroshilov, owed his position solely to the fact that he was Stalin's loyal henchman who had miraculously escaped the purges and had been moved sideways after his bungling of the campaign against Finland. His three deputies were men of staggering incompetence.

Stalin and Zhdanov, who was the Central Committee Secretary responsible for the army and industry, both fancied themselves as experts on military affairs, imagining that military history had stopped with the civil war. Vannikov, People's Commissar for the armaments industry, had the temerity to oppose the decision to stop the production of anti-tank guns, a weapon which was said to have done nothing to secure the triumph of Marxism–Leninism in Russia, and was promptly despatched to the Gulag. A similar fate awaited many other scientists and managers whose ideas had progressed a little beyond those of the Father of the People, or who were convenient scapegoats for the failures of a disastrously mismanaged planned economy.

Although Soviet reasoning and motives remain obscure and scholars are denied access to the archives and therefore rely in large part on guesswork, it would seem that Stalin still hoped to maintain his alliance with Nazi Germany, at least for the foreseeable future. The joint invasion of Poland was celebrated with a parade by the Wehrmacht and the Red Army in Brest Litovsk, a sordid event tactfully ignored by the Soviet press. Molotov crowed over the demise of Poland, describing it as 'this misshapen offspring of the Versailles treaty'. Stalin told Ribbentrop that the friendship of the peoples of Germany and the Soviet Union was 'forged in blood'. After the fall of France, Molotov congratulated the German ambassador on his country's 'brilliant successes'. But behind all these expressions of friendship and good will there was a growing uneasiness.

The inevitability of war between capitalist states was an unquestioned part of the Marxist–Leninist canon. The problem for the Soviet Union was how best to profit from this situation. The Germans offered the highest price, but it was one which brought dubious benefits. The Soviets had always argued that any future war would be fought on foreign soil and would result in minimal casualties. They consistently denounced the *cordon sanitaire* erected along its borders, but once it was removed they found themselves face to face with Nazi Germany with no buffer zone between them. Similarly, Stalin had welcomed Hitler's invasion of France, hoping for a long breathing space while the capitalist powers hacked one another to pieces. This also proved to be a dangerous fantasy.

The Soviets replied to the rapid defeat of France by promptly annexing the Baltic states and Bessarabia, but this did little to improve their strategic position. Some indirect, cautious and highly ambiguous advances were made to Britain, but the Soviets were terrified that they might provoke the Germans who were now masters of most of Europe. Nor were they comforted by the proviso in the Three-Power Pact that relations between the signatories and the USSR were not affected. Increasing German activity in Romania and the Balkans, along with Italian adventures in Yugoslavia and Greece, further confirmed their suspicions. Stalin may have imagined that Hitler would first have to settle accounts with Britain, and possibly the United States, before turning east, but felt it prudent to moderate the vicious and primitive attacks on the western powers which had been such a nauseating feature of the Soviet press in the early months of the war. At the same time it was decided scrupulously and punctually to meet the commitments of the trade treaty with Germany. The last goods train crossed the border into Germany minutes before the Wehrmacht launched their attack. Similarly, the Soviets hindered the movement of British shipping, provided meteorological information for use by the Luftwaffe for the bombing of Britain even though this was a serious breach of their theoretical neutrality, and handed over some 800 anti-fascist activists to the Gestapo, including the founder of the Austrian Communist Party.

Stalin continued to appease Hitler, while state after state joined the Three-Power Pact, by negotiating a spheres-of-influence agreement which the Germans made abundantly clear was a sham, and by dutifully sending vast quantities of raw materials essential to the German armaments industry, even though the Nazis obviously had no intention of paying. At the outbreak of war the Germans owed 239 million Reichsmarks for 1941 and 380 million roubles for the previous year. It was not until March 1941, by which time there were clear indications of German intentions to attack the Soviet Union, that Vishinsky dared to inform the Bulgarian Government that he 'disagreed' with their decision to allow German troops to enter the country to 'protect peace in the Balkans'.

On 27 March a group of officers, led by General Simovic, carried out a coup in Belgrade while the Yugoslavian Prime Minister and Foreign Minister were in Vienna putting their signatures to the Three-Power Pact. Moscow reacted swiftly to this blatantly anti-German act by signing a friendship and non-aggression pact with the new Yugoslav Government on 5 April at an impressive ceremony in the Kremlin. Less than twenty-four hours later, the Germans invaded Yugoslavia. The Soviets made no official comment on this flagrant act of aggression, and were no doubt relieved that they had not made any undertakings to come to Yugoslavia's assistance. All that happened was that Molotov complained to the Hungarian ambassador that his country's attack on Yugoslavia was unwarranted.

On 13 April, the day that Belgrade fell, the Soviet Union and Japan signed a non-aggression pact. The Japanese Foreign Minister, Matsuoka, travelled to Moscow from Berlin and was treated with exceptional cordiality. Stalin took the unprecedented step of seeing Matsuoka off at the railway station. He embraced him warmly and announced that fellow Asiatics had to stick together. It is doubtful whether this made much impression on the Foreign Minister, for he was spectacularly drunk after a prolonged vodka-drinking session with his host. On the platform Stalin also made profuse expressions of friendship to the German deputy military attaché, Colonel von Krebs, in the presence of officials from the British embassy. If he was still uncertain about Germany, at least Stalin knew that he no longer faced the prospect of a two-front war.

Stalin was provided with excellent intelligence about German intentions. Reports from Soviet agents in Berlin, Switzerland and Paris that Germany intended to attack the Soviet Union began to trickle in from the autumn of 1940. These were confirmed by the Soviet master spy stationed in Tokyo, Richard Sorge, who by 15 May was able to give the exact date of the invasion and an outline of Hitler's strategic concept. He was also able to give precise details of Japanese intentions. Sorge was arrested in October 1941 and hanged three years later. The Soviets did nothing to save him, and his wife was arrested and sent to a Gulag. All of the Soviet agents who had done such splendid work and who unfortunately decided to return to the Soviet Union after the war were either executed or disappeared in the Gulag archipelago. Stalin had no desire to spare the life of those who were witnesses to his folly.

On 5 May Stalin was formally appointed head of the Soviet Government with Molotov as his deputy. Schulenburg interpreted this as an attempt to place himself in a stronger position to save the peace. He promptly made a series of demonstrably friendly gestures towards Nazi Germany. He closed down the embassies of Norway, Belgium, Greece and Yugoslavia, countries which had been overrun by the Germans, and he established diplomatic relations with the pro-Nazi Government of Rashid Ali in Iraq. He also let it be known that he was prepared to make further economic concessions to Germany.

Great was Stalin's alarm when he heard of Rudolf Hess's flight to Scotland on 10 May. The British Government was at a loss to know what to do with Hess and his behaviour was so bizarre that they were undecided whether he was truly mad or merely pretending. Churchill promised to issue a full statement on the spectacular flight of Hitler's deputy but, prompted by Eden, the Cabinet silenced the Prime Minister. With no statement from the British Government, the Soviets had much upon which to brood. Stalin was convinced that this was part of an intrigue between the British and the Germans at the Soviet Union's expense. Although the suspicions were utterly baseless, at least they helped to persuade Stalin that the warnings from his agents were not founded on information planted by imperialist powers, and that the massive troop concentrations on the Soviet borders could not be ignored. But this only served to make him more anxious than ever about the Soviet Union's preparedness for war. On 5 May he addressed hundreds of new officers at a reception in the Kremlin, stressing the danger of a German attack for which the Red Army was not yet prepared. Therefore, diplomatic means would have to be used to postpone the attack until the autumn. By 1942 the Red Army would be in a far better position to fight the almost inevitable war with Nazi Germany. The Soviet Union could then count on the support of Britain and the United States, and Stalin was confident that the Japanese would not attack the Soviet Union. As part of the diplomatic initiative TASS issued a communiqué on 14 June which was designed as an invitation to the Germans to clarify their position and to begin new talks, while discounting any rumours of hostile intent on either side and reaffirming the non-aggression pact. The Soviet people, skilled at reading between the lines, were highly alarmed. Particular attention was paid to the sentence: 'As for the transfer to the northern and eastern areas of Germany of troops during the past weeks, since the completion of the task in the Balkans, such troop movements are, one must suppose, prompted by motives which have no bearing on Soviet–German relations.' The 'one must suppose' had a distinctly ominous ring. To many soldiers the communiqué was particularly demoralizing in that it appeared that the Government was blind to the danger of imminent war.

Stalin was still convinced that the Germans would begin a fresh round of negotiations and told the Defence Commissar, Timoshenko, on the evening of 21 June, referring to a flood of reports of an impending German attack: 'We are starting a panic over nothing.' That night Molotov asked Schulenburg to call on him and posed the question why Germany was dissatisfied with the Soviet Union. Schulenburg was unable to reply, and returned to the embassy to find instructions from Ribbentrop to deliver a declaration of war to Molotov. As German troops crossed the border,

Schulenburg went back to the Kremlin. Molotov's stunned reaction was to say: 'This is war. Do you believe that we deserved that?'

Meanwhile, Stalin discussed the situation with Timoshenko and Zhukov. He was still obsessed with the idea that nothing should be done which might be interpreted as a provocation. When told that a German deserter, a communist labourer from Berlin, had said that the invasion would begin early that morning, he ordered the man to be shot for spreading 'disinformation'. He suggested that ambitious German generals had sent the man to 'provoke a conflict' and thus force the peaceful Hitler's hand. Timoshenko and Zhukov disagreed and argued that the situation was critical. When members of the Politburo joined the party, a bewildered Stalin asked them what could be done. No answer was forthcoming until Timoshenko proposed alerting all the troops along the border. Stalin felt that this was likely to result in 'complications' caused by 'provocations' and suggested that the question could be settled peacefully. Finally an order was drafted shortly after midnight. It was a confusing document stressing the importance of not giving way to 'provocative actions of any kind which might produce major complications' and ending: 'no other measures to be taken without special authorization.' This left commanders completely in the dark. How were they to distinguish between 'provocative actions' to which they were not to respond and a 'surprise blow' which they were to counter? Timoshenko told General Boldin, deputy commander of the Western Military District, that comrade Stalin had not authorized the use of artillery against the Germans. Boldin yelled into the phone that such an order was absurd when the army was in retreat, the cities burning and the people dying. Timoshenko would not budge.

At 07.15 hours a second order was issued which called for the destruction of all enemy forces which had violated Soviet territory, but which insisted that the army was not to cross the border. There was still no mention of a state of war nor of a general mobilization. Stalin still imagined that the situation could be saved by negotiation. Moscow was in constant radio contact with the embassy in Berlin and Stalin even turned to the Japanese in the hope that they might be persuaded to mediate. By midday on 22 June Stalin had to admit that these grotesque efforts were pointless, and Molotov announced on the radio that the Soviet Union was now at war with Germany. At 21.15 hours on the same day Timoshenko issued Directive No. 3 which called for offensive action by all three of the western fronts. This astonishing directive was based on a total ignorance of the situation at the front. The Red Army was staggering from a series of shattering blows. The air force had been shot to pieces on the ground. Communications networks were disrupted, artillery stuck for lack of transport, tanks were without fuel or ammunition. Orders to regroup for a counter-attack led to further confusion and a weakening of defensive positions. Yet the first operational digest from the general staff spoke of the 'insignificant success' achieved by the Germans in some sectors. Old hacks from the civil war who had survived the purges, such as Voroshilov and Budenny, were completely out of their depth. Only in the south-western sector, where Zhukov was examining the situation and offering his advice, did the counter-attacks have a limited success. Elsewhere they were a disastrous waste of effort.

Stalin did not appear in public and did not speak to the nation until 3 July. He was shattered by the invasion, not least because it showed up the absurdity of his pretensions to infallibility. He behaved in an extremely erratic and nervous manner, spending most of the time at his *dacha* outside Moscow. On 23 June the General Headquarters of the Soviet High Command (*Stavka*) was formed with Stalin as chairman and comprising Molotov, Timoshenko, Voroshilov, Budenny, Shaposhnikov, Zhukov and Admiral Kuznetsov. A few days later a State Defence Committee (GKO) was formed. It was a far more important body with wider functions, overseeing all major military, economic and political questions. Stalin was again in the chair, and the committee was made up of Molotov, Malenkov, Voroshilov and Beria, the head of the NKVD. Stalin became Defence Commissar on 19 July and in August Commander-in-Chief. He was in close contact with the field commanders through his personal secretariat run by Poskrebyshev and was always excellently briefed. During the entire war he visited the front on only one occasion, in August 1943, but once he recovered from his initial shock, probably by 30 June when the GKO was formed, he was in absolute control.

Stalin's speech to the nation on 3 July had a remarkable effect. Speaking in a dull, slow voice with his thick Georgian accent, he addressed his mass audience as 'Comrades, citizens, brothers and sisters', admitted that certain losses had been incurred and called for an all-out effort to rid the country of the German fascist invader. He ordered a scorched-earth policy, the formation of partisan units and of a home guard (*opolcheniye*). For the moment the Soviet people forgot the monstrous crimes that Stalin had committed against his 'brothers and sisters' and saw in him a true national leader who appealed to their deep-rooted patriotism and assured them of a final victory. It was Stalin's equivalent to Churchill's promise of blood, sweat and tears, and was no less effective. There was no promise of any relaxation of the dictatorship, and the warning that there would be a merciless struggle against cowards, deserters and panic-mongers was a prelude to further ruthless purges by Beria and his henchmen.

At first 'Barbarossa' went like clockwork. Within three weeks the Germans had advanced more than 400 miles. On 3 July Halder wrote in his diary that the war would be over within two weeks. There were a number of reasons for these early successes. Although the Red Army was far larger than the Wehrmacht, it was extended along a lengthy frontier and was ineptly deployed to meet a concentrated mechanized attack. Many Soviet airfields had been built far too near the border and were destroyed in the first day of fighting. By midday on 22 June the Soviets had lost 1200 aircraft, most of which were destroyed on the ground. The railway system, which was not extensive enough to meet the needs of a modern army, was completely disrupted by bombing raids. The Germans had the advantage of a better trained and more experienced Officer Corps and the ordinary soldier was more highly skilled and better equipped than in the Red Army.

The only hope for the Soviets was to hold up the German advance and let time, space and natural resources work to their advantage. But the Germans pushed onward, fighting a series of skilful battles of encirclement, taking hundreds of thousands of prisoners and seizing vast quantities of arms, fuel and ammunition. This tactic worked most successfully in Army Group Centre. Flanked by armour, the infantry encircled Bialystok, Volkovysk, Novogrudok and, by 28 June, Minsk. On 16 July they had taken Smolensk. Army Group North met stiffer resistance and made slower progress, but reached Pskov on 8 July. Army Group South faced the hardest task of all. The area had the most natural barriers and in the vast expanses of the Ukraine the Red Army proved harder to pin down and encircle; but by the end of July Kiev was threatened. On 29 July Zhukov presented a cogent argument to Stalin that the most serious weakness in the Soviet position was on the central front. He suggested withdrawing behind the Dnieper, abandoning Kiev and sending reinforcements to the central front. Stalin exploded and told Zhukov that he was talking nonsense. Zhukov lost his temper, offered his resignation as Chief of Staff, and requested to be sent to the front. Stalin accepted his resignation and appointed Shaposhnikov as his successor.

By 8 August the Germans crossed the Dnieper and it became clear that Kiev would have to be abandoned. Budenny, commander of the south-western direction, requested permission to withdraw from Kiev to avoid encirclement by the 3rd and 16th Panzers led by Guderian and Kleist and to establish a defensive position on the Psel river. Stalin refused to agree to this request and relieved Budenny of his command. As a result of Stalin's refusal to allow a withdrawal from Kiev, the city fell on 19 September and the Germans took 655,000 prisoners, 884 tanks and 3718 guns.

After the fall of Smolensk, Brauchitsch, Halder, Bock and Guderian wanted to concentrate all efforts on an advance towards Moscow, thus reverting to arguments they had used during the planning stages of 'Barbarossa'. They claimed that Moscow could be taken before the end of August. Hitler's response was that 'Only completely ossified brains, absorbed with the ideas of past centuries, could see any worthwhile objective in taking the capital.' He insisted that the main object of the campaign was to seize the riches of the Ukraine and the Caucasus and to protect the northern flank by attacking Leningrad. The question was whether the two Panzer groups of Army Group Centre should be sent to support the drives towards Leningrad and the Sea of Azov, or whether Army Groups North and South should make do with what they had got so that all efforts could be concentrated on a major battle around Moscow. In the end von Leeb was ordered to take Leningrad, von Bock Moscow, and von Rundstedt was to drive on into the Caucasus. This was a hopeless dispersal of effort and a recipe for disaster.

In a sense Hitler judged the situation more realistically than did Halder. He realized that 'Barbarossa' had failed and that the Soviet Union could not be defeated before the onset of winter. Therefore it was essential to be in the best possible position to continue the campaign in the following year. Halder, however, thought that it was still possible to bring the campaign to a conclusion in a massive battle around Moscow. This operation, 'Typhoon', had to be postponed until the beginning of October since troops had been sent from Army Group Centre to assist in the envelopment of Kiev.

The Wehrmacht pushed on rapidly towards Moscow. The Moscow Volunteer Corps, in which many intellectuals served, was thrown into the battle without any training and was destroyed. Many of the men did not even know how to fire a rifle. A terrible fate awaited the many Jewish volunteers who were taken prisoner. In this remarkable battle of encirclement the Vyazma defensive line was broken, Vyazma was enveloped and the Germans took 663,000 prisoners, 1242 tanks and 5412 guns. Further south in a smaller operation the Soviet 3rd and 13th armies were trapped in the Bryansk pocket and a further 200,000 men were captured. Many Government offices and embassies were evacuated to Kuibyshev, on the Volga, others to different cities to the east. Panic seized Moscow. Refugees fled the city with everything they could carry. Communists destroyed their party cards. Soldiers hastily changed into civilian clothes. Public services ceased to function; even the police and the ubiquitous NKVD disappeared, to the relief of all, especially the looters. Stalin vanished on 16 October only to reappear two days later.

The defence of the capital was entrusted to Zhukov, a ruthlessly tough soldier who had been given command of the western front. He had already performed miracles in the defence of Leningrad, and he immediately set about bringing all available reserves to the defence of the capital, having no alternative but to give himself as long a breathing space as possible. The Soviets fought with great heroism against a superior enemy, and by dint of extraordinary sacrifices managed to wear down the attack. The Germans failed in their attempt to encircle Tula, an important industrial centre nearly 200 kilometres to the south-west of Moscow. The Panzers were halted a few kilometres from Moscow, and reconnaissance units had already entered the suburbs. By now the German offensive had run out of steam. They lacked reserves and matériel and their lines of communication were over-extended, their flanks dangerously exposed. Even without the freezing weather the German advance would have been halted.

On 5 December the Soviets launched their counter-offensive, striking north and south of Moscow. Although the attack did not attain Stalin's totally unrealistic objective of a triumphant general offensive on all fronts, it was a major triumph for the Red Army. The Germans were forced back some 100 to 250 kilometres and Hitler was obliged to place the entire front on the defensive. 'Barbarossa' had failed, and the Soviets had wrested the initiative from the Germans. England was now spared from any threat of invasion, the resistance movement throughout Europe was given fresh encouragement, and with the Japanese attack on Pearl Harbor on 7 December the war took on a wholly different dimension.

Churchill was spending the weekend at Chequers when news of the German invasion of the Soviet Union arrived at 4 a.m. Since the Prime Minister had ordered that he was not to be woken before 8 o'clock except in the event of an invasion of the British Isles, his staff waited anxiously to give him the good news. He was delighted and, without consulting the Cabinet or the Foreign Office, he broadcast to the nation that night. It was one of his finest addresses, although it contained much sensitive material. His position was unequivocal: 'Any man or state who fights on against Nazidom will have our aid. Any man or state who marches with Hitler is our foe.' Forgetting the conquests made by the Soviets since September 1939, he spoke of 'Russian soldiers standing on the threshold of their native land guarding the fields their fathers have tilled from time immemorial.'

The speech made an enormous impression in the Soviet Union, where suspicions that the British were likely to join the Germans in their crusade against bolshevism were deliberately fanned by official propagandists and had been made more credible by the recent dramatic arrival of Rudolf Hess in the British Isles. In Government circles the remark about the threshold of their native land was taken as *de facto* recognition of Soviet conquests in Poland, Finland, the Baltic states and Bessarabia.

The Cabinet made no criticism of Churchill's speech, but many had serious reservations about any close association with the Soviet Union in spite of the common enemy. Eden argued that the Soviet Union was every bit as bad as Nazi Germany and that half the population of Britain would be strongly opposed to an alliance with such a power. The service chiefs were convinced that the Soviet Union would be defeated within six weeks and that it would therefore be madness to send any aid which would either be destroyed or end up in German hands. The Deputy Chief of the Imperial General Staff, General Pownall, expressed a widely held view when he wrote: 'The Russians are a dirty lot of murdering thieves and double-crossers of the deepest dye. It is good to see the two biggest cut-throats in Europe, Hitler and Stalin, going for each other.' The Foreign Office, as one official remarked, treated the Soviet Union somewhat like a mistress who suddenly arrives at a wife's garden party. In such an atmosphere it is hardly surprising that when the Soviet ambassador, Maisky, requested economic and military aid, Eden told him that the British had far too much on their plates already.

Initially the British did precious little to help the Soviet Union, in spite of Churchill's extravagant promises in his radio speech. General Mason Macfarlane, renowned for his outspoken anti-Soviet views, was sent to Moscow as military attaché. A rather absurd figure, Colonel George Hill, who had been involved in Sidney Reilly's inept attempt to assassinate Lenin and Trotsky, was appointed liaison officer to the NKVD in Moscow. Stafford Cripps returned to his post as ambassador, but was not granted an interview with Stalin until 8 July. The first concrete measure was to send two submarines to patrol Russian northern waters in mid July.

Relations between the Soviet Union and Britain were strained from the outset. In his first note since the German invasion, Stalin demanded the immediate opening of a second front in France. When told that this was completely out of the question, he demanded 3000 fighters and an equal number of bombers. Although only one Hurricane was sent, Stalin was remarkably friendly to Cripps when he explained why it had not been possible to send the supplies requested. Cripps was a strong advocate of an immediate and generous response to the Soviet Union, both economically and politically. But Britain had little to spare and a political settlement, such as a discussion of post-war frontiers, was rejected out of hand by Eden and by the United States ambassador John Winant, even though with the Germans ripping through the Soviet defences the question was purely academic.

It soon became obvious that supplies were what the Soviets needed most, and it was equally clear that they could come only from the United States. Churchill made a passionate appeal for such assistance when he met Roosevelt at Placentia Bay in Newfoundland. Although the American military wanted to build up the defences of the Philippines, and the British wanted to keep everything for themselves, Roosevelt and Churchill ignored their objections and sent a joint note to Stalin promising that they would do everything possible to help and suggesting that a supply conference should be held in Moscow as soon as possible.

The Americans postponed the Moscow conference as long as possible and then insisted that supplies for Russia would have to come in large part from matériel allocated to the British. This infuriated the British, who were also smarting under Stalin's accusations that the Russians were fighting the Germans alone and were outraged by his totally unrealistic demand that they should send 25–30 divisions to the south of the USSR.

Although the Russians suspected that the British were insincere in their offers of help, the British furious at what they felt to be Russian ingratitude and lack of realism, and the Americans unenthusiastic about wasting supplies, the Moscow conference was a considerable success. But there were still many outstanding differences between the Soviet Union and the western powers. The basic problem, as Cripps pointed out, was that although the British were making considerable sacrifices to help the Russians, the amount they sent looked terribly insignificant compared with the frightful losses suffered by the Soviets. Cripps argued that Soviet suspicions could be overcome only if there was a comprehensive political agreement between the two countries. Churchill wanted to avoid making any commitments to the Soviets and used the American obsession with the principles of the Atlantic Charter as a convenient excuse to avoid the issue.

Although the British and the Russians were fighting a common enemy, they fought separate wars. No attempt was made to co-ordinate strategy and there was minimal exchange of intelligence information and technical data. The sum total of combined military operations was a comic opera raid on Spitzbergen and the joint occupation of Iran. The British were keen to secure the oilfields in Iran, and the Soviets were fearful that the Germans were planning a raid on Baku via Iran. Both wanted to secure a condominium over the railway which was the most important supply route to the Soviet Union.

On 25 August Soviet troops invaded Iran from the north while the British moved up from the south. The Persians offered virtually no resistance and the country was soon under the joint control of the two countries. Fears that it might prove difficult to get the Russians out of Iran after the war, voiced by Cripps among others, were discounted in Whitehall. Instead the British Government threatened the Shah with a Russian occupation of Teheran if he did not toe the line, a policy which horrified the ambassador, Sir Reader Bullard.

British public opinion was strongly pro-Soviet and calls for help for Russia and an early second front, which were taken up by politicians such as Beaverbrook and Cripps, found widespread resonance. This was a natural response to a nation which was fighting so desperately against a common enemy, but it was also part of a leftward turn in British politics in which demands for fundamental reform at home were combined with a somewhat idealized enthusiasm for the Soviet experiment. Churchill ordered the Ministry of Information to 'consider what action was required to counter the present tendency of the British public to forget the dangers of communism in their enthusiasm over the resistance of Russia', but it proved difficult to distinguish between enthusiasm for Russia and enthusiasm for communism. The Government gave generous subsidies to sympathetic organizations, and dyed-in-the-wool capitalists such as Beaverbrook were to hymn the praises of Soviet communism and to inform a credulous public that the millions who had died in Stalin's purges were all Nazi agents. In spite of such nonsense there was little danger of the communists gaining a foothold in British politics. The Communist Party increased its membership from 12,000 to 65,000 by September 1942, although it was still something of an exotic sect. Admiration for the Soviet Union did not mean that there was any enthusiasm for converting Britain into a carbon copy of the 'New Civilization'.

Relations between Britain and the Soviet Union remained strained, the Soviets insinuating that the British were fighting to the last drop of Soviet blood, calling for the immediate despatch of up to 30 divisions and demanding that Britain declare war on Finland, Romania and Hungary. The Foreign Office suggested that the Soviets had good reason to complain. They had been excluded from the discussions which had led to the publication of the Atlantic Charter, and they desperately needed a major diversion to relieve the pressure on their front, and supplies were still only a trickle. Britain needed the Soviets far more than they needed Britain, and it was only the heroic stand of the Red Army which saved Britain from invasion. Some sort of political arrangement was essential, even if it meant bringing up the difficult issues of war aims and the post-war settlement.

Eden presented these views rather lamely to Cabinet, but backed down when Churchill argued that the Americans would not accept any discussion of a post-war settlement. From Moscow, Cripps threatened to resign if a political agreement was not reached. To break the deadlock, Churchill suggested that Eden should go to Moscow, an idea which was welcomed by the Russians.

The Foreign Secretary's visit to Moscow was not a great success. Stalin demanded formal recognition of the annexations in the Baltic states and Finland, but Eden said that the British Government was unable to grant *de jure* recognition of the new frontiers because of a previous undertaking to the United States. Stalin had no patience with fine distinctions between *de jure* and *de facto* recognition and behaved in a manner which Eden found 'deplorable'. Nevertheless Eden returned to London convinced that Britain would have to recognize the Soviet Union's frontiers of 1941, and argued that the Russians might win the war virtually on their own, establish communist regimes throughout Europe, seize German industrial plant and become virtually independent from the United States and Britain. Churchill would not accept these arguments, Attlee threatened to resign if the Cabinet agreed to recognition, and Beaverbrook resigned because they would not. Faced with such opposition, Eden soon backed down and left it to Beaverbrook and Cripps to argue the case for recognition.

The British Government avoided the issue by presenting both sides of the argument to the Americans and asking them to decide. The result was a foregone conclusion; the Americans were horrified at the suggestion that the British might consider recognition of the 1941 frontiers, a policy which Sumner Welles found 'not only indefensible from every moral standpoint, but likewise extraordinarily stupid'. This left the British in the awkward position of having virtually nothing to offer the Soviets. There could be no question of a second front in Europe for a long time to come. The campaign in north Africa was lamentably unsuccessful and supplies to the Soviet Union were still little more than a trickle. The Cabinet was divided over the issue of the recognition of the frontiers, and the Americans were vehemently opposed. The Government was thus in no position to refuse the Soviet proposal that there should be a treaty between the two countries, but it was in a singularly poor negotiating position.

American intransigence over the recognition of the 1941 frontiers did not result from any reluctance to help the Soviet Union. With the capitulation of France and the growing threat of war with Japan, the Under-Secretary of State, Sumner Welles, began discussion with the Soviet ambassador, Oumansky, in July 1940. Little was achieved in the course of these talks. The ambassador adopted an uncompromising negotiating position and the American side was constrained by opposition in Congress to anything more than a few token gestures, while public opinion was still firmly opposed to any rapprochement. With a presidential election in November, Roosevelt was in no mood to run any risks.

Roosevelt had enormously increased the executive powers of the presidency with the Executive Reorganization Act of 1939 under which he issued a considerable number of executive agreements. While the Germans continued to overrun Europe, Roosevelt's views of foreign policy began to prevail over those of the isolationists and virulent anti-communists in Congress. The President was convinced that it was not the Soviet Union but Nazi Germany which had the means and the intention to challenge the vital strategic interests of the United States. He further considered Germany to be a far greater threat than Japan and was convinced that the defeat of Germany would automatically lead to the demise of Japan. In this 'Europe first' strategy the Soviet Union was by far the most valuable potential ally.

Roosevelt was often uneasy about Soviet expansion into eastern Europe, but he believed that it was motivated by a desire for security against the Nazi threat rather than blatant expansionism or an ideologically motivated crusade. He imagined that it would be possible to reach some Faustian bargain with the communist devil and leave the whole problem of frontiers until the end of the war. But this apparent realism was combined with a lofty Wilsonian vision which was enshrined in the Atlantic Charter. Whereas for the British the Atlantic Charter was seen as little more than a rather vacuous publicity stunt which should not be allowed to stand in the way of pragmatic policy-making, for the Americans it was a profession of faith. It enshrined the sacred principle of the self-determination of peoples. It proposed that the United Nations, led by the 'Four Policemen' – the United States, the Soviet Union, Britain and China – should replace the old balance of power diplomacy which was felt to have been the root cause of two world wars. Lastly it upheld the principle of economic liberalism and envisaged a world in which all restrictions to the free flow of trade and investment capital were removed. It was a programme as idealistic as it was absurd, and it took no account of the failure of Woodrow Wilson's identical programme as outlined in his 'Fourteen Points'. The self-determination of peoples was irreconcilable with the demands of power politics and could never be fairly applied to the ethnically mixed areas of central Europe. The United Nations would work effectively only as long as the 'Four Policemen' were in broad agreement. Free trade was incompatible with a socialist planned economy, a fact which was lost on the Americans who, in a richly comic episode, hoped to entice the Soviets to participate in the International Monetary Fund.

The Americans, like everyone else with the possible exception of Stalin, were convinced that Hitler would attack the Soviet Union and were determined to give the Russians every possible assistance in their struggle. Thus as early as January 1941 the 'moral embargo' on trade with the Soviet Union, imposed during the war with Finland, was lifted, much to the disgust of the British authorities who knew that some of these goods would end up in German hands. At the same time the wording of the Lend-Lease Act, which was being submitted to Congress, was changed so that all countries at war with Nazi Germany were eligible for assistance. In March the American Government informed the Soviets of their intelligence information about an imminent German attack, although some State Department officials opposed this step.

When the invasion began, Roosevelt was uncertain what to do. The attitude of Congress and of public opinion to this dramatic turn of events was not yet clear. He was advised that the Russians would be unable to put up much of a resistance and that supplies would be put to better use by the British. But within three weeks, by which time the Soviets had shown that they were prepared to make every sacrifice to defend their country, the President decided to act. Proclaiming Germany the paramount threat to the American way of life, he released $39 million in frozen Soviet assets. Congress did not invoke the Neutrality Act, so that the Soviets were free to purchase military equipment in the United States.

It took until November for Lend-Lease to be formally extended to the Soviet Union. There were complaints in Congress of Lend-Lease becoming a 'Lenin-Lease'; Catholics referred to Pius XI's encyclical outlawing any collaboration with communist countries, and Charles Lindburgh announced to an enthusiastic crowd that he would rather ally with Nazi Germany than with communist Russia. Gradually, however, public opinion began to swing in the same direction as the President and even the traditionally isolationist *San Francisco Chronicle* said: 'We should stop snapping at the tail of the Red Bear and instead help grab the Nazi monster by the throat.'

By the end of October, when Congress approved the second Lend-Lease appropriation which set aside almost $1 billion for the Soviet Union, only a handful of fanatical anti-communists actually wanted to see the Soviets defeated and few questioned the decision to send as much aid as possible. Hardly anything reached the Russians in time to help them in the struggle for Moscow, but this was not due, as some suspicious Soviet historians have suggested, to any conscious delaying tactics, but rather to excessive red tape and a shortage of shipping. The Soviets were given the same priority rating as the British and in the course of the war were to receive $11.2 billion worth of supplies, only a fraction less than the $13.5 billion sent to Britain.

CHAPTER FOUR

The War in the Mediterranean (March 1941–May 1943)

At the beginning of March 1941, Rommel reported to the OHL that he intended to go on the offensive as soon as possible. His immediate aim was to recapture Cyrenaica, and if all went well he intended to push on into Egypt and seize the Suez Canal. Both Halder and Brauchitsch strongly supported the idea of an offensive, but Halder felt that it would be impossible to advance any further than Tobruk. Brauchitsch, who was preoccupied with planning for 'Barbarossa' and who argued that supplies would not be available for such an ambitious strategy in north Africa, doubted whether Rommel would be able to advance much beyond Agedabia.

Rommel returned to Africa with a somewhat less ambitious programme. He ordered an offensive to secure the approaches to Agedabia. This proved a relatively easy task since the British had failed miserably to establish adequate defensive positions in the strategically vital bottleneck at Mersa Brega, a strip of land only eight miles wide between the sea and impassable salt marshes, which was the key to the whole of Cyrenaica. With his forces depleted by Churchill's decision to send troops to Greece, and thinking that the Germans would be unable to mount an offensive for several months, partly because of misleading intelligence gleaned from 'Enigma' decrypts, Wavell had left a minimum force of inexperienced troops in Cyrenaica. With obsolete and lightly armoured tanks and inadequate anti-tank guns, they were in no position to stand up to the Panzer IIIs and IVs. The British excused their decision to withdraw by claiming that they were trading space for time, but they had allowed Rommel to get through the defile and he now could make full use of his numerical superiority.

Wavell recalled O'Connor, the finest of his generals, who was on leave having been stopped by Churchill from driving on to Tripoli. He was appointed advisor to Neame, an exceptionally valiant soldier who commanded the troops in Cyrenaica, in spite of his lack of experience in desert warfare. A staff car in which O'Connor and Neame were travelling lost its way in the dark and they were taken prisoner. In a rapidly deteriorating situation Wavell, supported by the CIGS, Sir John Dill, and Eden (both of whom were visiting Cairo), decided to hang on to Tobruk while abandoning the rest of Cyrenaica. The defence of Tobruk was entrusted to General 'Ming the Merciless' Morshead and his Australians.

Rommel conducted an unconventional and irresponsible campaign, but it was one which paid off. Once through the Mersa Brega funnel he divided up his force into three. One part drove along the coast, a second went straight ahead and a third to the south, joining the central thrust at Mechili. Rommel was short of fuel and supplies, and his path was littered with broken-down vehicles and isolated units. But the British lacked determined commanders who were prepared to exploit Rommel's weaknesses in a series of counter-attacks which could have halted his advance. The British had inferior weapons, an inadequate communications network and poor aerial reconnaissance. Perhaps most important of all, they failed to exploit the endless possibilities afforded by the desert for a war of movement. If they stayed put they were either overrun or by-passed, and if they moved it was usually to retreat. Rommel's gamble paid off and he was convinced that he would soon be in possession of Tobruk in an operation which he claimed, with characteristic lack of modesty, would be a combination of Cannae and Dunkirk.

Rommel launched his attack on Tobruk on Good Friday, 11 April 1941. He soon ran up against carefully prepared defences and his advance was halted by accurate artillery fire against troops who were unable to dig shelters in the stony ground. His senior officers soon wanted to call off the attack, but he was convinced that the British were on the run and dreamed of a great victory. Far from abandoning Tobruk, the Royal Navy poured supplies into the town to meet the German attack, but Rommel was so obsessed with his vision of glory that he imagined that the ships sailing into Tobruk had come to evacuate the garrison. Rommel threw his exhausted troops against Tobruk and they were beaten back by Morshead's Australians. Refusing to take the blame for a poorly conceived plan, he found undeserved scapegoats in General Streich and Colonel Olbricht. The 25,000 men in Tobruk had denied him the victory he felt he deserved; in frustration he struck out at two officers who had served him well. Such shabby behaviour did little to tarnish his grossly inflated reputation for human decency and military genius, but it did earn him a mild rebuke from Brauchitsch.

Rommel was now in a very awkward situation. He had reached the Egyptian frontier, but he was denied the extra troops he needed to seize the Suez Canal. Hitler was about to launch his attack on the Soviet Union, a plan of which Rommel knew nothing, and therefore could not spare anything for north Africa. Halder, who hated Rommel, wrote in his diary: 'By exceeding his orders, Rommel has created a situation which has outstripped the supply capability at this time. Rommel is not up to the job.' Furthermore, without Tobruk Rommel had to bring the bulk of his supplies 1700 kilometres from Tripoli, wasting vast amounts of fuel in the process and offering an easy target for enemy raids. Halder sent a highly competent strategist, General Paulus, to north Africa to find out what Rommel, 'this demented soldier', was doing. Paulus arrived at Rommel's headquarters on 27 April and was appalled to see he was wasting his resources in a series of unco-ordinated raids while he rushed around the desert in a desperate attempt to gain an overview of the situation. Paulus insisted that he should concentrate on making a series of limited raids on Tobruk and not waste all his supplies in a massive attack.

While the OHL tried to rein in Rommel, Churchill was ordering Wavell to pay close attention to the defence of Crete, to get rid of the junta of colonels in Iraq headed by the pro-German Rashid Ali, to drive the Vichy French out of Syria, and rid Iran of German influence. There can be no doubt of Churchill's wisdom in ordering these operations. Control of Syria (which then included Lebanon), Iraq and Iran was absolutely essential to the British, both strategically and economically. Had they fallen into German hands, as they might well have done if Hitler had not been obsessed with the attack on the Soviet Union and if he had not had strong reservations about nationalist movements in the Middle East and in Asia, the British would have been in an exceedingly precarious position in the Middle East.

Churchill saw to it that 307 of the most modern British tanks were sent to the Middle East in preparation for an offensive codenamed 'Battleaxe' which was designed to drive the Germans out of north Africa. The tanks were poorly armed and lightly armoured Matildas and Crusaders, and were easy prey for the Panzer IIIs and IVs as well as the 88mm anti-aircraft guns used as anti-tank guns. Fifty-seven were lost en route when a ship hit a mine. But Churchill had read the decrypts of Paulus's report on the situation in north Africa and believed that the Germans were exhausted, at least until the 15th Panzer Division was up to strength. Churchill therefore urged Wavell to launch 'Battleaxe' as soon as possible, while the cautious Wavell insisted that he was not yet ready. Churchill was grasping at straws in his hasty reading of partial information gleaned from 'Ultra' decrypts, and goaded Wavell into dangerously premature action.

Wavell's first move was to throw the 7th Armoured Division, the 'Desert Rats' against Halfaya Pass which they had lost to Rommel on 27 May in the course of the appropriately named 'Operation Brevity' to relieve Tobruk. 'Hellfire Pass' had been converted by Captain Wilhelm Bach, a Lutheran pastor in civilian life, into a deadly trap for tanks. A battery of 88s had been dug in so that only the muzzles could be seen, and then only at a distance of fifty yards. The British attacked this fortress with slow-moving Matildas, without cover and without artillery or air support and armed with toy guns without high-explosive shells. The tanks were shot to pieces, the British losing a total of 99. Only by dint of a hasty retreat from the forward position at Fort Capuzzo were the British able to escape Rommel's skilfully planned outflanking movement, a characteristic right hook. Wavell reported to the Prime Minister: 'I am sorry to have to report that "Battleaxe" has failed.' Shortly afterwards Wavell was sent to India as Commander-in-Chief and was replaced by General Sir Claude Auchinleck.

The British failed to learn the lessons of 'Battleaxe'. Rommel had shown the deadly effectiveness of a mobile defence and had given a painful lesson as to how a combination of anti-tank guns and tanks could be used as offensive weapons. The Matildas were far too slow and had been used in the totally unsuitable role of anti-tank weapons in support of infantry. In spite of the deadly effect of the 88s, which could knock out tanks at distances up to 2000 yards, the British continued to build their worthless two-pounder as anti-tank guns and as tank armament. Traditionalists still insisted that the 3.7-inch AA gun should not be used against tanks, even though it had been shown to be as effective as the 88s.

Rommel prepared a fresh attack on Tobruk but was delayed by lack of reinforcements and supplies sent to the bottom of the Mediterranean by the Royal Navy. Meanwhile, Churchill urged Auchinleck to launch an attack, 'Crusader', before Rommel's forces were up to strength. Auchinleck preferred to wait until Rommel was ready to launch his offensive, and then attack from the rear.

'Crusader' was eventually launched on 18 November after Auchinleck had been constantly prodded by an impatient Churchill, who argued that: 'It is impossible to explain to Parliament and the nation how it is our Middle East armies had to stand for four and a half months without engaging the enemy while all the time Russia is being battered to pieces.' Churchill badly needed a victory to save his political life, having presided over an endless series of setbacks and disasters and with a number of ambitious politicians anxious to have his job. He needed a victory to guarantee the continued support of the Americans and to answer the surly complaints of the Soviets. But he also imagined that the offensive would be so successful that it would be possible to follow it up with 'Acrobat', an advance to Tripoli and Tunisia, to be followed by 'Gymnast', the invasion of French north Africa, and possibly 'Whipcord', the invasion of Sicily. To this end, men and supplies were poured into the Middle East in spite of the warnings of the CIGS, Sir John Dill, that the situation in the Far East was perilous and that Singapore was badly in need of reinforcements.

Auchinleck had an overwhelming superiority of aircraft, tanks, men and reserves but, as he wrote, his was 'an amateur army fighting professionals'. The British commanders had no grasp of the basics of modern mechanized warfare, dispersing their efforts rather than concentrating in powerful hammer blows. The basic plan was for 13th Corps (Godwin-Austen) to hold down the enemy along the frontier wire, ignoring the heavily defended Halfaya and Sollum passes to the right, while 30th (Armoured) Corps (Norrie) was to sweep around the German left flank and push on to the airfield at Sidi Rezegh and then to the Tobruk garrison which was to break out of the town to meet them. Rommel was quick to see the basic flaw in the execution of the plan: 'What difference does it make if you have two tanks to my one, when you spread them out and let me smash them in detail? You presented me with three brigades in succession.' The British obsession with 'seek out and destroy' missions led to disaster. Given the mobility of armour, they ended up chasing phantoms, dispersing their forces and being drawn into Rommel's skilfully positioned tank traps to be destroyed by the 88s and the long-barrelled 50mms.

Rommel held up the 4th and 22nd (Armoured) Brigades to the south with anti-tank weapons, and threw the 15th and 21st Panzer Divisions against the 7th (Armoured) Brigade at Sidi Reżegh. In the confusion Sir Alan Cunningham, commanding the 8th Army, imagined that the Germans were on the run with the 7th Armoured

Brigade ahead of them, the 4th to their rear and the 22nd on their southern flank. It soon became clear that the 7th Armoured Brigade had been smashed, the 7th Hussars losing virtually all their tanks, and the 4th and 22nd Armoured Brigades were badly battered, although still intact. Rommel now had a comfortable superiority in armour and he was convinced that he could finish off the campaign in a rapid and daring move which would cut off the British supply lines, force them to retreat to avoid outflanking, finish them off with a blow to the rear and continue the advance into Egypt.

On 23 November Cunningham requested permission to break off the offensive, withdraw and reorganize. Auchinleck flew up to the front, dismissed Cunningham who was exhausted, dispirited and at the end of his tether, and replaced him with Major-General Neil Ritchie who was given orders to continue the battle whatever the cost.

The situation was now hopelessly confused, with British and Axis troops aimlessly dispersed between Tobruk and the frontier. Rommel's 'dash to the wire' had run out of steam. He no longer had a firm grasp over the deployment of his forces and he managed to get himself lost one night, along with his Chief of Staff, among British and Indian troops. He was saved only by the fact that his command vehicle had been captured from the British and was therefore not challenged. General Bastico, Rommel's superior, had no idea where he was and his GI Ops, General Westphal, had to conceal from the OKH and OKW that Rommel had disappeared, was no longer in radio contact, and that his reports were undated, largely incomprehensible and gave no hints of his intentions.

While the two sides thrashed around in the desert, the New Zealanders advanced towards Tobruk, joining up with the break-out forces who had broken through the El Duda escarpment thus opening up the corridor to the garrison. On 26 November Westphal ordered the Afrika Korps to return to Tobruk and to disregard all orders to the contrary. Rommel was furious when he heard of this, assuming it was a British trap and threatening to have Westphal court-martialed. After a careful examination of the situation, Rommel decided that Westphal had been absolutely correct. The Germans once again seized Sidi Rezegh after two days of hard fighting, even though they were greatly outnumbered. The British still held the heights of El Duda, although this left Tobruk dangerously isolated. The Germans were now exhausted and staff officers proposed a tactical withdrawal from Cyrenaica. Rommel, however, would not listen to such a suggestion.

By the beginning of December the Afrika Korps only had thirty-four Panzers left. Rommel had been unable to restore an effective investing circle around Tobruk and could not break through to his men, who were surrounded at Halfaya Pass, Sollum and Bardia. He decided to retire through the Mersa Brega gap to El Aghelia to regroup, await reinforcements and prepare for a fresh offensive. The British chased him all the way to the Tripolitanian border, but in spite of numerical superiority their final attack was a costly failure. The Guards Brigade mounted a frontal attack which was repulsed, and a flanking movement by the 22nd Armoured Brigade resulted in the loss of sixty-five tanks. Further east the Axis troops held on to Badia until 2 January, and the force at Halfaya Pass surrendered two weeks later.

Auchinleck's decision to stand and fight resulted in an impressive but largely forgotten victory in which the Germans suffered losses almost as great as at the second battle of El Alamein, even though the British forces were half the number and the Axis forces stronger. Rommel had lost one-third of his command, the bulk of his Panzers were destroyed and 36,000 of his troops had been taken prisoner, the same number as at the second El Alamein. But far from being beaten, Rommel told his wife on 17 January: 'The situation is developing to our advantage and I am full of plans I dare not even discuss with my entourage. They would think I am insane.' Four days later he launched a counter-attack.

While Ritchie was preparing an offensive into Tripolitania, many of his aides advised him to prepare defensive positions lest Rommel should move first. Ritchie, told by GHQ intelligence that Rommel had not received any reinforcements, ignored these warnings, even though new tanks and fresh troops had been spotted by reconnaissance units. At this critical stage the British were temporarily unable to crack the German army codes, and nothing useful was gained from Luftwaffe decrypts. Rommel's intelligence was superior. He knew that he faced the 1st Armoured Division, freshly arrived from England and with no experience of fighting in the desert. When Rommel struck he therefore caught inexperienced troops on the wrong foot.

At first Ritchie imagined that Rommel's offensive was merely a reconnaissance in strength, but it soon became clear that he was hoping to encircle the entire 1st Armoured Division. This move was poorly executed, allowing the British to retreat in somewhat unseemly disarray. Rommel pursued the British at break-neck speed, smashing their tanks with concentrations of anti-tank guns and

Panzers. The 1st Armoured fell apart and fled. Ritchie, an inexperienced general who had been appointed well beyond his abilities, was at a loss to know what to do. Auchinleck flew in from Egypt to examine the situation, but he too felt that the tales of rout and disintegration were exaggerated and was uncertain whether Rommel would aim for Benghazi or go for the British lines of communication to Egypt. Ritchie attempted to counter-attack but this was anticipated by Rommel who feinted to the east, drawing Ritchie's armour away from Benghazi, then swiftly changed direction towards the coast, trapping the 4th Indian Division who fought their way out with great bravery. On 29 January Benghazi fell and with it the stores and fuel prepared for the advance into Tripolitania. The 8th Army retreated to Gazala, but Rommel lacked the supplies to follow with anything but light forces. There followed several months of preparation, training and waiting.

Churchill still desperately wanted a victory in the desert for political reasons and, misled by reports of relative numerical strengths, demanded another offensive. Auchinleck, who knew that numbers were far less important than quality and who believed that the superiority of German tanks could be overcome only by a ratio of three to two, argued for a postponement until he had built up his reserves.

Whereas Churchill was prodding Auchinleck, Hitler was holding back Rommel. He was interested in Russia, not north Africa, and he felt that Malta was the most important objective in the Mediterranean. Reluctantly Hitler gave way to Rommel's argument in favour of an attack on Tobruk in May, but ordered that he was then to halt his advance and release his air support for an attack on Malta.

Rommel's fresh offensive began on 26 May 1942. Ritchie's 8th Army was poorly dispersed behind the Gazala Line. His infantry and guns were placed in forward positions in strong points or 'boxes', easy prizes to be picked off by Rommel, while his mobile mass of manoeuvre in 30th Corps was scattered all over the place in isolated armoured brigades. It was a hopelessly outdated deployment, with immobile infantry fighting separately from the thinly spread armour. Rommel headed towards Bir Hacheim, at the southern end of the Gazala Line, with 500 Panzers and 10,000 other vehicles in order to turn the British left flank. The general consensus in the 8th Army was that such a move was impossible and that he would attack the Gazala Line head on. Thus only the 7th Armoured Division guarded the left flank; the other Division was miles away to the north waiting to see where Rommel's main blow would fall. British intelligence was so poor and the deployment of 30th Corps so unfortunate that the armour was never able to recover from the initial shock. The result was, as General Messervy, commanding the 7th Armoured Division, put it, 'an awful muck of a battle'. Rommel headed north at astonishing speed, overrunning divisional headquarters and taking Messervy prisoner. Within twenty-four hours the 7th Armoured Division was no longer a viable fighting force, its brigades having been picked off one by one.

In spite of the remarkable success of his offensive, Rommel's position was now very vulnerable and he could only hope that he would be saved by the habitually slow and unimaginative response of the British commanders. On his left were the strongly defended boxes of the Gazala line, on his right the remains of the British armour. His supply lines were dangerously stretched, his armour too far ahead of their supply trucks. Had British armour been able to mount a co-ordinated strike against his flank he would have been decisively beaten. The British threw themselves with great courage and determination at Rommel's right flank, but it was far too haphazard an effort to bring victory. Much of Rommel's armour was sitting in the desert without fuel, but the pathetic two-pounder British anti-tank guns could do little damage.

Rommel wanted to push on to Tobruk, but prudence dictated that he should secure his supply lines which were over-extended and threatened by the Free French at Bir Hacheim. His solution was typically daring. He decided to drive through the Gazala Line north of Bir Hacheim and join up with his forces pulled back to a bridgehead to the east of the gap. It was an unexpected move that would greatly shorten his lines of communication and was mistakenly taken by Ritchie to be proof that Rommel was on the run. Once again only piecemeal efforts were made to exploit the situation, and the counter-attack came too late to save the Green Howards and the East Yorkshires, who fought very bravely to save the 150th Brigade Group 'box' at Sidi Muftah. The Germans were now in control of the centre of the Gazala Line and had the option either to retreat or to push eastwards.

While Rommel sat in his bridgehead, known as the 'Cauldron', preparing for a fresh assault on Tobruk, Ritchie held endless meetings and discussed countless plans. Although he was at a loss to know what to do, he still believed that Rommel was beaten. Eventually 'Operation Aberdeen' was agreed upon, an attempt to crush the enemy in the Cauldron. It was an ineptly conducted attack which Rommel quickly put to rout, capturing Messervy's headquarters for the second time, which resulted in the loss of over 200 tanks, four regiments of artillery and an Indian brigade. Ritchie complacently reported to Auchinleck that 'the enemy's position is not too easy'.

Rommel's next move was to head south to lay siege to the Free French position at Bir Hacheim. After days of bombing by Kesselring's Stukas and bombardment by heavy artillery, the 4000 Free French, some of whom were German-born Legionnaires, were forced to surrender. Rommel wrote of them: 'nowhere in Africa was I given a stiffer fight'. It is greatly to the credit of the Afrika Korps that Hitler's directives to shoot the Free French, Jews, political refugees and commandos were ignored. The prisoners of Bir Hacheim were regarded as brave soldiers who deserved to be treated honourably.

Rommel now headed north east towards Tobruk, isolating the heavily defended 'Knightsbridge' area in a battle which cost the British 200 tanks in two days, thus virtually depriving them of armour, and threatening their remaining forces which were strung along the coastal area from Gazala to Tobruk. Ritchie now wanted to move the bulk of his army back behind the Egyptian frontier, even at the risk of losing Tobruk. Auchinleck instructed him to defend Tobruk by holding the western and southern perimeters. Churchill demanded that Tobruk be held at all costs, arguing that until it fell the Germans would be unable to move into Egypt. Ritchie had already allowed the bulk of his troops to head for the frontier and thus knew that there was little hope of offering a serious defence of Tobruk. Auchinleck had already said in January that Tobruk might have to be abandoned, and CIGS had offered no objections. On 21 June 1942 Tobruk fell. Sadly, it was also Auchinleck's birthday. Ritchie withdrew to a poorly prepared defensive position at Marsa Matruh. Rommel decided to press on deep into Egypt, certain that the British mixture of pluck and incompetence would not be able to halt his progress. On 25 June Auchinleck relieved Ritchie of his post and took over the direct command of the 8th Army. Hitler, although preoccupied with plans for an attack on Stalingrad, was delighted with the news. He promoted Rommel to Field Marshal and abandoned the attack on Malta so that Kesselring's air force could be used to destroy the Allies in the desert. He announced that the war had reached a turning point, and he saw the glittering prospect of the German armies driving up through Egypt and down through the Caucasus in a campaign which would lead to the defeat of both the

Soviet Union and Britain. Mussolini, not to be outdone, made both Cavallero and Bastico Field Marshals, prompting Ciano to remark that while the first appointment amused people, the second made them indignant. In anticipation of a triumphal entry into Cairo, Mussolini flew to north Africa and arranged for a white charger to be ready for the victory parade. He left a few days later, livid that Rommel had not seen fit even to pay him a courtesy call.

The situation for the Allies seemed desperate. Churchill, who was in Washington, described the loss of Tobruk as 'one of the heaviest blows I can recall during the war', and Roosevelt immediately ordered 300 Sherman tanks to be sent to the Middle East. If Rommel could deliver a final deadly blow he would be in the Delta within a few days, sit astride the Allied routes to India and the Far East, cut off the supply line to the Soviet Union via the Persian railway, seize the oilfields of Persia and Iraq, and probably force Turkey into the Axis camp. Syria and Palestine would be overrun, the Royal Navy would be forced to leave the eastern Mediterranean, and Russia's southern flank would be wide open. Auchinleck decided on a mobile defence rather than stake everything on a last-ditch stand at Mersa Matruh, an unsuitable location to fight it out with Rommel since it could be easily turned to the south. The 60-kilometre strip between the Qattara Depression and the sea, where there was nothing but a small railway station at El Alamein, offered a far better position. Should that fall, Auchinleck decided to continue the fight into the Delta or up the Nile, for the oilfields of the Middle East, not Egypt, were the prize which had to be denied the Germans.

Although hopelessly outnumbered, Rommel fought a textbook battle at Marsa Matruh and won his most remarkable victory. His shadow forces carried out a double battle of envelopment, to the north and to the south, picking off Allied formations one by one. It was a battle Auchinleck never wanted to fight. Had he been able to co-ordinate his forces he could have defeated Rommel, but he inherited the battle from Ritchie and intelligence provided him with an accurate picture neither of the dispositions of the 8th Army nor of the course of the battle. Retreating to El Alamein, Auchinleck told his Chief of Staff, Dorman Smith: 'The British pride themselves on being good losers. I'm a damned bad loser. I'm going to win.'

Auchinleck took full advantage of the brief breathing space afforded by the exhaustion of Rommel's troops to reorganize his army. In the place of ossified and immobile divisional organization and rigid 'boxes' which could be outflanked and surrounded by German armour, he created battle groups out of his brigades which gave the 8th Army a degree of mobility and flexibility without which it was helpless against an opponent who was a past master of armoured warfare.

Rommel had little to throw into the battle but energy and bluff. He had 86 tanks and 1500 infantrymen, most of whom rode in captured British vehicles. He intended to attack the centre of the British front, where he mistakenly believed he would find the bulk of the enemy's armour, and then to divide his forces into two, turning north to envelop part of the allied forces at El Alamein, the rest to the south. Signals Intelligence (*Sigint*) gave Auchinleck a clear indication of Rommel's intentions, and he used this information to maximum effect. It was in any case a plan which had little hope of success given the forces available to the Germans, and was typical of Rommel's wishful thinking.

Rommel launched his attack on 1 July but, making little progress, was forced to abandon the idea of a double envelopment for a single drive north to cut off the El Alamein box. Auchinleck's counter-attack was poorly executed by his subordinates and resulted in a head-on clash at Ruweisat Ridge, which at least held up Rommel's advance. Further south the New Zealanders, Australians and the 1st Armoured Division made quick work of the Italians when the Ariete Division made an ill-considered outflanking attempt. Rommel was forced to hold up his advance and rush to the help of his allies. He was obliged to use his armour in defence, particularly as an anti-tank weapon, and thus lost the mobility which was the secret of his success.

Auchinleck then hit the Sabratha Division on the left flank of the Axis forces, seizing the strategically important hill at Tell el Eisa, and compelling Rommel to abandon his plans for an advance and to hasten north to avoid disaster. Two days later Auchinleck again hit the Italians, routing the Trieste Division and forcing Rommel to send in units of the Afrika Korps to repair the damage. The German counter-attack failed and Rommel now had to abandon his dreams of an advance into Egypt. He was seriously worried that the Italians might collapse totally, leaving him in a critical situation.

On 13 and 14 July the Germans desperately tried to push forward, but were forced to go on the defensive. On the night of 15 July the New Zealanders and Indians seized Ruweisat Ridge from the Italians and took the bulk of the Brescia and Pavia Divisions prisoner. The Afrika Korps was now positioned in the centre and the two flanks were controlled by the Allies, the Italians having been put to flight. Rommel confided to his wife that the situation made him weep. Auchinleck had won a great victory, and had reserves been available he could easily have finished off the Axis forces in north Africa. Instead there were clear indications that the Germans were about to seize the Caucasus and would soon be on the borders of Persia. Churchill therefore ordered Auchinleck to go on the offensive, push Rommel back to a safe distance and then release part of the 8th Army for the defence of Persia and Iraq. Although the army was exhausted, poorly trained and much of its equipment defective, Auchinleck had no alternative but to obey.

The attack on the El Mreir depression, then on Point 63 on the Ruweisat Ridge, which began on 21 July was a disaster. Worst hit of all was the 23rd Armoured Brigade. Freshly arrived from England, without desert training and equipped with obsolete Valentine tanks, they were shot to pieces by the German anti-tank guns. A second attack on the night of 26th was no more successful. Once again poor co-operation between the armour and the other sections led to a serious dissipation of effort and allowed the Germans to counter-attack. Auchinleck saw no alternative but to call off the battle.

Churchill, ignorant of the true situation in north Africa and misled by Auchinleck's characteristically modest accounts of his very considerable achievements, fumed at what he considered to be inexcusable inertia. Rommel saw the battle in a truer light. He wrote: 'Although the British losses in this Alamein fighting were higher than ours, the price to Auchinleck was not excessive, for the one thing that mattered to him was to halt our advance, and that, unfortunately, he has done.' Rommel's Chief of Staff, General Bayerlein, described Auchinleck's achievement as 'marvellous' and confessed that the Afrika Korps knew all too well that they had suffered a serious defeat.

All this was lost on the British Prime Minister, who was still smarting under the humiliation of hearing that Tobruk had fallen while he was Roosevelt's guest in Washington, and he attributed the massive defeat of his Coalition Government's candidate at the Maldon by-election to Auchinleck's shortcomings. 'Defeat,' he wrote in his memoirs, 'is one thing; disgrace is another.' He utterly failed to see the significance of the battle of El Alamein, and went to Cairo to dismiss Auchinleck. Although it was an appalling break with the traditions of the army, Churchill the politician also dismissed two of Auchinleck's immediate subordinates, Dorman-Smith and Corbett. Corbett was an officer of very modest talents, but Dorman-Smith was one of the finest minds in the British army. His career was ruined by mediocre personalities who resented his unorthodox brilliance, and although he led a brigade with great distinction at Anzio he was removed from the active list of the army in November 1944 without even the courtesy of an explanation. In place of Auchinleck as commander of the 8th Army, Churchill appointed Gott, a disastrous choice based largely on 'Strafer's' earlier reputation as an independent and energetic spirit. Gott was killed shortly after his appointment and his place taken by Montgomery, whom both the CIGS and Auchinleck preferred. General Alexander was appointed Commander-in-Chief in the Near East.

Montgomery, with his energy, boundless (if unjustified) self-confidence and genius for self-promotion, was a breath of fresh air, but that he galvanized an army sunk in despair and defeatism – a 'dog's breakfast', to use a favourite expression – is pure myth. He was wise enough to take over plans devised by Dorman-Smith, who was probably the most brilliant staff officer in the British army. These plans had been initiated, developed and approved by Auchinleck and the positions prepared while Montgomery was still in England. It is typical of Montgomery that he was to insist to his dying day that the dispositions at Alam Halfa were his own, as was the plan of campaign. Like Auchinleck he knew that time was needed before launching an attack, but this did not lead to his dismissal by the Prime Minister. Unlike Auchinleck he knew how to handle Churchill, how to flatter him, spoil him and pour wine and spirits down his parched throat. Churchill was immensely impressed by Montgomery's accurate predictions of Rommel's intentions, but these were based on Auchinleck's and Dorman-Smith's assessments and on information gleaned from 'Ultra' decrypts.

The battle of Alam Halfa was a foregone conclusion. Montgomery inherited an excellent plan and had 777 tanks to Rommel's 200 which were also desperately short of fuel. He had complete mastery of the air. Rommel was a very sick man, unable to get out of his command truck. Montgomery's main contributions to the battle were the decision to dig in his tanks hull down and, above all, to keep a firm grip on the course of the battle.

Late on 30 August Rommel began his offensive, committing all his troops to the south of Alam Halfa Ridge. The 7th Armoured Division met the brunt of this attack and slowly gave ground until Rommel, already running seriously short of fuel, headed north towards the western end of the Ridge. The British, making good use of their new six-pounder anti-tank guns firing from well-entrenched positions, fought off the attack on the Ridge, which was not pressed with the Germans' customary verve. Repeated attacks failed and on

2 September Rommel ordered a retreat. He had virtually run out of fuel.

Montgomery lost the golden opportunity to counter-attack across Rommel's lines of communication which could well have led to the total defeat of the Axis forces. But he was always a painfully cautious and slow-moving commander whose basic tactic was what he called 'dog eat rabbit'. The 8th Army had been plagued by constant bickering between armour and the infantry. The British, who had invented the tank, were singularly inept in its use, wasting this valuable resource in heroic but pointless tally-ho charges in the glorious tradition of Balaclava, which simply resulted in them being shot to pieces. The tactical problem was, as Liddell Hart was to point out, somewhat like the child's game of paper, stone and knife. Guns stop tanks, but infantry stop guns. Tanks could destroy infantry and disrupt supply lines. It was a game Rommel played with great skill, but it was beyond the ability of the 8th Army. Auchinleck and Dorman-Smith had tried to overcome this problem by introducing battle groups on the German model, but Montgomery had no patience for what he described as 'cow-pat tactics'. He decided not to play the game at all, to dig in and let Rommel wear himself down. This worked splendidly, and Rommel complained bitterly to Kesselring: 'The swine does not attack!' But although Alam Halfa was a fine defensive battle, the counter-attack, 'Beresford', when it eventually came, was too little, too late. Rommel had already escaped.

Montgomery's plans for an offensive were characteristically cautious in spite of endless goading from Churchill. The Prime Minister needed a victory, and he needed one quickly. He was being challenged at home politically by Stafford Cripps and militarily by the advocates of an all-out bomber offensive. He needed to have something to show before the Americans landed in north Africa at the beginning of November, and he also needed something to placate Stalin who was endlessly grumbling that the British were not doing any serious fighting. Given the disparity in strengths, it is no wonder that the British won the battle, but it is truly amazing that Montgomery almost managed to lose it. Exact figures are impossible to calculate, but the British had about 230,000 men, the Axis about 90,000 of whom about 50,000 were Germans. Montgomery had about 1300 tanks to Rommel's 200 German tanks and 300 obsolete Italian models. Montgomery had overwhelming superiority in all forms of artillery and complete control of the air. Although Montgomery and Churchill made much of the strength of the

German defensive position, Rommel's 90,000 men were deployed along a front 45 miles long. The Dyle Line of 1940 was defended by 45,000 British troops along a 17-mile front, yet was deemed desperately weak. The German front was only 5 miles deep, including minefields, and was thus vulnerable to artillery fire from behind the British front. On top of all this, Rommel was seriously ill and had to return to Germany for treatment, leaving the planning for counter-measures to a British offensive in the hands of Generals Stumme and Thoma, neither of whom had much experience of desert warfare. The unfortunate Stumme died of a heart attack when he came under fire at the beginning of the offensive. Rommel was hastily recalled, only to find his defences badly dented and many of his valuable tanks lost in fruitless counter-attacks.

Montgomery's original master plan was for a breakthrough followed by a mopping-up operation of enemy infantry by his armour. He soon decided that this was too ambitious and beyond the capabilities of the 8th Army. The final plan called for the four infantry divisions of Leese's 30th Corps to punch two holes through the German and Italian left flank towards Kidney Ridge and Miteiriya Ridge. Then the armour of 10th Corps was to pass through these gaps and position itself defensively to the west, wear down the enemy and eventually pursue the stragglers as they left the battlefield. To the south Horrocks' 13th Corps was to make a diversionary feint. This cumbersome plan, which led to appalling congestion on a narrow front and divided armour and infantry in an unimaginative battle of attrition, was given the absurdly ironic codename of 'Lightfoot'.

The major question is whether the second battle of El Alamein needed to be fought at all. In military terms it was totally unnecessary. Rommel admitted that the 'Torch' landings spelled the end of the German army in Africa. He would have had to retreat to join his forces in Tunisia even without a British offensive. Had Montgomery waited until Rommel was forced to withdraw, he could have devastated the Axis forces with his overwhelming superiority in armour and in the air. The second battle of El Alamein was therefore fought for purely political reasons. It was Britain's last chance to fight alone and win alone before becoming a subsidiary power to the United States. It was for this reason that the second battle of El Alamein was made into a victory as great as Blenheim or Waterloo, with church bells ringing and screaming headlines. Montgomery, who had won the political victory that Churchill needed, was rewarded with every honour. Auchinleck, who had won the military victory without which the second El Alamein would have been impossible and who had saved Egypt, was disgraced.

Montgomery launched his attack on the evening of 23 October. By the morning it had ground to a standstill. The infantry was packed into narrow corridors, unable to penetrate to the far side of the enemy defences and subjected to mercilessly accurate artillery fire. Behind them stood the armour, unable to move until the way was cleared. To the south Horrocks's attack floundered on the minefields. Montgomery then ordered the armour of 10th Corps to clear the way through these narrow defiles. Lumsden, the corps commander, rightly objected to this misuse of tanks, arguing that to send them through minefields and against 88s in a narrow defile would invite a massacre. Gatehouse, who commanded 10th Armoured Division and was the most experienced tank commander in the British army, was equally appalled. The problem was compounded by the fact that two corps, one infantry and one armour, under two different commanders were fighting two battles on the same narrow ground. Inevitably the breakthrough failed, and Montgomery attempted to blame this failure on the cowardice and inertia of 10th Armoured Corps.

By 26 October the British were exhausted. Montgomery had lost 200 tanks and many of his infantry divisions had suffered crippling losses; 30th Corps was in disarray and needed a breathing space to recover. Montgomery now decided to try a fresh approach by ordering the 9th Australian Division on the right flank to head for the sea. Rommel's counter-attacks at Kidney Ridge were beaten back by anti-tank guns and bombers with the loss of one third of his tanks. On 28 October he tried again, but by now he was virtually out of fuel and suffered heavy losses from the RAF. Montgomery withdrew forces from his left flank to form a reserve for his final breakthrough in 'Operation 'Supercharge'.

Montgomery's attempted *coup de grâce* failed partly because of the incompetence of the 8th Army, but largely because of Rommel's superb generalship. He managed to pull back an army which was hopelessly outnumbered, immobilized by lack of fuel, subjected to endless attacks from the air, across country which offered no cover against an enemy who had an overwhelming superiority of tanks and motorized infantry. Montgomery was given a further bonus when on 3 November Hitler ordered Rommel to stand and fight. The following evening he was persuaded to allow Rommel to act as he saw fit. In spite of a thirty-six-hour delay, Rommel managed to escape because Montgomery's pursuit force was not ready to move – indeed, it had to be patched together from elements of various divisions. It was slow off the mark, widely dispersed and wasted its energy in short jabs towards the sea which missed the enemy they were supposed to trap. By 6 November the pursuit force was hopelessly stuck in the rain-sodden sand south of Mersa Matruh.

Montgomery and Churchill both used the rain as an excuse for the failure of the 8th Army to destroy the Afrika Korps, but this is as lame as it is convenient. While his experienced generals, such as Gatehouse, implored him to make a long dash to Tobruk to head off the enemy, Montgomery stuck to the tactics of a cautious bank manager: no advance without security. Rommel was amazed at Montgomery's slow response, but with only a handful of tanks left and precious little fuel he thanked his lucky stars that he had such a cautious opponent.

The 8th Army reached Tobruk on 13 November and Benghazi a week later. Rommel deployed his skeleton forces at El Aghcila, and Montgomery was so smitten by the Rommel legend that he fell for this outrageous bluff and waited for three weeks preparing an offensive. By the time it was launched Rommel had rested, reorganized and gone. The 7th Armoured Division under Harding caught up with Rommel at Mugta on the coast, but he fought his way out of the trap. Montgomery missed another golden opportunity to destroy Rommel's forces along the coast road to Tripoli, but although he had 450 tanks to the Germans' 50, the 8th Army moved so slowly that Rommel again escaped and was able to destroy the port installations at Tripoli before the British arrived on 23 January. A magnificent victory parade was held in Tripoli on 4 February, attended by Churchill. A week later Rommel withdrew across the Tunisian border.

The Americans had been reluctant to agree to the 'Torch' landings in north Africa. The British, with their piecemeal approach to strategy, found themselves in the Mediterranean and intended to exploit their position there to tighten the ring around Axis-controlled Europe, knock Italy out of the war and then establish a foothold on the Continent to deliver the final blow against Nazi Germany. It was a strategy of erosion and attrition which was to exploit any available opportunity. The Americans felt that the proper procedure was to decide where the decisive blow should be delivered and direct all efforts to that end. There was never any doubt in their minds that the object of Allied strategy should be the invasion of north-western France at the earliest possible date.

These differences in approaches to strategy were the cause of endless friction between the United States and Britain. The British felt that the Americans overlooked the enormous difficulties of mounting a full-scale invasion across the Channel against an experienced and skilful enemy. The Americans felt that the British were traumatized by the horrific experiences of the western front in the First World War and by a series of humiliating defeats in the Second, and lacked the drive and determination to mount a successful offensive.

There were further difficulties. Churchill frequently confided to his entourage that his principal war aim was the preservation of the British Empire and the status of Britain as a great power. This necessitated the total defeat of Nazi Germany, a policy with which the Americans were in total agreement, but as the US Army Planning Staff pointed out, it seemed that 'British deployments and operations apparently were undertaken primarily with a view to maintaining the integrity of the British Empire'. This was particularly true of the Mediterranean, where the Americans suspected that they were being lured into a side-show to protect British interests in the Middle East which would postpone the cross-Channel invasion.

At the 'Arcadia' conference held in Washington shortly after Pearl Harbor the Americans examined British proposals for future strategy. The United States agreed in a joint memorandum named 'WWI' to the British scheme for a tightening of the ring around Germany and a gradual wearing-down of German resistance by air bombardment, subversion, blockade and propaganda. The British conceded the possibility of a full-scale landing in western Europe by 1943, but suggested that these landings might instead be in the Balkans or the Mediterranean. It was also agreed that the major effort should be directed to the defeat of Germany, after which it would be the turn of the Japanese to meet the full weight of Allied military might.

The Americans soon began to have serious misgivings about 'WWI'. The humiliation caused by the evacuation of the Philippines, the losses inflicted on the Pacific fleet, the rapid advances made by the Japanese troops and the American public's demand for revenge all made it obvious that the war against Japan could not be regarded as simply a side-show. The US Navy understandably saw the Pacific as their principal theatre. The Joint Chiefs were therefore concerned that Germany should be finished off as soon as possible and felt that the British attitude was woefully dilatory. Army planners were in no doubt at all that the plains of north-western Europe were where the decisive battle had to be fought, and they were also convinced that the British notion that Germany would collapse by strangulation and attrition without the use of a land army in Europe was pure fantasy. The Americans were therefore determined that an army should be landed in northern France as soon as possible. The object was to defeat Germany, not to defend British interests or to dissipate America's immense resources throughout the world. The more they thought about the matter, the more it seemed to the Americans that they were being used and manipulated by the unscrupulous British to fight a war for their own selfish aims. Not even the exceptional diplomatic skills of Field Marshal Sir John Dill, who represented the British military in Washington, could quite allay these doubts.

In March 1942 Eisenhower, with the full approval of the President and of General Marshall, proposed that the United States should begin a build-up of forces in Britain which would amount to 18 divisions by early 1943 in 'Operation Bolero', followed by an invasion in April 1943, 'Operation Roundup'. A smaller force would be available by the summer of 1942 ready to invade in 'Operation Sledgehammer' if 'the German situation in western Europe becomes critically weakened', or if 'the success of German arms becomes so complete as to threaten the imminent collapse of Russian resistance'. The second condition for 'Sledgehammer' was clearly absurd. If the Soviet Union were to collapse it would be suicidal to throw nine British divisions and a maximum of three and a half American divisions against a minimum of twenty-four first-line German divisions in France.

At the beginning of April, Marshall flew to London to present these proposals to the British authorities. They were enthusiastically received and Churchill, in spite of the repeated warnings of the service chiefs that there could be no question of mounting 'Sledgehammer' in 1942, was so carried away by the proposal that he wrote to the President that Britain 'might however feel compelled to act this year'. This was an utterly irresponsible remark, for the War Cabinet Defence Committee and the Chiefs of Staff Committee had decided only two days earlier that any 'emergency operation' was unthinkable so long as German strength in the west remained at its existing level. The endless objections raised by the British to an early invasion were in such marked contrast to the readiness with which they had accepted American proposals in April that the Americans could easily be excused for their impatience and their suspicions of British duplicity.

The main reason why the British grasped at these proposals so eagerly, even though they were inadequately discussed and poorly conceived, is that they were under constant pressure from the Soviet Union to open the second front as soon as possible. The Soviets were deeply concerned that with the invasion of the Soviet Union the British might relax their efforts against Germany or even join the Germans in their anti-bolshevik crusade. Given that the German forces in western Europe still outnumbered the Allied divisions in the United Kingdom by more than two to one, there was little that the British could do, as Eden pointed out to Maisky on 22 June 1941 and as Churchill wrote in his personal letter to Stalin on 7 July, except step up the air offensive.

This was little comfort to the Russians, who persistently demanded land operations on the Continent. In the light of the Chiefs of Staff's report on the feasibility of even a raid, Churchill wrote to Stalin that he saw no way 'of doing anything on a scale likely to be of the slightest use to you . . . to attempt a landing in force would be to encounter a bloody repulse and petty raids would only lead to fiascos doing far more harm than good to both of us'. On 3 September 1941 Stalin suggested an offensive through the Balkans as a possible alternative to a landing in France. Churchill replied that this would not be possible without the help of Turkey and until the Allied position in the Middle East had been significantly strengthened. Stalin raised the question again during Eden's visit to Moscow in December, and approved the British suggestion for operations across the Mediterranean once north Africa was secure, with the remark: 'I think that is quite sound. The weakest link of the Axis is Italy.'

The situation was hardly altered when the the United States declared war on Japan on 8 December 1941, the day after the Pearl Harbor raid, or by Germany's declaration of war on the United States three days later. Allied forces in the United Kingdom were further depleted to meet the Japanese attack in the Far East. 'WWI' argued that an essential part of the strengthening of the ring around Germany was to gain possession of the whole north African coast and was thus consistent with British Mediterranean strategy. Although the Cabinet and the Chiefs of Staff agreed in principle to an invasion in the spring of 1943, they were still opposed to any 'emergency operation' across the Channel so long as German strength in the west remained at its existing level.

The British needed to placate the Russians and ensure that the Americans stuck to their 'Europe First' principle, and they thus made singularly disingenuous remarks about the possibility of operations across the Channel in 1942. Although they would contemplate such an operation only in the unlikely event of a major reduction of the German forces in France, the Chiefs of Staff informed Washington in April 1942 that the importance of helping Russia was so great that they should not be prevented 'from doing anything we can, however small, this summer'. This was both misleading and non-committal, as was Churchill's assurance to Molotov in June that the British were making preparations for a landing on the Continent in August or September 1942, a remark which was hastily followed by the proviso that: 'It is impossible to say in advance whether the situation will be such as to make this operation feasible when the time comes.' Molotov made it perfectly clear that the Soviets were not interested in any operation which drew off less than forty German divisions from the eastern front. This was hardly the case with the badly bungled raid on Dieppe.

The more the British planners looked at 'Sledgehammer' the less they liked it, and since it would have to be conducted largely by British troops, their view of the proposal was decisive. Roosevelt agreed with the substance of these objections, but suspected that they were part of a British tactic to wriggle out of their commitment to 'Roundup'. Meanwhile the Russians, facing the full weight of a renewed German offensive, had in the course of Molotov's visit to Washington in June extracted from the Americans what they subsequently claimed was a promise of a second front in 1942. In this awkward situation Roosevelt decided that American ground forces had to start fighting Germans somewhere, and he was now amenable to Churchill's suggestion for a landing in north Africa. On 8 July 1942 Churchill telegraphed President Roosevelt pointing out that conditions were unfavourable for 'Sledgehammer' and that an American landing in north Africa, 'Operation Gymnast', was 'the true second front of 1942'. 'Gymnast', a revival of proposals made in December during the Washington conference, was thus seen as the best alternative to 'Sledgehammer', the preconditions for which did not exist, and a possible way to meet Soviet complaints that nothing was being done to relieve them.

The American military were appalled at the President's decision to opt for 'Gymnast', which was now renamed 'Torch'. They realized what Churchill seemed incapable of understanding, that 'Torch' would divert resources from 'Bolero' and thus make it impossible to mount 'Roundup' in 1943. Eisenhower described the President's decision rather over-dramatically as 'the blackest day in history'.

Marshall decided to minimize the damage by adopting a different set of strategic priorities. More resources would be sent to the Pacific, and the stranglehold on the Third Reich would become a mere cordoning-off of the Germans. The Americans wanted a single landing at Casablanca with the immediate objective of controlling French Morocco. The British wanted a landing as far East as possible so as to control Tunisia. It needed the personal intervention of Churchill to the President to convince the Americans to land as far East as Algiers.

In August 1942 Churchill attempted to explain this strategy to Stalin in the course of his first meeting with the Soviet dictator. Stalin insisted that a firm commitment had been made to a second front in France that year and dismissed arguments that a landing on French soil was impracticable. In the end he professed to be convinced by the Prime Minister's arguments, claiming that he saw three principal advantages in the north African landings – that it would take the enemy in the rear, that it would put Italy out of action, and that it would involve the Germans in further difficulties with France.

On 7 November the Allied landings took place at Casablanca, Oran and Algiers. French resistance to the invasion was quickly overcome and by the end of December the Allies were in control of the whole of French Morocco and Algeria. The 8th Army continued its advance and reached the frontier of Tripolitania. The Germans reacted swiftly and, with a mixture of bluff and bravery, established a powerful defensive position in Tunisia. Rommel flew to Rastenberg in East Prussia and told Hitler that north Africa should be evacuated and the Axis forces in Italy strengthened in anticipation of an invasion. Hitler argued that the defence of Tunisia and Tripolitania was a political necessity, and decided to pour reinforcements into north Africa. For the Allies this proved to be a blessing in disguise. By failing to seize Tunisia in November they were to take a far bigger bag in May, and Italy was left virtually defenceless.

In January 1943 Roosevelt, Churchill and their respective chiefs of staff met in Casablanca to discuss future Allied strategy. Stalin was invited to the conference but declined on the grounds that he could not leave the active direction of the Soviet armed forces at such a critical moment. It was speedily agreed that the three main tasks for the coming year were to destroy the U-boats in the Atlantic, to concentrate on the bombing of Germany, and to give all possible aid to the Soviet Union. Much more difficult was the question of what to do in the Mediterranean. Churchill and Roosevelt agreed that the next step should be the invasion of Sicily. It was assumed that Italy, threatened by Allied air and sea power, would soon collapse and that the Germans would then be obliged to pour troops into Italy, the Aegean and the Balkans. In taking over from the Italians the Germans would be forced to move troops from the eastern front, thus relieving the Soviets, and also from north-western France, which would pave the way for 'Roundup'.

In a joint letter to Stalin, Roosevelt and Churchill argued that Hitler would soon know of the build-up of an Anglo-American invasion force in north Africa, Egypt and in the United Kingdom, but he would not know where it would strike. He would thus be compelled to spread his forces across the shores of France, the Low Countries, Corsica, Sardinia, Sicily, the heel of Italy, Yugoslavia, Greece, Crete and the Dodecanese. In reply to Stalin's request for further details, Churchill claimed that the invasion of north-western France would take place in August or September 1943. This was a hopelessly unrealistic claim which was to give rise to further recriminations from Moscow. Tunis and Bizerta did not fall until the middle of May, so that the conquest of Sicily was not complete before the end of August. This meant that there could be no cross-Channel invasion until the spring of 1944 at the earliest. Furthermore, the requirements in the Pacific had risen steeply so that the American Chiefs of Staff felt obliged to deflect men and materials to the Far East rather than to Europe and there was an acute shortage of landing craft.

The American military were bitterly frustrated by the results of the Casablanca conference. General Wedemeyer wrote: 'We lost our shirts . . . we came, we listened, and we were conquered.' They accepted the commitment to invade Sicily which, given the impossibility of launching a cross-Channel invasion in 1943, was a valid strategy, but they feared that they might become so embroiled in the Mediterranean that the British might be able to argue for a postponement of 'Round-up' even in 1944. Their 'Europe First' strategy had been based on the conviction that the war in Europe should be decided as quickly as possible so as to get on with the job of defeating the Japanese. Now they were being asked to underwrite the British strategy, which one American officer described as 'periphery pecking'. Admiral King used the opportunity afforded by this general disillusionment with the results of the Casablanca conference to press successfully for an extension of the war in the Pacific. The British in turn resented what they saw as a partial rejection of the prime commitment to the European theatre.

Meanwhile, Rommel decided to exploit his central position by holding up the ever-cautious Montgomery whose lines of supply were now becoming dangerously stretched, and by directing a blow against the inexperienced Americans. First he threw his crack 21st Panzers against the French garrison at the Faid Pass, which was quickly overrun. The Americans assumed that this was a feint, believing that the main attack would be directed against Fondouk. This proved to be an almost-fatal mistake.

On 14 February the Germans struck again with the 10th and 21st Panzer Divisions in a pincer movement from the Faid Pass and from a point further south, in an attempt to trap part of the American 1st Armoured Division. This was entirely successful, the Americans losing forty tanks. The Germans were unusually slow to follow up, as General Ziegler would not follow Rommel's advice to push on until he had received permission to advance from von Arnim, his immediate superior. A combat group from the Afrika Korps led by Rommel attacked further to the south, reaching Gafsa on 16 February. American, British and French troops, fearing that they would be trapped between Rommel's and Ziegler's forces, beat a hasty and disorganized retreat.

Rommel's plan for exploiting this situation, to push on through Tebessa in the direction of Bône, was frustrated by von Arnim and by the Comando Supremo in Rome. On 20 February he seized the Kasserine Pass. The Germans were now too weak to push far forward against massive Allied forces and Rommel decided to move east to meet the threat from the 8th Army to the Mareth Line. The Allies missed a golden opportunity to counter-attack and allowed Rommel to withdraw without serious loss. Even the much-fêted recapture of the Kasserine Pass was achieved without resistance. Rommel had taken more than 4000 prisoners and destroyed or disabled about 200 tanks. He had almost forced the Allies to retreat from Tunisia. It was a remarkable feat of arms and he was rewarded by being given command over all the Axis troops in north Africa.

Montgomery was ready for Rommel's attack on his position at Medenine which was launched on 6 March. With his carefully prepared defensive positions and with overwhelming superiority on the ground and in the air, Montgomery had little difficulty in forcing Rommel to break off the attack. Rommel was more convinced than ever that it was madness to remain in north Africa, and urged an immediate withdrawal to Tunis and Bizerta. When Hitler refused to accept this assessment of the situation he handed over command of the Army Group to von Arnim and flew to Italy and Germany to persuade his superiors to change their minds. His interviews with Mussolini and Hitler were to no avail, for the dictators shared a totally unrealistic appraisal of the situation in north Africa.

The Allies now began to tighten the ring. To the west the Americans had a tough time against the Germans. Even a commander as aggressive as Patton was unable to overcome the resistance of experienced troops such as those who defended the strategically vital Hill 322, and he began to gain the upper hand only when the Germans wasted their strength in a series of abortive counter-attacks. To the east Montgomery, with a two to one advantage in men and guns and a four to one advantage in tanks, began his attack on the Mareth Line on 20 March. A frontal assault at a singularly unsuitable sector of the front by Leese's 30th Corps was beaten back. Montgomery again showed his flexibility and improvisational skill (albeit obscured by his claiming that all his battles went according to carefully prepared plans) by altering the direction of his thrust towards the Tebaga Gap on the right flank of the Axis position. It was a skilful move but was somewhat ploddingly executed. The Germans made deadly use of their anti-tank guns and mounted a spirited counter-attack which allowed them to withdraw to the Wadi Akarit position. A quick hook towards the sea would have cut off their retreat, but Montgomery was again too slow to seize the opportunity.

On the night of 5 April the 4th Indian Division and the 51st Highland Division began their assault on the Wadi Akarit. It was successful, but Montgomery waited too long before sending in Horrocks's 10th Corps armour to exploit the gaps opened up by the infantry. Had he moved more quickly, the campaign in Africa might have been decided within the next few hours. By the time he moved the Germans had already counter-attacked, and they then swiftly withdrew to a new defensive position at Enfidaville, some 150 miles to the north.

The Axis forces, some 60,000 fighting men and less than 100 tanks, now defended a 100-mile arc around Tunis and Bizerta. They were surrounded by 300,000 men with 1400 tanks. The Germans and Italians fought very skilfully and beat back the first offensive by Alexander's forces from points all around the perimeter. But they were desperately short of fuel, ammunition and food. Allied command of the air and sea routes to Tunis and Bizerta resulted in the Axis forces being starved into submission. The final Allied offensive was painfully slow, and many opportunities to end the campaign swiftly were lost. At last on 7 May the British 6th and 7th

Armoured Divisions entered Tunis and the Axis forces surrendered. The exact number of prisoners taken is uncertain. It was certainly not the quarter of a million subsequently claimed by Alexander and Churchill, but it was probably more than the 150,000 claimed at the time. Whatever the number, the Axis had lost many of their finest troops who would have contributed greatly to the defence of Europe, and they had been driven out of a strategically vital area.

News of the fall of Tunis reached Churchill on board the *Queen Mary* as he sailed to the United Sates for the 'Trident' conference. The Joint Planning Staff proposed that the favourable situation in the Mediterranean should be exploited to the full. After the invasion of Sicily, southern Italy should be invaded and occupied, if necessary, as far north as Rome. A bridgehead was to be established in Yugoslavia, and the Dodecanese occupied. The Germans would be obliged to send forces to Italy and the Balkans. This was deemed to be the most effective way of preparing the ground for a cross-Channel invasion in 1944. The Americans were concerned that the British Mediterranean strategy would result in a further postponement of 'Roundup', which was now renamed 'Overlord'. General Brooke argued that operations in Italy and the Balkans would provide the best possible preconditions for 'Overlord'. The Americans, not entirely convinced, insisted that the invasion should take place on 1 May 1944 and that at least seven divisions should be withdrawn from the Mediterranean in preparation for the landings in Normandy. The British argued that a shortage of assault vessels, particularly of tank-landing ships (LSTs), would mean that an assault force of not more than five divisions could be landed in France in the spring of 1944. Since the Allies were preparing an eight division assault force against Sicily, the invasion of France would clearly be possible only under very favourable circumstances. The British continued to insist that their Mediterranean strategy would draw German troops away from northern France and thus make 'Overlord' possible; the Americans again argued that all efforts should be concentrated at the decisive point.

The 'Trident' conference established the supremacy of 'Overlord', but it was vague about future strategy in the Mediterranean. Eisenhower was instructed to take such measures as necessary after the invasion of Sicily to ensure the capitulation of Italy and the diversion of the maximum number of troops from the eastern and western fronts. This did not necessarily imply an invasion of Italy, a country whose terrain offered excellent opportunities for defending forces. Churchill was inspired by the vision of the 8th Army making a triumphal entry into Rome and argued vigorously for an invasion of Italy. He was strongly supported by the RAF, who had their eyes on strategic air bases in Italy from which they could more effectively conduct the bomber offensive against Germany. Marshall was not impressed by these arguments, but there were many Americans on Eisenhower's staff who favoured an invasion of Italy. Alternative plans were therefore drawn up for invasions of Sardinia and of Italy, so that when 'Operation Husky' was launched it was still uncertain where the Allies would strike next.

With the surrender of the German forces at Stalingrad at the beginning of February, the question of a second front was no longer quite as urgent a priority for the western Allies, but the Soviets were naturally concerned that their successes might lead to a lessening of Allied assistance. Soviet demands for a second front were as insistent as ever and arrived with what the Foreign Office described as 'boring monotony'. For failing to secure a second front Maisky was replaced as ambassador to Britain by Gusev, a thirty-eight-year old of neither brains nor charm, described by the British ambassador in Moscow as 'like a sea calf and apparently no more articulate'. Churchill was getting increasingly impatient with Soviet jibes and wrote to the Moscow embassy in June:

> Nothing will induce me in any circumstances to allow what at this stage I am advised and convinced would be a useless massacre of British troops on the Channel beaches in order to remove Soviet suspicions. I am getting rather tired of these repeated scoldings, considering that they have never been actuated by anything but cold-blooded self-interest and total disdain of our lives and fortunes.

Thus the defeat of the Axis forces in north Africa did nothing to improve relations between the Allies. The British and Americans disagreed fundamentally about future strategy, and the Soviets remained aloof, critical and suspicious. It was hardly an auspicious climate for the return of the Allied forces to Europe.

CHAPTER FIVE

The War at Sea and in the Air

The German admiralty did not begin serious planning for a naval war against Britain until the winter of 1938 when, in a series of war games, it was revealed that there were too few U-boats for an effective submarine offensive. Admiral Dönitz was an experienced officer who had commanded a submarine in the First World War, ending up as a British prisoner-of-war when he had the misfortune to be forced to abandon his UB 68 after blowing a ballast tank in the middle of a British convoy. In 1935 Dönitz began working on the development of his 'pack' tactics (*Rudeltaktik*), whereby a group of medium submarines of type VII was to operate under a single commander. Dönitz estimated that for an effective offensive against British shipping in the Atlantic, at least 300 U-boats were needed. At the outset of the war the German navy only had 57 U-boats fit for service, of which only 23 were suitable for operations in the Atlantic.

Dönitz's proposals for a large increase in the number of U-boats were rejected by Admiral Raeder, the Commander-in-Chief of the German navy. Whereas Dönitz believed the German navy should concentrate on attacking Britain's merchant navy and thus sever Britain's overseas lifeline, Raeder believed that the objective should be the destruction of the Royal Navy. Hitler supported Raeder and told him that he had until 1946 to prepare the navy for a show down with the British. In line with this thinking the German admiralty (OKM) favoured a smaller number of larger submarines which were heavily armed and which had a longer range. Dönitz believed that this scheme, outlined in 'Plan Z', was fundamentally flawed in that it would take far too long to build a fleet that would be strong enough to take on the Royal Navy, whereas a crash programme of U-boat construction offered a viable alternative.

Dönitz was soon proved correct. When the war began the Germans were in no position to fight an effective naval war with only a handful of U-boats and three pocket battleships. Nevertheless, they were to have some impressive successes in the early stages of the war. Between September 1939 and March 1940 the Germans sank 148 ships in the Atlantic totalling 678,130 GRT, and a further 267,443 GRT were sunk by mines off the British coast. The aircraft carrier *Courageous* was sunk on 17 September and the battleship *Royal Oak* a few weeks later. The *Deutschland* raided merchant shipping in the north Atlantic and another battleship, the *Graf Spee*, chased shipping in the south Atlantic and the Indian Ocean. The Royal Navy failed to take effective action against the U-boats and destroyers which were laying mines off the British coast; in fact, they did not even notice what was happening. This appalling negligence was only partially offset by the gallantry of the minesweeper crews and by the spectacular hunt for the *Graf Spee* by the cruisers *Exeter*, *Ajax* and *Achilles* which ended with the scuttling of this prize battleship in Montevideo on 17 December 1939.

The Norwegian campaign showed up a number of weaknesses in German naval operations. Staff work was poor and reconnaissance inadequate. Individual commanders were not given sufficient freedom of action, the fleet commander was tied down by precise orders from Raeder, and Hitler had the unfortunate habit of ordering individual ships about with total disregard for overall strategic or tactical considerations. The Germans were, however, saved from disaster by the even greater incompetence of the Royal Navy, whose signals they were able to decode.

The second phase of the battle of the Atlantic lasted from June 1940 until March 1941. Once France was overrun the Germans were able to build U-boat pens on the Atlantic coast, thus significantly reducing the time it took to reach their operational positions. On 17 August Hitler ordered unrestricted submarine warfare against Britain, and although Dönitz had an average of only twelve boats in operation at any given moment, this was enough to allow them to hunt in packs. The Royal Navy was preoccupied with the defence of the British Isles against the threat of imminent invasion and thus was unable to provide adequate defence for merchant shipping in the Atlantic.

The Germans had some remarkable successes in 1940, and had they followed Dönitz's advice and concentrated on building more U-boats they could have dealt the British a very serious blow indeed. Hitler was not particularly interested in the navy, and was preoccupied with planning the invasion of the Soviet Union. Raeder still hankered after more heavy surface raiders, even though they had proved to be something of a disappointment. The *Bismarck*'s battle with the *Hood* and the *Prince of Wales* showed what German sailors could do when they had the chance, but the battleships were seldom given the freedom of action they needed. Since there were so few of them the heavy ships were very vulnerable, and the *Bismarck* was sunk only because it was hopelessly outnumbered. Nevertheless the battleships *Scharnhorst* and *Gneisenau* and the heavy cruisers *Scheer* and *Hipper* were highly effective against merchant shipping in the Atlantic.

The U-boats were greatly hampered by lack of aerial reconnaissance, and it was not until January 1941 that the German navy was given the support of the Focke-Wulf 200 'Condor', a four-engined long-range aircraft. They were ideal for spotting convoys, but as only two aircraft per day were available there were far too few to be effective. By now the threat of invasion was over and the Royal Navy could greatly strengthen their convoy escorts and concentrate on hunting U-boats. In March 1941 the Germans lost five U-boats with exceptionally experienced commanders. This forced them to move their operational area away from the coast to the greater safety of the mid Atlantic, and a new stage in the battle of the Atlantic began.

Between June 1940 and March 1941 the British lost more than three million GRT and they were losing ships faster than they could be replaced. This was cause for great concern, but it was not enough seriously to disrupt the British war economy. The Germans estimated that they would have to sink 750,000 GRT per month in order to bring Britain to its knees, a target figure which was never reached by the U-boats. In their most successful month, November 1942, the U-boats sank 650,000 GRT. Raeder was now becoming convinced that the navy should concentrate on U-boat construction and defeat Britain before turning against the Soviet Union. Hitler, however, believed that the defeat of the Soviet Union would force Britain to end the war, and thus refused to give the navy the resources they needed for a successful U-boat offensive.

The third phase of the battle of the Atlantic, from April to December 1941, was marked by the increasing involvement of the United States in the war. President Roosevelt's determination to do everything 'short of war' to help the British was a further headache for Dönitz, and Hitler insisted that the Americans should not be given any grounds for entering the war. In September the US Navy took over the operational command of Allied warships escorting convoys in the western Atlantic, and thus became an active ally of the Royal Navy. Hitler did not react to this provocation but insisted that American ships should be attacked only in the war zone around the British Isles. Roosevelt had given the British fifty destroyers which could not be distinguished from their sister ships still in service in the US Navy. To avoid any unfortunate incidents, Hitler instructed Dönitz to stop any attacks on these destroyers, which were among the U-boats' worst enemies.

Single U-boats were useless against greatly strengthened convoy escorts, and from August 1941 they hunted in packs of about fifteen. They were immediately successful. At the beginning of September, twenty out of a total of sixty-three ships in Convoy SC 42 were sunk off the southern tip of Greenland. They would have been even more successful had the British not begun to crack the German naval code 'Hydra', which enabled them to read the U-boats' signals and thus divert convoys and direct accurate attacks against the packs. Particularly vulnerable were the tankers used by the U-boats for refuelling on the high seas. They were sunk in such numbers that the Germans were able to rely only on their submarine tankers, the 'milch-cows', which were capable of carrying 720 tons of diesel fuel for more than 12,000 miles.

On 17 October the US destroyer *Kearny* was damaged by a torpedo from U568, and two weeks later another US destroyer, *Reuben James*, was sunk by U552. Roosevelt took this welcome opportunity to secure the revision of the Neutrality Law of 1939 and ordered US merchant vessels to be armed. Dönitz would have liked to launch a pre-emptive strike against the US Navy in September, but the increasingly threatening situation in the Mediterranean obliged him to concentrate his forces around Gibraltar. The Japanese attack on Pearl Harbor came as a complete surprise to the Germans, and they were thus unable to launch a lightning attack on the east coast in December.

With the perfection of radar detection, improved aerial reconnaissance and increasingly swift and accurate information from the British Government Code and Cypher School (GC and CS) at Bletchley Park, the German surface ships became virtually worthless. Their port facilities in France were also particularly vulnerable to bombers. The sinking of the *Bismarck*, in which 'Ultra' information played no role, in May 1941 was a terrible blow to German naval prestige, and henceforth the heavy ships played an ever-decreasing role in the battle of the Atlantic.

Between January and July 1942 the U-boats were able to cause havoc against inexperienced American crews off the east coast of the United States, their task made easier by the introduction of a new version of 'Enigma' in February whose 'Triton' code the specialists at Bletchley

Park were unable to crack until December. In August the 'Interlocking Convoy System' was introduced, which greatly increased the efficiency of convoy defence and which made optimum use of aerial reconnaissance and radar. This resulted in a reduction of losses, which had reached 600,000 GRT in July. In this fourth phase of the battle of the Atlantic, a total of three million GRT was sunk in seven months.

In the next phase, from August 1942 to May 1943, the U-boats concentrated on attacking convoys in the north Atlantic where they were out of range of protecting aircraft. The U-boats adopted a tactic of 'raking' the ocean which proved most effective. In December 'Ultra' was again providing decrypts of wireless traffic between the U-boats so that the convoys were able to take evasive action, which saved many hundreds of thousands of tons of shipping, but in March 1943 a further drum was added to 'Enigma' so that 'Ultra' was unable to provide any further information for several months. Meanwhile the German Naval Radio Cypher Service (*xB-Dienst*) managed to read some of the Allied convoy codes and was thus able to detect changes of course. But by May 1943 the tide was beginning to turn against the U-boats, when of the 118 in service 38 failed to return.

In 1942 the Allies lost a total of 7,699,000 GRT and were able to build 7,182,000 GRT. At the same time the Germans were building U-boats faster than the Allies could sink them. In the same year Dönitz got 238 new U-boats and 87 were sunk – a net gain of 151. In November the British formed the Anti-U Boat Warfare Committee, with Churchill in the chair, to discuss means of combating Germany's most dangerous weapon. At the Casablanca conference in January 1943 it was agreed that the removal of the U-boat menace was a top priority and an essential precondition of a successful invasion of northern France.

Although there was no question that the convoy system was the best way to protect merchant shipping, there were differences of opinion about whether it was also the best way to sink U-boats. Both the Royal Navy and the RAF were intensely bored with convoy duty and wanted a more offensive strategy. Studies conducted by Coastal Command showed that convoys were still the best way of catching U-boats. Aircraft on spotter-patrol operations took far longer to sight U-boats than they did on convoy protection duty. The difficulty was that although the convoys lured the U-boats, the escort ships could not leave the convoy to chase and kill them, enabling the U-boats to make successful 'hit-and-run' raids. To overcome this difficulty the Royal Navy created 'support groups' made up of highly trained U-boat hunters using the latest centimetric short-wave radar (ASV – the land version was called H2S) and heavier depth charges which could be thrown ahead.

The support groups could range freely in pursuit of U-boats, unlike the escort groups, but they still faced a number of difficulties. The work called for very skilled crews, and few officers could match the experience of men like Captain F.J. Walker who commanded the first support group. Short-wave radar sets were in short supply, and Bomber Command had the first priority. 'Operation Torch' made heavy demands on shipping, so that very few vessels were available for support-group work. It was not until March 1943 that the support groups could become fully operational.

It took even longer to overcome the problems of the most effective use of aircraft for anti-U-boat operations. Coastal Command was subordinated to the Admiralty in April 1941 for operational purposes, but as the most junior command within the RAF it was starved by Bomber Command of the aircraft and equipment it badly needed. The major problem was the lack of Very Long Range (VLR) aircraft, such as the Liberator, without which they could not reach the 'Atlantic Gap' or 'Black Pit' in mid Atlantic. They played an important dual role in that they guided surface vessels to the attack, and they forced U-boats to remain submerged, thus preventing them from attacking the convoys. Even as late as February 1943, there were only 18 VLRs in operation against the U-boats. Roosevelt, realizing the importance of the U-boat campaign, transferred Liberators from the Pacific to the Atlantic, in spite of the outspoken opposition of Admiral King. Portal, however, allocated them to Bomber Command, insisting that the Americans wanted the aircraft to be used for high-level bombing raids. There was thus only one under-equipped squadron (No. 120), stationed in Iceland with five Mark 1 Liberators, which helped to win the battle of the Atlantic. The bomber offensive remained the absolute priority, and the Air Ministry persisted in seeing Coastal Command as a side-show. Air Chief Marshal Sir Philip Joubert de la Ferté, AOC-in-C Coastal Command, argued in February 1942 that at least part of the bomber offensive would have to be sacrificed and long-range aircraft diverted to the protection of sea communications if Britain were to survive the year, but such views were regarded as dangerously heretical in the Air Staff. 'Bomber' Harris went even further, denouncing Coastal Command and its incessant demands for more aircraft as 'merely an obstacle to victory'. Churchill did not intervene decisively in the debate, but at least he saw the problem when he wrote: 'The issue of the war depends on whether Hitler's U-boat attack on Allied tonnage or the increase and application of Allied air-power reach their full fruition first.'

Bomber Command attacked the U-boat pens between January and May 1943, but it was a futile and wasteful effort. Sixty-seven aircraft were lost in these raids and not a single U-boat was destroyed or even damaged. A further seventy-four bombers were lost in raids on the U-boat yards in Germany, with no tangible results. Coastal Command had argued in favour of bombing the pens while they were under construction in the summer of 1941, but Bomber Command had insisted that everything had to be concentrated on the bomber offensive against Germany. Once the construction of the pens was complete, it was too late. They proved to be truly bomb-proof. Convoys and support groups were clearly the only answer to the U-boats. In March 1943 the Atlantic Convoy Conference was convened in Washington to clarify the command situation. Convoy defence was now in the hands of the British and the Canadians, the latter having sole responsibility for convoys west of the 'Chop Line' (47 degrees west) and the Commander-in-Chief Western Approaches for the eastern Atlantic.

The outward convoy ONS 5 was attacked by the U-boats on 29 April and twelve of the convoy's forty-two ships were sunk. It cost the Germans six U-boats, which was a painful loss but not enough for them to question their basic strategy. Dönitz regrouped his U-boats for attacks on SC130 and its B7 escort group. Not a single Allied ship was lost in this attack and five U-boats were sunk.

This combination of organizational change and technical innovation forced Dönitz to abandon attacks with his packs. It was a victory in many ways as important as the battle of Britain, but one which has been almost forgotten. Support groups made systematic hunting of U-boats possible without leaving the convoys unprotected. Aircraft carriers and VLR aircraft filled the gap in mid Atlantic. New weapons, such as the 'Hedgehog' salvo firer for depth charges and the airborne homing torpedo, greatly increased the chances of a kill. The high-frequency radio direction finder (HF/DF or 'Huff-Duff') was invaluable to the escort vessels and aircraft, and centimetric radar made it possible to track the U-boats and meet the threat of surface raiders by night. Above all, the outstanding seamanship and courage of the escorts and support groups was a match for the exceptional skill and valour of the U-boat crews. They too were few, but their ability to make the very best use of their resources was to show that training and teamwork were more important than mere numbers. On 24 May Dönitz wrote in his diary: 'Losses, even heavy losses, must be accepted if they are accompanied by proportional success in tonnage sunk. But in May one U-boat was lost for every 10,000 GRT sunk, when not so long before one U-boat was lost for 100,000 GRT sunk. Thus our losses so far in May have reached an intolerable level.' In the month of May the Allies sank forty-one U-boats and the battle of the Atlantic was finally won. Among the casualties was Dönitz's son, Peter, who was serving on U954.

The U-boat war continued and German technical improvements resulted in some successes. Radio direction-finding equipment was greatly improved and the 'Hagenuk' receiver enabled the U-boats to detect centimetric radar emissions and take evasive action. The development of the schnorkel made U-boats far more difficult to detect. The electrically powered XXI U-boats and the smaller type XXIII could move incredibly fast under water with a top speed of 18 knots. None of this equipment was given the priority it deserved and the first eight type XXIIIs were not operational until February 1945, but they were enormously successful and none was lost. They were the only new type U-boats to become operational, even though by the end of the war 63 type XXIIIs and 119 type XXIs had been launched.

In 1942 the Germans removed their surface ships from the Atlantic. The battleships *Scharnhorst* and *Gneisenau*, along with the heavy cruiser *Prinz Eugen*, which were stationed at Brest, were subjected to such heavy aerial bombardment that it was decided to bring them back into the North Sea. On 12 February they made a successful dash through the Channel, prompting *The Times* to declare: 'Nothing more mortifying to the pride of sea power has happened in home waters since the seventeenth century.' The *Prinz Eugen* was severely damaged by a torpedo from a British submarine in Norwegian waters on 23 February, and four days later the *Gneisenau* was put out of action by bombs while docked at Kiel. Most important of all, the withdrawal of these ships marked the end of the offensive in the Atlantic by German surface vessels.

It soon became clear that *The Times* was crowing too loudly and too soon. The presence of these heavy ships in Norwegian waters, among them the *Tirpitz*, was a permanent threat to the convoys to Russia via Murmansk. In spite of 'Ultra' decrypts which showed that the *Tirpitz* did not intend to go to sea, the Admiralty ordered the dispersal of the escort to PQ 17 in July 1942 when they heard of the concentration of German heavy ships in Alta Fjord. This left the convoy defenceless against the U-boats and Luftwaffe, and twenty-three of the thirty-four ships were sunk. Hitler was unaware of the psychological effect of the heavy ships and took note only of the fact that they played no direct part in the sinking of ships on the Murmansk route. By January 1943 he came to the conclusion that the German navy had failed in its historic mission and concluded that: 'The heavy ships are a needless drain on men and materials. They will accordingly be paid off and reduced to scrap. Their guns will be mounted on land for coastal defence.' This outburst prompted Admiral Raeder to tender his resignation. He was replaced by Dönitz who, although he continued to exercise direct command over the U-boats, persuaded Hitler to reconsider his decision to scrap the surface fleet. He knew only too well that this act of petulance would simply hand the Allies a splendid and bloodless victory.

As the battle of the Atlantic showed, there were many in Britain, including the Prime Minister at times, who believed that Bomber Command would win the war. Even in 1942 this seems in retrospect to have been an astonishing notion. For the first two years of the war Bomber Command was small, poorly trained and badly equipped, capable only of delivering pinpricks to the enemy. This is somewhat surprising given that the ability to mount a strategic bombing offensive and deliver the 'knockout blow' was the *raison d'être* of the RAF as an independent force. Strategic bombing was clearly outside the spheres of activity of either the Royal Navy or the army, and this fact made it possible for the RAF to resist attempts by the two senior services to subordinate it to their command during the inter-war years. For all the talk of 'the bomber always gets through' the RAF had only some two hundred Wellingtons, Whitleys and Hampdens available for operations on a daily average, which was clearly not enough for an effective air offensive. This turned out to be a blessing in disguise. Inskip, as Minister for the Co-ordination of Defence, and Air Vice-Marshal Peck favoured fighters over bombers, the former for economic, the latter for professional reasons. Financial exigencies diverted the RAF from its self-appointed role as an offensive bomber force into an essentially defensive posture. Penny-pinching thus saved the country in 1940.

At the beginning of the war Bomber Command cooked up a number of schemes for bombing Germany, but they were never put into practice. Few of these plans were even feasible. They had no idea of the effectiveness of German air defences. There were serious doubts as to whether they could find, let alone hit, the appointed targets. There was no satisfactory way of assessing likely physical damage, and no way at all of judging the effect on enemy morale. Bombing by day was deemed too dangerous, but bombing by night was hopelessly ineffective. The plan to bomb the Ruhr, which had been the Air Staff's main strategic goal, had to be abandoned as unrealistic.

A strategic air offensive was, therefore, a gamble for which the British were not yet ready. The Government did not wish to risk the opprobrium of being the first to unleash large-scale bombing raids in which countless innocent civilians were bound to be killed. They also had an obsessive fear of retaliation and a curious concern not to cause any damage to private property. In the early stages of the war, daylight raids on shipping proved very costly and the results were disappointingly meagre. Night actions were hardly more promising and were largely confined to dropping some rather fatuous leaflets. In such operations accuracy was of little importance, and it was not long before the same tactic was applied with bombs. The result was 'area bombing', the indiscriminate dropping of bombs by night. It was designed to undermine enemy morale, and with a bit of luck the odd bomb might hit a worthwhile target. High explosives were deemed more damaging to the enemy than propagandist prose, and the Nazis were for once rather more to the point in describing it as 'terror bombing'. Area bombing was dictated not only by the inability of Bomber Command to find and hit specific targets, but also by the desire of members of the War Cabinet to reap revenge for the German bombs which had fallen on Britain. This was hardly a sound foundation for an effective strategy. On July 8 1940 Churchill wrote to Beaverbrook:

> When I look round to see how we can win the war I see that there is only one sure path. We have no Continental army which can defeat the German military power. The blockade is broken and Hitler has Asia and probably Africa to draw from. Should he be repulsed here or not try invasion, he will recoil eastward, and we have nothing to stop him. But there is one thing that will bring him back and bring him down, and that is an absolutely devastating, exterminating attack by very heavy bombers from this country upon the Nazi homeland. We must be able to overwhelm them by this means, without which I do not see a way through.

It was an appalling over-simplification of the strategic situation and was to have disastrous effects, but it seemed compelling in 1940. Apart from a side-show in north Africa, how else could the British fight anything other than a defensive war against Germany? There were still plenty of ways of losing the war, but it was difficult to think of any other way it might be won.

From the beginning it was agreed that the 'exterminating attack' would be aimed not at the enemy's war industry, communications system or military installations but against civilians so that their nerve would crack and they would overthrow the regime which had dragged them into war. Portal, writing as C-in-C Bomber Command at about the same time, claimed that the bomber provided the 'means by which we can undermine the morale of a large part of the enemy people, shake their faith in the Nazi regime, and at the same time and with the very same bombs, dislocate the major part of their heavy industry and a good part of their oil production'. At first the Air Staff did not agree with this approach, claiming that the main aim of bombing must be 'material destruction' and that 'moral effect' was a subsidiary, if important, by-product. Calls for revenge for the Blitz greatly strengthened the argument in favour of bombing civilians to undermine their morale. Portal, now promoted CAS, reversed the Air Staff's formula so that material damage was now seen as a desirable side-effect of the attack on enemy morale. Prime targets such as oil installations were now ruled out on the grounds that they were not in densely populated areas.

The strategy of terror bombing was questionable not only on moral grounds. As late as 1941 Bomber Command had only 400 operational aircraft on any one night, whereas the Germans had sent 712 bombers over London on 19 April. In May 1941 it was also estimated that 50 per cent of Bomber Command's bombs were falling harmlessly in open country. The effect of much heavier bombing than the RAF was able to deliver was also questionable. Raids on Madrid in the Spanish Civil War, or on London and Coventry during the Blitz, had not caused morale to collapse – indeed, it had in many individual cases strengthened the determination to fight on until final victory. The absurd notion that the Germans were made of weaker moral fibre, a widely held British prejudice, stood in the way of the development of an effective bombing strategy. Not only were Germans no easier to terrify, they also had the misfortune to live in a brutal totalitarian regime which made short shrift of pessimists and cowards. The bomber offensive was to have, in the final stages of the war, a shattering effect on civilian morale, but the SS and Gestapo made certain that this did not affect the security of the regime.

The experience of the early raids, such as the 'Abigail–Rachel' raid on Mannheim on the night of 16–17 December 1940, was hardly encouraging. The bombs fell in a widely dispersed pattern, thus minimizing the effect. By April the following year it was calculated that the average error of a properly aimed bomb was 1000 yards, and a few months later studies showed that in a series of attacks on the Ruhr only one in ten of the bombers got within 10 miles of their designated targets, and with a new moon it dropped to one in fifteen. Lacking effective navigational equipment, most crews released their bombs according to the estimated time of arrival (ETA), so it is hardly surprising that so many bombs fell wide of their mark. All this merely strengthened the arguments of those who favoured indiscriminate bombing, even though most raids caused minimal damage and had an insignificant effect on morale.

For the first four months of 1941 Germany's synthetic oil plants were designated the primary target. This had been singled out as the weakest point of the German war economy, and Portal promised that 855 sorties per month for four months would result in the destruction of the seventeen major synthetic oil plants. This soon proved to be an empty boast. In the first three months only 221 sorties were made, which caused minimal damage. This failure resulted in demands for more bombers. In the summer of 1941 the Air Staff called for a bomber force of 4000 machines by the spring of 1943. Portal imagined that this force would be capable of destroying forty-three German towns with a total population of over fifteen million and thus obtain 'decisive results against German morale'. On 31 July the Chiefs of Staff drew up a paper for the Prime Minister in which they insisted on the supreme importance of the bomber, which alone could 'produce the conditions under which other offensive force can be employed'. A massive bomber offensive, it was argued, would destroy German morale and could very well render a continental invasion unnecessary. It was a document born of despair. The Royal Navy was suffering terrible losses in the Atlantic and the army was being thrashed by the Afrika Korps. In such a situation the RAF seemed to offer the only glimmer of hope.

A statistical analysis by D.M.B. Butt of the War Cabinet Secretariat of the effects of bombing raids, which was completed in August 1941, showed that the Chiefs of Staff's confidence in the efficacy of bombing was misplaced. The report concluded that an average of only one-fifth of all aircraft despatched actually reached the target area, and the target area was generously defined as 75 square miles around the target. From this report the Air Staff concluded that a vast bomber force was needed to guarantee the desired effect, and the Chiefs of Staff, who saw no other possible way of beating the Germans, had to agree. Sceptics suggested that since the bombers were producing such pitiful results it would be a waste of limited resources to build the 4000 bomber force foreseen in 'Target Force E'.

By this time Churchill was beginning to doubt whether the bomber would have quite such a decisive effect on the course of the war. He warned that the moral and physical effects of bombing had been greatly exaggerated and suggested that accuracy was the major problem which had to be overcome. In spite of these reservations he remained an enthusiastic supporter of the bomber offensive. If not decisive it was a 'heavy, and I trust a seriously increasing annoyance'. Portal countered the Prime Minister's scepticism by a spirited defence of the bomber strategy. Churchill then reminded him that: '. . . he is an unwise man who thinks there is any certain method of winning this war, or indeed any other war between equals in strength'.

The situation at Bomber Command which Air Chief Marshal Sir Arthur Harris inherited in February 1942 was not a happy one. The Berlin raid on 7–8 November resulted in a loss of 28.76 per cent of the aircraft claiming to have reached their destinations. One hundred and twenty aircrew were lost in a raid which caused nine deaths and thirty-two injuries. Stafford Cripps began to ask questions in the House of Commons as to whether building up the bomber force was the best use of resources. Churchill was appalled at these losses which could not be justified by results, but Bomber Command insisted that were their men to believe anything other than that they were winning the war, the effect on morale would be disastrous. Harris was determined to restore morale and to concentrate the RAF's efforts on the bombing of Germany.

Bomber Command's first major raid under Harris's command was against Lübeck on 28–29 March. It was a target of minimal importance but it was on the coast and therefore easy to find, was poorly defended and its wooden houses were ideal for testing the efficacy of a heavy attack with incendiary bombs. For Harris it was more important to destroy a town of moderate importance than to fail to destroy an important industrial centre. Thomas Mann's birthplace was burnt to the ground, prompting him to broadcast a blood-curdling warning to his fellow countrymen that this was a taste of things to come. A total of 312 died in the raid. Industrial damage was slight, the effect on morale exaggerated, but the news of the city's destruction was gleefully received in Britain. Raids on Rostock between 24 and 26 April produced even better results. Heavy damage was sustained by the Heinkel, Neptune and Arado works and 100,000 people had to be evacuated. Goebbels confided in his diary that the raid had put the Führer in a very bad humour, but he was somewhat mollified by the reports of the 'Baedeker' raids on England's historic centres, among them Bath, Exeter, York and Canterbury. Yet in spite of this success the major war factories were back in full production within three days. Other raids in April against Essen, Cologne, Dortmund, Hamburg and Kiel produced equally meagre results.

The most successful raid of all was against the Renault works at Billancourt, outside Paris, on the night of 3–4 March. A large percentage of the planes actually arrived on target. Flares were used to make precision bombing possible, resulting in the highest concentration of bombs yet achieved. Only one bomber out of a total of 236 was lost. The new direction-finding device 'Gee' was helpful, but the range was limited, the margin of error great and it was soon jammed by the Germans. Excellent new planes such as the Lancaster and the Mosquito were brought into service. The problem was how to use this new equipment and the benefits of experience to bomb a major industrial centre, which was bound to be heavily protected, and to cause the maximum damage.

Harris decided that numbers provided the answer, and in May he suggested saturation bombing using a force of one thousand planes. It was an incredible idea since it involved using virtually all of Bomber Command's planes in one raid augmented with planes from other commands, but its theatricality greatly appealed to Churchill, who warmly approved. Harris scratched together 1043 bombers, more than a third of which were manned by instructors and advanced pupils. It was a terribly dangerous gamble which, had it gone seriously wrong, would have had disastrous consequences. The raid, codenamed 'Millennium', was directed against Cologne on 30 May, the night of a full moon. An unprecedented quantity of bombs were dropped – nearly 1500 tons – and sixty-two aircraft were lost, but the results were far less impressive than had been hoped. Within two weeks industrial production in Cologne was back to normal.

Harris was determined to keep up the pressure and mounted a further thousand-bomber raid on Essen on 1–2 June. The results were again disappointing. Heavy cloud cover made it almost impossible for crews to identify their targets and no damage at all was done to the Krupp works. Nothing daunted, Harris sent another thousand bombers against Bremen on 25–26 June. Again the weather was bad, losses high and the damage done far less than suggested by the analysis of photographs. This was the last of the thousand-bomber raids until 1944. The propaganda effects of the raids at home had been considerable, but they were of dubious military value. Bombing had been wildly inaccurate and losses unacceptably high. Harris still believed that he could win the war from 18,000 feet, but he also realized that the great day would have to be postponed until he had far more aircraft with greatly improved navigational and bomb-aiming equipment. He also needed control of German airspace to conduct such massive raids. He did not have any fighters with sufficient range to penetrate deep into enemy territory, and the 'Circus' operations in northern France had produced disappointing results. Bombers were used here to lure enemy fighters which could then be destroyed by their own fighter escorts. 'Circuses' did divert some Focke-Wulf 190s and Messerschmitt 109s from other theatres, but they were not destroyed in sufficient numbers to have much impact. Fighter sweeps or 'Rhubarbs' were equally disappointing. Harris also now had to contend with critics of Bomber Command who regarded raids with less than a thousand bombers as insignificant. Daylight raids, such as that against the MAN works at Augsburg where U-boat motors were built, resulted in unacceptably high losses, and minimal damage was done.

In a daylight raid on the U-boat yards at Danzig, a target at the limit of the Lancaster's range, on 11 July only two aircraft were lost, but once again the damage was minimal. Accuracy was still a major problem, as was shown in a remarkable low-level daylight raid on the Creusot works (an operation which some joker codenamed 'Robinson'). The raid was carried out at such low levels that the only Lancaster lost crashed after hitting a building, and yet the damage caused was disappointingly small. Analysis of routine raids revealed some shocking figures. In eight attacks on Essen in March and April, 90 per cent of the aircraft had dropped their bombs between five and one hundred miles off target. In August the Pathfinder force was formed to ensure that the target area was clearly identified. The experience of 1942 was not particularly encouraging. On a number of raids the Pathfinders failed to find the target; on others they failed to mark what they found. The new direction-finding system 'Oboe' was not operational until the end of the year, and centimetric radar for target identification (H2S) was first used in January 1943. In 1942 Bomber Command failed to solve the problem of precision bombing and thus was faced with the choice of continuing with area bombing or halting the bomber offensive. In such circumstances, more of the same seemed to be the only choice.

Faulty intelligence, wishful thinking, chauvinistic prejudice and dubious logic combined to convince the Air Staff that Bomber Command was creating the preconditions for winning the war. In November 1942 Portal made the astonishing claim that in the next two years his bombers would kill 900,000 Germans, seriously injure one million others and render twenty-five million homeless. In addition, one-third of German industry would be destroyed. Experts had long since pointed out that Germans lacked a sense of humour and would therefore be unable to cope with long hours in air-raid shelters. Unlike the ever-cheerful and optimistic British with their endless fund of good jokes, their morale would crack, and with the destruction of Germany's fighting potential the Third Reich would be unable to continue the war. Allied intelligence failed to note that there was a substantial increase in war industrial production in Germany in 1943 and 1944, and that the bombing raids had no serious effects on civilian morale.

This analysis no longer met with automatic approval, although few questioned the morality of the wilful massacre of almost one million civilians. Churchill announced that: 'There are less than seventy million malignant Huns – some of whom are curable and others killable,' and later suggested that if they wished to avoid the bombers they could abandon the cities where munitions work was carried on and could 'watch their home fires burning from a distance'. Bishop Bell of Chichester led the opposition to the bombing of civilians, but his pleas fell on deaf ears. Churchmen who take strong moral stands in wartime are usually regarded as tiresome troublemakers, especially by their colleagues, and civilians who have the impertinence to present sound military arguments against a strategy such as area bombing are doubly irritating. The good bishop's supporters were mostly pacifists, a far smaller group in the Second World War than in the First, but they were unable to rouse the conscience of a nation which was numbed by the Blitz and the desire for revenge.

Gradually an alternative to area bombing seemed feasible. The victory at El Alamein and the defence of Stalingrad showed that the German army was not invincible. With the 'Torch' landings, an alternative strategy could be considered. The First Sea Lord, Sir Dudley Pound, felt that Portal's belief that the war could be won only by making German civilians homeless and by destroying industry was unduly pessimistic. He suggested that the RAF should go for the German fighter force and then begin precision bombing of serious military targets. Brooke feared that the building up of a bomber force of 4–6000 aircraft would take resources away from the army and make it impossible to mount an invasion. With only 200 operational Lancasters, heavy losses and a large number of obsolete aircraft, this did not seem an unreasonable fear.

The bomber offensive of 1942 had one positive result. It forced the Luftwaffe on to the defensive and it now devoted most of its resources to the struggle for air supremacy over the Reich. It was possible to send only a few bombing raids to England, none of which had any serious effect on Britain's war potential. Altogether 900,000 men and women were now serving in flak units in the west, operating 75 per cent of Germany's 88s which would have been better used against

Soviet tanks. The Luftwaffe still had an impressive fighter force in the west. The night fighters were equipped with the 'Lichtenstein' radar direction finders, the anti-aircraft guns were employing better tactics with tangible results, the early warning system had been greatly improved and the defensive chain of the 'Kammhuber Line' was extended from Denmark to Paris. For the Germans the major problem was that they had a vast area to protect with only limited resources, and it was clear that, as in the Soviet Union and in north Africa, they were losing the strategic initiative in the air war.

At the Casablanca conference in January 1943 it was agreed that the bomber offensive could not win the war as 'Bomber' Harris continued to insist, but should be used to soften up the enemy to the point where ground forces could finish off the job. The directive on Allied bombing policy stated: 'Your primary object will be the progressive destruction and dislocation of the German military, industrial and economic system, and the undermining of the morale of the German people to the point where capacity for armed resistance is fatally weakened.' Primary targets, in order of priority, were: U-boats yards, the aircraft industry, transportation, oil installations and other war industrial targets. Harris promptly changed the wording of the directive to read that these raids were 'aimed at undermining the morale of the German people' and used this revised version as a sanction from on high for continued area bombing.

The Americans, whose 8th Air Force was stationed in England, were more scrupulous in their reading of the Casablanca directive and insisted on the precision bombing of designated industrial targets. Their daylight raids over France in 1942, often with heavy RAF fighter protection, showed that precision bombing could bring satisfactory results at a low cost. Their first raid in Germany, on Wilhelmshaven on 27 January 1943, was also successful. Fifty-three planes reached the target and only three were lost. But it soon became apparent that this result was due largely to good luck. German fighters inflicted severe losses on the USAAF in subsequent raids. The Germans were increasing fighter production in spite of the raids, and were withdrawing fighters from other theatres to fight the battle of Germany. Heavily armoured B–17s, flying in close formation at high altitudes, were an easy prey for the German fighters. The Junkers 88s and Messerschmitt 110s were fitted with night sensing devices which enabled them to home in on the British bombers, and the obliquely mounted cannons (*schräge Musik*) enabled them to shoot at the bombers' highly vulnerable under-bellies. It was a very risky business for the German pilots, but it resulted in a large number of kills.

Bomber crews were becoming demoralized and increasingly 'balked at the jump', as Air Vice-Marshal Bennett reported. They saw no reason why such high risks should be taken to achieve such modest results. They were beginning to lack the determination necessary to drive home successful attacks. More and more crews dumped their bombs into the North Sea in order to improve their performance against the night fighters, and there was an alarming increase in the number of 'fringe merchants' whose main concern was for their own safety.

That the German fighters were the main problem was firmly stated in the plan drawn up by US General Eaker and adopted at the Washington conference in May 1943 as the 'Pointblank' directive. The Eaker plan, entitled 'The Combined Bomber Offensive from the United Kingdom', called for a combined offensive by the USAAF and the RAF against German fighter strength, followed by the destruction of 'selected segments of German industry'. Eaker made no mention at all of enemy morale, and the 'Pointblank' directive was a clear repudiation of Harris's area bombing strategy. Harris did not allow himself to be swayed by this directive and ensured that it was amended to include the undermining of morale as a 'primary objective', even though the attack on the Luftwaffe was seen as a 'first priority'. In other words, Bomber Command would continue as before and leave the destruction of German fighter strength to the 8th US Air Force.

In spite of the profound disagreements between the British and the Americans over bombing strategy, Bomber Command and the 8th Air Force did manage to combine in a ten-day raid on Hamburg from 24 July to 2 August 1943. The results of the raid were horrific. Between 40,000 and 50,000 died and a further 40,000 were injured; 61 per cent of dwelling places were destroyed. Worst of all was the terrible fire storm of the night of 27–28 July. The heat from incendiaries falling in great concentration in an area of 22 square kilometres reached 1000 degrees Centigrade, causing an immense suction which in turn resulted in winds of over 150 miles per hour which uprooted trees, destroyed houses and flung humans into the flames. The effect on morale was considerable as horrified Germans heard of the effects of the raid and promptly wondered when the same would happen to them. Allied losses were relatively slight: some 1000 aircrew were lost. The use of the radar jamming device 'Window' proved most effective; small strips of aluminum foil rendered the Kammhuber Line totally useless. But the victory was largely illusory. Only 10 per cent of the city's industrial capacity was affected and

Hamburg was back to business as usual within a remarkably short space of time. The post-war estimate was that Hamburg had lost 1.8 months' production, an amount which was comfortably made up elsewhere.

The Americans, who had participated in the 'round the clock' bombardment of Hamburg, continued with their policy of precision bombing by daylight. The losses were terrible. In the second raid on Schweinfurt on 14 October they lost sixty bombers, or more than a quarter of the aircraft that reached the target. Although the Allies aimed to destroy the German aircraft industry, the production of fighters doubled in 1943 and both Bomber Command and the 8th Air Force suffered heavily as a result. It was not until the end of 1943 that the Allies had effective fighter escorts for their bomber fleets when the USAAF took delivery of the P–51B 'Mustang' long-range fighter which had the range of a bomber and was superior in every way to the German fighters.

'Bomber' Harris was still convinced that he could win the war before the invasion, confidently predicting that the forthcoming large-scale bomber offensive would 'cost Germany the war'. The 'Battle for Berlin', which raged from November 1943 to March 1944, was a series of raids, about half of which were aimed against the capital of the Reich. Far from leading to the defeat of Germany, it very nearly caused the destruction of Bomber Command. In the course of the battle Bomber Command lost 1047 aircraft, and a further 1682 were badly damaged. The RAF could not sustain these losses and the offensive had to be halted. Terrible damage was done to Germany and thousands were killed, but war industrial production continued to increase and morale did not crack. Harris's strategy proved to be an appalling and costly mistake.

The Americans were considerably more successful. During 'Big Week' in February 1944 the USAAF attacked a series of centres of the German aircraft industry. The 8th Air Force joined with the 15th Air Force, stationed in southern Italy, to carry out thirteen major strikes. The fighters came up to fight and the Mustangs shot them down in large numbers. Spaatz claimed that the Luftwaffe lost 600 fighters in six days. These figures may well be exaggerated, but General Galland reported that the Luftwaffe lost 1000 pilots between January and April. There is no doubt that 'Big Week' was a considerable victory and a decisive turning point in the struggle against the German fighters. The fighters no longer stood between the Allied bombers and their strategic objectives. By breaking the back of the German fighter force the Americans had also prepared the ground for the success of 'Overlord'.

Until September 1944, when the Combined Chiefs resumed direct control over strategic bombing, Harris and Bomber Command were subordinated to the Supreme Allied Commander for 'Overlord'. The directive of 14 September designated German oil production as the principal target. The Americans had long insisted that if the German armed forces were denied oil their planes could not fly and their tanks could not move, and General Spaatz had been attacking oil targets for several months. Portal was enthusiastically in favour of the oil plan, and Tedder supported it, although he thought it was a trifle narrow in scope. Harris was opposed, clinging to his vision of area bombing as the way to win the war and seeing the proposed strategy as further evidence of Spaatz's stupidity. When Churchill told Harris that Spaatz was a man of limited intelligence, Harris replied: 'You pay him too high a compliment.' To Harris the oil plan was yet another 'panacea' which, along with the demands of the Admiralty to go for the new U-boats, and of the army who wanted ground support and SOE with their exotic plans, was yet another attempt to divert Bomber Command's resources away from its war-winning task. The Allies now had command of the air and Bomber Command could go about its task by day with relatively low losses. The bombing raids continued with such intensity that for Bomber Command the only serious problems were a shortage of bombs and the opposition of Sir Charles Portal.

In January 1945 Harris offered his resignation, but Portal felt obliged to refuse it in order to preserve the morale of Bomber Command. Area bombing continued against the remains of 'Fortress Germany', a structure which no longer had a roof, and was to reach a terrible climax in the Dresden raid between 13 and 15 February. Dresden was an ideal target for Harris. It was densely populated, had little military significance and was therefore lightly defended, and its wooden houses made it, as Harris suggested, 'more like a fire-lighter than a human habitation'. In many ways it was a repeat of the Hamburg experience, and the number of dead was probably about the same. The police chief reported 25,000 dead and 35,000 missing.

Dresden was the high point of terror bombing and has become symbolic of the horrors of conventional warfare against civilian targets. The Soviet Union was said to be delighted with the results and saw the raid as an admirable finale to the Yalta conference, but it soon appeared that the raid had been militarily pointless and morally dubious. Churchill had always been an enthusiastic supporter of area bombing, and appeared to see nothing wrong in slaughtering civilians. (He had once suggested that Bert Harris should send his bombers to destroy the 'foul race' of Hindus.) But on 28 March he minuted the Chiefs of Staff Committee:

> It seems to me that the moment has come when the question of bombing of German cities simply for the sake of increasing the terror, though under other pretexts, should be reviewed. Otherwise we shall come into control of an utterly ruined land . . . . The destruction of Dresden remains a serious query against the conduct of Allied bombing . . . . I feel the need for more precise concentration upon military objectives, such as oil and communications behind the immediate battle-zone, rather than on mere acts of terror and wanton destruction, however impressive.

The Prime Minister agreed to a redraft of this minute by Portal which expressed his reservations in less drastic terms, but he continued to have serious doubts about area bombing. He asked Harris over dinner at Chequers: 'What will lie between the white snows of Russia and the white cliffs of Dover?' (when he had finished with the destruction of Germany).

In the final stages of the war the combined bomber offensive was directed primarily against oil targets, and half of Bomber Command's sorties were by day. With absolute air supremacy the attacks were a complete success and the German war machine was brought virtually to a standstill. Even Harris had to admit that the final offensive was a triumph, but in doing so he called his own strategy into question.

That the Luftwaffe was unable to match this offensive was no reflection on the skill and courage of the German pilots, nor on the excellence of their machines and equipment; it resulted from a total inability to adjust to a changed situation. The Luftwaffe had been designed as an offensive weapon and when the destruction of Hamburg showed up the inadequacy of the defence the Chief of Staff of the Luftwaffe, General Jeschonnek, committed suicide. Goering now believed that greater emphasis should be placed on fighters, but Hitler demanded a resumption of the air offensive against England. Speer was convinced of the necessity to build fighters and created a 'Fighter Staff' to see that they were produced. Against Hitler's wishes the percentage of fighters was increased, so that of the 40,593 machines built in 1944 (a figure which is ample testimony to the ineffectiveness of Allied bombing), 25,285 were fighters.

In 1943 Messerschmitt produced the prototype of a jet-propelled fighter, the M262. When Hitler heard that the plane could be modified to carry bombs he ordered that it should be developed as a *Blitzbomber* to act in a support role to the army to meet the threatened invasion. This caused delays in the production programme, which was further held up by Allied raids on the Messerschmitt works. By D-Day not a single *Blitzbomber* was operational. The M262s produced as fighters and armed with rockets proved deadly against the Allied bombers, but there were far too few to turn the tide.

Similar errors were made with the V-bombs (*Vergeltungswaffen* = revenge weapons) which were developed at the Luftwaffe's experimental station at Peenemünde. The programme was delayed by bombing raids on the factories and the launching pads so that they were not ready to meet the invasion, and the V1 was first fired en masse against London on 13 June 1944. A total of 9300 rocket propelled 'doodlebugs' fell on England in the following months, but only about one-quarter of them fell on London as German agents acting as spotters had been turned round by British counter espionage and relayed false information back to Germany. With an 800-kilogram warhead the V1 was a frightening weapon which had a considerable effect on civilian morale. All manner of ridiculous schemes for revenge for the 6184 dead were mooted, including the use of poison gas against German civilians, but they were scotched by Eisenhower's characteristically sensible appeal to 'keep our eyes on the ball and use some sense'. Bombing raids against the V1 installations mounted in operation 'Crossbow' absorbed half the efforts of Bomber Command for several months and resulted in the deaths of 3000 aircrew. Far more effective against the 'doodlebugs' were the jet-engined Gloster 'Tempests' and 'Meteors' barrage balloons and anti aircraft guns firing proximity fuses.

The V2 rocket was an even more alarming weapon. It travelled faster than the speed of sound and entered the stratosphere, and therefore could not be intercepted. The delivery of one tonne of explosives without prior warning was highly alarming. It was, however, a very inaccurate weapon and once again the spotters relayed faulty information so that the bombs were unknowingly aimed at sparsely populated areas south of London. Altogether, 1115 V2s were fired at England and killed 2724 people; 2050 others were fired at Antwerp and Brussels.

The German wonder weapons thus did not have the effect that was expected. Jets and rockets were the weapons of the future. The development of a superb jet fighter was held up by the decision to develop a fighter bomber. As 'Bomber' Harris told Churchill, the bomber was a 'passing phase' and the future belonged to the rocket, the perfect instrument for terror bombing. But at this critical stage of the war the Germans were investing a great deal of inventive genius and industrial effort in a weapon which turned out to be militarily worthless and therefore counter-productive.

CHAPTER SIX

The War in Asia (September 1931–July 1944)

During the night of 18 September 1931, units of the Japanese army stationed in Kwantung blew up some three feet of line on the railway near Mukden. Claiming that the attack had been launched by the Chinese, the Kwantung army opened fire on Chinese troops and seized Mukden and Changchin.

The Mukden incident was planned by a group of dissident officers who were determined to force the Japanese Government to reject the system of international co-operation established at the Washington conference of 1921–22. They wished to break away from a liberal and capitalist system which seemed to them to be based on a set of alien values which subordinated Japan's traditional interests to the needs of the western powers, and which was designed to frustrate the country's legitimate aspirations in the Asian Pacific.

The action of the Kwantung army was hardly an isolated act of disobedience by a clique of extremists. There was considerable support for the action at home, where anti-Government agitation was growing under the impact of the depression and the stringent deflationary policies of an administration committed to economic orthodoxy and to the preservation of the Washington system.

Prime Minister Wakatsuki was not the man to act forcefully against this unilateral action by the military, and those who were disturbed by the turn of events, particularly in the diplomatic service, found themselves without support. Even critics of the army did not want to go back to the status quo before 18 September. The official version of events was that Japan had acted decisively in punishing Chinese lawlessness and was thus upholding international treaties. But by acting unilaterally the Japanese were soon accused of violating the Nine-Power agreement. The Chinese Government denounced the Japanese for this breach of international law, refused to deal with them bilaterally and called for an emergency meeting of the League of

Nations. Unfortunately for the Chinese, London and Washington were unwilling to take their side, and were prepared to accept the Japanese assurance that it was a minor incident and that the status quo would be swiftly restored. The Soviet Government was alarmed by the Japanese action, but for the moment was prepared to accept their version of events.

The Kwantung army was encouraged by the response of the powers to China's pleas, and decided to extend their operations to drive the Chinese forces from Manchuria and even from Inner Mongolia. On 8 October Chinchow was bombed, and it was now abundantly clear that China was the victim of premeditated aggression. The Council of the League of Nations called upon the Japanese to return to the positions they had held on 18 September. The Japanese Government responded by proposing that the League should send a commission of enquiry to Manchuria. The Commission, headed by Lord Lytton, duly went to Manchuria, but fighting in Shanghai between Japanese and Chinese troops and the establishment of a puppet regime in Manchukuo without international consultation were clear indications that Japan had no intention of respecting the treaties, regardless of all protestations to the contrary. The Lytton Commission's report, which condemned Japanese actions, made it impossible for Japan to maintain the pretence that they were acting within the framework of existing treaties and, rather than give up an 'independent' Manchuria, Japan withdrew from the League.

Contrary to Chinese hopes, the western powers did nothing beyond criticizing Japan in the vain hope that such expressions of disapproval would eventually convince the Japanese of the error of their ways. The Soviet Government, in spite of its routine denunciations of Japanese imperialism, appeared willing to negotiate with Japan and was even prepared to grant *de facto* recognition to the Manchukuo Government. With the world in the midst of a severe economic crisis it seemed likely that the Japanese would be able to get away with little more than a few empty expressions of disapproval, and Chinese hopes for an anti-Japanese front were all in vain. Unable to win any support against Japan, and engaged in full-scale fighting with the communists, the Chinese signed the Tangku truce in May 1933 which gave tacit recognition to Japan's occupation of Manchuria. The Great Wall now separated China from the Japanese sphere of influence.

The aim of Japanese diplomacy was now to obtain recognition of Japan's new status as the dominant power in the western Pacific by negotiating a bilateral agreement with the United States and by revising the naval treaties so as to grant Japan parity with Britain and the United States. It was hoped that if these modifications could be agreed upon, the Washington system could continue under a new guise. These hopes were not unreasonable. The British Government was willing to appease the Japanese within the framework of the Nine-Power treaty, just as they hoped to appease Germany while maintaining the Stresa front. Roosevelt, who had just been elected President, was more concerned with domestic economic recovery than with international affairs and did not feel the same sense of obligation towards the Washington system as his predecessor, Herbert Hoover. The new administration showed itself willing to enter bilateral discussions with the Japanese and thus neglected the international ramifications of the outstanding issues. Neither Britain nor the United States paid any attention to Soviet calls for an anti-fascist coalition which was the main goal of Soviet foreign policy after the seventh Comintern conference of 1935, at which Germany and Japan were singled out as the greatest threats to world peace and security. At the same time, Britain and the United States were pursuing contradictory policies in China. The American Silver Purchase Act of 1932 had a ruinous effect on the Chinese economy because the currency was silver based. Britain responded by sending the Leith-Ross mission to China which proposed Anglo-Japanese co-operation to stabilize the Chinese economy, in return for which the Chinese might be prepared to offer *de facto* recognition of the regime in Manchukuo. The Japanese turned down this British initiative, preferring to negotiate directly with the Chinese. The Japanese military, although divided as to whether they should concentrate on meeting the perceived Soviet menace or to go for total mobilization against as yet unspecified opponents to carve out an Asian Empire, rejected out of hand the idea of co-operating with the British to help China. Leith-Ross and his commission helped create a new Chinese currency based on sterling. This stabilized the Chinese economy and strengthened British influence in China, but further undermined the Washington system.

The triumph of the 'total mobilization' group in Japan, determined to bring the Asian Pacific under Japanese domination, marked the end of any pretence to preserve the Washington system. In November 1936 Japan signed the anti-Comintern pact with Germany, thus aligning itself with the revisionist powers in Europe. The appointment of Prince Konoe Fumimaro as Prime Minister marked another turning point. Konoe was an outspoken imperialist and militarist who had no patience with international trade agreements and wished to exclude the western powers from Asia.

During the night of 7 July 1937, Chinese troops hired by a local warlord fired on Japanese soldiers near the Marco Polo bridge in Peking. Although the Japanese launched a punitive attack against these mercenaries, Prince Konoe's Government did not wish to use the incident as an excuse to extend the war in China. Influential circles in Japan, however, demanded that the Chinese should be punished for their insolence and the Prime Minister agreed to send three divisions to China. Chiang Kai-shek, determined to assert his authority in Peking and goaded by communist calls to resist Japanese imperialism, also decided to send troops from Nanking to the north, at the same time appealing to the powers for help. Although the Japanese insisted on describing the affair as an 'incident', a full-scale war soon developed in which the Chinese troops were driven from northern China.

Chiang counted on German support in his struggle against Japan but the Germans, anxious not to weaken the anti-Comintern pact, sought a negotiated solution. None of the other western powers wished to become involved and they were content to issue platitudinous statements deploring the bloodshed in Asia. The Soviet Union, unable to convince the powers to take joint action against Japan in the spirit of its collective security policy, decided to send modest amounts of arms to Chiang. The Japanese had no clear idea of their goals in China. Full-scale commitment to the war against the Chinese would make it impossible to pursue their aims of crushing the Soviet Union or of imperial expansion in the Asian Pacific. In addition, the alienation of the Chinese people would make a mockery of their anti-western and pro-Asian crusade. The Japanese therefore contrarily announced that they were fighting to uphold the rule of law and basic human decency and spoke of the need for co-operation between China and Japan, while at the same time mobilizing for total war.

While the German ambassador to Nanking, Trautmann, worked energetically for a settlement, the League and the United States condemned Japanese lawlessness and thus encouraged Chiang to refuse anything but a return to the status quo. Any hope of a negotiated peace was ruined when, on 13 December, Japanese troops entered Nanking and promptly massacred some 200,000 innocent civilians. The murderous brutality of Japanese militarism and the appalling hypocrisy of the ideology of Asian co-operation were now blatantly obvious to all the civilized world.

It was also painfully clear to the Germans that their hopes for a negotiated settlement were unrealistic and that they would have to choose between China and Japan. There was no doubt about what that choice would be. The Japanese were no longer prepared to parley with Chiang and were determined to establish a puppet regime in China. The United States and Britain began to discuss a common strategy to meet the threat of Japanese aggression. The Soviet Union stepped up its propaganda campaign against Japan and announced its willingness to increase aid to China. Thus by the beginning of 1938 the Sino-Japanese war had become a central issue in international affairs.

For Japan the major problem was how best to wage the war. The Konoe Cabinet wished to localize the fighting, which was already placing an intolerable strain on Japanese resources, so as to avoid the expense of a full-scale campaign. Unable to find a Chinese Franco to replace Chiang, they were at a loss to know how to occupy and control such a vast country. At the same time they wished to be free to pursue their aggressive policies against the Soviet Union and in the Asian Pacific, which would be impossible if a total commitment were made to the war in China. The expeditionary army argued that nothing short of the occupation of more than half of China – the northern provinces, the port cities including Canton, and the Yangste as far as Hankow – would bring the war to a satisfactory conclusion. This argument was accepted by the general staff and the War Department.

Konoe and his Foreign Minister, Ugaki, resented the independence of the military, and wished to limit the war in China, negotiate with Chiang and the western powers, and concentrate on an anti-Soviet policy by strengthening the anti-Comintern pact. This was a hopelessly contradictory policy. Ugaki would not offer peace terms which were acceptable to Chiang and the nationalists, for he was adamant that northern China should remain under Japanese control as a springboard for an attack on the Soviet Union. Co-operation with the British and the Americans was hardly a realistic possibility if the anti-Comintern pact were simultaneously to be strengthened. His attempt to steer a middle course was bound to fail, particularly when, a few weeks later, the Germans occupied Bohemia and Moravia and thus put an end to the illusions of all but the most purblind appeasers. None of these considerations was acceptable to the Japanese army, who secured Ugaki's dismissal within four months of his appointment.

Konoe now talked of a 'new order' in Asia – in other words the repudiation of the Washington system and the creation of a Japanese Empire in the Asian Pacific. At the same time he hoped to strengthen the anti-Soviet alliance with Germany. His public statement on 3 November 1938 was a clear rejection of the Washington system and suggested that Japan's aim was to rid Asia of western influence. Subsequent Japanese efforts to reassure the western powers that co-operation was still possible could not be accepted without an unequivocal repudiation of this statement of intent, and this was not forthcoming. The State Department denounced the new policy as arbitrary, unjust and unwarranted and the Japanese Government did nothing to make them change their minds. The German Government continued to support Japan's policies in China but would not consider an alliance directed solely against the Soviet Union, wanting Japanese support in any future war with Britain and France. The Japanese harassed the British concession in Tientsin in order to show the Germans the sincerity of their anti-British sentiments, but would not make any binding agreements with Germany that might oblige them to become involved in a European war before they were ready. The result, therefore, was that Japan further alienated the British without getting any closer to Germany.

Border clashes with Soviet forces on the Manchurian–Mongolian border soon escalated into a major armed conflict in which the Japanese suffered an embarrassing defeat. It was, however, a salutary lesson in that it discouraged those who were keen on a war with the USSR. The Soviet forces, led by General Zhukov, were superior in armour, aircraft and artillery to the Japanese and fought with great skill and deadly effectiveness, even though they were operating in difficult terrain 400 miles from the nearest railhead. It was a demonstration of the quality of the Soviet armed forces which the Germans foolishly ignored when planning 'Operation Barbarossa'.

The Nazi–Soviet non-aggression pact signed on 23 August 1939 was a further setback, coming shortly after the United States announced the abrogation of the 1911 Commerce and Navigation treaty which, given the vast quantities of essential supplies including oil, scrap iron and steel supplied by the United States, was a shattering blow. The Americans saw no reason why they should continue to supply the Japanese with materials which were used against their Chinese Allies. Japan was now dangerously isolated and still saddled with the war in China. The Soviet Union had renounced the popular front and embarrassed the Chinese, both communist and nationalist, but the anti-Comintern pact, around which Japanese European policy had revolved, was now in ruins.

With the German successes in Europe and the continuation of the Nazi–Soviet pact, Japanese leaders began to consider a new approach to international politics. It was proposed that Japan should seek a rapprochement with the Soviets, still the main suppliers of arms to Chiang, in order to create an anti-democratic alliance which would include the Axis powers and which would be aimed against Britain and the United States. This scheme was attractive to those who favoured a southward expansion and the creation of a Japanese Pacific Empire. It was also assumed that China, once it was no longer supplied by the Soviets, would soon sue for peace and the protracted, frustrating and hideously expensive war would then at last be over. The fatal mistake in this calculation was that Britain and the United States, far from abandoning China, reacted by increasing their support and formed what was to prove to be an unbeatable alliance which would dash all these absurdly unrealistic hopes.

Even the more moderate Japanese politicians, such as the Prime Minister, Abe, and the Foreign Minister, Nomura, who realized the importance of American imports and the disastrous consequences of a breach with the United States, imagined that they could patch up relations with the Americans while at the same time hanging on to large chunks of China and going ahead with plans to build the new order in Asia. Advocates of closer ties with China, including Henry Morgenthau and Harold Ickes, were gaining ascendancy in the United States and were supported by the President. They imagined that by the strengthening of China, Japan could be deterred from further expansion, just as it was hoped that strengthening Britain would restrain Hitler. The Japanese, meanwhile, had not abandoned the idea of a war with the Soviet Union and a rapprochement with Moscow never became official policy. But it was impossible to try to bring the war in China to an end while at the same time preparing for war against the Soviet Union. The only possible way out of this dilemma was either to abandon most of the gains made in China or to improve relations with the Soviet Union.

After the fall of France on 22 June 1940, the Japanese decided to exploit the weakness of Britain and France to improve their position in China. They therefore demanded that the Vichy Government close the route through Indo-China to China and that Britain close the Burma road. Churchill appealed to Roosevelt for help against this provocation, but the President was anxious not to provoke the Japanese at a time when the situation in Europe was so desperate. The American fleet remained stationed in Pearl Harbor as a warning that the Japanese should not go too far, but that was all. Churchill therefore had to agree to close the Burma road. For the British this was a humiliating surrender, and as some 10,000 tons of supplies reached China every month via this route it was a serious blow to the Chinese. The Japanese also exerted pressure on the Dutch, whose hold over their empire had necessarily weakened after their defeat by the Germans, to guarantee supplies of petrol, rubber and tin from the Dutch East Indies and thus lessen their dependence on supplies from the United States. These triumphs, the indirect result of the glittering successes of the Germans in Europe, encouraged those who wanted closer ties with Germany and a more active and aggressive policy in the Pacific.

The advocates of a southern advance also wanted to eradicate all traces of western influence at home. Konoe Fumimaro, who was reappointed Prime Minister in the summer of 1940, was the man chosen to carry out the necessary reforms. His ideas were inchoate and confused and were not simply borrowed from fascism, which was after all very much a western ideology. He rejected modern industrial capitalism as a system which tied Japan too closely to the western powers, and he hoped to create a self-sufficient Asia dominated by Japan. He wanted constitutional reform in order to strengthen the executive, end the squabbles between the army and the navy and bring the military under civilian political control. Konoe imagined that the Chinese as fellow Asiatics would co-operate with a determinedly anti-western Japan, overlooking the fact that the Chinese preferred to be supported by the west than massacred and exploited by a people whom they had every reason to detest in spite of the colour of their skin. Konoe's Foreign Minister, Matsuoka Yosuke, was an outspoken proponent of the new order and proposed a strengthening of Japan's ties with the Axis powers so as to realize his dream. A non-aggression pact with the Soviet Union and a rapprochement with Chungking would provide the preconditions for the exclusion of the Anglo-Americans from Asia.

The United States reacted to such ill-considered and provocative talk in Tokyo by cutting off supplies of aviation fuel, lubricating oil and certain grades of scrap iron as a warning to the Japanese that they could not exploit the situation in Europe to their advantage. Both Germany and Japan were increasingly concerned with the United States' determined stand against Japanese ambitions in the Pacific and their support to Britain in its struggle against Germany.

Such was the background to the German–Japanese alliance. The Japanese hoped that it would deter the Americans or, if that failed, that they would have German assistance in a war which alone they had only a slender chance of winning. The Germans imagined that an alliance would restrain the Americans from becoming directly involved in the war in Europe. Thus Mitsuoka was perfectly correct when he described the pact as a military alliance aimed against the United States.

Once again the Japanese made a serious miscalculation. Washington, far from being deterred by the Axis pact, was more determined than ever to resist Japanese ambitions in the Pacific. When the Japanese invaded and occupied northern Indo-China the United States reacted by cutting off all scrap iron shipments to Japan, the Dutch in Batavia refused to meet all of Japan's demands for oil, and the British decided to reopen the Burma road. American support for China was shown by their sending a volunteer air force, known as the 'Flying Tigers' and commanded by Colonel Claire Chennault, a very devious character who set about training Chinese pilots and flying combat missions against Japanese positions. At the same time the American plan 'Dog', which called for a purely defensive strategy in the Pacific, meant abandoning Asia to the Japanese, for the British would be incapable of holding on to Singapore and Hong Kong without substantial American assistance and the Americans were unwilling to establish defensive positions west of Hawaii. The American policy of resisting Japan was further weakened by the 'Europe first' strategy.

Japanese policy in 1940 was even more confused. The Government imagined that it might be possible to reach an agreement between Chiang's regime in Chungking and Wang Ching-wei's puppet Government in Nanking. A basic treaty between Tokyo and Nanking which imposed the most humiliating terms on a Government that had neither legitimacy nor popular support infuriated Chiang and the nationalists and strengthened their resolve to resist the Japanese. Similar confusion existed among the strategic planners. The army wanted to finish the job in China and then go for British and Dutch colonies in Asia. The navy thought in terms of grabbing the Marshalls and the Bismarck Archipelago. The army did not relish the idea of a war with America which this would almost certainly entail; the navy thought such a war inevitable. The war plan of December 1940 reflected these differences and uncertainties and contained no clear-cut strategic objectives. Matsuoka tried to form an alliance of the four great revisionist powers – Japan, Germany, Italy and the Soviet Union – at precisely the time when the Germans were busy putting the finishing touches to their plans for 'Operation Barbarossa'. Stalin did not take the warnings of an impending breach with Germany seriously, and therefore did nothing to improve relations with the Japanese which would have secured his rear. Hitler had no reason to discuss German–Russian relations with the Japanese, and Ribbentrop studiously ignored the Japanese ambassador's attempts to get the Germans to act as intermediaries between Tokyo and Moscow. Although thoroughly informed of worsening relations between Germany and the Soviet Union, Matsuoka continued to pursue his fantasy of including the Soviets in the anti-Comintern pact. In March 1941 he set off for Europe to meet Hitler and Stalin and realize his ambition.

The talks between Matsuoka and Hitler were inconclusive. Hitler stressed that German–Russian relations were deteriorating rapidly and would not consider a four-power pact. Matsuoka would not commit Japan to attack Singapore and the British possessions in Asia, even in co-operation with the Germans. In Moscow he met with a warmer reception. The Russians were at last anxious to avoid a war on two fronts and therefore quickly signed a five-year treaty of neutrality under the terms of which Japan would not become involved in a war between Germany and the Soviet Union. The treaty also recognized the Japanese conquest of Manchuria, so that the Soviets were abandoning the Chinese, communist as well as nationalist, in the interests of guarding their rear in anticipation of a future war with Germany.

Matsuoka left Moscow in a state of near paralytic intoxication, but felt that he had good cause for such excessive celebration. In fact, he had gained nothing. The Soviets were now free to devote all their efforts to meeting the threat from Nazi Germany, whereas Japan was further isolated. As the Soviet Union backed away from China, the Americans, British and Dutch formed a closer association with the Chinese, creating the ABCD coalition directed against Japan. Even Japan's Allies were loath to give any help. The Germans were deeply suspicious of the motives behind the talks in Washington between American and Japanese officials and wanted a firm commitment from the Japanese to attack Singapore.

Konoe's absurd four-power policy was clearly bankrupt with the German invasion of the Soviet Union on 22 June 1941. He drew the obvious conclusion and insisted that Japan would now have to abandon the Axis powers which had brought them nothing, and try to improve relations with the United States, since a war between Japan and a combination of America, the Soviet Union and Britain was unthinkable. Such a necessary reorientation of Japanese policy was, however, unacceptable to Mitsuoka and the military, for it would mean abandoning their plans for an Asian co-prosperity sphere. They, too, were uncertain what to do next. Mitsuoka, convinced that

Germany would soon defeat the Soviet Union, suggested an immediate attack on Russia. The military tended to adopt a wait-and-see attitude to the campaign in the Soviet Union, having learnt their lesson in Mongolia, and stuck to their southern strategy. Their first objective was southern Indo-China, a strategically important region since it served as the vital link between China and its Anglo-American suppliers. At the same time, forces were to be mobilized for an eventual war with the Soviet Union. Konoe, still imagining that he could keep the lines open to Washington, was forced by the supreme command to accept their northern and southern strategies.

At the end of July Japanese troops occupied southern Indo-China, having first obtained permission from the Vichy Government. The United States and Britain promptly froze all Japanese assets. This convinced the Japanese that they might soon find themselves at war with the ABCD nations and that therefore it might be prudent to abandon the northern strategy against the Soviet Union. Since the United States imposed a strict oil embargo on Japan, those who argued for a southern strategy, which would open up the riches of the Dutch East Indies, had a more compelling case. Differences within the military were now over how this could best be achieved. The army preferred to begin with Malaya, while the navy, with its anti-American obsessions, wished to attack the Philippines. Admiral Yamamoto Isoruku, Commander-in-Chief of the combined fleet, believed that if war with the United States was inevitable, Pearl Harbor should be attacked in a lightning raid which would put the Americans temporarily out of action and give the Japanese time to build a strong imperial defensive system in the Pacific.

On 6 September 1941 the Japanese leadership agreed on the need to go to war unless the British and Americans stopped helping Chiang Kai-shek, settled trade relations and desisted from any military build-up in Asia. The Emperor and some of his advisors imagined that this document left the door open for further negotiations, but the military knew perfectly well that it meant war. The American Government made it abundantly clear that relations with Japan would not be normalized until they withdrew from China, and added that all the ABCD powers were united on this point. The Japanese were unable to meet the American conditions, War Minister Tojo insisting that the Japanese presence in China was the cornerstone of the Great East Asian Co-prosperity Sphere and thus could be neither abandoned nor modified. Konoe did not want war with the United States, for the simple reason that he felt it was bound to be lost, but he was powerless to resist Tojo and the army who were determined to fight.

On 16 October Konoe's Cabinet resigned so that a new Government could be formed that was not bound by the agreement of 6 September. The new Government, headed by Tojo, had no intention of avoiding a conflict with the United States, but was prepared to postpone the decision to go to war, calling for a policy of 'perseverance and patience'. The military, although they agreed that there was no chance of winning a protracted war of attrition against the United States and that nor was there a possibility of winning the war in a swift campaign, still argued for war as the only way that Japan could break out of the encirclement by alien and hostile powers. Those civilians who sensibly suggested that if the war could not be won it would be wiser not to start it, were told that things might turn out differently in the long run. The most the military were prepared to concede was to give the diplomats until 30 November to reach a satisfactory arrangement with the Americans. Since such an agreement would involve the Americans ending their support of the Chungking Government or loosening their ties to the ABCD entente, there was little doubt in anyone's mind that Japan was heading for war. The Americans found out about the proposal from 'Magic' intercepts, and decided to negotiate for time, but this prompted such a reaction from China and Britain that the Americans changed their minds and decided not to negotiate. Cordell Hull's note of 26 November made it clear that America would not modify its position. On 1 December the Emperor of Japan issued the order to go to war. At dawn on 7 December the Japanese struck at Pearl Harbor, beginning a war which had resulted from a fatal mixture of folly, aggressiveness and national hubris.

The Japanese quickly inflicted a series of shattering blows on the British and the Americans, and their planners' prediction that the war would begin with a series of victories was triumphantly vindicated. With the sinking of the *Prince of Wales* and the *Repulse* it seemed that the era of British naval supremacy in the Pacific had ended. Hong Kong fell within days of the beginning of the war, the British were ignominiously driven from Malaya, and on 15 February Singapore, on which British defences in the Pacific hinged, fell almost without a fight. Rangoon was occupied on 7 March, the Burma road was closed once again and most of Burma was soon in Japanese hands. General Wavell's command over the American, British, Dutch and Australian (ABDA) troops collapsed, leaving the East Indies open to the invaders.

The Americans fared no better. The attack on Pearl Harbor destroyed the Pacific Fleet, but owing to a serious intelligence error the

Japanese did not realize until a few hours before the attack that the aircraft carriers *Yorktown* and *Hornet* were in the Atlantic. They also failed to destroy the oil storage and harbour installations at Pearl Harbor, which were a more valuable target than a largely obsolete fleet which could soon be rebuilt. Pearl Harbor, the key to all future naval operations in the Pacific, was still a usable harbour and was still in American hands. It took some time for this comforting lesson to sink in. General MacArthur's defence of the Philippines was sadly incompetent, and the Americans were soon forced to surrender their final defensive positions in the Bataan Peninsula and Corregidor, the Gibraltar of the Pacific. MacArthur left for Australia, vowing that one day he would return and seek revenge for this humiliation. In the battle of the Java Sea, the first exercise in joint command, the Japanese scored yet another victory. The Allies lost five cruisers and six destroyers; the Japanese seized Java and its valuable oil resources.

The Japanese were now in possession of a large Empire in the Pacific, which they immediately began to exploit with incredible brutality under the cruelly mocking slogan of 'co-prosperity'. They were still uncertain as to what to do next. Admiral Yamamoto wanted to keep up the naval offensive so as to finish off the US Navy and deny the Americans the breathing space they needed to build up their enormous resources for a war of attrition. The army wanted to consolidate the gains that had been made and felt that the navy's strategy would leave Japan seriously over-extended.

The Americans were similarly divided. Admiral King wanted an offensive against the Japanese, but the army still held to the 'Europe first' strategy and managed to resist King and MacArthur's calls for a massive build-up in the Pacific. But the Americans soon began to make good use of what they had. In May the battle of the Coral Sea, the first engagement at sea in which the rival fleets never came in sight of one another and which was fought entirely by aircraft, was a moral victory for the Americans. The Japanese lost less tonnage but more aircraft and, most important of all, failed to dominate the approaches to Australia. Admiral King asked the British to send a carrier to the Pacific, but this was refused for fear that the Japanese were about to attack Madagascar. King never forgave the British for failing to come to America's aid at a moment of real need, and Churchill was later bitterly to regret this unfortunate decision, which had been based on faulty intelligence.

The failure to defeat the Americans at the battle of the Coral Sea meant that the Japanese were unable to attack Australia, a proposal which had been strongly opposed all along by the army. Hitler made it clear that he did not wish to see the Japanese in India, partly because he greatly admired the British Raj, which he saw as a model of how a handful of racially superior folk could lord it over millions of inferiors, and also because he did not want to end up face to face with the Japanese in the Middle East. In such a situation Admiral Yamamoto's ingenious plan to lure the American fleet to its destruction was readily accepted. The bait was Midway Island, some 1100 miles north-west of Pearl Harbor. Yamamoto argued that since it could be used as a base to attack the Pacific coast of America, the United States would commit its remaining aircraft carriers to its defence. In a final naval engagement the Japanese could therefore finish off the task they had begun at Pearl Harbor. The Japanese had suffered a serious loss of face, though little material damage, in the Doolittle raid on Tokyo and were worried that the Americans might use Midway for further bomber raids on the Japanese homeland. The naval staff therefore accepted Yamamoto's arguments in favour of a pre-emptive strike. A huge fleet was assembled for this task, but unfortunately American cryptographers were well aware of his plan to attack Midway Island at the beginning of June 1942. Brilliant intelligence work and a great deal of luck brought the Americans a tremendous victory which was a decisive turning point in the Pacific war. The Japanese were never to regain the initiative at sea. On the second day of the engagement American dive-bombers caught the Japanese aircraft on deck where they were refuelling and re-arming. The Japanese lost four aircraft carriers, the Americans one, the *Yorktown*.

Not overly deterred by this setback, the Japanese continued their advance by attacking the American base at Guadalcanal in the southern Solomons, and Buna and Port Moresby in Papua. Neither campaign went well and they soon degenerated into long slogging matches in which the Japanese were faced with serious supply problems. It was not until February 1943 that the Americans were able to win the battles in Guadalcanal and New Guinea and then begin the slow process of pushing back the enemy across the Pacific.

Although Britain had suffered a humiliating defeat with the fall of Singapore, and although Churchill's survival as Prime Minister was open to doubt, at least until the much puffed-up victory at El Alamein, Far Eastern affairs excited very little interest in Britain. It all seemed very remote and rather insignificant. Only 30,000 British troops died in the entire Pacific war, and it was not until the full details of Japanese atrocities against prisoners-of-war and civilian internees were widely known that the public became more concerned with

Asian affairs. In America there was no question that Japan was seen as enemy number one. No American could forget or forgive Pearl Harbor or the treatment meted out to GIs during the 'Bataan Death March'. The nation swore revenge, and anti-Japanese sentiments were fanned by the press leading to outbursts of crude racism. Awaiting the day of reckoning, Americans of Japanese descent who had the misfortune to live on the west coast were interned in camps and their property seized. Similar treatment was given to the Canadian Japanese.

Both Britain and the United States were overly fearful that the Japanese might be successful in creating a new Asiatic identity in which age-old resentments against the west could be exploited to their advantage. Britain particularly feared that India would succumb to such siren calls, while the Americans were more concerned about China. The Americans were deeply suspicious of Britain's imperial ambitions in Asia; the British thought the Americans clumsy, naïve and hypocritical. The Americans had long been singing the praises of Chiang Kai-shek and found it hard to swallow the criticisms of the military on the spot who found Chiang's regime far from ideal and the contribution of the Chinese nationalists to the Allied war effort less than satisfactory.

In 1942 a major problem was how to keep the Chinese supplied. General Stilwell, who commanded the American forces in China, Burma and India and who was Chief of Staff to Chiang Kai-shek, wanted to open a new supply route through Burma. General Chennault, with the vociferous support of Joseph Alsop, the columnist who was serving on his staff, and of the intriguing Madame Chiang Kai-shek, announced that he could defeat Japan if he were only given a few more planes, and he constantly attacked Stilwell's land strategy. Stilwell was supported by Marshall and was thus able to hold his own against Chennault.

There were also differences between the Americans and the British in their attitudes towards China. The Chinese, both nationalist and communist, complained that the British treated them as inferiors and that they were slow to abandon age-old colonial attitudes. The Americans were quick to negotiate away their extra-territorial rights, and did so without consulting the British who were obliged to follow suit, much to Chiang's delight. It was an excellent move since it scotched Japanese attempts to fob off the Government in Nanking as the authentic and independent mouthpiece of the Chinese people. In an atmosphere of rivalry rather than comradeship, the Americans accused the British of being indifferent to the fate of China. The British were annoyed at the wide-eyed innocence of much of this enthusiasm for Chiang's China and were hardly surprised when, in the course of the war, it changed into bitter disillusionment.

Stilwell thought that Chiang and his men were a 'gang of thugs' who did nothing to fight the Japanese and used American money and equipment to pursue their own selfish political aims in China. Other American officials were quick to discover that much of their $500 million loan had ended up in the pockets of the ruling clique. There was a growing belief among many American China watchers that Mao's communists were much better at killing the Japanese, were far from being extremist ideologues and shared more values in common with the Americans than with Chiang Kai-shek and his cronies.

The British shared little of the Americans' initial enthusiasm for Chiang's regime, and the Prime Minister was more impressed by Madame Chiang's well-shaped legs than by her husband's statesman-like sagacity or soldierly valour. Many British officials regarded Chiang as a fascist surrounded by self-serving, corrupt and incompetent followers. They had no respect for the nationalist army and were suspicious of China's political ambitions in south-east Asia. Keynes, as treasurer of Lady Cripps's United Aid to China Fund, estimated that 90 per cent of the money sent to China ended up in the pockets of Chiang's associates. In spite of such warnings, Sir Stafford Cripps, and many other left-leaning intellectuals, managed to convince themselves that the Kuomintang regime was admirably democratic and progressive.

Behind these differences between Britain and America over policy towards China lay a fundamental disagreement over the future of the British Empire. Most Americans, including the President, felt that the Empire would have to go, to be replaced by regional arrangements in which the United States would play an important role. Most British officials, although they resented American criticisms and found much of their rhetoric on the subject of Empire tiresome and superficial, felt that fundamental reform was necessary. They inevitably came up against the adamantine opposition of the Prime Minister, whose ideas on the Empire were reactionary in the extreme and who was strengthened in his outdated prejudices by Amery and Grigg in the Cabinet and by Lord Linlithgow in India. The miserable performance of the British in Singapore, Burma and Hong Kong provided ample material for the critics of the Empire, as sorry tales of corruption, inefficiency and the prejudicial treatment of natives were revealed. In the Foreign Office it was generally felt to be lamentable that the Government had no colonial policy, and hopes that the principles of the Atlantic Charter would also apply to the colonies were somewhat dampened by the certain knowledge that such would be totally unacceptable to the Prime Minister. For the Americans, Churchill's archaic vision of Britain's imperial role was a very serious menace in that it might be exploited by the Japanese to build an Asiatic front.

Nowhere was this more apparent than in India. Subhas Chandra Bose's attempts to enlist German and Japanese support for Indian independence had yet to be revealed as a preposterous misjudgement. As the Japanese advanced towards India it was felt that some constitutional concessions would have to be made or India would be lost. Churchill found a masterly solution to the problem. In March 1942 he sent Stafford Cripps to India with proposals that full dominion status should be granted after the war and that the political parties should advise the Government of India until that time. Although Cripps greatly exceeded his instructions, thus reducing Linlithgow to apoplexy, he got nowhere, just as Churchill had hoped. Congress would accept nothing short of full independence and Cripps had made a serious miscalculation by volunteering for a fruitless mission at a time when he posed a serious political threat to Churchill. Congress then began a campaign of civil disobedience and the British Cabinet, including the Labour members, decided to imprison Gandhi and the Congress leaders. Churchill did not improve the situation by making a number of dismissive and insensitive public statements on India. Chiang appealed to Roosevelt to help the British Government to see reason and insisted that Congress represented the will of the people. Gandhi also appealed to the President, but the effect was rather spoilt by his critical reference to the Negro problem in the United States. Even the greatest enthusiasts for Indian independence doubted whether a country led by the world's leading proponent of non-violence would be particularly effective against the Japanese. Roosevelt's proddings of the British Government were dismissed by Eden for their 'meandering amateurishness' and the British were not impressed by the overworked and irrelevant analogies drawn between the Philippines and India or lofty reminders of the glorious anti-colonial struggle of 1776.

The vast majority of Americans regarded the Japanese as their chief enemy, resented the apparent lack of British willingness to co-operate in the Pacific, and found it hard to understand the British obsession with Germany. For all the talk of a 'Europe first' strategy, many American military leaders, frustrated by Britain's Mediterranean tactics and their obvious lack of enthusiasm for an early second front, were placing increasing emphasis on the Pacific, and even Marshall was threatening to pull out of Europe if the British continued to drag their feet over the invasion of France. By the end of 1943 the Americans had more troops, aircraft and ships employed against Japan than against Germany. Conversely, the British authorities and public showed relatively little interest in the war against Japan. Once the shock and dismay at the loss of Singapore had abated, the war seemed comfortably remote and until the barbaric treatment of Allied prisoners of war by the Japanese was made public there were few cries for revenge.

Many Americans, including the President, felt that Britain was pursuing purely selfish aims in the Pacific by attempting to hang on to as much of its Empire as possible. There was a suspicion in many circles that the Americans were being duped by the British into fighting an imperialist war while they felt that they ought to be fighting to end imperialism and to secure the freedom of the Chinese, Indians and all the other enslaved Asiatics. Other Americans were more realistic, but no less suspicious of the British. For them the war opened up glittering commercial prospects and the opportunity to secure naval bases to guarantee the new order of a *pax americana*.

The matter was further complicated by the fact that neither the British nor the Americans had a clear strategy. Cadogan described British planning in Asia as 'a blind man searching for a black cat in a dark room'. The American Joint Chiefs were similarly undecided. General MacArthur favoured an offensive in the south western Pacific from New Guinea to the Philippines; the US Navy wanted to concentrate in the central Pacific so as best to deploy their aircraft carriers. There were excellent strategic arguments in favour of both these routes, and at the 'Trident' conference in Washington in May 1943 it was decided to adopt both simultaneously so as to avoid a head-on collision between MacArthur and the Navy. Such a strategy would also keep the Japanese in a state of uncertainty, forcing them to disperse their forces. The disadvantage was that this two-pronged offensive strategy required large forces and lengthy preparation, thus giving the Japanese time to improve their defences. Although approved by Churchill, this proposal virtually excluded the British, whose naval forces in the Bay of Bengal were to provide what Admiral Leahy rather contemptuously described as a 'diversionary effort'.

The American thrust in the Pacific was further delayed by a wasteful and time-consuming effort to drive the Japanese from the Aleutians. Around 100,000 troops supported by large naval and air forces took six months to achieve a minimal strategic gain. The attack on the Solomon Islands began at the end of June 1943. The offensive was poorly co-ordinated since MacArthur was given strategic control of the campaign, Admiral Halsey tactical control, and the forces stationed at Pearl Harbor were under the command of Admiral Nimitz. The troops were inexperienced and morale was low, but overwhelming American superiority in the air and at sea guaranteed the success of this first attempt at 'island hopping'. The Japanese were forced to withdraw in order to shorten their defensive perimeter.

In the central Pacific the main attacks were against Makin and Tarawa in the Gilbert Islands. The attack on Tarawa Atoll led by Rear-Admiral 'Terrible' Turner and Major-General 'Howlin' Mad' Smith was very costly, the Americans losing one-third of the 5000 men who landed on the first day. The Japanese failed to exploit this advantage and mounted a series of suicidal *banzai* attacks against overwhelming firepower. Meanwhile, MacArthur moved up the coast of New Guinea and Admiral 'Bull' Halsey seized the Solomons. The Marshalls were now within striking distance, beyond which lay the Marianas and the Carolines which held the key to MacArthur's main objective, the Philippines.

By contrast, British efforts in Burma were pitiful. Chiang made a preposterous proposal for a massive offensive with fifteen Chinese divisions from the east and ten British divisions from the west coupled with a seaborne attack on Rangoon. Since the troops, the ships and the airpower were not available for such an enterprise, it was all pure fantasy. Wavell opted for a landing on the Arakan coast in northern Burma close to the Indian border. The advance began in December 1942 and was painfully slow. The Japanese counter-attack resulted in the British and Indian forces being driven back to their starting points on the Indian border by May. The dramatic antics of Brigadier Orde Wingate's Chindits in harassing Japanese lines of communication were strategically worthless but provided a much needed boost to morale and appealed to the Americans, who otherwise had little respect for British efforts.

The British and Americans argued at length over how the command in south-east Asia should be reorganized and who should be appointed. Eventually the Americans agreed to the nomination of Lord Louis Mountbatten who, although young and still largely unproven, was felt to have the necessary dash and diplomatic flair to command SEAC. At American insistence 'Vinegar Joe' Stilwell was appointed Deputy Supreme Commander and he retained operational control over American and Chinese troops in Burma and remained as Chief of Staff to Chiang Kai-shek. Further confusion was created by uncertainties over the area to fall under the new command. The Americans were anxious not to cause Chiang any offence, while the

British had fewer scruples in dealing with the Chinese leader, although Mountbatten was careful to pander to his sensitivities. The Americans continued to believe that China would play a vital role in the defeat of Japan, but the British saw little point in pouring money and resources into this bottomless pit of oriental inefficiency and corruption. They discounted Chiang's imaginative claims for China's military prowess and felt that it was better that his regime should collapse than that resources needed against Japan should be wasted in an effort to keep it going. Americans were entranced by Madame Chiang Kai-shek and imagined that China was a freedom-loving democracy. They were horrified at the possibility that China might drop out of the war and did everything possible to stop criticism of this admirable ally in the press.

While Roosevelt waffled on about China, causing Stilwell to dismiss him as a 'flighty fool' who made him 'puke', Churchill was under no illusions that China was either a great power or a model of democracy. Americans tended to dismiss such British reservations about the Celestials as evidence of their patronizing attitude to other races. The British felt, as one official phrased it, that the 'dawn of intelligence' in America with regard to China was long overdue. Many British China experts felt that the Kuomintang was distinctly fascist, and that China entertained all manner of territorial ambitions and might eventually prove as great a menace as Japan. Most British officials, however, adopted a sceptical wait-and-see attitude towards China which was both realistic and avoided the bitter sense of disillusionment felt by the Americans when they finally realized the fatal shortcomings of their protégé.

For the Americans the main problem was what to do for the best in China. Should they concentrate on building up the Chinese army as Stilwell wanted, bomb Japan from Chinese bases as Chennault proposed, or concentrate on recapturing Burma? Roosevelt tended to support Chennault, and Stilwell was becoming increasingly fed up with 'Peanut', as he called Chiang, for his inactivity and rapacity. As the war progressed, the importance of China waned. The success of the American strategy in the central Pacific and the Soviet guarantee that they would declare war on Japan once the fighting in Europe was over meant that China was no longer particularly important for the defeat of Japan. China was now relegated to a flank position that needed protection but was hardly a major concern. Americans were also beginning to ask whether Chiang's regime was quite as democratic as they had at first imagined, and suggestions were made that much of Chiang's book, *China's Destiny*, had an unpleasantly fascist flavour. On top of all this was a growing uncertainty about the future of China. What would be the outcome of the struggle between the Kuomintang and the communists? Were the communists devoutly pro-Moscow, or were they a distinct national variant of communism with genuine popular support? Above all, what would be the Soviet Union's territorial demands on China after the war, and would these demands force Chiang into the Japanese camp? China was ceasing to be a model ally and was rapidly becoming a problem.

The Americans were getting increasingly annoyed with the British for dragging their feet over Burma. Marshall and Stilwell still placed top priority on opening up a new Burma road through Ledo to Yunan. The British argued that the road would take too long to build and would thus not offer the Chinese any immediate relief, and that the supplies travelling via the Burma road would be about enough to provide for the troops needed to guard it. There was also a growing feeling in Britain that Burma was hardly a worthwhile strategic objective. Churchill felt that the reconquest of Burma was like 'a man attacking a hedgehog by pulling out its bristles one by one'. At Casablanca in January 1943 it was agreed to mount 'Operation Anakim', a seaborne offensive on Rangoon coupled with a Chinese and British land offensive, in the next dry season. 'Operation Culverin', a landing in Sumatra designed to outflank the Japanese, a particular favourite of Churchill's, was also discussed but had to be abandoned. Landing craft were not available and the Americans still insisted on the priority of the Burma road. Later, plans such as 'Tarzan', involving landings on the coast of Burma, were also dropped. SEAC, with its dashing young supreme commander, was being pushed into the sidelines and was internally riven with jealousies and resentments. The Americans decided that SEAC was an acronym for 'Save England's Asiatic Colonies'. This further underlined the basic dilemma facing the Americans in Asia. On the one hand they posed as the champions of anti-colonialism, and yet on the other their closest allies were colonial imperialists. The more progressive and imaginative British officials and Cabinet Ministers found themselves stuck between a stubbornly reactionary imperialist Prime Minister and the exasperatingly naïve and ill-informed anti-colonialism and nativist views of the Americans. Some of Roosevelt's pronouncements on Asia were so staggeringly absurd that the British Foreign Office wrongly refused to take them seriously, convinced that they were high-minded liberal noises designed purely for political effect.

American attitudes towards India vividly illustrate this problem. With Gandhi in prison and apparently intent on starving himself to death, and with the appalling famine in Bengal, American anti-colonialists had ample material for their accusations against British imperialism. Roosevelt told Stalin at Teheran that he thought the best solution for India was reform from the bottom, 'somewhat on the Soviet line'. Stalin was shocked at this suggestion and pointed out that this would mean revolution, adding that he had no great quarrel with British imperialism, given the remarkable military contribution of the British Empire to the common cause.

The high-minded anti-imperialist rhetoric of the Roosevelt administration did not fit very comfortably with demands for bases throughout the Pacific which were voiced particularly stridently by the US Navy. Roosevelt prefered the idea of bases controlled by the United Nations. The British were not entirely averse to this idea, and were already beginning to think in terms of a moderate peace settlement with Japan. Deprived of its overseas possessions and utterly defeated, Japan would pose no military threat. The Emperor should remain to provide the necessary continuity and Japan should be swiftly readmitted to the community of nations. Gradually the Americans came to share this view.

Well aware that the British were preparing an offensive, the Japanese decided to launch a pre-emptive strike in Arakan in February 1944 so as to draw General Slim's troops away from their strategic objective of Imphal. Slim was the first to move, and his strategy of establishing strongholds which were supplied by air proved most effective. The second Chindit operation was dramatic but disastrous. Wingate was killed in an air crash and his successor, Lentaigne, marched north to join Stilwell's Chinese force. The Chindits had been unable to disrupt the Japanese attacks on Imphal and Kohima where the British were caught badly off balance. Slim quickly corrected the situation and his strategy paid handsome dividends. He held on to Imphal and Kohima, keeping them going in the largest air-supply operation in the entire war, and then, when the Japanese were worn down, he launched a shattering counter-attack. The Japanese were pushed back to the Chindwin, losing more than half of their men and most of their guns, tanks and equipment. Only the monsoon saved them from total defeat. It was a magnificent feat of arms, the worst land defeat in Japanese history, and it won Slim the right to be considered the finest British commander in the Second World War. These events were overshadowed by the opening of the second front in Europe, and however striking the victory of the 14th Army, it was not enough to undo the terrible losses to British prestige in 1941 and 1942.

In the spring of 1944 the Americans continued their advance in the Pacific. MacArthur finished off the campaign in New Guinea by July and the way was now open for him to return, as promised, to the Philippines. The remains of the five Japanese divisions were left for the Australians to mop up in some very fierce and totally unnecessary fighting. MacArthur and the Americans won the victory and the glory in New Guinea, while the Australians had done most of the hard fighting for which they got little credit.

In the central Pacific the Marshall Islands were attacked and the Japanese base at Truk in the Carolines was destroyed. In June four successive strikes by carrier-based aircraft were spotted well in advance by radar and the Japanese lost 218 aircraft in the 'Great Marianas Turkey Shoot'. Two of the Japanese carriers were sunk by torpedoes. Admiral Spruance was bitterly disappointed when the Japanese fleet managed to slip away during the night, but he had won a splendid victory. The Japanese lost a total of 480 aircraft and thereby lost control of the Philippine Sea. Success in the Marianas was guaranteed. Saipan, where the Japanese commanding general oddly committed ritual suicide in order to encourage his troops in their final attack, Tian and Guam were captured by the Americans, providing bases for the B29s to strike at the Japanese heartland. On 18 July 1944, General Tojo resigned.

After this tremendous success in the Marianas, King and Nimitz wanted to push on to Formosa, or possibly Iwo Jima and Okinawa, a strategy which appealed to the air force for it would give them bases from which to pound away at Japan. MacArthur, however, was obsessed with his promise to return to the Philippines. MacArthur and King argued out their differences in front of Roosevelt at a meeting in Hawaii in July. After three hours of MacArthur's impassioned oratory the President finally gave way, although the Chiefs of Staff favoured the central Pacific thrust on strategic grounds. It is reported that MacArthur's performance gave the President a severe headache.

With such advances in the Pacific it became abundantly clear that Burma was essentially a side-show and that China would not play a decisive role in the defeat of Japan. In May Churchill told the Commonwealth Prime Ministers: 'We must regard ourselves as junior partners in the war against Japan.' Britain could do little but secure the defence of India, open the land route to China and hold down as many Japanese troops as possible in Burma. SEAC decided that it would take far too long to establish a land route to China and therefore proposed a new plan, 'Axiom', involving operations against Sumatra and Malaya which would open up the China Sea and extend SEAC's boundaries to include Hong Kong. Stilwell still believed that the quickest route to Japan ran through Burma and China, and he thus violently opposed 'Axiom'. The American Joint Chiefs, convinced that 'Axiom' was dictated purely by British colonial ambitions, promptly squashed the proposal.

Successes in the Burma campaign opened up the possibility of pushing ahead with the overland route as well as an offensive across the Chindwin and an assault on Rangoon. The British Chiefs of Staff wanted Britain to support the American central-Pacific thrust with naval forces and finish off the job in Burma. Churchill still hankered after 'Operation Culverin', the landing in Sumatra, and dismissed Burma as a 'disease-ridden country' that was hardly a worthwhile objective as long as parts of the British Empire remained in Japanese hands. Eden agreed with the Prime Minister that Singapore and Malaya were prime objectives and that the strategy proposed by the Chiefs of Staff would bring no political advantages but merely relegated Britain to tagging along in the wake of the Americans. It was suggested that the Sumatra–Malaya approach would earn Britain the gratitude of the peoples of Asia for freeing them from Japanese tyranny and would serve to undo the shame of previous defeats. The result of these differences was a serious rift between the Prime Minister and the Chiefs of Staff which at times was so acute that the Chiefs seriously considered resigning.

British strategy in south-east Asia was thus the subject of endless waffling, muddle and mismanagement. Little was done to overcome American suspicions. Finally, a compromise was reached. Churchill got his way with a commitment to press on to Rangoon and Singapore, and the Chiefs of Staff got an agreement that the British would assist the Americans in the central Pacific. It was a compromise which did not disguise the fact that Britain's role was embarrassingly subordinate, and did nothing to assuage American suspicions and resentments.

By now the Americans had begun to reconsider the role China was to play in the defeat of Japan. The Joint Chiefs felt that the China theatre would not be the scene of any major effort. As long as the Chinese were able to hold down the Japanese forces, all was well and the central-Pacific advance could continue. Stilwell had reached the conclusion that Chiang had to go, since his policy was simply one of 'delay, while grabbing for loans and post-war aid, for the purpose of maintaining his present position, based on one-party Government, a reactionary policy and suppression of democratic ideas'. Stilwell was determined to stand up to Chiang, but the Chinese leader fought back and managed to secure Stilwell's recall in October. Roosevelt had signed the order for 'Vinegar Joe's' return to the United States but he had largely lost interest in Chiang and in China and was prepared, as Stilwell put it, to 'harpoon the little bugger' as soon as he saw fit.

A number of influential figures had become equally disillusioned with Chiang. Morgenthau thought the time had come for the Chinese to 'fish or cut bait', and did not wish to send Chiang and his 'bunch of crooks' any more money. Others, including the President, objected to his reluctance to reach an agreement with the communists and began to think that the overthrow of Chiang might well be in the best interests of the Allied war effort. All this was based on a profound ignorance of the situation in China. The Kuomintang would never make its peace with the communists, who in turn were bent on nothing less than absolute power. Chiang might well have been a disaster, but no one could bring about the unification of the two main political forces in China so that they could play a more active role in the war against Japan.

Many American observers were impressed by the popularity of Mao's communism with its fervent nationalism, and wondered whether it was really and truly communist. Encouraged by Stalin's talk of Chinese 'margarine communism', they were ready to accept the argument that they were agrarian reformers who were refreshingly honest when compared with the corrupt hangers-on in Chungking. Although some British officials, among them the colourful Sir Archibald Clark Kerr, who had been ambassador to China before being posted to Moscow, had similar starry-eyed notions of Mao Tse Tung and his followers, there was general agreement in Whitehall that co-operation between the Kuomintang and the communists was impossible. China was increasingly seen as a liability, and SEAC commanders were unenthusiastic about the campaign in northern Burma about which Stilwell and the Americans were still keen, in spite of the fact that advances in the central Pacific had made the opening of the Ledo road less urgent. Stilwell, who referred to his Limey allies, with the notable exception of General Slim, as 'pig fuckers' and their gallant supreme commander as a 'pisspot', did everything he could to discredit the British and to destroy the last vestiges of Allied unity.

CHAPTER SEVEN

The United States and the War

The endless and often bitter arguments between the interventionists, who argued that since public opinion polls showed that the vast majority of Americans were in favour of full support for Britain, even at the risk of war, therefore the majority was on their side, and the isolationists, who pointed out that 80 per cent opposed a declaration of war, were largely ended with the Japanese attack on Pearl Harbor. The outrage at a day which would 'live in infamy' was deeply and widely felt, but it was soon to subside. Throughout its remaining forty months the war seemed remote, the sacrifices demanded by the state were little more than inconveniences, and a massive advertising campaign had to be launched to remind Americans that there was a war going on in distant parts. As one American remarked: Europe had been occupied, Russia and China invaded and Britain bombed, while alone among the great powers the United States was 'fighting this war on imagination alone'.

Contrary to the advice of some of his closest advisors, among them the Secretary for War, Stimson, Roosevelt asked Congress for a declaration of war only against Japan, not against Germany and Italy. Hitler was soon to oblige those who wanted war between the United States and the Axis powers by declaring war himself. He was determined to stop the flow of supplies across the Atlantic, and he wanted to oblige his Japanese allies. He was convinced that sooner or later the Americans would declare war on Germany and he wanted to fire the first shot. Roosevelt knew that this was coming by means of the decrypts of diplomatic traffic between Berlin and Tokyo, and therefore preferred to bide his time and allow Hitler and Mussolini to make the next move. He did not have to wait long. The Axis powers declared war on the United States on 11 December.

On hearing the news of the Pearl Harbor attack, Churchill announced that he would travel immediately to Washington. Roosevelt was eager to meet Churchill but, fearing that public opinion would not take too kindly to the visit, he suggested a secret meeting in Bermuda and offered as an excuse his concern for Churchill's safety. In London there was some concern that Churchill was throwing himself at the Americans, but as usual the Prime Minister got his way and, accompanied by Lord Beaverbrook, Pound, Portal and Dill, he set sail on the *Duke of York* on 13 December bound for the 'Arcadia' conference in Washington.

The main achievement of the conference was an agreement on the wording of a declaration to be made on behalf of the United Nations. The British hoped to get social security included as a war aim, but Roosevelt was fearful that this would be seen by conservative Congressmen as an attempt to create a world-wide 'New Deal' and therefore insisted that it should not be included. Churchill was appalled by Roosevelt's suggestion that certain concessions should be made to India. Churchill subsequently claimed (inaccurately) that he 'reacted so strongly and at such length that he never raised it verbally again'. Roosevelt also wished to include religious freedom in the declaration, but the Soviets objected. Eventually he convinced Litvinov, the Soviet ambassador, that 'religious freedom' simply meant freedom to have a religion or not. Churchill was so impressed by this sophistry that he proposed that Roosevelt should become Archbishop of Canterbury should he fail to win the next election. It was agreed that all the Allies were to sign the declaration. An American official fortunately pointed out at the last moment that the hapless King Zog of Albania had been overlooked.

The declaration was a high-minded document which announced that the signatories were fighting a common fight for the defence of 'life, liberty, independence and religious freedom, and to preserve human rights and justice in their own lands as well as in other lands'. The substance of the document was that the signatories undertook not to make a separate armistice or peace. Churchill later remarked that it 'set forth who we were and what we were fighting for'. The first part of this statement was partly true, the second manifestly false.

Churchill's major fear had been that the Americans would fail to realize that Germany's defeat would assure the defeat of Japan and that the reverse was untrue. He was greatly relieved to learn at his first meeting with the President that in spite of Pearl Harbor he was absolutely committed to the 'Europe first' strategy. The Prime Minister could therefore inform the Cabinet that the outstanding question was 'not *whether* but *how*' to apply this strategy. Roosevelt also approved the suggestion for a landing of American troops in north Africa, codenamed 'Operation Gymnast', which would give them an opportunity to fight on the other side of the Atlantic. He also wanted the USAAF to begin the bombing of Germany from bases in England as soon as possible.

The Army Chief of Staff, General Marshall, raised all manner of objections to 'Gymnast'. There were serious logistical problems to overcome, the French were likely to offer stiff resistance and a setback would be disastrous for morale. The poor performance of the British in Libya and the need to support Allied troops in the Pacific played into Marshall's hands and forced the postponement of 'Gymnast'.

Marshall was not alone in resenting Roosevelt's enthusiastic support of Churchill's strategy. Most senior officers saw no reason why the United States should play second fiddle to a country like Britain and sacrifice their men to an ill-considered, ineffectual, selfish and imperialistic strategy. General Stilwell spoke for many when he complained that: 'The Limeys have his [FDR's] ear, while we have the hind tit.'

Roosevelt knew that unity of command was essential for the effective conduct of the war, and feared that these tensions would make this impossible. In order to get the British to agree to a single commander over all the Allied forces in the south-west Pacific Roosevelt had to propose that the job should go to Wavell. The British Chiefs of Staff merely saw this as an attempt to shift the blame for an inevitable defeat on to them. Churchill managed to overcome the further objections of his Chiefs of Staff to the suggestion that the Combined American and British Chiefs of Staff should meet permanently in Washington by suggesting that they should try it for a month to see whether it was a satisfactory arrangement.

Although there was a considerable degree of reciprocal respect between Roosevelt and Churchill, relations between the two men were often strained. The President pointed out that: 'It's in the American tradition, this distrust, this dislike and even hatred of Britain – the Revolution, you know, and 1812; and India and the Boer War, and all that. There are many kinds of Americans of course, but as a people, as a country, we're opposed to imperialism; we can't stomach it.' To Churchill and the British this anti-imperialism and sanctimoniousness was tiresome humbug. Negotiations over an economic pact were seriously endangered by British fears that the American concept of economic democracy would lead to the abolition of imperial preference. Roosevelt felt that the British attitude to India amounted to an invitation to the enemy to occupy the country. Yet in spite of these differences and disagreements 'Arcadia' was a success and set the tone for later meetings. On his return to London Churchill told the King that Britain and the United States were now married after many months of 'walking out'. Like most marriages it was beset with tensions, misunderstandings and recriminations, but at least it lasted.

From the outset there was no doubt in Roosevelt's mind how the war would be won. With the enthusiastic support of Henry L. Stimson, whom he had made Secretary of War even though he was a life-long Republican, and of General Marshall, he set about mobilizing the full industrial potential of the United States. America would win the war from Dearborn, Michigan by building up vast reserves of matériel, shipping it to north-west Europe and crushing the Germans under its weight. The foundations of this industrial strategy had already been laid. As early as 1938 Roosevelt had sent Bernard Baruch to Europe to assess the danger posed by Hitler to the United States. Baruch had recommended a massive increase in defence spending, but Roosevelt was still reluctant to act. Although he agreed with Baruch that Hitler was a real menace to American interests, the economy had yet to recover from the depression, and isolationist sentiment was very strong. In such a situation the President acted like any other politician and set up a committee. The War Resources Board was made up of a group of distinguished businessmen who duly produced a report on what was to be done in the event of war. In 1940, while the Nazi armies were marching across western Europe, Roosevelt created a number of other defence agencies, dividing responsibilities between them and thus retaining the final authority.

Roosevelt felt obliged to bring into his administration those 'economic royalists' who had been among the strongest opponents of the New Deal, the businessmen and financiers whom he had recently denounced as monopolists, price-riggers and reactionaries. But he knew that he had to rely on such men if his policies were to be effective and if the nation were to be united. He was similarly committed to bi-partisanship. Stimson, a prominent New York lawyer with a long list of important corporate clients, was an outstanding administrator who gave the Army and War Department the decisive leadership it had been sadly lacking. James Forrestal, Under-Secretary and later Secretary for the Navy, was a man of similar background and talents. He had been in the Wall Street firm of Dillon Reed, an investment house with close ties to the corporate world. Stimson and Forrestal were outstanding examples of the new men who entered the administration during the war. They had never been enthusiasts for the New Deal; they were privately educated patricians, at ease in the world of power, influence and wealth; they were incorruptible and dedicated to public service. Roosevelt, who came from a similar social background, found it easy to work with them, as did New-Dealers like Harry Hopkins, an intimate of the President and head of Lend-Lease, Harold Ickes, the Secretary of the Interior, Henry Morgenthau at the Treasury, and the Vice-President, Henry Wallace. They were united in their determination to prepare the country for war and then to fight it as effectively and to win it as quickly as possible.

The Harvey Bundys, Robert P. Pattersons, John J. McCloys and Robert A. Lovetts who played key roles in the War Department did not set out primarily to further the interests of big business and were not privy to a vast capitalist conspiracy. They were scrupulously honest and selfless public servants whose major concern was to create the preconditions for victory, and yet they helped to create a megalithic 'Military–Industrial Complex' which eroded the democratic process and undid some of the achievements of the New Deal. It was perhaps an inevitable process given their basic attitude, which was admirably summed up by Stimson: 'If you are going to . . . go to war in a capitalist country, you have to let business make money out of the process or business won't work.' The decisions of the War and Navy Departments on contracts, the allocation of raw materials and the ordering of priorities favoured the large, efficient and powerful corporations. As a result big business got bigger, fed by low-interest loans, secure contracts, tax incentives and vast profits without risk. Many small businesses were crushed by the giants and to many it seemed that 'free enterprise' was little more than the freedom of the giants to frustrate efforts by the Government to free the market from the effects of monopoly.

In January 1941 the Office for Production Management was created as an attempt to ensure the co-operation of capital and labour. The trade unionist Sidney Hillman and William Knudsen from General Motors were joint directors but were too mindful of their constituents to be able to work effectively together. In January the following year the War Production Board was formed to control the entire process of the mobilization of industry. The agency was headed by Donald Nelson, a thoroughly likeable if somewhat indecisive executive from Sears, Roebuck and Company. The major weakness of the Board was that Nelson allowed the Army and Navy to control procurement, and thus he was unable to make effective decisions on production priorities. This had unfortunate consequences for all aspects of war production, including Lend-Lease.

The Army and Navy dealt directly with big business which had the capability, the capacity and the experience to undertake innovative and large-scale programmes. The WPB was unable to control the allocation of contracts to small or large businesses, so that big business got an increasingly large share of the contracts. In 1940 some 175,000 small companies were providing 70 per cent of the manufacturing output of the United States and one hundred large corporations produced the remaining 30 per cent. By March 1943, by which time aggregate production had doubled, the situation was reversed: the one hundred companies now produced 70 per cent of the total production. Nelson recruited the president of the General Electric Company, Charles E. Wilson, to supervise production from raw materials allocated by the WPB, but this had no effect either in curbing the autonomy of the service departments or in halting the growth of big business.

Small business also had its champions, among them Robert A. Taft of Ohio, the brilliant conservative 'Mr Republican'; James E. Murray, an enormously wealthy small businessman, New Dealer and crusader against monopolies and cartels; and Wright Patman, a hard-hitting Texan Democrat on the Banking and Currency Committee. Their Senate Committee on Small Business held hearings which led to the passing of the Murray-Patman Act which required the WPB to look after the interests of small concerns and established a Smaller War Plants Corporation to act as an intermediary between the services and small business and which had a revolving capital fund to provide investment capital for small businesses willing to convert to war production. None of this had much effect on reversing the trend towards the concentration of economic power in the hands of the few, and the conversion to a war economy and its conversion back to a peacetime economy was done in a manner which further threatened small business. The protection of the interests of small business was an attempt to preserve an essential part of the American dream. It was a dream that bore increasingly less resemblance to reality as the exigencies of war destroyed what was left of 'free private enterprise'.

In 1933 Roosevelt had suspended the Sherman Anti-Trust Act of 1890 and had designed the National Industrial Recovery Act to enable industry to agree on production quotas, wages and prices in order to help overcome the effects of the depression. The Supreme Court threw out the act, big business expressed its total aversion to the New

Deal, and economic recovery was not forthcoming. Roosevelt now no longer believed in the economic and political virtues of big industry and became a determined opponent of the trusts. The Attorney General, Francis Biddle, and his assistant in charge of the Anti Trust Division, Thurman Arnold, were zealous scourges of the trusts and singled out giants such as Standard Oil and Du Pont for harsh treatment. Stimson and Forrestal objected strongly to this hounding of the trusts, claiming that the efforts of these fanatics were undermining war production and arguing that anti-trust legislation should be ignored for the duration of the war. In spite of his earlier misgivings, Roosevelt was now convinced that the big corporations were alone capable of doing the job of supplying the armed forces, and agreed with this view. Biddle and Arnold were thus without effective support and had to concede defeat. Biddle kept up the fight, enquiring into the dubious activities of some major corporations including Du Pont. Although it was an uphill struggle against Stimson and Forrestal, at least he was able to win a few rounds and keep alive the principles of anti-trust legislation.

The War Labor Board placed a limit on wage increases in order to curb inflation, but this affected hourly and not weekly wages. With large amounts of overtime, wages rose by an average of 70 per cent during the war, a greater rate of increase than profits. Although rivalry between the two union federations, the AFL and the CIO, remained intense, union membership increased by 50 per cent during the war, in part because of the WLB's decision in favour of a 'maintenance of membership' policy whereby union members who did not resign from their union after two weeks had to remain as dues-paying members until the contract between the union and the firm expired. The trend towards big Government and big business during the war was thus matched by the growth of big labour.

Few believed that the prosperity of the war years was due to deficit spending on a massive scale. Workers attributed it to the skill of their union negotiators, businessmen to their cunning in the marketplace, and farmers to their lobby in Washington, the Farm Bureau Federation. The sheer volume of war contracts resulted in an enormous increase in productive capacity and a corresponding demand for labour, so that the effects of the depression were overcome even in many of the economically backward areas. Taxation covered only half of Government spending; the remainder had to be borrowed. Borrowed money paid for the goods which provided the jobs which paid the money which in turn fuelled consumption on an extraordinary scale. For most Americans the war was a period of plenty after the horrors of the depression. Their country and their homes were unaffected by the war and the percentage of those who died or were seriously wounded in defence of the American Way of Life was relatively small. Life was good, the mood was optimistic, the war a distant unpleasantness which for most was easy to tolerate. The world's greatest producer of guns was also the greatest producer of butter.

The Government statistics are truly staggering. The federal budget was $9 billion in 1939; by 1945 it was $166 billion. In the first six months of 1942 orders for military equipment were greater than the aggregate yearly production of the entire American economy. Industrial production rose by 96 per cent during the war, creating seventeen million new jobs. Although there was a slight drop in the production of consumer goods, it was so insignificant that it scarcely had an effect. The war economy thus took little away from the civilian market, which in turn was fuelled by the new prosperity. The production of consumer goods failed to increase at the same rate as the rest of the economy, and inflation was the inevitable result. The Government made determined attempts to curb this inflation but was not wholly successful.

Even though life in wartime America was better than anywhere else in the world and was far more pleasant than it had been during the height of the depression, rationing and shortages were seen as tiresome reminders that a war was on. Now that the average consumer had the money, it was aggravating that steaks or cigarettes were not always freely available. Shortages led to the promotion of the sale of paperback books, and to save material the two-piece swimsuit was advertised as being both patriotic and sexy. Men's suits were mostly unfashionably single-breasted and were sold with only one pair of trousers. With the increase in personal incomes there was a flourishing black market, and luxury goods sold particularly well. *Gourmet* magazine complained that the epicure had to make do with smoked salmon, since caviar was no longer readily available. The department stores also did excellent business. The average sale of $2 in 1940 had risen to $10 by 1944.

Madison Avenue was quick to exploit the possibilities of the war. Formfit claimed that its brassieres were 'for the support you need in these hectic days of added responsibility', the GI returned to his Penelope to find everything unchanged but for the Nash Kelvinator refrigerator in the kitchen, and Yehudi Menuhin played the Mendelssohn Concerto to encourage the purchase of war bonds and to underline, as Morgenthau pointed out, that both artist and composer were *verboten* in Nazi Germany. The advertising industry was in no doubt that Americans were fighting for a consumers' paradise which would be created once the war was over, when massive factories such as Henry Ford's Willow Run bomber plant near Detroit would retool to produce every imaginable gadget for ultra-modern homes fit to welcome the returning heroes.

The ever-ingenious American businessman seized every opportunity offered by the war to increase sales. Coca-Cola managed to persuade the Government that its five-cent drink was essential to maintain the health, efficiency and morale of the armed forces. The Army and Navy encouraged the company to send its product overseas and to establish bottling plants abroad. These were to form the basis of its world-wide Empire. Parker Pens pointed out the morale-boosting effects of writing letters to the troops and was able to ensure a reasonable supply of Lucite, the plastic from which the famous '51' was made, even though the material was also used for bomber noses. Philip K. Wrigley waxed poetical over the merits of his chewing gum which banned 'Monotony, Thirst and Nicotine', three of Hitler's secret weapons designed to undermine productivity in war industry. Andrew Jackson Higgins, a colourful and resourceful manufacturer of motor-boats, put pictures of Hitler, Mussolini and Hirohito in the men's lavatory with the caption: 'Come on in brother, take it easy, Every minute you loaf here helps us plenty.' It is uncertain to what extent such measures contributed to the increase of Higgins's total sales from $400,000 in 1935 to $120 million by 1943.

As in all belligerent countries, the number of women in the workforce greatly increased during the war. Some six and a half million women entered the labour force between 1941 and 1945, most of them married and middle-aged. Although their wages were considerably lower than men's, they had the satisfaction of doing their bit for the war effort and thereby earning some extra money which enabled their families to enjoy some modest luxuries and an enhanced status. Women spent more on themselves. Sales of women's clothes doubled during the war as they clamoured for the shorter, pleatless and zipperless economy skirts.

The prosperity of the war years had a dramatic effect on white America, but blacks, as usual, did less well. America was still a society which practised apartheid, and Roosevelt did little to change the situation beyond making some rousing speeches designed more to appease his wife than to help the blacks. The President was too much of a politician to risk losing the support of Southern Congressmen by taking such drastic steps as supporting anti-lynching legislation. Thus, in the original industrial boom in 1940 and 1941, although most unemployed whites found jobs, the blacks still remained without work. Business, organized labour and Government were determined to keep the blacks in their place, and they made sure that there was no anti-discrimination clause in Government defence contracts. In such a situation many blacks had at least some sympathy for the Japanese, who claimed to be fighting for the liberation of the coloured peoples from white domination. Some blacks even suggested that they had no quarrel with Adolf Hitler, who had no blacks to torment, and that their struggle was against home-grown racism, not against international fascism.

When blacks began to enlist in the armed forces they did so in large numbers. Sixty per cent more blacks enlisted as a proportion of their share of the total population than did whites, but they were treated abominably. The Air Corps and Marine Corps, self-styled elites, would not accept blacks. In the navy they were given menial duties such as mess orderlies, and in the army they served in segregated non-combatant units as labourers with the pioneers, cooks and batmen. It was widely believed that blacks were inferior to whites, should never be allowed to become officers and made poor combat soldiers. Stimson announced that: 'Leadership is not imbedded in the Negro race yet and to try to make commissioned officers to lead men into battle – coloured men – is only to work a disaster to both.' General Marshall, a Virginian, agreed.

Towards the end of 1940, A. Philip Randolph organized the Negro March on Washington Committee to protest against the absurdity that a Jim Crow army was being prepared ostensibly to fight for freedom. Randolph was an outstanding labour leader, head of the Brotherhood of Sleeping Car Porters, a militant socialist and a devout Methodist. He was able to win over the support of moderate black leaders, including Walter White of the National Association for the Advancement of Colored People (NAACP), for a march on Washington under the slogan 'We Loyal Negro American Citizens Demand the Right to Work and Fight for Our Country'.

Roosevelt was determined to stop the march, but was unable to get any concessions from the army. They had already reluctantly allowed a few black combat units and black aviators and had to tolerate a black brigadier-general, but they would not give way to Randolph's demand for integrated combat units. The Under Secretary of War, Patterson, claimed that such units were 'impossible' and suggested instead that blacks should be 'inspired to take pride in the efficiency of Negro units'. Thanks to the intercession of Mayor La Guardia of New

York, the President agreed to discuss the issue with Randolph at the White House. Roosevelt tried to charm Randolph, but the black leader had not come to Washington to listen to the President's anecdotes, and he demanded action. A committee was appointed to examine the question, but Randolph would not call off the march, announcing that 100,000 blacks were ready to descend on the capital to demand their rights. On 25 June 1941 Randolph called off the march and accepted Executive Order 8802 which stated that 'there shall be no discrimination in the employment of workers in defense industries or Government because of race, creed, color, or national origin'. A Fair Employment Practices Committee was established to investigate complaints. This was a major step forward in the struggle for civil rights, but it did not affect segregation in the armed forces and the FEPC soon came under criticism as a toothless organization.

The war changed little, and blacks found it very hard to work up much enthusiasm for a war which seemed unlikely to bring them any benefits. They gained little from increased employment and suffered endless humiliations from segregation, of which one of the more bizarre was the refusal of the army and the Red Cross to mix blood plasma from blacks and whites. There were some ugly race riots during the war, the worst in Detroit in June 1943 which resulted in the deaths of twenty-five blacks and nine whites. Six died in riots in Harlem in August. In June soldiers and sailors attacked Mexican 'zooters' in Los Angeles. The police arrested the victims, not the perpetrators. In none of these incidents did the President show the leadership essential if the situation were to improve. Although well advised by men such as Governor Earl Warren of California and La Guardia in New York, he did nothing but condemn 'mob violence'. Southern influence in the White House was too great for the President to take any decisive action. Blacks became increasingly frustrated and radicalized. They had done much to win the war abroad, but it seemed that they were losing the war at home. The war years offered a great opportunity for a radical improvement of race relations, as Gunnar Myrdal pointed out in his classic study *An American Dilemma*, published in 1944, but the opportunity was lost.

At the time of Pearl Harbor, Japanese Americans were a tiny minority without political significance. There were about 127,000 of them, mostly living on the west coast of whom 47,000 'Issei' had not been permitted to naturalize after the Immigration Act of 1924 which put a stop to Japanese immigration. The 80,000 remaining Japanese were divided between the American-born known as 'Nisei', and their third-generation children known as 'Sansei'. All three groups of

Japanese Americans suffered from all manner of discrimination, and in most states they were denied the right to vote or to own land. Excluded from American society, they preserved their own language, culture and religion and were thus seen as an alien element within the American melting pot.

Immediately after Pearl Harbor all Issei were treated as enemy aliens, but the restrictions placed upon them were not excessively onerous. Stimson announced that he was opposed to discrimination on the grounds of race, but this high-mindedness did not last for long. Rumours were rife that a Japanese–American fifth column was responsible for the Pearl Harbor disaster, and it was soon reported that the Japanese fleet was heading for Los Angeles, directed by the same sinister people. Japanese fishermen were immediately suspected of complicity in this foul plot, and many were arrested. Not a single charge could be substantiated. California was soon in the grip of racist hysteria which affected even men as fundamentally decent as the Attorney General, Earl Warren. It was a purely racist outbreak that took no account of the military situation or of individual loyalty. The Commanding Officer of the West Coast Defence Command, General DeWitt, summed up the general feeling succintly: 'A Jap's a Jap . . . It makes no difference whether he is an American citizen or not . . . I don't want any of them.'

Executive Order 9066 of February 1942 gave the War Department the right to designate military areas and then evacuate them. Stimson used this power only on the west coast, and exclusively against Japanese Americans. He delegated his authority to DeWitt, who at once set about moving the Japanese Americans from the coastal areas of Washington, Oregon and California. They lost almost all their property or were forced to sell at absurdly low prices. No other state wanted them. The governor of Idaho announced that: 'The Japs live like rats, breed like rats and act like rats. We don't want them.' Internment in camps therefore seemed to be the only answer, and by September 100,000 Japanese Americans were locked up in camps with totally inadequate facilities and intolerable living conditions. Even though life in these camps was harsh and disrupted traditional family patterns, thus causing severe generational conflicts, many Japanese Americans preferred to remain in them rather than risk the vicious hatred of their fellow Americans outside. It is also hardly surprising that few Japanese Americans volunteered to fight for a country that had denied them their rights and freedoms. About 1200 volunteered to form the 442 Regimental Combat Team along with a Japanese battalion recruited in Hawaii. They fought valiantly in Italy but were, of course, rigorously segregated. Others who refused to take an oath of loyalty to the United States, almost always as a protest against the way they had been mistreated, were rounded up in a special camp where they were subjected to further humiliations which in turn led to increasing militancy.

The Supreme Court upheld all these Government actions, although there were dissenting opinions. Mr Justice Frank Murphy accurately described the expulsion of the Japanese Americans from the west coast as 'legalized racism'. There was no military justification for this act and it was nothing more than the continuation and intensification of deep-rooted racist policies. It was not until 1968 that Japanese Americans were partially compensated for the property they had lost during the war. Canada, where the Japanese were similarly treated, did not make such a move for another twenty years.

Italians fared much better, even though the majority of Italian Americans were supporters of Mussolini and were strongly isolationist. They had two points in their favour: they were white, though regrettably not 'Anglo-Saxon', and they had political influence. Roosevelt lost many Italian votes in November 1940, in large part because of his condemnation of Italy for stabbing France in the back, and Democrat politicians were concerned about the Italian–American vote in the 1942 congressional elections in states such as Massachusetts, New York and Connecticut. They made sure that enemy alien laws were not applied harshly against Italians and that there was no overt discrimination against them. The war did much to integrate Italians into American society and although many were perhaps sorry that Italy lost the war, few were disappointed that the United States was victorious. It was an ambiguous attitude which was acceptable because of a certain patronizing attitude towards the Italians. Whereas the Japanese were totally alien and totally depraved and the Germans a deadly enemy, it was often difficult to take Mussolini's Italy quite seriously as an opponent.

The attitude of most Americans towards Jews was bound to be affected by the war and by the Nazi persecution, but sympathy for the fate of the European Jews came too late to be of much help. As in most other countries, a fatal mixture of anti-Semitism, red tape and bureaucratic indifference resulted in precious little being done to help those Jews who tried to escape from Hitler's clutches. There was never a majority in Congress willing to amend the 1924 Immigration Act. Breckinridge Long, Assistant Secretary of State in charge of immigration, was a vicious anti-Semite who hid his true feelings behind an implacably patrician facade. He was unalterably opposed to any changes in immigration policy, censored news of the final solution, and blocked efforts to ransom Jews. Most American Jews also opposed the mass immigration of their co-religionists on the grounds that it would lead to an increase of anti-Semitism, and in the case of many German Jews they were resentful of their abilities and high social standing.

Although there was never a really serious challenge to his presidency during the war years, Roosevelt had to contend with many opponents of the New Deal, both within his own party and among Republicans. Conservative Republicans had opposed aid to Great Britain and the Soviet Union until Pearl Harbor, and were determined to wrest the control of the party from Wendell Wilkie and the liberals and to undo the New Deal. They were supported in this endeavour by the Southern Democrats who stood for reduced Government spending, white supremacy and the assertion of states' rights against those of the federal Government.

Roosevelt was totally absorbed with fighting the war and was unwilling to devote much energy to the defence of the progressive social programmes which his opponents found so objectionable. With general prosperity there was little electoral benefit to be gained from a liberal policy. Most Americans complained about high taxation and the shortage of luxuries rather than the lack of subsidies and Government programmes for the disadvantaged.

The Office of Price Administration and its colourful and pugnacious head, Leon Henderson, were the objects of particular loathing and scurrility, in turn giving Henderson many excellent opportunities to counter-attack, which he did with much relish. In the course of 1942 a number of key commodities such as meat, coffee and shoes were rationed and prices were frozen at levels determined by the OPA. To the right the OPA, led by a veteran New Dealer, was nothing less than socialism and had to be stopped. Henderson, for all his very considerable abilities, was in no position to defend himself effectively. He was unable to control wages or the price of agricultural products. Worst of all, there were no available means of curbing inflation. The enormous increase of Government expenditure had put more money in people's pockets, but war production reduced the quantity of consumer goods so that demand far outstripped supply. Higher taxation, which would have counteracted this tendency, was politically unacceptable. Price controls were extended with the Price Control Act passed in October 1942, and the act also provided for the control of wages. This measure was only partially successful, but without a more rigorous fiscal policy inflation remained a problem, while price controls were a major irritant to merchants and were circumvented by a flourishing black market.

For inflation to be curbed and for the budget deficit to be kept within reasonable limits, taxes had to be increased. The Secretary of the Treasury, Henry Morgenthau Jr, although an advocate of voluntary saving to curb inflation, proposed some major increases in taxation in March 1942. These included increases in taxes on corporations and on high incomes, increases in death duties and in the taxes on luxury items, and the plugging of a number of tax loopholes. Opponents of these proposals suggested a sales tax, but Morgenthau pointed out that this would place an unfair burden on lower-income groups. A protracted debate ensued and a decision was postponed for fear that higher taxation would have an unfortunate effect on the congressional elections. It was not until October 1942 that Congress passed a Revenue Act which, although it did increase personal and corporate income taxes, contained a highly regressive 5 per cent tax on incomes above $624 per annum. Morgenthau accepted this inequitable tax only because it was slightly preferable to a sales tax and, along with price and wage controls, it did something to curb inflation.

The Republicans made substantial gains in the congressional elections in 1942 so that with their allies, the Southern Democrats, they had a comfortable majority. An analysis of the election by the Democratic Party showed that discontent with the OPA and its outspoken head, annoyance at the series of setbacks in the war in the Pacific, a widespread feeling that labour was being unduly favoured by a refusal to bring in wage controls while at the same time controlling prices, and disaffection with a swelling bureaucracy were the major factors accounting for the drop in support for the Democrats. Roosevelt took the hint. He dropped Henderson, shelved all social reform programmes and waited for the onslaught on the New Deal.

The Republicans came to Washington in 1943 determined to put an end to the left-wing, un-American, collectivist, inefficient and overstaffed New Deal. One by one the work-relief agencies of the New Deal were dissolved under this attack. The National Resources Planning Board, which provided a home for all manner of detestable Keynesians and crypto-socialists, was denied funding as was the Farm Security Administration, a key New Deal organization which protected farm labourers and small-holders and was thus the object of particular loathing by the propertied. The Rural Electrification Administration was also starved of funds. Schemes to improve social security and increase teachers' salaries in poor districts were voted down. The House Un-American Activities Committee, under the chairmanship of the appalling Martin Dies of Texas, began to root out people suspected of communist sympathies, or even of nudism, from the federal employ. The victims of this vicious witch-hunt were to be vindicated by the Supreme Court three years later. The Smith-Connally Bill of 1943 greatly restricted the right to strike and forbade union contributions to political campaigns.

In 1943 Morgenthau requested that $12 billion be raised by new taxes to defray increases in Government expenditure and to reduce the rate of inflation. Roosevelt, fully aware of the reaction to such a proposal on the Hill, reduced the Treasury's figure to $10.5 billion. Congress replied by passing a revenue Bill which provided a mere $2 billion in additional taxation and which included some attractive tax breaks. Roosevelt vetoed the Bill but Congress, for the first time in history, overrode the presidential veto, thus enacting a Bill which was foolish, selfish and in defiance of the administration.

In preparation for the 1944 presidential elections, Roosevelt proposed a comprehensive package of unemployment benefits, social security and educational opportunities for veterans. It was a skilful political move, for even conservative Congressmen felt that veterans were worthy of the nation's gratitude. They in turn would be grateful to the President for the GI Bill. Roosevelt knew that a programme of social reform, such as that proposed by Beveridge in Britain, would have no chance of success, but at least one important sector of the population could be covered by such a scheme, which might later be extended to all Americans. In March 1944 the Senate voted unanimously for the Bill.

In his 'State of the Union' address in January 1944 the President called for a second Bill of Rights which would guarantee security and prosperity for all. These rights would include the right to employment, to adequate wages, to a decent education, medical attention and financial support in the event of sickness, unemployment or old age, and freedom from monopolies. The speech warmed the heart of liberal America, but there was nothing of substance behind the dazzling rhetoric. During the election year Roosevelt stressed his economic Bill of Rights and the GI Bill, but avoided tendentious foreign-policy issues. He announced that he had only two war aims: to defeat the enemy and to prevent Germany and Japan from ever starting another war. With American troops going from success to success, landing in France in June 1944 and back in the Philippines in October, Roosevelt as Commander-in-Chief could only benefit. Few could argue with his professed war aim of world peace, and he did not make Woodrow Wilson's mistake of describing how he intended to achieve this lofty ambition.

For the Republicans, Dewey attempted to capture the middle ground by accepting the fundamental principles of the New Deal and by rejecting isolationism. He attacked the Roosevelt administration by suggesting that it was being led by the nose by the Soviet Union and Britain, who were determined to achieve their sinister and selfish post-war aims. He suggested that it was a one-man Government whose leader was so frail as to be unlikely to last out his term of office and whose mental capacity was declining rapidly. He suggested that the communists were gradually taking over the Democratic Party, that they controlled the CIO–PAC, and that the New Deal was essentially a communist front organization. Dewey claimed that the President had pardoned Earl Browder, the communist leader who had been imprisoned for passport fraud, in order to secure his help in the presidential election. The communists willingly complied, Dewey announced, because under a Roosevelt administration the American form of Government could be more easily changed. Dewey was able to convince many Catholics that Roosevelt was delivering the world to atheistic communism, and six million Polish electors became increasingly concerned that their mother country would be handed over to the Russians by the Roosevelt administration.

The President was warned by his advisors that the Republicans were making considerable gains with their claims that he was soft on communism, but although he lashed out against such 'misrepresentation, distortion and falsehood' he did not let himself get misled into conducting an apologetic and defensive campaign. He promised victory, a lasting peace and post-war prosperity. The picture he painted was comfortable and coincided with the desires of most Americans, the majority of whom believed that Roosevelt was capable of realizing this dream. The election was an easy victory, although his majority was somewhat reduced. The gain of twenty-two extra seats in the House of Representatives was not enough to change the balance of forces on the Hill.

For all the promises made during the campaign, it was clear that the Administration would continue on the same course. In foreign affairs there was indication that the President was moving to the right. When Cordell Hull resigned, Roosevelt made a number of curious senior appointments to the State Department including men of immense wealth such as Edward Stettinius, Nelson Rockefeller and William L. Clayton, or those of barely concealed fascist sympathies such as Julius C. Holmes and James C. Dunne. Henry Wallace was appalled, comforting himself with the hope that the President was like an oarsman 'looking one way and rowing another'. In the weeks after Yalta, Roosevelt made a number of impressive rhetorical utterances on the post-war world, but these were devoid of any substance. On 12 April 1945 he died as a result of a massive cerebral haemorrhage.

In Europe the war years were marked by a distinct left-turn in domestic politics resulting from a widespread desire for a more equitable and just society as compensation for past sacrifices and as a guarantee against a repetition of the horrors of war. In America, Roosevelt announced that 'Dr Win-the-War' had taken the place of 'Dr New Deal'. Americans had enjoyed exceptional prosperity during the war and saw no further purpose in social services for which they no longer had any need and which served only to help minorities whom they were determined to exclude. Only in the case of war veterans was it agreed that comprehensive social services should be provided at the taxpayers' expense. Americans rejected the welfare state as communist inspired. Their vision of the future was of a consumer society which rewarded hard work and individual initiative. It was a vision which for many was soon a reality. As the war ended there were more jobs, money and commodities than ever before. The memories of the depression had faded, the wartime restrictions were lifted. Americans settled down to enjoy the good life and saw little need to worry about social reform or even politics, whether domestic or foreign. Prosperity seemed a just reward for past efforts, and those who did not share in it had surely only themselves to blame.

CHAPTER EIGHT

Europe under the Nazis

Hitler's vision of a German-dominated Europe went far beyond any previous notions of power politics and hegemony. The guiding principle of his 'New Order' in Europe was racial. Thus the 'Nordic' peoples – Scandinavian, Dutch and Flemish – were to form the basis of the new Europe and stand united against the vast hordes of racially inferior Slavs in the east whose lands would be seized and exploited by Germanic colonists.

At first the Germans moved cautiously. Their long-term aims were disguised behind conventional if harsh occupation policies. France was divided into occupied and unoccupied zones, but Alsace-Lorraine was not formally annexed, nor was Luxembourg. Hitler intended to annex eastern France from the mouth of the Somme to the Argonne and Lake Geneva, thus incorporating Champagne, Burgundy and the Franche Comté into the Reich. A truncated France would never again be able to challenge Germany.

In Belgium the mining areas of Eupen, Malmedy and Moresnet were annexed in May 1940. Hitler proclaimed Wallonia in the south to be ancient German land and that the Flemish areas were an integral part of the 'Greater Germanic Reich'. The Germans permitted the Flemish National Association (VNV) to act as the political voice of the Flemish, but although the party was entrusted with important administrative posts by the occupation forces, its political aim was unification with Holland rather than with Germany. The Germans therefore sponsored a new party, the German–Flemish Association (DEVLAS), whose professed aim was the unification of Flanders and Germany.

In Wallonia there was already a home-grown fascist movement led by Léon Degrelle and the Germans indulged in some remarkable sophistry by announcing that the Walloons, in spite of the fact that they spoke French, were a Germanic race. No such bending of principles was need in the case of the Dutch, whose National Socialist Movement (NSB) under Anton Mussert worked for an autonomous Flemish state within a 'Federation of Germanic Peoples' under the leadership of Adolf Hitler.

Denmark was at first left as a theoretically sovereign state under military occupation, but Fritz Clausen's Danish National Socialist German Workers' Party (DNSAP) was seen as a useful ally with whose help Denmark would become a German province. In the person of Vidkun Quisling Norway provided the world with a new synonym for an unprincipled traitor. Curiously enough the Germans supported Quisling only because they could find no one else who was willing to co-operate with them, and they treated him with the contempt which he so richly deserved.

German occupation policy was dictated by three main considerations: military security, economic exploitation and racial domination. In the occupied countries each of these factors was given differing importance according to the role that was designated to it within the 'New Order'. In those countries where Germany's interests were largely political, a civil administration was established. Thus in Holland the civil administration was in the hands of Reich Commissar Seyss-Inquart who ran the country with the help of senior Dutch civil servants. He had little sympathy for Mussert's posturings. The Dutch fascist leader was merely allowed to establish a consultative Cabinet which had virtually no power. He was of little use to his masters except as a recruiting officer for the SS and as an enthusiastic persecutor of Dutch Jews. In much the same manner, Quisling's 'National Government', formed in February 1942, was completely controlled by Reich Commissar Terboven.

The General Government of Poland was also run by a civilian, Hans Frank, who ruled the unfortunate country from his court in Cracow and who was answerable directly to Hitler. The Baltic states of Estonia, Latvia and Lithuania formed the 'Ostland' satrapy of Heinrich Lohse, the Gauleiter of Schleswig-Holstein. Although he was nominally under the Minister for the Occupied Territories, Lohse was virtually independent and co-opted the local civil service. Although Himmler singled out the Lithuanians as racially worthless, it was generally considered that the Baltic peoples were 'racially related to the Germans' and they were encouraged in their hope that they would eventually enjoy a degree of autonomy within a greater Germany. Lohse felt that the Ruthenians were racially inferior, and they were therefore not allowed their own administration. The Reich Commissar for the Ukraine, Erich Koch, held a similar view of his subjects and Ukrainians were allowed only minor administrative posts at the communal level. Many Ukrainians were also permitted to give full vent to their basest instincts by joining the German army or the police, or by working as guards in the concentration camps.

Occupied France, Belgium, Greece and Serbia were regarded as being of essential military and strategic importance and therefore remained under military control. Belgian Nazis flocked into the ranks of the SS, but they were allowed little say in the running of the country. King Leopold appeared to be far too obsequious to the conquerors and too concerned with his creature comforts, and thus lost the sympathy of Belgian patriots without gaining that of the occupation authorities. Belgium was eventually given a civil administration in July 1944 under Josef Grohé, the Gauleiter of Cologne-Aachen.

Denmark had a unique position in that it was originally under neither civil nor military administration. The Danish Government remained in office, and even the armed forces were left untouched. The German Government transmitted its requests to the Danish Government through the traditional diplomatic channels. In October 1942 the German ambassador in Copenhagen was replaced by an SS plenipotentiary, SS Gruppenführer Best, who tried unsuccessfully to include a number of Danish Nazis in the Government. The Nazis made the grave mistake of allowing an election in March 1943 which resulted in the total repudiation of the German-backed Prime Minister, Erik Scavenius, and the Danish Nazis got a miserable 2 per cent of the popular vote. After this debacle, and with the Danish authorities insisting that those charged with sabotage of German military installations should be tried in Danish civil courts, the Germans imposed martial law on 29 August. The King was made a prisoner-of-war, Parliament was dissolved, the armed forces disbanded and the country was ruled by the German army.

With the failure of the *Blitzkrieg* against the Soviet Union, the economic exploitation of the occupied territories became a primary concern. Those who were not members of the 'racial community' were to be brutally forced to serve the German war machine. In the summer of 1941 there were already three million foreign workers in Germany. The longer the war lasted, the more the Germans were dependent on foreign labour. On 21 March 1942 the Gauleiter of Thuringia, Fritz Saukel, was appointed 'General Plenipotentiary for the Use of Labour' and he immediately began rounding up workers in the occupied territories. Whereas the workers recruited in western Europe were treated little differently from German workers, the 'eastern workers' (*Ostarbeiter*) were slaves. They were housed in dreadful camps, subjected to terrible punishments and given starvation rations. They were treated slightly better only towards the end of the war when it became obvious that half-dead workers were not particularly productive. In March 1944 Saukel estimated that of the five million foreign workers only 200,000 were volunteers, and the definition of 'volunteer' was exceedingly flexible. By the end of the summer the number of foreign workers had risen to 7.6 million. Many of them were Soviet prisoners-of-war who were treated with special brutality and whose destiny was particularly tragic. Of the 5.7 million Soviet prisoners-of-war, 3.3 million died in captivity. Many of those who survived were executed as deserters on their arrival back in their proletarian homeland or disappeared into the Gulag archipelago. For them the 'Saukel Action' was merely another stage in a life of endless suffering.

Of the more than 7 million foreign workers, 2.8 million were Soviet citizens, 1.7 million Poles, 1.3 million French, 590,000 Italians, 280,000 Czechs, 270,000 Dutch and 250,000 Belgians. About half of the agricultural workers and one-third of the workers in the armaments industry were foreigners. The ruthless exploitation of foreign labour, particularly that of the eastern workers, exposed as a complete sham the Nazi vision of a new Europe freed from the menace of 'Jewish bolshevism' and enjoying the benefits of German cultural supremacy. Some of Hitler's entourage suggested that certain concessions should be made to the European peoples in order to counteract the mounting opposition to German domination by giving them a stake in a more attractive future. Hitler rejected all such suggestions out of hand, insisting that any concessions would be taken as signs of weakness.

All the the Nazis could offer was a crusade against bolshevism, which some found attractive. 40,000 volunteers from the 'Germanic peoples' were to join the SS, but the SS soon ceased to be a racial elite. An increasing number of non-Germanic recruits were allowed into the ranks of the SS, the racial purists comforted by the thought that 'German mothers do not weep for dead foreigners'. By 1944, 150,000 Frenchmen, Ruthenians, Ukrainians, Albanians and Croats along with Bosnian and Turkish Muslims had joined the SS. Indian prisoners-of-war were also recruited by the SS and fought in France with singular lack of distinction. In the Soviet Union Cossacks, Georgians and Armenians were among the 'eastern troops' in the

Wehrmacht and Waffen-SS. They were used to put down the liberation movements in their own regions and later terrorized eastern Europe. Only in the case of General Vlasov and his 'Russian Army of Liberation' (ROA) did the Germans make any effort to win the support of anti-bolshevik elements in the Soviet Union. At first Hitler felt that Vlasov might be too independent and had him silenced, but by the autumn of 1944 the Germans were in need of all the help they could get and Himmler decided that this dubious character was a potentially valuable ally against the Soviet Union. In November 1944 a Committee for the Liberation of the Russian Peoples was formed at an imposing ceremony at the Hradschin in Prague. Vlasov then recruited a rag-tag army from Soviet prisoners-of-war, eastern workers and Soviet soldiers in the Wehrmacht and Waffen-SS. The troops were militarily worthless, frequently ran amok and were later disposed of by the appropriate Soviet authorities with customary brutality.

The vast majority of the people in occupied Europe had little to hope for but survival. A minority took a more active course, either as collaborators or in the resistance movements. As repression increased, with mass murder and deportations, slave labour and economic exploitation, plunder and the denial of the last vestiges of independence, the resistance grew in strength and determination, encouraged by increasing signs that the Nazi empire was collapsing. The resisters saw their task as assisting the Allies to defeat Germany by attacking 'Fortress Europe' from within. They differed widely in their political aims, which ranged from conservative nationalism to militant communism.

In the summer of 1940 the British Government set up the Special Operations Executive (SOE) to co-ordinate subversion and sabotage in occupied Europe. Churchill was much taken by what he called the 'Ministry of Ungentlemanly Warfare', and hoped that Germany could be defeated with a combination of bomber offensive, blockade and subversion. Hugh Dalton, the Minister of Economic Warfare, was appointed head of the new organization and, fired by a vision of stalwart anti-fascist proletarians casting off the fascist yoke, a romantic notion typical of a Wykehamist socialist remote from the working class, he took up Churchill's challenge to 'set Europe ablaze'. Although there was ample indication that guerilla activity in these early stages of the war was failing to have any significant impact, it was fondly believed in Whitehall that militant resisters were widespread and merely needed co-ordination to become deadly.

Active resistance began in France in the summer of 1941. The communists with their underground party organization were in the best position to conduct guerilla operations. Now that the Soviet Union was fighting for its life, the communists felt obliged to end their tacit support for Nazi Germany as the ally of the Soviet Union, and partisan groups – *Franc-Tireurs et Partisans* (FTP) – went into action carrying out a number of assassinations and acts of sabotage. The Germans reacted by executing a large number of innocent hostages and imposing harsh communal fines, which in turn served only to increase the hostility of the French to the occupying forces. Vichy's Minister of the Interior, Pucheu, also took harsh measures against the partisans since the three major partisan groups were based in unoccupied France. Former soldiers and Christian democrats, led by Henri Fresnay and Georges Bidault, formed their own partisan group, *Combat*, and socialist trades unionists founded another, *Libération*. In occupied France the socialists formed *Libération-Nord* and the right created the *Organisation Civile et Militaire* (OCM). These and other smaller groups established contact with de Gaulle's Free French in London, and in January 1942 Jean Moulin was sent by de Gaulle to France to co-ordinate these resistance groups. Moulin overcame a number of political obstacles with great skill, and in May 1943 the *Conseil National de la Résistance* (CNR) was formed in Paris. Shortly afterwards Moulin was arrested by the Gestapo, tortured and killed.

With the increasing activities of the resistance groups in France, the SS under Gruppenführer Oberg took over policing duties from the military authorities. He co-opted the French militia, which was the cause of further bitterness among French patriots, and strengthened the appeal of the resistance. The armed resisters of the *Maquis* were provided with weapons by SOE and in February 1944 were combined as the *Forces Françaises de l'Intérieur* (FFI). The *Maquis* was particularly active in the mountainous regions of southern France and tied down a large number of German troops. The resistance played an important role during the Normandy invasion – General Eisenhower estimated that they were worth fifteen divisions. On 10 June 1944 troops of the SS Panzer Division *Das Reich* took a terrible revenge for activities of the FFI which had seriously slowed down their advance towards the Normandy battlefields. At Oradur-sur-Glane all adult males were executed and the women and children locked in the church where they were either shot or burned alive. The village was razed to the ground in a lasting symbolic act of Nazi brutality.

Relations between the French resistance and the western Allies were never smooth. The resisters complained that the Allies did not take them seriously and failed to provide them with the arms they needed. They bitterly resented British and American air raids on French towns and argued that they could do the job better if they were given the tools. The Allies tended to underestimate the effectiveness of the resistance and exaggerated the political differences between the various groups to the point of believing that France was on the brink of a civil war which the communists, as the most experienced and effective resistance group, would win. Co-ordination between the Allied forces and the resistance was poor, resulting in unnecessarily high losses and to the unfounded communist charges that de Gaulle was trying to destroy the resistance for selfish political reasons. Yet in spite of all these difficulties, the resistance played an important role both militarily and politically as the advance guard of the patriotic struggle against Nazi tyranny.

In Belgium the illegal political parties, the universities and the Catholic Church under the leadership of Cardinal van Roey kept alive the ideal of a free Belgium and did much to immunize the population against Nazi propaganda. An active resistance group, *L'Armée Secrète*, was recruited from the different political parties and carried out a number of actions against the occupation forces and collaborators. The communist-led *Front de l'Indépendence* (FI) was the most effective of the armed resistance groups. The *Légion Belge* was largely made up of former soldiers and was determined not only to co-operate closely with the Allied forces after the Normandy landings but also to ensure that Belgium did not fall into the hands of the communists as soon as the Germans left.

Whereas the communists played a key role in the resistance in both France and Belgium, and the fear of a communist takeover after the liberation was widespread, elsewhere in western Europe the communists were of little significance. In Holland all the resistance groups were loyal to the monarchy and to the constitution and there was almost complete agreement between them and the Government-in-exile in London, which also worked closely with SOE. In the early stages of the occupation the universities at Leyden and Delft were centres of the resistance, but they were closed down and many professors and students were sent to concentration camps in Germany. There were outbreaks of strikes during the occupation, first in protest against the provocative activities of the Dutch Nazis in 1941 and then in April and May 1943 when the German army ordered all Dutch prisoners-of-war to be once again interned. This protest was put down with the utmost brutality by Reich Commissar Seyss-Inquart, which in turn had the effect of winning recruits for the resistance organizations, such as the *Orde Dienst*, the *Knokploegen* and the *Rad van Verzet*. Unfortunately the Abwehr and the SD managed to crack the codes used by the Dutch resistance when transmitting to England in an operation codenamed the 'England Game' (*Englandspiel*), with the result that agents and supplies dropped into Holland were captured on arrival and the resistance was infiltrated by German agents. Nevertheless the resistance groups combined in September and October 1944 to form the *Binnenlandse Strijdkrachten* (Home Forces) under the command of Prince Bernhard. A railway strike greatly hindered the movement of German troops and supplies moving up to Arnhem and Nijmwegen. The strike continued until the liberation, and the Germans responded by starving the country. In the 'starvation winter' of 1944–45 10,000 people died of hunger in the province of Limburg alone.

In Denmark the situation was complicated by the fact that the country still had a legal national Government so that resistance amounted to treason, and the exiled 'Danish Council' in London had no influence at home. SOE pressed for sabotage action, but the Danish Government was anxious not to provoke the Germans. It was not until early 1943, after the German defeat at Stalingrad, that sabotage activities began, most of them carried out by SOE agents dropped into Denmark. German reprisals were countered by strikes and culminated in the proclamation of martial law by the German occupation authorities. The Danish resistance reacted by forming a 'Freedom Council' which co-ordinated the efforts of the different resistance groups. Its first major test came in June 1944 when the Germans imposed a curfew in Copenhagen. The Freedom Council called for a general strike, which was entirely successful and the curfew was lifted. After a second general strike in September the Germans interned the entire Danish police force and deported its officers to Germany. In the winter of 1944 Danish resistance groups carried out a series of actions against German troops as they withdrew from Scandinavia back to the Reich. The Soviets still refused to recognize the Danes as Allies, for they could not forgive the Government for joining the anti-Comintern pact in 1941, even though it had done so under duress. The western Allies had no such qualms and eventually the Soviets gave way. Denmark took part in the founding congress of the United Nations and was thus formally accepted as an Allied power.

Norway had a remarkably well-organized and effective resistance movement which was led by the President of the Supreme Court, Paal Berg, and by the head of the state Church, Bishop Berggrav. The

'Home Front' was supported by socialists and trade unionists as well as by conservative patriots. The military side of the resistance, *Milorg*, established arms depots and built up armed forces ready to support an Allied landing as well as carry out a number of spectacular sabotage actions. The most impressive of these was the destruction of the heavy-water plant at Rjukan in co-operation with Norwegian agents from England. The political wing of the resistance organized a series of strikes which in turn led to the proclamation of a state of emergency in September 1941, which was followed by a wave of arrests and deportations to Germany. Many Norwegians avoided labour service in Germany or recruitment into the Wehrmacht by fleeing to Sweden or by joining the Home Front in the mountains. In October 1944 Soviet troops entered northern Norway, and the resistance systematically attacked the German troops as they withdrew from Finland and Norway.

The Poles built up an elaborate resistance network in close contact with the Government-in-exile of General Sikorski in London. The military side was first called the Association for Armed Struggle (ZWZ) and from February 1942 was known as the Home Army (AK). It took its orders from the Commander-in-Chief in London. The Political Co-ordination Committee (PKP) amounted to a virtual underground Government with a Council of National Unity representing the exiled parliament and an official delegate from the Polish Government in London. The dilemma facing the Polish Government and underground was that it was fighting a war on two fronts against both the Germans and the Soviets. They were determined to restore the frontiers of August 1939 and thus were in continued conflict with the Soviets, even after 22 June 1941. At first these problems were pushed into the background. All of Poland was occupied by the Germans and the Red Army was the only means by which they could be driven back. The Polish underground therefore supplied the Soviets with intelligence and conducted sabotage actions on the lines of communication to the eastern front. The communists had their own partisan movement, the People's Army (AL), which was independent from the AK and subservient to Moscow. The partisan movements, both nationalist and communist, had no shortage of recruits. The extreme brutality of German rule in Poland was such that people flocked to the partisans as the only hope of saving Poland from abject slavery.

On 26 April 1943 the Soviets finally broke off diplomatic relations with the Polish Government in London and sponsored a rival, communist-dominated Union of Polish Patriots in Moscow and an underground parliament, the National Patriotic Council (KRN), organized by Boleslaw Bierut. The London Poles still imagined that they could convince the Russians to drop these communist-sponsored organizations by co-operating as far as possible with the Red Army and by stepping up sabotage operations against the Germans. For this they needed weapons from SOE, but the British concentrated on western and south-eastern Europe and regarded Poland as being within the Soviet sphere of operations. Flights to Poland from Britain were also a major difficulty, although almost 500 sorties were made prior to the Warsaw uprising. The planes were from SOE, the pilots mainly Polish volunteers. The Poles resented this reluctance on the part of the British, but the Home Army, commanded since June 1943 by General 'Bor' (Komorowski), was supplied with enough arms to launch 'Operation Hurricane', an intensification of sabotage actions and attacks on German troops to assist the Soviet advance. The Soviets were scarcely appreciative of these efforts. They refused to assist the Home Army, promptly disarmed all units on establishing contact with them and shipped these dangerously bourgeois nationalists off to the Gulag. In such circumstances it was hardly surprising that some units of the Home Army found themselves fighting the Germans, the Soviets and the Polish-communist Berling Army. On 27 July 1944 the Soviets broke with the London Poles and recognized the National Committee of Liberation in Lublin as the legitimate Government of Poland.

The Home Army had long been planning a national uprising designed, in General Bor's words, to demonstrate the 'existence of Poland'. On 27 July the London Poles informed Eden that an uprising in Warsaw was imminent and asked for military assistance. The Chiefs of Staff felt that it was operationally impossible to give the insurgents any material help, and therefore turned down the request. On 29 July Moscow Radio broadcast an appeal to the population of Warsaw to rise up and join battle with the Germans. Three days later the uprising began. The Red Army was held up on the Vistula and could not get to Warsaw, but Vishinsky told the British and American ambassadors that the uprising was utterly irresponsible and that the Soviet Government had no intention of helping. Stalin referred to the Warsaw insurgents as 'criminals' and made it plain that he was delighted to see them massacred by the Germans under SS Obergruppenführer Bach-Zelewski with the able assistance of the infamous Kaminski Brigade, made up of Soviet prisoners-of-war. On 4 October the insurgents were forced to surrender. Warsaw was flattened as 16,000 members of the Home Army were killed along with 150,000 civilians. At the last moment the Soviets allowed American planes to land on their airfields, but it was far too late to afford the Poles any help and it was also too late for them to save face. The Home Army called off 'Hurricane', for it was obvious that any hope of a positive result from co-operation with the Soviets was futile. Once the whole of Poland was occupied by the Red Army, the Home Army was dissolved. Its new leader, General Okulicki, was arrested and with the representative of the London Poles, Jankowski, tried in Moscow and despatched to a prison camp to serve a lengthy sentence.

In the Reich Protectorate of Bohemia and Moravia a resistance movement was also formed at the very beginning of the German occupation. It centred around the intellectuals and students who were particularly affected by the closing of the university in Prague and the arrest of the entire student body following a demonstration on the Czech national day, 28 October 1939. They were joined by ex-officers and civil servants. The supporters of Benes founded the Central Political Organization (PU) and the former soldiers the National Defence (ON) under the command of General Ingr. The various resistance groups were co-ordinated by the Central Command of the Home Resistance (UVOD) which remained in close contact with the exiled Government in London.

At first these Czech resistance groups concentrated on propaganda, passive resistance and the gathering of intelligence. The communists, controlled by Klement Gottwald from Moscow, began sabotage activities as soon as the Germans invaded the Soviet Union, and mocked the passivity of the non-communist resistance. On 27 May 1942 Czech agents, who had been carefully trained in England, assassinated Heydrich, who had been appointed Reich Protector the previous September and who had established a reign of terror of a brutality remarkable even by Nazi standards. In retribution the Germans razed the village of Lidice to the ground, shot all the males and sent the women to concentration camps along with such children as were deemed unsuitable for 'germanization'. The German security forces proved so efficient that they virtually wiped out the Czech underground, and none of the agents dropped by SOE lasted for more than a few hours before being rounded up.

The communists called for combined national committees at the local level, but the non-communist groups were rightly suspicious of their motives. It was not until the Red Army reached the Carpathians that the democratic parties agreed to the formation of a Slovak National Council which included communists and which organized an uprising coinciding with that in Warsaw. Although the Slovak uprising was an impressive affair, it was crushed by the Germans since the Red Army failed to cross the Carpathians in time to give the Slovaks the assistance they desperately needed. It was not until April 1945 that the Red Army enabled Benes to return to Kosice in Slovakia with the exiled Government. On 5 May, by which time Hitler was already dead, the Czechs began their uprising in Prague. It was a largely symbolic gesture. Two days later the European war was over.

It was part of the irony of the war that the collaborators often created a climate in which the resistance could organize, and that the resistance frequently did little but provoke terror and destruction. There were decent men among the collaborators and cynical villains among the resisters, but in the final count it was the resisters who stood up against tyranny, injustice and oppression and had a vision of a better and freer world. The true tragedy is that few of these dreams were realized.

For the European Jews collaboration was made virtually impossible by Nazi racial fanaticism, and there could be no Jewish Quislings, Musserts or Degrelles. Avraham Gancwajch, a former Zionist, acted as an informant in the Warsaw ghetto. Some members of the *Judenräte* imagined that they could save their own skins if they co-operated with the Nazis. The Jewish police rounded up the victims for deportation. The two presidents of the Dutch Jewish Council, Asscher and Cohen, collaborated with the Germans, arguing that otherwise things would be worse. A bitter joke among Dutch Jews was that when only Asscher and Cohen were left and the SS demanded that one of them be deported, Cohen said to Asscher: 'It had better be you Abraham – lest worse befall the rest of us.'

For Jews, collaboration could at most amount to an attempt to save one's own skin. Resistance could never be much more than an act of collective desperation. The Jews were herded together in ghettos and camps and were under constant police supervision. Only as victims were they united. They had widely differing political ideologies; many were confused by a lingering nationalism and there was precious little that could bind them together to resist. They had no Government-in-exile, no help from the Allies and no traditions of national independence. In many instances they were not only persecuted by the Nazis but also rejected by their own countries. As Emmanuel Ringelblum wrote in his basement in the Warsaw ghetto, for most Jews the best that could be hoped for was an honourable and dignified death, befitting an ancient people with a history stretching back over the centuries.

When German troops marched into Austria and Czechoslovakia,

they were accompanied by special troops (*Einsatzgruppen*) from the security police who seized Jewish property and made a large number of somewhat haphazard arrests. In the same manner, Himmler and Heydrich sent the *Einsatzgruppen* into Poland where they disappropriated and isolated the Jewish population. Dr Hans Frank, head of the 'General Government', that part of Poland which had not been absorbed by either the Reich or the Soviet Union, ordered all Jews to wear the star of David. Jews were forbidden to use the railways, forced into slave labour and herded into ghettos in the larger towns such as Lodz, Warsaw, Cracow, Lublin and Radom. Jews from Vienna and Czechoslovakia were also sent to these Polish ghettos.

In September 1939 Heydrich told the army Commander-in-Chief, Brauchitsch, that he intended to create a 'Jewish reservation' somewhere in Poland so that the Reich could be freed from Jews. But the idea of a reservation near Lublin was never taken very seriously and Hitler said that it was not a satisfactory solution to the Jewish problem. There is every indication that in these early stages mass murder was already regarded as preferable to a reservation. On 21 September 1939 Heydrich ordered the leaders of the *Einsatzgruppen* to treat their oral instructions as to the final goal of his Jewish policy as absolutely secret. Since every other form of persecution was apparent to all, he can only have meant murder.

Special units of the security police were given specific orders to 'liquidate' the Polish intelligentsia, and although there is no documentary evidence it would seem likely that similar orders were given to begin the mass murder of Jews. SS Obergruppenführer Udo von Woyrsch and his *Einsatzgruppe* went on the rampage in Galicia, and elsewhere in Poland countless Jews were murdered. A number of SS men were court-martialed for the murder of Jews, for the SS was subject to military law, but Hitler issued a general amnesty at the beginning of October 1939 and a few days later removed the SS from military and civil jurisdiction. The bandmaster of the *Leibstandarte Adolf Hitler* could breathe a sigh of relief. He had been charged with the murder of fifty Jews in Blonie and now was immune from prosecution.

With the murderers and bully-boys in the SS restrained only by SS law, there followed an endless series of murders of Polish Jews, while the slaughter of the intelligentsia and the murder of patients deemed 'unworthy of life' in the hospitals and psychiatric clinics continued apace. The euthanasia programme was ordered directly by Hitler and was organized by Philipp Bouhler from the Reich Chancellery. Known as T4 (the offices were at Tiergartenstrasse 4 in Berlin), the extermination agency was kept secret, its officers working under assumed names and the link with the Chancellery carefully disguised. It was only a short step from the mass murder of the incurably sick and the mentally disturbed to the mass murder of Jews. The arguments used in both cases were identical. After visiting the ghetto in Lodz in November 1939, Goebbels remarked that the destruction of these 'animals' was a 'surgical task' which had to be performed, otherwise Europe would be destroyed by the 'Jewish disease'. Hitler also believed that the Jewish problem was 'clinical' rather than 'social'. This argument was forcefully presented in the propaganda film *The Eternal Jew*, which showed the Jews migrating along the same routes through Europe as rats and thus spreading plague and pestilence. The Jews as the spreaders of disease whose destruction was therefore justifiable on strictly hygienic grounds was a widely believed myth. A map to this effect can still be found in a popular historical atlas from a highly regarded publishing house in the Federal Republic of Germany.

There were a number of considerations which restrained those Nazis who were anxious to begin the systematic murder of Jews. Hitler still hoped to win over the British and did not wish to alienate the Americans, and feared that large-scale massacres of Jews might have an unfortunate effect on public opinion in those countries. The persecution of German Jews was not generally regarded with revulsion in Britain or the United States, but even in more rigorously anti-Semitic circles mass murder might well have been considered a trifle excessive. There were also a number of complaints from the army in Poland that the brutal treatment of Jews by the SS created a negative impression among the troops, and objections were raised to the plunder of Jewish property by SS officers. General Blaskowitz, the Army Commander East, repeatedly complained about the outrageous behaviour of the SS and warned that the inhuman treatment of the Jews would serve to arouse the sympathies of the Poles and of Catholics, who would become united in their opposition to Nazi Germany.

The SS did not have a 'Führer order' to murder Jews, and therefore found it somewhat difficult to answer the moral objections of a number of senior army officers. Heydrich complained that the order to exterminate the Polish intelligentsia had not been published to the army and that therefore the SS appeared to be acting in an arbitrary and lawless manner. Hatred of Jews was said to be the mark of a true National Socialist, and outrages against Poles were excused as revenge for the murderous activities of Poles against Germans in September 1939. Hitler made it perfectly clear which side he was on. He silenced

Brauchitsch's timid objections and raved about the 'Salvation Army attitude' of the military. At the end of October he placed Poland under civil administration and Heinrich Himmler, as 'Reich Commissar for the Strengthening of the German Race', was ordered to 'eradicate the harmful influence of populations alien to the German people and which present a danger to the Reich and to the German racial community'.

In June 1940 Heydrich pointed out to Ribbentrop that there were already three and a quarter million Jews in the territory under German jurisdiction and argued that since emigration could no longer solve the problem, a 'territorial final solution' had to be found. Shortly afterwards, Rademacher of the 'Jewish Section' (*Judenreferat*) of the Foreign Office suggested that France should hand over Madagascar as a resettlement area for four million Jews. Himmler would appoint a governor for the island which would be administered by Heydrich's security police. The idea was developed by Eichmann, enthusiastically endorsed by Himmler and approved by Hitler. Just as Karl Paasch had argued in 1892 for his New Guinea plan, it was assumed that the Jews would be unable to survive the inhospitable climate and the tropical diseases of the island. Europe would be free of Jews, who would eventually die out in their new home.

In the summer of 1940 Hitler hinted that he intended to exterminate the European Jews. Goebbels also decided that the time had come to get rid of them. At a time when Hitler was beginning preparations for his great ideological war against the Soviet Union, the Madagascar plan was dropped and gradually replaced by plans for systematic genocide. The planners of this war for *Lebensraum* suggested that some thirty to forty million Soviet citizens would die in the crusade against bolshevism, and in March 1941 Hitler told the officers designated as commanders of 'Operation Barbarossa' that he intended to destroy bolshevism and to eliminate the commissars and political functionaries along with the 'Jewish-bolshevik intelligentsia'. In none of these statements or orders was there any mention of an intention to begin the mass murder of Jews. On the other hand, it was quite clear that the SS was about to murder a large number of Jews and that they would not be subject to any legal restraints or tormented by any moral qualms.

The leaders of the *Einsatzgruppen* were given intensive training in preparation for their work in the Soviet Union. They were told that they would have to exterminate four distinct groups: Soviet functionaries, 'inferior Asiatics', Gypsies and Jews. On 17 June 1941 Heydrich told the commanders of the four *Einsatzgruppen* that the murder of Soviet Jews was merely the first stage of a programme to kill all European Jews. Immediately after the invasion of the Soviet Union the *Einsatzgruppen* began their work. *Einsatzkommando* 3 proudly reported on 25 November 1941 that they had to date executed 1064 communists, 56 partisans, 653 people suffering from mental illnesses, 44 Poles, 28 Russian prisoners-of-war, 5 Gypsies, 1 Armenian and 136,421 Jews. By the beginning of December 1941 more than 400,000 Soviet Jews had been murdered, among them the 35,000 victims of the massacre at Babi Yar in Kiev in September. In the first nine months after the invasion the SS murdered some 750,000 Jews.

Although many German soldiers were appalled at these mass murders, most preferred to ignore them. Some actively participated. War on the eastern front was brutal, and soldiers gradually became indifferent towards all forms of barbarity. General von Reichenau, commanding the 6th Army, issued an order in October 1941 in which he told his troops that they were not only 'soldiers bound by the rules of the art of war, but also standard bearers of an inexorable racial idea'. It was therefore essential for them to 'have a complete understanding of the necessity for the hard but necessary atonement of Jewish subhumanity.' Reichenau's text was adopted by von Rundstedt, praised by Hitler and issued by Brauchitsch to all German units on the eastern front. Manstein and Hoth produced their own orders which were couched in even more extreme language.

The army not only supported the murderous activities of the security police by such orders, it also provided logistical support and allowed them to take Jewish prisoners-of-war from camps run by the Wehrmacht. It was not only units of the Waffen-SS which helped the *Einsatzkommandos* with the mass executions; army units also took part on a number of occasions. The complicity of the army in the murder of Soviet Jews is beyond all doubt, although individual soldiers bravely resisted and refused to compromise either their moral standards or their human decency.

In March 1941 Hitler discussed the future of Poland with the Governor General, Hans Frank. He announced that his long-term aim was the 'germanization' of Poland, but that was a process which would take fifteen to twenty years. His immediate aim was to make Poland free from Jews (*Judenrein*). Since he had already abandoned the Madagascar plan, and since there was no discussion of deporting the Polish Jews to the Soviet Union, it would seem clear that Hitler had already decided that they should be murdered. Heydrich's statement to the *Einsatzgruppen* commanders on 17 June 1941 that all European

Jews would be killed could never have been made without an orde[r to] that effect from Himmler, which in turn depended on a decision by Hitler, for which there is sufficient supporting evidence.

On 31 July Goering signed a document, which was almost certainly prepared by Heydrich, which called for 'all the necessary organizational, practical and material preparations to be taken for the complete solution of the Jewish question in German-controlled Europe'. Heydrich was instructed to 'present a plan for the preliminary steps for the execution of the intended final solution of the Jewish question'.

At the end of August a murder squad under Christian Wirth, which had gained considerable experience in the use of carbon monoxide to kill mental patients in the euthanasia programme T4, was sent to Lublin. The euthanasia programme had been temporarily halted due to public protests, particularly by the churches. Wirth was placed under the direct command of Odilo Globocnik, the SS and police chief in Lublin, a former gauleiter of Vienna and intimate of Himmler's, who called him 'Globus' (globe). His task was described as 'special duties for the Führer' and he was paid from Hitler's personal chancellery. The first major step in 'Operation Reinhard', the codename for the murder of the Polish Jews, was the construction of an extermination camp at Belzec, to the south-east of Lublin, which began in November. By March 1942 Wirth could begin his programme of mass murder using carbon monoxide in the T4 tradition.

Himmler had serious reservations about the mass shooting of Jews. He had witnessed such executions near Minsk and found the spectacle troubling. He ordered the investigation of a more 'humane' method of killing, by which he meant one which did not place so much strain on the executioners. Carbon-monoxide gas, which had already been used to kill some 70,000 in the euthanasia programme, seemed ideal. The *Einsatzgruppen* were provided with mobile gas chambers, 'S wagons', in which at least 100,000 Jews died.

The camp at Belzec had hardly begun to function when work on a second camp at Sobibór began. A third camp was built at Treblinka under the supervision of a euthanasia specialist, Dr Eberl. All three camps were small, cheaply built and designed solely for mass killing. Christian Wirth was given overall responsibility for the three camps, and his staff of almost one hundred people conducted the killings. Most of the guards were Ukrainian prisoners-of-war. The camps were almost entirely financed by the sale of property taken from the victims. Some one and a half million Jews were killed in these three camps, the vast majority from Poland.

The largest and most notorious of the death camps was at Auschwitz (Oswiecim). In addition to an old Austro-Hungarian cavalry barracks, 40 square kilometres were seized in the autumn of 1939 and seven villages cleared to make way for the camp, which at first housed Polish political prisoners. In May 1940 Rudolf Höss, a Nazi veteran, convicted terrorist and previously in charge of the camps at Dachau and Sachsenhausen, was appointed commandant. On 1 March 1941, almost four months before the German invasion of the Soviet Union, Himmler visited the camp and ordered that it should be extended to house 100,000 Soviet prisoners-of-war who were to work as slaves in agricultural enterprises run by the SS and in an artificial rubber factory for IG Farben. In the course of the summer of 1941 Himmler told Höss that the Führer intended to eliminate all the Jews he could lay his hands on, and that Auschwitz would play a vital role in this task because of the excellent railway connections.

On 3 September some 600 Soviet officers were gassed in an experiment conducted at Auschwitz using a powerful granular delousing agent, Zyklon B. A further 6000 Soviet prisoners-of-war were gassed in the following weeks, along with as many as 100,000 Jews. The mass murder of Jews at Auschwitz thus began in the autumn of 1941 and ran parallel to the mass shootings in the Soviet Union. In order to accommodate an increasing number of victims, Höss expanded the camp, building Auschwitz II at Birkenau which was designed exclusively for mass murder, and Auschwitz III at Monowitz for IG Farben's slaves.

In September 1941 Himmler ordered the building of a new camp at Majdanek, near Lublin, which was intended to form part of a racial Maginot Line running from East Prussia to Galicia. Since the camp was in the territory of the General Government of Poland, it was designated as a prisoner-of-war camp so as not to fall under the jurisdiction of Hans Frank. It was staffed by men who had proved themselves proficient as torturers and tormentors at Buchenwald, and the camp served as both a prisoner-of-war camp and an extermination plant for Jews and sundry undesirable Gentiles. A further camp was built by the RSHA at Theresienstadt to the north-west of Prague. It was designed for German Jews who had been decorated in the First World War or who had proof of similar distinguished service to the Fatherland. They were given a temporary reprieve from deportation to the death camps in the east and compared with their fellow sufferers they were given favoured treatment. Heydrich's motives for building this special camp were purely cynical and tactical. Most of the German Jews were fully assimilated and it was felt that were they to be sent directly to the gas chambers there might be some awkward questions asked by friends concerned about their fate.

The deportation of Jews from Germany, mostly to Poland, had begun as early as December 1939. In October 1940, 6500 Jews from Baden and the Saarpfalz were deported to Lyon without the Vichy officials being consulted. The oldest member of this group was aged a hundred and four, and one-third of them were over 60. They were intended to be the first batch of up to 270,000 Jews to be dumped on the reluctant Vichy authorities. The French protested vigorously to the armistice officials in Wiesbaden, with the result that the Germans were a little more restrained in their attempts to unload their unwanted Jews on the anti-Semitic Vichy authorities.

In March 1941, 5000 Viennese Jews were deported to the General Government, but it was not until October 1941, when it seemed that victory over the Soviet Union was imminent, that Kurt Daluege, the head of the 'Order Police', began the systematic evacuation of Jews from Germany in order to render the Reich *Judenrein*. Between mid October and mid November 20,000 German Jews were deported and confined in the ghetto at Lodz where they were to wait their turn to go to the death camp at Chelmno, where three gas trucks stood ready. The Chelmno camp was an improvisation, designed as a stop-gap until the big camps were ready to receive their victims. Prisoners were killed on arrival – there were no barracks for them to stay in.

From the middle of November to February 1942 a further 40,000 German Jews were deported to Warsaw, Riga, Minsk and Kowno. Most of them were murdered by the *Einsatzgruppen* on arrival. Thus by the autumn of 1941 there was no question that all European Jews were to be murdered and that the decision for this 'final solution to the Jewish question', as the Nazis brutally called it, had been taken at the very highest level. When the German authorities in Belgrade enquired on 12 September 1941 whether Serbian Jews were to be sent to Russia or to the General Government, the RSHA replied that they were to be shot on the spot. Similarly, a junior official in the Ministry for Occupied Territories instructed the Reich's Commissar for the Baltic on 25 October 1941 to kill all German Jews who were unable to work, by means of equipment to be provided by T4. No orders of such momentous impact could have been given without the sanction of an 'order from the Führer'. The fact that there is no written order to this effect signed by Hitler is totally irrelevant, since there are virtually no such orders on any topic. The suggestion that the lack of a written order is proof that Hitler did not know what was going on, or that he was a weak dictator who allowed the murder of millions to occur behind his back, would be ignored as frivolous attention seeking were these bizarre notions not held by a number of otherwise competent historians.

If Hitler were indeed unaware of the mass murder of Jews, at least until 1943, then he was one of the very few senior officials who did not know what was happening. At a press conference on 18 November 1941, Rosenberg announced that the 'biological eradication of the European Jews' was about to begin. On 16 December, Hans Frank told his senior functionaries that the Jewish question 'must somehow or other lead to successful annihilation (*Vernichtungserfolg*)'. Paul Wurm, who was on the editorial board of Streicher's appalling journal *Der Stürmer*, told Rademacher, the expert on Jewish questions in the Foreign Office, that he had heard from a senior Nazi official that 'a number of Jewish bugs would soon be exterminated'.

Initially it had been assumed that the 'final solution' would take place at the end of the war, but the invasion of the Soviet Union was in part a racial crusade against 'Jewish bolshevism' and was marked from the outset by the murderous activities of the *Einsatzgruppen* and Waffen-SS. The decision to murder all the Jews of Europe in the middle of the war presented Eichmann and his staff with many difficulties, all of which they overcame with ghastly efficiency. Transportation was a major problem, but in many instances the shipment of victims to the death camps took precedence over military requirements. Thus 1200 Jews were sent from Rhodes to Auschwitz, and this meant that no transport was available for the German troops when they were forced to evacuate the island shortly afterwards. Many Jews were skilled craftsmen who were desperately needed in the war industry, but complaints from industrialists were answered with the statement that 'economic considerations should not be taken into account in dealing with this problem'.

On 20 January 1942 a conference was held at the former Interpol headquarters in Berlin, am Grossen Wannsee 56–58, to discuss the 'final solution'. The 'Wannsee conference' did not mark a significant new step in the mass murder of Jews which was already in full swing, but it did reaffirm the determination to continue the extermination of the Jews before the end of the war, and it also established the principle that Jews who were capable of working should be given a temporary reprieve from the gas chambers. As a result of this decision, doctors such as Josef Mengele had to decide which prisoners were able to work and which should be sent directly to the gas chambers. Participants at the conference included representatives from the

Reich's Chancellery, the Nazi Party, the Foreign Office, the Department of Justice, the Four-Year Plan and the Ministry of the Interior, so that all relevant branches of the Government were informed.

The systematic deportation and murder of the European Jews which now began met with some resistance among those who were reluctant to hand over their fellow citizens to Nazi murderers. In Belgium 25,000 Jews, most of whom were fully assimilated, fell into the hands of the Germans, but 40,000 others were saved. The Dutch reacted strongly to the deportation of the Jews, although Dutch Nazis co-operated enthusiastically. There were a number of protest strikes, but 100,000 of the 125,000 Dutch Jews were sent to the death camps. In Norway 728 Jews were killed and 1000 survived. The Danish showed remarkable courage and resourcefulness in saving their Jewish compatriots. Himmler's henchmen managed to lay their hands on only 100 Jews, and some 7000 were spirited away to Sweden and safety.

Even in the satellite countries there was some reluctance to become accessories to mass murder. In Slovakia the Government of Monsignor Jozef Tiso was urged by the Vatican to stop the deportation of Jews. Unfortunately 58,000 Jews had already been deported and only 25,000 remained, of whom 8000 died after the failure of the Slovak revolt. Romanian troops and police took an eager part in the mass murder of some 350,000 Jews in Bessarabia, the Bukovina and southern Russia where they assisted *Einsatzgruppe* D. Yet in spite of this enthusiastic butchery, the Romanian dictator Antonescu refused to allow the deportation of Jews from Romania since he did not want to spoil his chances with the Allies should he be obliged to begin armistice negotiations. In this manner the lives of 300,000 Romanian Jews were saved.

Vichy France had an appalling record of anti-Semitism. Discriminatory legislation was introduced before it was demanded by the Germans. Vichy authorities greatly assisted the work of the SS by clearly stamping the identity cards and ration books of Jews, whether French or foreign, with a large 'JEW'. Foreign Jews were interned ready for shipment to the death camps. French Jews were easily identified and were soon to follow. It is remarkable that three-quarters of French Jews survived, and it is obvious that had the French authorities been less obliging even more would have been saved. About 42,500 Jews were deported in 1942, about one-third of them from Vichy. The number declined to 22,000 the following year, largely as a result of Vichy's second thoughts about the outcome of the war. In 1944 only 12,500 were deported. Approximately one in ten of those sent east were French Jews.

Germany's allies were even less co-operative, and many Jews from France saved their lives by escaping to Italy where they were safer than in Vichy or occupied France. The Italian fascists had never wholeheartedly supported Nazi racial theory, and although there were some enthusiastic anti-Semites in the party, they remained an isolated minority whose influence depended on the support of Italy's powerful ally. Some 8000 of Italy's 40,000 Jews were deported, the vast majority by the Germans from their zone of occupation after the fall of the fascist Government. In Hungary Admiral Horthy, like Antonescu, was fearful of the consequences of compliance with the RSHA should Germany lose the war. As in Italy, it was only when the Germans occupied Hungary on 19 March 1944 that the deportation of Jews began on a massive scale. In all, 430,000 of Hungary's 650,000 Jews were sent to Auschwitz where at least 280,000 died.

Occupation by the German army is not, however, of itself an adequate explanation for the sudden increase in deportations. Finland was occupied by the German army and was directly threatened by Himmler, but not a single Jew was deported. Italians openly resisted the Germans' attempts to round up Jews, and yet there were no reprisals. The 'final solution' was possible only because native anti-Semites were given a free rein and were no longer restrained by Governments which did not share Nazi Germany's racial fanaticism. They were also able to rely on the support of those in charge of the Jewish communities and other prominent Jews in the Jewish councils (*Judenräte*). Jewish leaders felt that resistance to the Nazis was futile and refused to believe that nothing but death awaited them. In some instances they were able to bribe the SS. In June 1944, forty-five members of the Weiss family, the richest Hungarian Jews, were given permission to travel to Portugal. Later in the year, 2000 relatives of prominent Hungarian Zionists were allowed to go to Switzerland. The best-known instance of such bribery turned out to be without effect. In April 1944 Eichmann proposed that one million Jews should be set free in return for 10,000 trucks. This was almost certainly a trick designed to give the Hungarian Jews a false sense of hope and to secure the continued co-operation of the Jewish leadership. The Nazis showed extreme cunning in avoiding mass panic and revolt by exploiting to the full the natural human tendency to refuse to believe the worst and to hope that co-operation would lead to milder treatment. Resistance indeed proved futile. The uprising in the Warsaw ghetto in April and May 1943 was an act of desperation following the deportation and murder of hundreds of thousands. Virtually none of the insurgents survived.

The Allies were well aware of the Nazi genocide, and yet did practically nothing to stop it. Churchill learned of the mass murders at Auschwitz on 7 July 1944 from the Jewish Agency for Palestine. He took up the suggestion that the railway lines from Hungary to Auschwitz should be bombed, but the RAF insisted that it was impossible to interrupt the railway and that bombing the gas chambers would have to be done by day and was thus a task for the USAAF. Many factors combined to stop any effective action being taken to stop the mass murder of European Jews. Anti-Semitism was widespread in Britain and America and rampant in the Soviet Union. Churchill was told that 1.7 million had already died at Auschwitz, which was in fact a gross exaggeration, and it was felt that were such figures made public they would not be believed and would be seen as a repeat performance of the horror stories of the First World War, all of which had subsequently been shown to have been the inventions of propagandists. In the middle of a war the fate of the Jews seemed peripheral to those whose moral vision was further blurred by prejudice. The most popular argument was that the best way to save all the victims of Nazism, Jew or gentile, was to end the war as quickly as possible. Bombing raids on the death camps were seen at best as a diversion from this aim and, at worst, as one officer at Bomber Command phrased it, as kowtowing to world Jewry.

In Germany the fact that Jews were being murdered on a vast scale was widely known. There was little outright sympathy among the German people for this crime, even though anti-Semitism was widespread and was actively encouraged by the regime. Although murder seemed to most Germans to be excessive, the moral sense of too many was blunted. This could even work to the regime's disadvantage. Reports by the Security Service (SD) showed that the attempt to stir up moral indignation by broadcasting details of the murder of Polish officers by the NKVD at Katyn were completely unsuccessful. It was widely felt that this outrage was nothing compared with the activities of their own regime against the Jews. In the final stages of the war most Germans were numbed by endless bombing, terrorized by Himmler's police, terrified of reprisals for the crimes committed by their fellow countrymen, and had braced themselves for the arrival of avenging bolshevik hordes. In such an atmosphere there was little room for sensitive moral judgement or thoughtful reconsideration. Even Himmler imagined that he could obtain better terms from the Allies by an exceptional act of mercy. On

27 November 1944 he ordered an end to the killing of Jews and the destruction of the gas chambers and crematoria.

By this time more than three million Jews had died in the death camps: at Auschwitz (at least one million), Treblinka (about 900,000), Belzec (more than 600,000), Sobibor (250,000), Majdanek (about 200,000) and Chelmno (152,000). In addition, some two million Jews in the Soviet Union were murdered by the *Einsatzgruppen* and their assistants, the 18,300 men of the SS brigades of the Command Staff of the Reichsführer SS, who probably killed even more than the *Einsatzgruppen* and the Wehrmacht. Hundreds of thousands of Gypsies, prisoners-of-war and sick prisoners were murdered, and countless others were worked to death or died in the cattle trucks on the way to the camps. More than five million Jews died in this monstrous crime which remains unique in human history.

The Government of a great nation, whose cultural achievements were second to none, ordered a massacre on a stupendous scale and according to totally irrational criteria. The Jews are a religious community, and there is no such thing as a Jewish race. The Nazis ordered the elimination of an entire race which existed only in their depraved imagination, regardless of any objective criteria such as age, political convictions, social status, gender or personal attitudes. Orthodox Jews were spared if they were not considered to be Jewish by the racial experts of the SS, while those who had never had any contact with Judaism were destroyed as being racially suspect. These murders were thus motivated not by economic or political considerations, nor were they a response to a real danger, they were uniquely inspired by a pathological ideology which defies comprehension. This fanatical vision was realized by a ruthlessly efficient bureaucracy, by a modern industrial society and by men who in many ways were disturbingly normal and ordinary. The result was a catastrophic collapse of moral values, not only in Germany but among almost all who came into contact, however remotely, with these terrible events.

CHAPTER NINE

Two Countries at War: Britain and Germany

On 1 September 1939 Neville Chamberlain proposed to the Labour Party that they should join his Government. The executive of the Parliamentary Labour Party refused. They would not serve under a man who Attlee claimed treated them like dirt, nor in a Cabinet dominated by the 'guilty men' of Munich. Chamberlain's was not a serious offer, any more than was that made to the Liberals, for he saw no pressing need for a National Government. He was still convinced that Hitler was bluffing and that the war would remain limited and 'phoney'. He argued that Hitler would not risk a full-scale war for fear of British retaliation, thus showing an astonishing lack of understanding of the German leader and a totally misplaced confidence in the striking power of the RAF. He rejected all proposals to create a controlled war economy, and only the poverty and the appalling state of the nation's health, revealed when children evacuated from the slums descended upon 'respectable' Britain, shattered this feeling of complacency. Even then, self-help rather than Government action seemed to offer the best remedy. Chamberlain wrote: 'I never knew that such conditions existed, and I feel ashamed of having been so ignorant of my neighbours. For the rest of my life I mean to try to make amends by helping such people to live cleaner and healthier lives.'

Against the drab background of the Chamberlain administration, the exotic figure of Winston Churchill stood out in dramatic relief, heightened by his immense skills as a self-publicist. Whereas Chamberlain blandly proclaimed in April 1940 that Hitler had 'missed the bus', Churchill knew that there was no alternative to a long bloody struggle until Hitler and his regime were totally crushed. Chamberlain was brought down by a combination of anti-appeasement Conservatives, the Labour Party and the economists, planners and social engineers eager to grasp the opportunity afforded by the war to realize their schemes for a better society. Churchill was the man they needed to defeat Hitler, but he was also the man who had crushed the General Strike in 1926 and who was (wrongly) believed to have ordered the troops to fire at the striking miners in Tonypandy in the Rhondda Valley in 1910. The big question was whether this extraordinary man, in his determination to fight the war with every ounce of national strength, would see the necessity for far-reaching social reform. It turned out that Churchill's Coalition Government was the greatest reforming administration since the Liberal Government of 1905. The Prime Minister devoted almost all his energies to fighting the war, and the reformers got on with their job on the home front while his attention was diverted.

When Churchill became Prime Minister on 10 May 1940 he was a man without a party. Chamberlain continued to serve as leader of the Conservative Party, and although humiliated and mortally ill he served Churchill loyally until his death from cancer in November 1940. In October Churchill took over the leadership of the party, but this was a largely symbolic gesture to make sure that no one else got the job. Churchill did not punish the men of Munich, and only the dreadful Sir Samuel Hoare was sent off as ambassador to Spain. For the time being none of the Churchillians was given a top job. Eden became Secretary for War; Duff Cooper, the only Minister to have resigned over Munich, was appointed Minister of Information. Amery went to the India Office, Lord Lloyd to the Colonial Office, and Beaverbrook became Minister for Aircraft Production. Harold Macmillan, Robert Boothby and Harold Nicholson also got junior appointments. Three Liberals were appointed: Churchill's bosom pal Sir Archibald Sinclair, Harcourt 'Crinks' Johnstone and Dingle Foot. None was given a position of great importance. Labour obtained eight ministerial and eight junior ministerial positions. The party had two of the five seats in the War Cabinet. During the course of the war Attlee skilfully managed to increase the number of ministerial posts held by Labour so that by April 1945 they had ten ministerial and seventeen junior ministerial positions. The appointment of the trade union leader Ernest Bevin as Minister of Labour was the most outstanding of these Labour appointments.

When Churchill became Prime Minister there was a widespread feeling of defeatism throughout the country. The Foreign Secretary, Lord Halifax, was in favour of negotiating a peace settlement, and the Chief of the Imperial General Staff, Field Marshal Ironside proclaimed the end of the British Empire. Large numbers of 'enemy aliens' were interned, including many German Jewish refugees. Macmillan, Boothby and Amery called for a Committee of Public Safety with dictatorial powers, to replace the War Cabinet. After Dunkirk the country braced itself for invasion and defeat. In such an atmosphere there were persistent calls for the punishment of the men of Munich, reaching a peak at the time of Dunkirk when Peter Howard, Michael Foot and Frank Owen published, under the pseudonym 'Cato', the grossly unfair and distorted book *Guilty Men*, a true masterpiece of British political pamphleteering. Churchill was determined not to split the Conservative Party as Lloyd George had done in the First World War, and he moved cautiously, picking off the appeasers one by one and sending them gracefully out to pasture or posting them to distant parts.

With the old guard out of the way and with a comfortable Conservative majority, Churchill was able to create the closest thing to a dictatorship that Britain has seen in modern times. In his first great speech in the House of Commons as Prime Minister, he said:

> I have nothing to offer but blood, toil, tears and sweat. You ask, what is our policy? I will say: it is to wage war, by sea, land and air, with all our might and with all the strength that God can give us. . . . You ask, what is our aim? I can answer in one word. Victory – victory in spite of all terror, victory however long and hard the road may be.

This was rousing stuff. It inspired the people and confounded the defeatists, and Churchill never wavered from this single-minded course. But it totally ignored the widespread feeling that victory was not enough, and that a better and more just society should emerge from the war. The Prime Minister pursued victory to the exclusion of everything else, but within the Conservative, Labour and Liberal parties there was a consensus that far-reaching social reform was necessary. This worked entirely to the benefit of Labour. On the day that Churchill promised 'blood, toil, tears and sweat' Attlee told the Labour Party conference: 'I am quite certain that the world that must emerge from this war must be a world attuned to our ideals.' He was perfectly correct. Churchill won the war, but Attlee was to win the peace.

Behind the back of a resolutely reactionary Prime Minister, the foundations were laid for universal social security, family allowance, fundamental reform of the educational system, a national health service, town and country planning, full employment and the state control of key industries. The Labour Cabinet Ministers, particularly Attlee, Ernest Bevin, Hugh Dalton and Herbert Morrison won the respect of their Conservative colleagues and of the civil service. They were moderates who were passionately committed to ameliorating the conditions of the working class and set about their task with dedication and efficiency. They gained the experience they needed when the 1945 election returned the Labour party to power, and they had shown the electorate that they were amply qualified to conduct the affairs of state. Labour had been able to bring down Chamberlain's Government, in spite of its huge majority, and had been brought into Churchill's administration because only a united country could survive such a series of crushing defeats, retreats and evacuations and hope for a final victory. The way was now wide open for the dissemination of social democratic ideas in the armed forces, the information services and the BBC. The British were all in the same boat, and that boat was being steered in the direction of the promised land over which would fly the Butskellite flag.

In the 1945 general election campaign there was much talk of the struggle between 'state socialism' and 'free enterprise' by politicians who were in fundamental agreement over the need for a mixed economy. The war had offered a golden opportunity to the Conservative left, whose manifesto was contained in Harold Macmillan's book *The Middle Way* (1938), whose outstanding achievement was R.A. Butler's Education Act of 1944, and whose intellectual leader was a liberal, John Maynard Keynes. They were organized in the Tory Reform Committee whose prominent members included Lord Hinchingbrooke, Peter Thorneycroft and Quintin Hogg. They were still a minority in a party which they were not to dominate until the 1950s. This ideology was later christened 'Butskellism' when R.A. Butler, as Conservative Chancellor of the Exchequer, continued the fiscal policies of Hugh Gaitskell when Churchill was returned to office in 1951. It was the politics of the wartime consensus which was to set the tone of British politics until the victory of Margaret Thatcher in 1979.

Keynes was the most brilliant exponent of this view and for this reason was later to be particularly reviled by the post-war counter-revolutionaries. He was given an office in the Treasury in June 1940 and exercised a powerful influence over financial policy throughout the war. Although he was fully aware of its injustices and its exploitative nature, he accepted capitalism as the least objectionable and the most efficient economic system. The fundamental question for him was how capitalism should be regulated and controlled so that its harmful effects could be ameliorated. This view was echoed by all the major political parties, including Labour. Revolutionary change was never on the agenda, and in spite of all the rhetoric to the contrary, there was general agreement that capitalism could be made to work and, with suitable adjustments, was not irreconcilable with a reasonable degree of social justice. Some, like the Chairman of the Labour Party, Harold Laski, managed to convince themselves that capitalism was on its last legs and entertained apocalyptic visions of some ghastly native form of fascism. But even Laski was full of admiration of Churchill as a war leader, as was his most consistent critic, Aneurin Bevan, who said of him: 'His ear is so sensitively attuned to the bugle note of history that he is deaf to the raucous clamour of contemporary life.' For the left, Churchill's sins were largely those of omission, not of commission. Churchill was unable to stem the tide of reform. Laski was silenced by laconic asides from Attlee. The extremists on the left and right were small splinter groups with no influence. The far left were seen as stooges of the Kremlin, while the far right were discredited by their ideological proximity to Hitler and Mussolini.

The most telling argument for this vision of the future was the practical experience of the war itself. As so often happens in times of real hardship, there was a genuine feeling of community, of needing to help one another out, and of the obligation for each to do his part for the common and worthwhile cause. Class barriers remained rigid, but it was generally agreed that the deprived deserved better and that the privileged should be required to make some sacrifices. There was a pleasant relaxation of the more extreme social conventions and the classes rubbed shoulders in air-raid shelters and the overcrowded railway compartments. It was even reported that perfect strangers spoke to one another without formal introduction. Rationing helped to create a partly illusory impression that the poor were a little better off and that the rich were a trifle less privileged. For this reason rationing was welcomed, and a majority felt that it should be continued after the war. 'Fair shares' became a powerful slogan after it was introduced by the Board of Trade in 1941. The war showed that unemployment could be overcome, miners given a minimum wage, income tax increased, and the basic needs of ordinary people met. Evacuation and the Blitz exposed the unacceptable undernourishment, lack of education and frightful housing that so many people had to suffer. Such injustices were widely felt to be unnecessary and unacceptable, and their alleviation became an unofficial war aim. At the insistence of the War Cabinet, Churchill inserted a vague promise of social security amid the general waffle of the Atlantic Charter.

The leftward swing of British politics happened long before the Nazis attacked the Soviet Union, but after June 1941 British public opinion demanded the closest possible co-operation with the Soviets. The view held in right-wing circles and unfortunately blurted out by the Minister of Aircraft Production, Colonel Moore-Brabazon, that it was a good thing that Britain's two greatest enemies were now at each other's throats, was regarded by the vast majority of people as treasonable. 'Guns for Russia' was a popular slogan, and ambitious politicians such as Beaverbrook and Stafford Cripps were quick to use support for the Soviet Union and the demand for an early second front to further their cause. It was widely believed that the Soviet Union was fighting Britain's war with insufficient help and that every Russian killed was one Englishman less to die.

Enthusiasm for the genial pipe-smoking Uncle Joe with his taxi driver's cap and his admirably progressive country placed the propaganda specialists at the Ministry of Information in a difficult situation. They attempted to draw clear distinctions between Britain and the Soviet Union and yet emphasize that they were fighting for a common cause, but this inevitably led to a favourable presentation of the Soviet case. The Ministry sponsored a Penguin special, *100 Questions about Russia*, in order to present a balanced picture, but the answers were all highly complimentary. Most specialists on Soviet affairs were sympathizers, fellow travellers or communists, and critical accounts of Soviet life would do nothing to help the war effort. As a result, far from stealing the thunder of the left as the Ministry intended, their publications helped to create the impression that the Soviet political system was at least in part responsible for the Soviet Union's success in withstanding and beating back the Nazi attack.

All this enthusiasm for the Soviet Union was somewhat troubling to the Government and the Foreign Office. Churchill ordered the Ministry of Information to 'consider what action was required to counter the present tendency of the British public to forget the dangers of communism in their enthusiasm over the resistance of Russia'. The Ministry considered the matter but was at a loss to know what to do, finally suggesting that the best thing was to work closely with the Soviet embassy who were best able to keep British communists under control. The Foreign Office sponsored the Anglo-Soviet Public Relations Committee which was chaired by the unimpeachably respectable Lord Horder, the King's physician, and whose members were prime representatives of progressive and enlightened opinion, including H.G. Wells, J.B. Priestley and H.N. Brailsford. Even so, the Committee sponsored such horrors as the hymn of praise to the Soviet constitution of 1936 by the Cambridge communist economist Maurice Dobb, and Leonard Woolf's announcement that Soviet democracy was 'no less magnificent than liberal democracy'.

Communist and sympathetic organizations flourished in such a climate. The Joint Committee for Soviet Aid and the Russia Today Society were communist organizations. The fellow-travelling Society for Cultural Relations with the USSR was frequently consulted by the Foreign Office and the BBC. Communist propaganda efforts were financed by the Government, blessed by bishops and accompanied by the massed band of the Brigade of Guards. Mrs Churchill chaired the Aid to Russia Appeal, which met with an enthusiastic response. Sidney and Beatrice Webb's frightful *Soviet Communism: A New Civilization* was reprinted, but without the question mark at the end of the title. At Faber and Faber the impeccably conservative T.S. Eliot refused to publish George Orwell's *Animal Farm* on the grounds that such anti-Soviet propaganda was politically undesirable. The Foreign Office and the Secret Service became infiltrated with communist agents. An astonished House of Lords heard Lord Beaverbrook, a capitalist of the purest water, proclaim that he was much impressed by the Stalin philosophy.

In spite of all this enthusiasm for the Land of the Red Dawn, communism remained an insignificant factor in British politics. Membership of the Communist Party rose from 12,000 in 1941 to 65,000 by September 1942 but very few, not even party members, were intent on converting Britain into a carbon copy of the New Civilization. The party remained something of a sect, with very little influence. Enthusiasm for Russia meant for most people a demand for the welfare state, for more nationalization, for all-out war on the Blimps and Moore-Brabazons, for a degree of workers' control, for the all-out prosecution of the war and for an early second front. Ironically it was the Labour Party, whose leadership was consistently critical of the Soviet Union and its policies – far more so than the Conservatives – who were to be the political beneficiaries of this enthusiasm for the Soviet Union.

Three weeks after the battle of El Alamein, on 1 December 1942, when the tide of war was at last beginning to turn, Sir William

Beveridge published his report on the future of the social services. This old-fashioned, arrogant and rather stuffy Liberal technocrat overnight became a popular hero. His report called for comprehensive social security 'from the cradle to the grave' based on a national health service, family allowances and the maintenance of full employment. His declaration of war on the 'five giants on the road of reconstruction' – Want, Disease, Ignorance, Squalor and Idleness – was exactly in tune with the times, and his report was the fundamental document of the new consensus in British politics.

It was a cautious and conservative document. It involved virtually no redistribution of income, it insisted that everyone should pay their own way, it emphasized individual thrift and it accepted that 8.5 per cent of the population would probably be unemployed after the war. Nevertheless it was widely felt to be revolutionary and therefore undesirable. Churchill had little sympathy for the report and wanted to put it on the shelf and get on with the business of winning the war. The Confederation of British Employers announced that the proposals would cause such an increase in production costs that the export industries would be ruined. Keynes, although very sympathetic to such ideas as a family allowance, insisted that the country could not afford the scheme. The *Daily Telegraph* warned that this was a major stride towards socialism. The Chancellor of the Exchequer, Kingsley Wood, argued that the plan would be too expensive, that income tax would have to rise to the unacceptable level of 4s 8d in the pound and that 'the weekly progress of the millionaire to the post office for his old age pension would have an element of farce but for the fact that it is to be provided in large measure by the general taxpayer'. Lord Cherwell, Churchill's scientific guru, argued that the British Government would have to go cap in hand to the Americans after the war and that they would be unlikely to want to subsidize the social services. A Conservative Party committee's report on the proposals was severely critical. From the left of the Conservative Party Harold Macmillan thought that the report was wildly extravagant and could not possibly be afforded after a ruinous war. From the right wing of the Labour Party Ernest Bevin squabbled with the Labour backbenchers who wanted immediate implementation of the Beveridge blueprint and proclaimed his dissatisfaction with the proposals for family allowances and workmen's compensation, adding that he saw no reason why doctors' private practices should be disrupted. But the overwhelming majority of the people, even the rich, supported the proposals.

Churchill tried to avoid discussion of the Beveridge Report and attempted to confuse his critics by telling his radio audience on 21 March 1943 that he favoured a 'national compulsory insurance for all classes for all purposes from the cradle to the grave' and that he was against unemployment because 'we cannot have a band of drones in our midst, whether they come from the ancient aristocracy or the modern plutocracy or the ordinary type of pub crawler'. No one really believed that this was a change of heart, for he had vetoed a Labour proposal to nationalize the coal industry and had tried unsuccessfully to wind up the Army Bureau of Current Affairs (ABCA) which he felt was tendentiously left-wing. The Conservative heavyweights gave him no support. Eden, who was temperamentally sympathetic to the Tory reformers, was distressed at Churchill's refusal to address the problems of post-war reconstruction, and was tempted to make a bid for the party leadership with the support of the left wing of his party. Beaverbrook was far too much of a maverick and was loathed by so many within the party that he was incapable of providing the leadership needed for an electoral campaign. The professional politicians of the 1930s had been largely replaced by the Prime Minister's curious clique, so that the Conservative Party was left with no proper sense of direction, leaving the field wide open to Labour.

The Government's White Paper on education was published in July 1943 and was seen by the opponents of the Beveridge Report as an admirable diversion. Most Conservatives found the proposals admirable. They applauded the provision of compulsory religious instruction and the elitist principle of separating children with 'different types of aptitude': in effect, the middle class to the grammar schools and the riff-raff to the secondary modern schools. The public schools, those bastions of educational and social privilege, were untouched and convenient tax loopholes enabled them to raise their fees without losing pupils. Public opinion warmly endorsed the proposals to provide universal secondary education, to raise the school leaving age to sixteen (although no date was set for this measure, which was not put into effect until many years later) and to abolish all fees in the state sector. Although the Labour Party conference of 1942 committed the party to the principle of comprehensive schooling, this did not become a major issue in the debates over the Bill. There were, however, some controversial points. Some Tory reformers joined with Labour backbenchers to defeat the Government by 117 votes to 116 by demanding equal pay for women teachers, the only significant defeat for the Coalition in a division. Churchill entertained the preposterous notion that the Government's defeat over equal pay would be seen in Germany as evidence of war weariness, and he went to the House the following day, called for a reversal of this vote in what he saw as a vote of confidence, and as a result of this outrageous blackmail gained a substantial majority. A similar attempt to raise the school-leaving age to sixteen by 1951 was defeated and the Education Bill thus did not specify a date. For all its shortcomings, the Education Bill was the most far-reaching educational reform ever enacted in Britain.

Manpower was an acute problem in the early stages of the war and it was made worse by Churchill's support for the bomber offensive which necessitated an additional 850,000 workers. Sir John Anderson chaired a committee to solve this problem and proposed that men and women from the ages of eighteen to sixty should be obliged to perform 'national service'. The conscription of women was accepted by the War Cabinet in spite of Churchill's opposition, making Britain the first country ever to adopt such a measure. Neither Hitler nor Stalin followed this example, feeling that women's prime purpose was to breed and to provide heroes with a little recreation. Unmarried women between the ages of twenty and thirty were required to join the auxiliary services or work in industry. In the course of the war the age groups liable for service were driven steadily upwards.

The National Service (No. 2) Act became law in December 1941 and was widely approved. Almost the only criticism of the legislation was that it should have come sooner. Some of the old volunteers complained that compulsion would be the death of idealism. Industrial managers grumbled that they were having to make do with the scrapings from the bottom of the barrel as deferments from military service became increasingly difficult to obtain. The allocation of manpower became a decisive means of controlling industrial production and was used by Bevin to force management to improve wages and working conditions.

The experience of the war was that industry could be effectively controlled and directed and that even in the midst of the horrors of war capitalism could be made more humane. The war hastened this reform of capitalism, the realization of the vision of such upper-middle-class reformers as Beveridge, Cripps, Attlee and Keynes. To those on the left who felt that capitalism in any form was grossly unjust and ruthlessly exploitative, all this was a cruel swindle and the reformers were merely patching up a decaying structure. They were correct in their insistence that this was not a socialist agenda; indeed, it was supported by an increasingly important section of the Conservative Party. The great reforms of the post-war Labour Government were mostly based on the deliberations of Tory-dominated committees. The Reid Report recommended the nationalization of the coal industry, the McGowan Report that of electricity, and the Bank of England was taken into public ownership as a result of the Macmillan Report. Although Bevan's National Health Service was in many ways radically innovative, it was still based on the proposals of a White Paper produced by a Conservative Minister of Health, Henry Willink.

When Britain was fighting with its back to the wall, threatened by invasion and destruction from the air, the nation's rulers realized that the country could not survive without the active participation of the ruled. This was something that Churchill fully understood, and his outstanding achievement was to unite the country in the bleakest hours of 1940 and to make the people share his unshakeable conviction that in the end they would be victorious. For this he earned the undying affection of his countrymen, including his frequently exasperated colleagues and his political opponents. 'Morale' thus became a key to victory and was minutely recorded and analysed by Mass Observation. Within strict budgetary and political limits the people had to be given what they wanted and concessions had to be made to public opinion. Londoners had to be allowed to use tube stations as air-raid shelters, rationing had at least to appear to be more equitable even if it could always be circumvented by the rich, production committees were permitted so that workers had a greater say over their lives, and a commitment was made to the creation of a welfare state which no political party could have afforded to ignore.

Parliament was largely silenced by the need for security, and normal party politics were suspended for the duration of the coalition. Local Government was shown up as hopelessly inefficient during the evacuation. In the place of such forums there arose a vigorous democratic spirit which affected the daily life of the people on the factory floor and at the street corner. This never became part of a new participatory democracy, because as soon as the war was over there was a general feeling that the traditional institutions had proved their worth and that the old elites had done a good job. Most of the temporary civil servants and experts who had injected new life into the system returned to their peacetime jobs and the old bureaucracy was restored.

Looking back at the war, the British people were proudest of the moment when in 1940 they had 'stood alone' against the new barbarism of Nazi tyranny. Like so much else about the war, this was almost pure myth. Without the largely unwilling support of hundreds of millions in Asia and Africa, Britain could never have survived. Churchill could conjure up the vision of the British Empire lasting a thousand years, but this was empty rhetoric. Gandhi rejected the suggestion of the Cripps mission that India should be given its independence after the war by announcing that he could not accept 'post dated cheques upon a bankrupt Empire'. The fall of Singapore showed to all the world just how bankrupt the Empire had become, and gave great encouragement to the independence movements.

At the end of the war the nation faced what Keynes called a 'financial Dunkirk'. Victory had been won, but the country was hopelessly in debt to the United States, the Soviet Union was in control of all of eastern Europe, industry was run down, fuel running short, and there was the bleak prospect of bread rationing and austerity. One woman spoke for many when she told Mass Observation: 'I was happier when I lay listening to bombs and daring myself to tremble; when I got romantic letters from abroad; when I cried over Dunkirk; when people showed their best sides and we still believed we were fighting to gain something.'

The situation was very different in Germany. Britain had a far higher standard of living and was therefore able to make greater cuts in consumption without causing undue hardship. In both countries there was approximately a 10 per cent reduction in consumption in the first year of the war, but in Germany this was enough to cause noticeable shortages. The regime had attempted to prepare for war with its policy of autarky and with a large-scale rearmament programme, but it had not been successful. The country was not prepared for a lengthy war and attempts to mobilize the economy were a miserable failure.

It has often been suggested that the regime opted for a partial mobilization of the economy in order to maintain morale and because the *Blitzkrieg* strategy made it unnecessary to do more. Rapid campaigns did not require lengthy and extensive preparation and the shortages in the domestic market could be made good by foreign conquest. In fact the limited preparation for war was the result, not of deliberate policy but of inefficiency, and the regime had no strong commitment to preservation of existing levels of consumption. By the end of August 1939 rationing was imposed which provided for one pound of meat per head per week, a quarter of a pound of butter, 62.5 grams of cheese and one egg. Rationing was imposed much later in Britain and was less stringent. On 4 September 1939 a wage freeze was announced. Income tax was increased sharply, as were the taxes on alcohol, tobacco, theatres and travel. By 1942 taxes had doubled. The drastic reduction in available consumer goods resulted in a four-fold increase in private savings between 1938 and 1941. While the cities were reduced to rubble, the building societies encouraged their clients to save up for a pleasant home after the war.

Until 1942 there was a reduction in the number of women employed, caused by the provision of benefits for soldiers' wives which enabled many of them to leave their jobs. There were strong ideological reasons for such a measure. As late as April 1944 Hitler insisted that women should be employed in industry only if their work was absolutely essential, 'otherwise we will distort National Socialist peacetime reconstruction'. In spite of Hitler's concern that women's place was in the home, there was a higher percentage of women wage-earners in Germany than in England or the United States before the war. By 1944, 51 per cent of all German workers were female. In Britain the figure was 37.9 per cent and in the United States 35.7 per cent.

Very few Germans were enthusiastic about the news of the outbreak of war, and the giddy atmosphere of August 1914 was not recaptured. The regime was concerned about this lack of martial spirit, clearly observable in the last days of peace, and on 26 August 1939 it made undermining the military power of the nation (*Wehrkraftzersetzung*) a capital offence. This gave a terrifying power to the Gestapo which Heydrich ordered should be used to the full. He ordered the 'brutal liquidation of such elements' deemed to be guilty of hindering the war effort. Failure to provide adequate blackout became a war crime, and listening to foreign radio was described as 'mental self-mutilation'. Special courts condemned to death those found guilty of such heinous offences.

The spectacular successes of the German army in the early campaigns silenced all but the regime's most principled critics. Food, raw materials and labour poured in from the occupied territories. The Führer was regarded with slavish adoration and hymned as the 'Greatest General of All Time'. With the Soviet Union as the loyal ally of Nazi Germany even the Communist Party could voice no criticism, and those soldiers who had misgivings about Hitler's strategic abilities were a dwindling and powerless handful. The news of the failed attempt to assassinate Hitler in the Bürgerbräukeller in

Munich in November 1939 was greeted with appalled indignation and was widely believed to be the work of sinister Englishmen and Jews. The demand that England should be razed to the ground was widely voiced, particularly among the working class.

Although they did not have the faintest idea what it was all about, in 1940 the German people were enthusiastically behind the war effort. Even Goebbels had to confess to representatives of the German press that he did not know what *Lebensraum* meant. This vagueness helped to create an atmosphere of expectation of great things to come, for which the people were prepared to make considerable sacrifices. It was a situation that was exploited with great skill by politicians and propagandists. In the autumn of 1940 Robert Ley, the leader of the German Work Front, revealed the details of Nazi Germany's equivalent to the Beveridge Report. This 'Social Work of the German People' promised a comprehensive programme of care for the aged, a health service, programmes for spare time and holidays (Ley was also head of 'Strength Through Joy' [KdF] which organized travel and holiday camps), a review of wages, professional education and training, and a crash programme for building subsidized housing.

Social services from the cradle to the grave were, of course, to be provided only for 'citizens of the Reich of German or similar type of blood' and were designed to strengthen the 'racial community'. Old-age pensions were to be given only to those who had fulfilled their 'duty to work' and who had 'committed themselves unconditionally to the good of the nation'. 'Anti-social elements' and 'racial vermin' had no claim to support. The Aryan infant was cared for by the 'Aid for Mother and Child' in the National Socialist People's Welfare (NSV) whose boss, Erich Hilgenfeldt, was Ley's bitter rival but who had Hitler's full support and therefore could not be touched. The principle behind the entire programme was to increase the individual productivity of the 'soldiers of labour' and to purify the German race. In spite of lengthy discussions, nothing concrete ever came of these proposals. The regimentation of labour and mass murder took the place of this negative utopian vision. 'Racial renewal' was to take place through genocide, euthanasia, sterilization and discriminatory legislation. Health was no longer seen as a personal matter but a social concern. Under the slogan 'your health is not yours alone!' a new concept of racial hygiene was developed, based on optimum performance for the good of the 'racial community'.

The eastern *Lebensraum* was to be an enormous racial laboratory. Himmler, in his capacity of Reich Commissar for the Strengthening of the German Race, consulted with Rosenberg's Ministry for the Occupied Eastern Territories and the Racial Political Office of the NSDAP and produced a 'General Plan East'. The 'racial frontier' was to be pushed some 300 miles eastwards, and between thirty and fifty million people of 'alien race' were to be evacuated to Siberia where it was assumed by many of the experts that they would obligingly die. Fourteen million 'racially worthwhile aliens' would be allowed to remain as slaves for the German settlers. Anthropologists at the Kaiser Wilhelm Institute in Berlin were given the task of preparing criteria to decide who measured up to these standards and who belonged to the 'undesirable clans'.

If all this were not difficult enough, Himmler's helpers soon discovered that there was a desperate shortage of suitable Aryans to people the eastern Empire. The much-vaunted 'people without space' began to look embarrassingly like a space without people. Germans from south Tyrol who had been designated as settlers in France in 'Burgundy Gau' were now seen as potential settlers in the Ukraine. Racially promising Slav children were to be 'germanized' in the SS *Lebensborn* homes. But there were still not enough Germans. Himmler therefore decided to establish 'Marches' around Leningrad, in the Crimea and around Memel along with thirty-six 'settlement fortresses'. It was a mad vision, to which Hitler and Himmler clung until the very end of the war.

By December 1941 it was clear that the *Blitzkrieg* strategy had failed and that it would be a long haul until the promised 'final victory'. After the defeats at El Alamein and Stalingrad many Germans began to doubt that victory was possible at all. This widespread pessimism afforded Goebbels the opportunity for his finest hour. As Hitler faded from public view and seldom even addressed his people on the radio, Goebbels, who had fallen out of favour as a result of his endless amorous entanglements, suddenly leaped to the forefront. In two astonishing speeches in February 1943 and July 1944, masterpieces of inflammatory demagogy, he called for an all-out effort for 'total war' which alone would lead to a 'total victory'. Although continuing to live the luxurious and decadent life of a *grand bourgeois*, Goebbels preached his own version of war socialism. He announced that the bombs that had levelled Germany's cities had also destroyed all class barriers and freed the people from the 'ballast of civilization'. With pseudo-religious pathos he called for sacrifice, discipline, frugality, absolute obedience and unshakeable faith in Germany's destiny.

Goebbels may have given comfort and hope to some, but his

vision was a hopeless distortion of reality. The new equality in the cities was an equality of suffering and homelessness, the solidarity of his version of socialism was that of people in desperate straits. None of this applied to the rural areas, which were virtually untouched by the war until the final months and where there was usually enough to eat.

Hitler enjoyed the company of Goebbels and his charming and endlessly cheated wife, Magda, and he also badly needed his skills as a propagandist as the tide of war turned against him. Goebbels thus became one of the most powerful figures in wartime Germany. Conversely Goering, once the most powerful of Hitler's paladins, lost most of his power and influence. His Luftwaffe was shot to pieces and he lost his control over the war economy, first to Fritz Todt and then, when Todt was killed in an air crash in February 1942, to Albert Speer who was appointed Armaments Minister. Himmler subjected most of Europe to the terror of his SS and had the domestic affairs of the Reich firmly in his hands even before he was formally appointed Minister of the Interior in August 1943. In the background Hitler's secretary, Martin Bormann, took over control of the Nazi Party when Hess departed for Scotland in May 1941, and he exploited the possibilities of this position to the utmost to enhance his power. Bormann controlled the right of access to Hitler and was able to read his mind, pander to his fondest prejudices and manipulate him like no other. In the final stages of the war he was to become the second most powerful figure in the Reich and he could even push aside such rivals as Himmler, Goebbels and Goering and outwit Hans Heinrich Lammers who, as head of the Chancellery, was his most powerful rival. In such a situation the administration of Germany disintegrated into a number of rival fiefdoms, all of which were in a state of almost permanent upheaval and murderously intent on realizing their increasingly unreal aims.

Among the new elite of Bormann, Himmler and Goebbels, Albert Speer was very much the odd man out. He was only thirty-seven years old when appointed Armaments Minister, but had already distinguished himself as a brilliant administrator. By profession an architect, he had attracted Hitler's attention for his planning of the Nazi rallies at Berlin and Nuremberg. He delighted Hitler with his plans for the rebuilding of Berlin in a dreadful neo-classical style much favoured by the Führer. Speer was admired not only by Hitler for his organizational abilities and his architectural genius; the industrialists with whom he had to deal as Minister were also much impressed by his talent. He was a typical amoral technocrat and manager who unthinkingly and devotedly served an immoral system.

Speer extended the system of production committees which had been created by Todt and which were chaired by industrialists. In the 'Central Planning', which met once a fortnight, raw materials and labour were allotted to firms deemed best suited to undertake a specific job. The results were immediate and spectacular. In spite of the Allied bombing offensive, the production of heavy Panzers increased six-fold between 1941 and 1944 and that of aircraft by 350 per cent. Industrial production reached its peak in 1944, as did Allied area bombing.

Speer's pragmatic, managerial and unideological approach to industrial production, which favoured the large-scale producers who had already benefited greatly from the concentration of economic power under the four-year plan, was strongly opposed by Himmler and the SS. The leading economic expert in the SS was Dr Otto Ohlendorf, an economist and expert on Italian syndicalism and corporatism, who was director of research in the World Economic Institute at Kiel and who was also head of the Security Service (SD). He had commanded *Einsatzgruppe* D in the Soviet Union, which was responsible for the murder of some 90,000 people. He then returned to Berlin where he chaired a committee on foreign trade in the Ministry of Economics and was a powerful member of the Central Planning staff. Ohlendorf still kept his position as head of Section III (SD) of the RSHA. As a 'liberal' Nazi he wanted to break up the monopolies, combines and cartels and actively to support the aspirations of the lower middle class. Speer's efforts, however impressive the results, were anathema to such champions of the middle classes as Ohlendorf, but he did share Speer's technological approach and faith in professional expertise, although in his case it had to be combined with absolute ideological commitment.

This curious conflict became part of a broader discussion about the future of the German economy. By the summer of 1944 at the latest, the dream of *Lebensraum* in the east had had to be abandoned by all but the most wishful of thinkers. Large corporations began to move their assets away from what was designated as the Soviet occupation zone. Economic experts began to think of an economically powerful western Germany which could form part of a bulwark against bolshevism. It was a ludicrous and dangerous notion, based on the assumption that the American plutocrats would remove themselves back across the Atlantic and that Germany would soon dominate Europe both economically and politically. Nevertheless there were within it elements of the plans for western European integration which were realized after the war. Such post-war planning, an open admission of defeatism, had to be conducted in the utmost secrecy, and this Himmler, Ohlendorf and the SD were able to provide.

For the vast majority of the German people the main concern was how to survive. Only a small minority managed to delude themselves that the much-vaunted 'wonder weapons' would turn the tide. Most Germans hoped that the end would come as soon as possible and remained unimpressed by Goebbels' frantic efforts to terrify them with his blood-curdling visions of the consequences of unconditional surrender. But the news of the attempt on Hitler's life on 20 July 1944 was greeted with almost universal horror. The German people were still unable to free themselves from the spell of the man they had adulated for so many years, even at a time when he had brought the country to the brink of total ruin. It was only some months later that SD reports on morale indicated that people had at last begun to think that perhaps a golden opportunity to end the war had been lost.

Given the enormous popularity of the regime in the early years, the opposition groups had to contend with the widely held view that they were traitors and perjurers. The socialist trade unionists gradually formed an underground organization ready for the time when the regime would collapse. Although they were unable to do anything to bring down the regime, they were to play a vital role in the development of free and democratic institutions in the western occupation zones after the war. The communists were restrained from taking an active part in the resistance until Germany invaded the Soviet Union, although some party members refused to accept the Ribbentrop–Molotov pact. Along with individual acts of sabotage the communists concentrated on espionage, at which they were remarkably successful. Lieutenant Schulze-Boysen in the Luftwaffe Ministry, and Arvid Harnack in the Ministry of Economics, along with Rudolf Roessler who had access to information from Hitler's headquarters, were the key figures in Germany of the 'Red Orchestra', a European-wide Soviet spy ring which was broken up in the autumn of 1943 and most of its members were executed. Most of those who survived were rounded up by Stalin's henchmen and either executed or imprisoned as adventurers and deviationists.

The leading figure in the conservative bourgeois opposition was Carl Goerdeler, Lord Mayor of Leipzig until 1937 when he resigned in protest against the removal of a bust of Felix Mendelssohn-Bartholdy which stood near the town hall. He established close contacts with opponents of the regime in the civil service, the underground political parties, the army, business and the intelligentsia. Goerdeler used his position as foreign representative for Bosch to get in touch with a number of influential people in Britain, France and America. At the outbreak of the war the socialists and trade unionists established contacts with the Goerdeler group. However, in spite of his extensive knowledge of foreign affairs, Goerdeler entertained totally unrealistic nationalist ideas and imagined that Germany could survive the war with the frontiers of 1937 intact and with the addition of Austria, south Tyrol, west Prussia, Posen, the Sudetenland and even the German-speaking districts of Alsace and Lorraine. He imagined that the western Allies would accept this settlement as a necessary bulwark against bolshevism. He was, furthermore, an authoritarian who wanted a strong executive and the sovereignty of an elite, not of the people. Nor was he entirely free of anti-Semitism, and he imagined that he could win over Himmler and Goebbels to his side.

The 'Kreisau Circle', named after the ancestral home of Count Helmuth von Moltke, was a resistance group which included aristocrats such as Peter Yorck von Wartenberg, Fritz-Dietlof von der Schulenberg and Adam von Trott zu Solz along with trade unionists and socialists, among them Julius Leber, Adolf Reichwein and Wilhelm Leuschner. They were impatient with Goerdeler's prevarications, and with their socialist contacts and their slightly idealistic Christian socialism were not involved in planning to assassinate Hitler, but rather to develop blueprints for a humane and moral society once the Nazis had gone.

Closely associated with the Kreisau Circle was the activist group around Colonel Claus Schenk von Stauffenberg which included officers such as Henning von Tresckow, Mertz von Quirnheim, Werner von Haeften, Friedrich Olbricht and Helmuth Stieff. They found the Goerdeler group reactionary and were disgusted with their endless humming and hawing. Although most of Stauffenberg's associates were from ancient aristocratic families, they shared none of Goerdeler's fears of a far-reaching democratization of German society or of co-operation with the Soviet Union. They also realized that Goerdeler's territorial ambitions were hopelessly unrealistic. Stauffenberg established contact with the National Committee for a Free Germany (NKFD), which had been created in 1943 from German prisoners-of-war in the Soviet Union, among them General

Paulus, along with a selection of communists and sympathizers. He also worked closely with the communist underground in Germany, much to the disgust of Goerdeler and his conservative associates.

Stauffenberg and Moltke and those around them believed, often with regret, that the only alternative to Nazism was far-reaching reform along social-democratic lines. This clearly distinguished them from those who, at terrible personal risk and with enormous courage, hoped to preserve as much of the status quo as possible by means of a revolution from above along traditional Prussian conservative lines. The conservative and the church opposition to Hitler was paralysed by this fear of socialism and with no popular support at home vainly looked to Britain and the United States for help. This also condemned them to inaction, as the western Allies would make no commitments until they had seen positive results.

There was agreement on two main points: Hitler obviously had to be removed, and the military were the only people in a position to carry out such a coup. Goerdeler wanted Hitler to be arrested and put on trial. The soldiers pointed out that this would present impossible security problems and that only when Hitler was dead would the military be absolved from their oath of personal allegiance which the vast majority took with deadly seriousness. The conspirators were under increasing pressure to act. The military situation was rapidly deteriorating and it looked as if there would soon be little left of Germany to save. As early as April 1943 Hans von Dohnanyi, the son of the composer and brother-in-law of Dietrich Bonhoeffer, and an associate were arrested and their chief of staff in the counter-intelligence division of the OKW (*Abwehr*), Hans Oster, was suspended from duty. In January 1944 Moltke was arrested for warning a fellow conspirator of his impending arrest, and the Kreisau Circle disbanded. In July a number of communists and social democrats were arrested, among them Reichwein and Leber.

The only conspirator who had regular access to Hitler's conferences was Stauffenberg in his capacity as chief of staff to the Commander-in-Chief of the reserve army, another leading conspirator, General Olbricht. Stauffenberg had lost an eye, his right hand and two fingers of his left hand and was thus obliged to attempt to use a bomb to kill Hitler. On 11 and 15 July 1944 he had taken the bomb in his briefcase to the Obersalzberg but had not activated it because neither Goering nor Himmler attended the conference. The next opportunity was on 20 July when Hitler returned to his 'wolf's lair' in East Prussia. The conspirators decided that they could wait no longer. The bomb went off, but the effectiveness of the blast was diminished by the flimsy construction of the temporary building in which the conference was held. Although four people died in the explosion, Hitler was protected from the blast by a heavy table and suffered only minor injuries.

The putsch was singularly badly organized. Communications from Hitler's headquarters were not cut off. It was not until Stauffenberg arrived back in Berlin that 'Operation Walküre' was launched. The Government had had time to recover from the initial shock. It was known that Hitler was still alive, and OKW countermanded all orders issued by the conspirators. Stauffenberg, Haeften, Merz von Quirnheim and Olbricht were immediately arrested and were shot the same evening by members of the army they had hoped to save from further slaughter. Hitler spoke on the radio that evening of a 'tiny clique of ambitious, unscrupulous and at the same time criminal and stupid officers' who had tried to stab him in the back as he stood at the front. Most Germans were appalled at such murderous treason. All those who were in any way implicated in the plot were rounded up by members of a special 400-man commando of the SD. Thousands were bestially murdered in the dungeons of the security police, and Hitler followed their martyrdom with prurient interest. Some were prudent enough to commit suicide before being handed over to Roland Freisler's 'People's Court'. Among them were Beck, von Kluge and Rommel. The last, with cynical hypocrisy, as the immortal 'Hero of Africa', was given a state funeral with full military honours.

CHAPTER TEN

From Moscow to Kursk
(January 1942–August 1943)

At the beginning of January 1942 the *Stavka* met to discuss plans for a counter-offensive to drive the Wehrmacht away from Leningrad and Moscow and to crush the German forces in the south. Stalin was in an overly optimistic mood, insisting that the Germans, having been defeated at the gates of Moscow and being ill equipped for winter warfare, were an easy prey. Much to Zhukov's horror, he therefore called for a general offensive on all fronts. The Red Army lacked the resources, particularly artillery, for such a grandiose operation, which even under optimum conditions would have been a dangerous dissipation of effort. Zhukov therefore argued in favour of exploiting the weaknesses of Army Group Centre and insisted that offensives to the north and south would be doomed to failure. None of this had any effect. Stalin had made up his mind before the *Stavka* met, and directives had already been sent to the front commanders.

The offensive was to be carried out along the entire front from Leningrad to the Crimea so that Soviet forces, who suffered from acute shortages of food, fuel and ammunition, were spread so thinly across almost one thousand miles of front that there could be little chance of success. From his bunker in the Kremlin Stalin issued meaningless orders to terrified commanders, while his entourage shielded him from the harsh realities at the front. By moving armies from one point on the front to another he further undermined the efforts of his front-line commanders, who were doing their utmost to make the best of an almost impossible situation. Soviet forces either ran up against German strong points, were worn down and beaten back, or they advanced through the spaces between them and were encircled by skilful counter-attacks. It soon became obvious that Stalin had seriously underestimated the enemy and that little could be achieved without concentrating on decisive points of attack.

By March the Soviet leadership began to discuss the strategic options for the spring. The general staff argued in favour of a strategic defensive, concentrating on the central sector around Moscow, in which the enemy would be worn down attacking well-prepared positions and further weakened by counter-attacks. This strategy was designed to prepare the ground for a major offensive. Marshal Timoshenko, supported by his commissar, N.S. Khruschev, submitted an alternative proposal to Stalin for a massive offensive in the south. Stalin supported a modified version of Timoshenko's proposal and agreed to an offensive against Kharkov to be launched in May. At the same time he proposed a number of partial offensives, thus making a nonsense of the general staff's defensive strategy. Zhukov agreed with the general staff's assessment of the importance of the central sector but argued that an offensive should be mounted to wipe out the massive German bridgehead in front of Moscow from Rzhev to Demyansk.

At the end of March Stalin called a meeting of the State Defence Committee to discuss these different proposals. Brushing aside Marshal Shaposhnikov's arguments for an 'active defence' and Zhukov's insistence on concentrating on the central front, Stalin ordered a 'simultaneous attack and defence' with a concentration on the Moscow sector. The general staff and the *Stavka* agreed that the new German offensive would be directed against Moscow, in spite of detailed intelligence information coming from 'Lucy' and 'Werther' in Berlin and Switzerland which showed that the Germans intended to strike in the south. Stalin discounted the information provided by his superb network of agents, simply because it did not coincide with his assessment of German intentions. When he was provided with the full details of the drive to the Caucasus he blamed his tireless and devoted agents for falling for what he was convinced was a mere feint.

The Germans had begun their planning for the 1942 offensive as early as November the previous year. Rundstedt, commanding Army Group South, requested permission to withdraw to prepare for a fresh offensive towards the Caucasus in the spring. Hitler would not allow the offensive to halt, and accepted Rundstedt's resignation. He then flew to Mariupol, realized that Rundstedt had been perfectly correct, and ordered the Army Group to withdraw to the Mius. On 8 December he called for a halt to all offensive operations on the eastern front. This prompted his generals to request a strategic withdrawal, whereupon Hitler issued his 'Halt Order' on 16 December calling for 'fanatical resistance' to the last man and expressly forbidding any withdrawal. Guderian and Hoepner, two of Germany's leading tank experts, were dismissed for refusing to carry out this order to the letter. The commander of Army Group North, Leeb, realizing that nothing would persuade Hitler to withdraw from the highly vulnerable Demyansk salient, offered his resignation, which was gratefully received. Bock was ill and the command of his Army Group Centre was given to Kluge. Brauchitsch, who had been subjected to constant and bitter attacks from Hitler, took advantage of a convenient heart attack to offer his resignation, which was eagerly received by his Führer who published the news of the Commander-in-Chief's departure in such a way as to create the impression that he, along with the army group commanders and some other leading generals, was responsible for the failure of 'Barbarossa'. Hitler now appointed himself Commander-in-Chief, thus further strengthening his hold over the army.

Hitler's plans for a new offensive, outlined in Führer Directive No. 41 of 5 April 1942, were dictated by his ideological and economic obsessions and paid little attention to the more traditional strategic and political considerations of the General Staff. He was determined to seize the oilfields of the Caucasus, claiming that Germany would be unable to continue the war without additional oil supplies and that the Russians would be forced to sue for peace once they had lost their principal source of fuel. A further objective in the south was Stalingrad, which was to be rendered of no further use as an industrial and communications centre. The final objective was Leningrad which, as the breeding ground of bolshevism, had to be destroyed. The armies of the central sector were ordered to stand fast.

The generals were appalled by Hitler's directive, for it ran against all the basic principles of their military training. A major advance on the southern flank, without any pressure being applied on the centre, meant that the Germans would be caught between the bulk of the Red Army and the Black Sea, opening up the possibility of a devastating counter-attack. Their fears became even greater when they learned that their flank would be protected by Allied troops in whom they had little confidence. The key to the whole situation, and the most vulnerable point, was Stalingrad, which covered the flank of the advance into the Caucasus and controlled the land bridge between the Volga and the Don as well as the route north to Moscow.

Timoshenko's offensive against Kharkov, the details of which had been gathered by Lieutenant-Colonel Reinhardt Gehlen's intelligence unit, *Fremde Heere Ost*, began on 12 May with a massive bombardment of Paulus's 6th Army. The plan was over-ambitious and far beyond the capabilities of the Red Army, and was compromised by inaccurate intelligence reports. Timoshenko planned a pincer movement around Kharkov, the main push coming from the south from the Izyum salient. The 6th Army took a tremendous beating in the initial assault, but Timoshenko was far too slow in sending in his armour and motorized infantry to exploit the gaps in the German position.

Von Bock, temporarily back in command of Army Group South, Rundstedt's replacement Reichenau having died of a heart attack, ordered an immediate counter-attack using plans already drawn up for 'Operation Fredericus', a strike from the north and south to wipe out the Izyum salient. Army Group Kleist to the south of the bulge cut through the Soviet 9th Army and threatened the rear of the 57th Army. Paulus's 6th Army swept down from the north, threatening to cut off Timoshenko's left hook. At the Soviet general staff Vasilevsky insisted that Timoshenko should pull back to meet the deadly danger posed by Kleist, but Stalin, having spoken to Timoshenko, decided that this was a needlessly cautious approach and ordered the offensive against Kharkov to continue. The following day when Kleist had severed the lines of communication within the salient, Vasilevsky, supported by Khruschev, Timoshenko's commissar, pleaded with Stalin to call off the offensive, but the Soviet dictator refused. On 19 May Timoshenko ordered the offensive to halt, but his troops were already encircled and had to attempt to fight their way out of the German trap. By now it was too late. Thousands of Soviet soldiers died in endless assaults against German gun emplacements, but the ring would not break. Five Soviet generals lost their lives on the battlefield, including one suicide, and the Germans took 241,000 prisoners. It was a brilliant feat of arms by the Wehrmacht, and Halder had every right to claim that it was his greatest achievement.

Kharkov was not the only disaster to befall the Red Army. In the Crimea Manstein ripped apart the armies commanded by the *Stavka* representative, Mekhlis, an appalling creature even by Stalinist standards. The Deputy Defence Commissar was vicious, vindictive and grossly incompetent. The Russians lost 176,000 men and almost all their 350 tanks on the Crimean front. Stalin's ludicrous comment to Zhukov was that this disaster was further proof of the folly of fighting a defensive war.

Having seized the Kerch Peninsula, Manstein turned his attention to Sevastopol, a heavily defended fortress bristling with enormous guns in concrete emplacements, surrounded by minefields, trenches and underground fortifications. To crack this impressive nut Manstein ordered a five-day barrage featuring 'Karl', a mortar which fired a two-ton projectile, and 'Big Dora', an artillery piece with a ninety-foot barrel with a range of 50 kilometres. Having been thus softened up it took several weeks of ferocious hand-to-hand fighting before the Soviets finally abandoned their fortress and the Germans were masters of the entire Crimea.

On the Leningrad front Vlasov's army had been cut off in the marshlands behind the river Volkhov. Passageways were cut through to Vlasov, but they were rapidly closed off by the Germans and on 24 June Vlasov, realizing that the situation was hopeless, ordered his men to disband and fight their way singly out of the death-trap. Vlasov was captured by the Germans and began to recruit the 'Russian Liberation Army' (ROA), a worthless collection of misfits, fanatics, opportunists and assorted criminals whose avowed intention was to overthrow the bolshevik regime.

These successes on the Volkhov, at Kharkov and in the Crimea placed the Germans in an admirable position to launch their offensive as outlined in 'Plan Blue'. Weichs's 2nd Army and Hoth's 4th Panzers, positioned around Kursk, were to drive to the Don at Voronezh and then head south-east in the direction of Stalingrad. They were to be joined by Paulus's 6th Army breaking out west of Kharkov. Army Group A of Army Group South, made up of Kleist's 1st Panzers and Ruoff's 17th Army, was to head for the Caucasus.

On 19 June the operations officer of the 23rd Panzer Division, Major Reichel, crashed in a light plane just inside the Soviet lines. He carried with him plans for the opening phase of 'Operation Blue', the attack on Voronezh. The plans were sent to Stalin who, in spite of aerial reconnaissance photographs which confirmed the Reichel papers, promptly dismissed them as a German plant, chastised Soviet intelligence for their incompetence and gullibility, and promptly ordered an offensive to the north of Kursk, centred on Orel. Plans for this offensive had just been completed when the Germans launched 'Operation Blue'.

Although he remained obsessed with the supposed threat to his centre, Stalin eventually agreed to set up a separate Voronezh front, the effectiveness of which was greatly hampered by his personal direction and his firing of perfectly competent generals as scapegoats for his unfortunate decisions. The Red Army managed to withdraw the bulk of their troops and to fight some effective rearguard actions which were to win them the grudging admiration of the Germans, but the defence was greatly hampered by Stalin's reluctance to send in reserves from the Moscow sector. Further south the south-western front was ripped to shreds by Kleist and Ruoff, prompting the *Stavka* to set up a Stalingrad front under Timoshenko, with Lieutenant-General Bonin as Chief of Staff and Nikita Khrushchev as Commissar.

Stalin thus reluctantly abandoned his disastrous obsession with holding on at any cost and agreed to withdrawal in the south. He also ordered offensive operations around Leningrad and by the Kalinin, and western fronts near Rzhev. Blaming the disasters of the past months in part on poor political work, Stalin purged the army's political administration, *GlavPURKKA*, and intensified the indoctrination of an increasingly demoralized army.

By retreating, the Red Army denied the Germans the chance to fight a massive battle of encirclement, but Hitler now tried to trap them with his armour. Führer Directive No. 45 of 23 July called for a temporary halt of the advance towards Stalingrad and ordered a battle of encirclement around Rostov using Hoth and Kleist's Panzer Armies. In 'Operation Edelweiss', List's Army Group A was then to occupy the coastline of the Black Sea where it would be joined by the bulk of 11th Army, which would cross the Kerch Straits. A further force was to advance towards Batum, taking the oilfields of Maikop and holding a line from Tiflis to Baku. Army Group B, now commanded by von Weichs, was ordered to seize Stalingrad and establish a defensive line on the Volga in 'Operation Heron'. In the north Leningrad was to be taken by the beginning of September in 'Operation Magic Fire' (soon to be renamed 'Northern Light'), which was to be conducted by Manstein and his 11th Army, much to his disgust.

Directive No. 45 was an absurdly ambitious plan which took no account of the relative strengths of the Wehrmacht and the Red Army. Halder confided in his diary that he found Hitler's attitude 'sick'. The hard-pressed and under-supplied Wehrmacht was called upon to fight along a dangerously extended front. Once again there was no concentration on a single objective, but rather three separate offensives against objectives which lacked a close strategic relationship. Hitler brushed aside all objections, imagining that the Russians were close to defeat. Rostov had fallen on the day that Directive No. 45 was issued, and although the Soviets had escaped total encirclement they had suffered terrible losses. The Germans now controlled the Donbas, the Caucasus was seriously threatened and the defences of Stalingrad were pitifully weak.

Stalingrad was placed on a war footing on 19 July and 180,000 citizens of a population of half a million were sent to prepare defensive positions around the perimeter of the city. Meanwhile, livestock and industrial plant were transported to the far side of the Volga. Timoshenko was dismissed and replaced by Gordov as commander of the Stalingrad front. Vasilevsky was sent from Moscow to appraise the overall situation. The Red Army fought desperately to maintain at least a few bridgeheads on the inside of the Don bend before Stalingrad. Paulus was hopelessly outnumbered and was held up by a series of stubborn if chaotic counter-blows, but the Red Army was now threatened by Hoth's 4th Panzer Army which Hitler had directed away from the drive to the Caucasus, and was now threatening Stalingrad from the south-west. The defence of Stalingrad was further hampered by Stalin's unfortunate decision to split the Stalingrad front into two, with two commands, two staffs and two forces, both with their headquarters in Stalingrad and both defending the same objective.

Gordov was no match for Paulus who, with considerable skill, smashed the Soviet forces to the west of the Don, and on the night of 21 August most of the 16th Panzer Division crossed the Don. Two days later, mechanized units reached the Volga north of Stalingrad and established a bridgehead. By 10 September Hoth's 4th Panzer Army had reached the Volga to the south of Stalingrad. Stalin refused to consider evacuating civilians and industry from the city which bore his name, insisting that this would be seen as tantamount to surrender.

Meanwhile, to the south Ruoff's 17th Army raced through the Kuban, and Kleist's 1st Panzer Army headed for the Caucasus. Here the Soviets were particularly vulnerable since many of the local populations welcomed the Germans as liberators from the tyranny of Stalinist Russia. Stalin despatched Beria and his henchmen to the Trans-Caucasian front where they wreaked a terrible revenge on the hapless peoples who sympathized with the invaders. Not only the Volga Germans, but many of the other minority groups, particularly those who espoused Islam, were subjected to an orgy of mass murder, deportations, slave labour and imprisonment which constitute one of the darker chapters of these terrible times.

Although the Red Army was reeling back at Stalingrad and in the Caucasus, the Germans were beginning to pay a heavy price for their successes. Paulus's problem was that as he got nearer to Stalingrad his flanks became increasingly exposed. He was thus faced with the choice of weakening his offensive punch or over-extending his lines of communication. Thus the decision to send the 4th Panzer Army against Stalingrad resulted in Army Group A being spread too thin, a problem that became more acute as the advance progressed. The 4th Panzer Army was also painfully slow in working its way towards Stalingrad and was poorly positioned, the Soviets tenaciously hanging on to areas which were to provide admirable launching-pads for their counter-offensives.

At the end of August Stalin appointed Zhukov Deputy Supreme Commander and sent him to Stalingrad. He lacked adequate reserves and was constantly prodded by Stalin to make a series of wasteful piecemeal counter-attacks. On 13 September he discussed the situation with Vasilevsky in Moscow and came to the conclusion that the Germans would be unable to reach the strategic objectives they had set for themselves in 1942. Their armies at Stalingrad and in the Caucasus had suffered heavy losses and the lines of communication were seriously over-extended. Their weakest point was the flank of the Stalingrad attack where the Romanians were stationed. This point was west of the Don, so German armour at Stalingrad could not be used to counter the blow.

The plan proposed by Zhukov and Vasilevsky offered the only possible effective solution to the problem, but time was running desperately short. The Germans were already fighting in the streets of Stalingrad while the Soviets discussed this strategy, and it was agreed that forty-five days were needed to prepare the counter-attack. It was therefore absolutely essential that the Soviet troops in Stalingrad should deny the Germans the rapid victory which they anticipated. Hitler, convinced that the Russians were without reserves and on the point of collapse, was furious at the slow progress of the German troops as they fought from house to house in this terrible battle. Halder, who found Hitler's persistent underestimation of the enemy 'grotesque', persistently pointed out the danger to the flank and warned that Army Group A was wearing itself out in suicidal frontal assaults against the city. The atmosphere at Hitler's headquarters at Vinnitsa was icy. On 24 September Halder was replaced by Zeitzler, who agreed with his predecessor and with

Paulus that the attack on Stalingrad should be broken off. Hitler would not listen to such advice and the battle for Stalingrad continued. Although the Germans occupied most of the city, the Soviets were able to maintain a bridgehead on the west bank of the Volga which enabled them to bring supplies and reserves across the river in spite of crippling artillery fire and persistent attacks from the Stukas.

For Hitler the battle for Stalingrad had become a question of prestige. It served no useful strategic purpose to take the city, since German troops controlled the Volga to the north and to the south. Nor was the capture of Stalingrad essential to the conduct of the campaign in the Caucasus.

Plans for the Soviet strategic counter-offensive were outlined at the end of September and given the codename 'Uranus'. *Stavka* proposed a massive pincer movement to the west of Stalingrad with troops from Vatutin's south-west front and Rokossovsky's Don front sweeping down from the north, concentrating their attack on the hapless Romanians, while units of Yeremenko's Stalingrad front worked their way up from the south. Further refinements of the plan shifted the main blow further west, from the Don front to the south-west front.

In mid October Paulus made a final attempt to batter his way through to the Volga. After several days of murderous fighting, he almost succeeded. Chuikov's 62nd Army was split in half as the Germans reached the river and his right flank was smashed. The Tractor Factory, which had continued to produce and repair tanks and which had been defended to the last man, was now in German hands. Goebbels' propaganda machine screamed of victory on the Volga. But Chuikov's men were still clinging to their bridgehead on the west bank of the Volga and Paulus's troops had fought themselves to a standstill. On 11 November the Germans launched yet another massive attack in Stalingrad and blasted another gap through Chuikov's bridgehead some 500 metres wide. As the Volga was beginning to freeze it became increasingly difficult to ferry supplies across the river, and the Red Army was desperately short of ammunition. The situation in Stalingrad was critical 'Uranus' had to be launched immediately if the city were to be saved. By taking the full weight of the German attack the remaining Soviet troops in Stalingrad created the best possible conditions for the success of the counter-offensive. It was almost impossible for the Red Army men at Stalingrad to believe, but they were beginning to win the battle.

The Soviet counter-offensive began on 19 November at 07.30 hours. By the end of the day troops from the Don front and the south-west front had cut through the Romanians and advanced 60 kilometres. The following day the Stalingrad front began its offensive, and the pincers joined around Stalingrad at Kalach on the Don on 23 November. Vasilevsky estimated that there were about 90,000 German troops trapped in Stalingrad. In fact there were 220,000, with 100 Panzers, 1800 guns and 10,000 trucks. On the evening of 22 November, Hitler ordered Paulus to make a stand at Stalingrad, but he replied that he did not have sufficient strength to establish an all-round defence. His army group commander, von Weichs, and the Chief of the General Staff, Zeitzler, agreed with this assessment and proposed a break-out. Manstein, who had been ordered by Hitler to beat back the Soviet counter-offensive by creating an Army Group Don out of the 6th Army, the 4th Panzer Army and the Romanian and Allied troops, also quickly reached the conclusion that under no circumstances should the 6th Army remain in Stalingrad. Hitler, having been assured by Goering that the Luftwaffe could deliver 500 tons of supplies per day to the troops in Stalingrad, repeated his order on 24 November that Paulus should not retreat. In fact the Luftwaffe, in spite of heavy losses and truly heroic efforts, managed to deliver a daily average of only 105 tons of supplies, but at least they succeeded in evacuating 42,000 wounded from the cauldron.

Manstein's immediate problem was to plug the gaps in his front to the south and west of Stalingrad and to keep his lines of communication open to Army Group A in the Caucasus. For this purpose he stitched together two support groups. The first, under General Hollidt, soon got stuck in a defensive battle on the Chir and was unable to fulfil its mission as outlined in 'Operation Thunderclap' for the break-out from Stalingrad. The second, under Hoth, was somewhat more successful with 'Operation Winter Storm', but it too was brought to a halt some 50 kilometres before its objective. Manstein's plan was highly elaborate and unorthodox, but it was also far too ambitious given the forces available. Paulus in Stalingrad had no clear idea what he intended, and he had not yet got permission for a break-out.

Although Manstein's plan failed to reach its objectives, it forced the Soviets to change their next move. Initially they had planned 'Big Saturn', a drive south to Rostov so as to cut off the bulk of Army Group Don and Army Group A at Stalingrad and in the Caucasus. Stalin now felt that the situation was too precarious to risk such an operation and he ordered 'Little Saturn' – an attack to the south-east against the Chir front and the Italian 8th Army on the Don. 'Little Saturn' was launched on 16 December and Manstein was quick to realize the danger posed to Rostov and to Army Group A. By 20 December the Red Army had driven through the Italians on a 100-kilometre front and was heading for the sea of Azov. Hollidt's troops on the Chir were also partially overrun, and Manstein was obliged to send troops from Hoth's support group to strengthen the left flank of his army group. This in turn obliged Hoth to withdraw to the position he had held before 'Winter Storm', thus making a break-out from Stalingrad virtually impossible.

On 10 January the Soviets opened another offensive against Stalingrad with the greatest artillery barrage they had yet mounted. Within four days they captured the airfield at Pitomnik and, on 22 December, the last of the German airfields in the Stalingrad pocket at Gumrak. Now the 6th Army could be supplied only by parachute drops and the wounded could no longer be evacuated. Paulus begged Hitler for permission to capitulate so that further senseless bloodshed could be avoided, but to no avail. He was appointed Field Marshal to stiffen his resolve to fight to the last. By 25 January the German troops in Stalingrad were trapped in two cauldrons. On 31 January Paulus surrendered in the southern cauldron; the remaining Germans forces surrendered two days later. A total of 100,000 Germans fell at Stalingrad and of the 90,000 taken prisoner, only a handful survived.

Stalingrad was a great victory for the Red Army, but its importance has perhaps been exaggerated. It was hardly a turning point in the war. The German army had suffered a setback, but it was far from defeated. The third battle of Kharkov was to show that the Wehrmacht was still an awesomely professional fighting machine full of aggressive spirit. The Germans had suffered a worse defeat in north Africa, and it was not until the battle of Kursk that the Russians were able to beat the Germans at their own game. It is still a matter of debate whether Paulus and Manstein should have disobeyed orders and allowed the 6th Army to fight its way out of Stalingrad. Paulus was, in any case, temperamentally incapable of such defiant action in spite of his very considerable professional skill. Most important of all, the 6th Army's heroic stand held down very large numbers of Soviet troops and thus enabled Manstein to extricate Army Group B from the Caucasus. Had the 6th Army surrendered earlier, the situation would have been disastrous. Nevertheless, the psychological effect of the Soviet victory was enormous. The Russians had shown that the Germans could be beaten, and Nazi propaganda about Slav subhumans and the weakness and decadence of the Soviet state began to ring a trifle hollow. On the German side there was a growing feeling that Hitler had betrayed his own troops and was beginning to show alarming signs of irrationality.

As early as 28 December Zeitzler had managed to get Hitler to agree to a withdrawal of Kleist's Army Group A from the Caucasus. Some of these troops were able to squeeze through the Rostov bottleneck and cross the Don. Some 400,000 men retreated to the Kuban bridgehead. Hitler insisted that they should remain there, hold down Soviet forces and prepare for a fresh offensive to seize the Caucasus oilfields. His military advisers saw this as a pointless waste of effort and argued that these forces should be withdrawn over the straits to Kerch and then used to rectify the situation in the south.

Meanwhile, the northern flank of Army Group B on the Don was attacked by the Voronezh front and the south-west front and was pushed back across the Donets on a 350-kilometre wide front from Voronezh to Voroshilovgrad. In a two-pronged attack to the north and south of Kursk the Soviets created a wide salient to the south of which lay Kharkov, which was encircled and captured. The Germans were now in a precarious situation, even though the retreat from the Caucasus had been a brilliant achievement. Given the distance, the dreadful weather and the persistence of Soviet attacks, the speed and economy with which it had been conducted was remarkable. But Manstein was now faced with a critical threat to his left flank. He therefore proposed to shorten his right flank by withdrawing from the Don and the Donets to the Mius, and to prepare a counter-offensive. Hitler at first refused, insisting that coal from the Donets basin was essential to the German war economy, but in the course of a stormy four-hour interview Manstein managed to persuade him to change his mind. In a subsequent meeting at Manstein's headquarters Hitler turned down Manstein's proposal for a westward swing which would pin the Soviets to the coastline of the Sea of Azov, and opted instead for an offensive against the massive salient at Kursk, to be known as 'Operation Citadel'.

Stalin had full details of the German build-up for the offensive against the Kursk salient from 'Lucy', who provided daily reports of OKW decisions, from other agents who had infiltrated the German administration in occupied Russia, and from the British who provided 'Ultra' decrypts of German deployments. His first reaction was to call for a pre-emptive strike, but his generals warned him against such a move. It was then decided to go on the defensive although Stalin, mindful of the earlier failures of the Red Army in defence, still toyed with the idea of a spoiling attack. The salient, an area about half the size of England, was stuffed with armour and infantry and awaited the next move.

At the end of February and the beginning of March, Manstein plugged the gaps on his front and forced the south-west front armies back across the Donets, and on 14 March he recaptured Kharkov. Belgorod fell the following week, but the spring thaw and consequent mud brought the campaign to a temporary halt. These German successes brought them back to the starting point for their offensive of the previous summer, but they were in a far weaker position relative to the Red Army. They had suffered terrible losses and lacked reserves. Soviet war industry was greatly out-producing that of Germany and they were now manufacturing 2000 tanks per month. In the south the Soviets outnumbered the Germans seven to one, in the centre and north four to one. Zeitzler was at least able to use this unequal situation to persuade Hitler to allow some modest withdrawals to straighten the front.

But time was running out for the Germans. The Allies would soon be landing in Europe, and two summer offensives had failed to bring the Soviet Union to its knees. The most that could be hoped for was that in 1943 a series of partial offensives would cause the Soviets such severe losses of men and materials that they would be obliged to seek a political solution. This in turn was possible only if the Germans were able to maintain their superiority in mobility and in flexible and imaginative leadership. Such ideas, however, ran counter to those of the Führer. Hitler was not interested in a political solution, for that would involve some degree of compromise. Nor would he agree to a flexible defensive strategy, sticking to his belief that to withdraw was to admit defeat. This obsession with standing fast enabled the Red Army to destroy entire German armies.

By the spring of 1943 there was widespread disillusionment with Hitler's leadership and a growing feeling that the *Gröfaz* (Greatest General of All Time) was losing his grip. A group of senior officers including Manstein, Zeitzler, Milch and Guderian argued in favour of creating the post of Supreme Commander East so that Hitler's meddling with strategic decisions and operational orders could at least be reduced. Other officers favoured a more drastic solution. A group of younger officers around Colonel von Treschow, the senior staff officer of Army Group Centre who was close to General Beck and to Goerdeler, argued that Hitler had to be assassinated. With the knowledge of General Oster of military intelligence and General Olbricht of the reserve army, a bomb was planted in Hitler's plane when he visited Army Group Centre in Smolensk on 13 March 1943, but it failed to detonate.

The commanders of the two army groups involved in 'Citadel' insisted that the offensive should be launched as soon as possible before the Red Army had time to improve their defences. Hitler, however, wished to postpone the attack, awaiting the arrival of the new Panzer Vs ('Panthers') and VIs ('Tigers') and the provision of extra armour for the Panzer IIIs and IVs. But the longer the attack was postponed the longer the Soviets had to prepare their anti-tank positions in the salient, and bring in the new model of the T–34 and the brand new heavy KV–85, and greatly increase the number of self-propelled guns.

The German attack on the Kursk salient was launched on 5 July. Model's 9th Army from Army Group Centre attacked from the north and Hoth's 4th Panzer Army from the south. The Germans ran up against carefully prepared anti-tank positions and met with fierce resistance. The fighting was particularly intense in the southern part of the salient as the SS *Totenkopf*, *Adolf Hitler* and *Das Reich* drove towards Prokhorovka, eventually to be driven back with heavy losses in a series of counter-attacks. To offer some relief to their forces in the Kursk salient, the Soviets mounted a limited offensive against the Orel salient to the north against the 2nd Panzer army and the flank of the 9th Army. The success of the operation came as a welcome surprise to the *Stavka* and it obliged Army Group Centre to devote all its efforts to the defence of the Orel salient. Coupled with the failure to reach Prokhorovka, this setback forced the Germans to abandon 'Operation Citadel' on 13 July, and they thus had to admit that they had suffered a crushing defeat.

The battle of Kursk, the 'greatest tank battle of all time', was an appalling bloodbath, veteran soldiers insisting that it was the most brutal engagement of the war. Precise figures of the losses of men and equipment on both sides will never be known, but the decisive factor was that the Germans had been defeated at the game they knew best. Their elite armoured units, equipped with the latest Panzer models and manned by fresh troops, had been smashed and the Soviets had finally won the strategic initiative. Kursk, not Stalingrad, was the turning point of the war on the eastern front.

Model's troops, which had been used in 'Citadel', were now withdrawn to strengthen the Orel salient, but the Germans were hopelessly outnumbered as the Soviets attacked with three fronts –

the west front (Sokolovsky), the Bryansk front (Popov) and the central front (Rokossovsky). On 31 July the Germans withdrew from the Orel salient to a defensive position, the curiously named 'Hagen Line' east of Bryansk. Throughout the rest of the summer Army Group Centre was subjected to a series of Soviet attacks but was able to stand firm until events on the southern front forced them to retreat.

A major Soviet summer offensive was launched in the south against the Mius–Donets bend by Voroshilovgrad on 17 July. The operation met with a limited success and Malinovsky's south-west front was able to establish a bridgehead across the Donets at Izyum which proved to be a valuable launching pad for further operations. On 16 August they pushed on towards Stalino. A further offensive to clear the Belgorod pocket, formed as the 4th Panzer Army had advanced towards Prokhorovka, was launched on 3 August and met with complete success. The attempt to cut off Kharkov by driving down from the Kursk salient through Poltava to the Dnieper failed, but a push towards Kharkov from the south-east was successful and on 22 August the city was once again in Soviet hands. The Soviets had now removed the Kursk salient by pushing forward either side of it beyond Kharkov and Orel.

The northern flank of Manstein's forces was now dangerously exposed and either he would need large numbers of reserves to strengthen his position or he would have to evacuate the Donets basin and retire to the Dnieper. Unable to provide the reserves, Hitler agreed to a withdrawal to the Dnieper and the creation of the East Wall, a defensive line running north through Kiev and Pskov to the Estonian border. The Soviet breakthrough in the direction of Kiev had separated Army Group Centre from Army Group South, and Kluge was obliged to abandon Smolensk, Bryansk and Roslavi, scenes of the greatest German triumphs in 1941, in order to rectify this threatening situation. On 4 September Hitler also agreed to the evacuation of the Kuban bridgehead which had long since become a strategic liability.

The Germans fought skilfully as they withdrew to the East Wall, and the Soviets again dissipated their strength in an over-ambitious offensive strategy directed across the entire front. But by October the German forces were seriously weakened. Most infantry divisions were down to one-third of their strength. Between July and September the Germans had lost 1560 Panzers and had only 2300 left, of which only 700 were fit for action, and they had to face 8400 Soviet tanks. The Panzers therefore had to rush hither and thither to act as a 'fire brigade' to meet immediate dangers, and were no longer able to fight as proper divisions. The Red Army outnumbered the Wehrmacht by at least four to one, had far greater manpower reserves and was supported by a vastly superior war industry.

Although the Soviets were getting the upper hand, they were still prepared to discuss a negotiated peace with the Germans. Under the aegis of Alexander Kollontai, one of the few old bolsheviks who had survived the purges and who was serving as Soviet ambassador in Sweden, negotiations began in December 1942 between Kleist, from Ribbentrop's personal staff, and Edgar Clauss, a rather dubious figure of German extraction. In June the Soviets let it be known that Alexandrov, head of the European section of the Foreign Office, was prepared to discuss a separate peace. The Soviets were deeply suspicious of their western allies who refused to reach an agreement on the frontier issue, excluded them from the administration of occupied Italy and constantly delayed the second front. They let the Germans know that they were convinced that the western powers were prepared to let them fight to their last drop of blood so that they could then take over Europe by pushing aside an exhausted and ruined Soviet Union. Kleist was instructed not to contact Alexandrov, but in September 1943 the Soviets made a concrete offer: the Soviet Union would be guaranteed the Russian frontiers of 1914 and there would be a comprehensive trade agreement with the German Reich. Hitler forbade any such negotiations for fear of appearing weak, because of the effect such talks were likely to have on Germany's allies and because he believed that the Soviet move was designed merely to obtain political concessions from the British and the Americans. The Soviet Government's motives are impossible to discern, but it is perhaps indicative that the 'National Committee of Free Germany', made up of German communists, sympathetic intellectuals and gullible prisoners of war, desisted from denouncing the Nazi regime until the peace feelers were finally rejected, and were content merely to call for an armistice. The British and Americans knew about the Soviet–German talks, but were unimpressed. They were convinced that the Soviet Union had suffered so much that they would not accept a compromise solution.

At the back of Hitler's mind was his conviction that the alliance between the 'plutocratic' British and Americans and the 'Jewish bolshevik' Soviets would fall apart. He imagined that if he could beat back the Allied landings in northern Europe he could force the western powers to negotiate a peace. Thus, in Directive No. 51 of 3 November 1943 he announced that: 'The danger in the east remains, but a greater danger now appears in the west: an Anglo-Saxon landing!' This meant that the forces in the Soviet Union would be denied any significant reinforcements while the defences in the west were improved. Yet Hitler still refused to permit a further shortening of the front and a withdrawal from the Crimea. When the Soviets renewed their offensive in October it was therefore against a greatly weakened opponent who was badly off balance and lacked adequate reserves.

That the Soviet Union had withstood the German invasion, contrary to all expert predictions, and had now gained the strategic initiative was a remarkable achievement. It was widely believed that this was due in large part to appeals by the Government to national pride, and to a degree of ideological relaxation. Whereas it is true that millions of Soviet citizens volunteered to do their patriotic duty in the popular militia (*opolchenie*) and in the labour battalions which built the lines of defence, the Stalinist system was not going to rely on anything as subjective as patriotism or the spirit of self-sacrifice. The volunteers soon found that there were no weapons, and the labour battalions wondered why nothing had been done to prepare for an invasion and why Nazi Germany had, up until the last moment, been said to be friendly. All males capable of bearing arms who were born between 1905 and 1918 were drafted. In the western regions martial law was imposed. In December 1941 all workers remotely connected with war industry were placed under military law and could thus be shot as deserters if they failed to turn up for work. Holidays were suspended for the duration of the war, the normal working day was extended to up to twelve hours, and overtime was made compulsory.

The most remarkable achievement on the home front was the removal of entire factories from the western regions to the Volga, behind the Urals, Siberia, Kazakhstan and central Asia. Most of these factories were rebuilt in the harsh winter of 1941–42 and quickly began normal production. Workers lived in the most unimaginable squalor, suffered from acute undernourishment and worked exceedingly long hours. Clothing was almost impossible to obtain and footwear was no longer available at all. The average 'housing' for a worker in the coal industry during the war was a mere 12 square feet. Such suffering was bearable only because it was blamed principally on the Germans, not on the viciousness and incompetence of the Soviet authorities as had been the case in the past. The scale of this operation was truly staggering. By November 1941 more than 1500 factories had been moved and in October alone 80,000 railway wagons removed 198 factories from Moscow. Along with this plant and equipment went ten million people who had to be housed and fed, however poorly.

Apart from the privileged few who lived in obscene luxury, the vast mass of Soviet citizens existed on the brink of starvation throughout the war. Rations were minuscule and frequently not available. The Germans overran almost half of the agricultural land and slaughtered most of the livestock. Tractors, trucks and draught animals were needed by the army and were taken from the collective farms. All able-bodied men were needed in the armed forces and in war industry so that only the very young, the very old and women remained on the land. Workers on collective farms who failed to meet the frequently ludicrous norms were accused of sabotage. Workers and peasants were given small allotments in which they grew most of their food and they sold the excess on the black market at astronomical prices. Some unscrupulous characters were able to make enormous fortunes from the sufferings of others, and by turning over part of their profits on the black market to the state defence fund they were celebrated as national heroes.

In spite of the loss of most of the industrial west with its valuable sources of raw materials and the agricultural produce of the Ukraine, Soviet industry made a truly astonishing recovery. Thanks to rigid control over resources, tightly centralized control, skilful improvisation and the ferocious exploitation of labour in 1942, 25,436 aircraft and 24,688 tanks were produced. The Soviets received relatively few weapons from their allies, and much of what they got was obsolete, but the large numbers of trucks provided by Lend-Lease made up for serious deficiencies in transportation.

Under the impact of war the much-vaunted 'socialist national relations' began to fall apart. Many Soviet citizens had suffered appalling injustices under Stalinist terror and were misguided enough to welcome the Germans as liberators, but most people felt that a home-grown dictatorship was preferable to an imported one, and comforted themselves with the fond belief that once the war was over the regime was bound to relax its grip. The Volga Germans, most of whom had lived in Russia for generations and whose loyalty was unquestionable, were nevertheless accused of collaboration and deported to Siberia under appalling conditions. Few survived to tell the story. In the Caucasus and the Black Sea regions many of the nationals were deported and replaced by Russians and Ukrainians. Particularly affected were the Moslems, about one million of whom were evicted from their homelands. Crowded into camps in remote areas, those who managed to survive lived an inhuman existence, forbidden to use their mother tongue and denied any further education.

The Stalinist principle of guilt by association applied to these nationals. Entire peoples, not individuals or groups, were branded as collaborationists and herded into cattle trucks. The Karachai, Kalmyks, Chechens, Ingushis, Crimean Tartars, Greeks, Meskhetians and Balkars, along with countless other smaller groups, were shipped off to Siberia, Kazhakhstan, Uzbekistan and Kirgizia. About one and a half million were transported, one million arrived, few returned. It is small comfort that all these peoples were all subsequently rehabilitated. The struggle for basic rights in their homelands continues.

Great Russian chauvinism and the search for scapegoats, both officially encouraged during the war years, led to a distressing resurgence of anti-Semitism. Although Soviet Jews were to suffer an unimaginably terrible fate in the hands of the Germans, and there could be no possible question about their attitude towards Nazi Germany, they frequently became the victims of vicious discrimination as the ever smouldering Russian anti-Semitism broke into destructive flame. The wartime experience of many Soviet Jews, trapped between Nazi murderers and Soviet anti-Semites, was to have profound repercussions in the post-war years.

Deportees from the Baltic states, Poland, Bessarabia, the Northern Bukovina, Moldavia, and the Caucasus were herded together in the Gulag with Volga Germans, Crimean Tartars and 'defeatist elements', among whom were those Soviet soldiers who had been taken prisoner by the Germans and had made their way back to a grateful motherland. It was they, not the starry-eyed volunteers of official propaganda, who provided the slave labour which built the airports and hangars in the Urals, the roads in Siberia, the Arctic ports and Magadan, the capital of the Kolyma region. Hundreds of thousands died in these camps. The authorities estimated that those given heavy labour survived an average of three years. The ten-year sentence automatically given to 'defeatists' was thus virtually a sentence of death. In 1944 the American Vice-President, Henry Wallace, was taken on an official tour of Magadan. He was much impressed by what he saw at this notorious camp, which was ironically called the 'Far Northern Construction Project'. He was delighted to find the prisoners brimming with good health, the food excellent, the recreational facilities exemplary.

The Red Army, having suffered a series of catastrophic defeats, was rapidly demoralised and desertion, cowardice, indiscipline and sheer panic were widespread. Self-inflicted wounds were commonplace. To stop the rot disciplinary units were strengthened as was SMERSH, the military counter-intelligence service. The commissars were given sweeping powers and the NKVD troops terrorized faltering units. Officers and commissars who allowed their units to retreat were automatically demoted or hauled in front of a court-martial.

The state relaxed its persecution of the Church during the war years, and as a result there was a remarkable religious revival. On 22 June 1942 the Metropolitan Sergei called upon the faithful to defend the country and he issued a series of epistles praying for victory. These prayers were backed up by the Dimitry Donskoi tank column financed by church collections. In 1943 Sergei appealed to the priests in the occupied areas not to collaborate with the enemy, and expressly condemned Bishop Polikarp of Kiev for his pro-German activities. Shortly afterwards he announced that support of fascism was a betrayal of the Church and that any collaborators would be excommunicated. Stalin responded by closing down the League of Militant Atheists, allowing the election of a new patriarch, toning down anti-religious propaganda and easing restrictions on religious instruction. The Church prayed for Stalin's good health and long life and proclaimed him to be 'the incarnation of all that is best and brightest, all that constitutes the sacred spiritual heritage of the Russian people, the legacy of their ancestors'. Church dignitaries were afforded all the privileges of the Soviet elite and were lavishly decorated at the end of the war.

The arts, like religion, were given marginally more freedom, but the results were not very impressive. Ilya Ehrenburg's dreadful novel *The Fall of Paris*, which had been slightly rude about the Germans but considerably more outspoken about the appeasers, was allowed to be published. This was considered to be a major step forward in the direction of freedom of expression. The vast bulk of literary output during the war was of even lower standard, and those who attempted to be mildly critical, such as M.M. Zoshchenko or K.A. Fedin, were promptly brought to heel. For the most part Soviet artists were content to wallow in patriotic sentimentality, hymn the praises of great historical figures such as Alexander Nevsky, Peter the Great or Kutuzov, and produce endless cliché-ridden panegyrics to the heroic front-line soldier or the self-sacrificing father of the people, Josef Stalin. Dimitri Shostakovich, whose wartime works included the Leningrad Symphony and the second piano trio, was virtually the only artist who managed to produce lasting works of art which did not fall foul of the party line.

The war further enhanced the power and influence of the Communist Party. It became directly responsible for the mobilization and training of manpower, for the reorganization, reallocation and evacuation of industry and for wartime agitation and propaganda. Within the armed forces it was directly responsible for discipline and morale, and in the early years it exercised a profound influence over purely military matters through the system of dual command.

At first this development was partially disguised. The catastrophic failures of the early months of the war could scarcely be claimed as evidence of the far-sighted wisdom of the party or of the scientific achievements of Marxism–Leninism. Once the situation began to stabilize, the party of Lenin and Stalin was depicted as the head and the heart of the great patriotic struggle.

During the war the party became increasingly involved in economic affairs, and the need to recruit the most capable irrespective of social origins led to a further professionalization of the the cadres. During the war 32.1 per cent of new members were workers and 25.3 per cent peasants, but 42.6 per cent were classified as 'intellectuals', a group which included white-collar workers. The new recruits were younger and better educated. They were also almost exclusively Great Russians. In the disruption caused by the eastward movement of the population and of industrial plant, the local party organizations were often the only bodies able to make quick and effective decisions, the various commissariats having often lost direct contact with their enterprises. When the local party organs were unable to resolve these difficulties they had the advantage of immediate access to more senior officials.

Naturally enough the party became militarized during the war. By the end of the war 25 per cent of the armed forces were party members and a further 20 per cent were in the *Komsomol*. By 1945 half the members of the Communist Party were in the armed forces. The more prestigious the branch of the service the greater was the percentage of party members, and party members were more likely to be decorated. Party members accounted for 74 per cent of the Heroes of the Soviet Union, and a further 11 per cent were in the *Komsomol*. On 16 July 1941 political control over the armed forces was tightened by the introduction of political commissars. This was deeply resented by the Officer Corps, who regarded most of the commissars as incompetent amateurs, toadies and careerists whose activities had a disastrous effect on morale. The system was modified in October 1942, by which time it was clear that the loyalty of the military was unquestionable and that the activities of the commissars were counter-productive. The party, ever mindful of the dangers of 'bonapartism' and 'caesarism', was deeply suspicious of independent military power and was determined to maintain a degree of political control over the armed forces. In the struggle for power between the military and the party, the military as the architects of victory were to make substantial gains and to assure for themselves a powerful position within the Soviet state which they were determined to maintain in peacetime.

CHAPTER ELEVEN

Italy and the Balkans

(July 1943–October 1944)

On 10 July 1943 Montgomery's 8th Army and Patton's 7th Army landed on the south coast of Sicily. The Allies caught the Germans by surprise. In an operation involving 'the man who never was', phoney plans for the invasion of Sardinia and Greece were planted on a corpse which was washed ashore and fell into German hands. Hitler was taken in by this deception, although Kesselring, who commanded the troops in Italy, felt that the plans were a hoax and believed that the Allies would land in Sicily. 'Operation Husky' was badly planned and poorly executed. Although the landings were marginally more efficiently conducted than for 'Torch', 47 of the 134 British gliders landed in the sea and a counter-attack by the Hermann Goering Division drove the invaders back to the beaches. The situation was saved only when naval guns were levelled against the Panzers. Faced with such unequal firepower, the Germans were obliged to withdraw.

The Germans had inadequate forces for the defence of Sicily and 'Ultra' informed the Allies of their movements and intentions. Complete air and naval supremacy, plus the enthusiasm of the Italian troops for surrender rather than for fighting, guaranteed the success of the operation. The crucial mistake made by the Allies was not to block off the German retreat across the straits to the mainland where they could regroup. Patton's army dashed across the island then headed eastward, reaching Messina on 17 August. Montgomery took a painfully long time to cover a shorter route along the east coast. General Hube had time to build a defensive front which was punctured only when fresh troops were brought in from Tunis.

The Germans retreated across the straits in a brilliantly conducted operation which resulted in minimal casualties. Had the Allies followed quickly they could have scored an overwhelming victory, but the Americans were still worried that a campaign in Italy would lead to further postponements of 'Overlord', while the British were obsessed with security. Montgomery unleashed a massive artillery barrage on empty country before crossing the straits. A vast quantity of ammunition was wasted, the Germans had ample time to withdraw and only three unfortunate stragglers were taken prisoner. Churchill and Brooke now began to think that success in Italy might make 'Overlord' superfluous if it were followed by an attack on the south of France or through the Balkans to Vienna. The Americans became seriously concerned that the British were trying to ditch the invasion of north-western France, and constant mutterings of 'Passchendaele' and 'Dunkirk' did nothing to assuage their fears. The real trouble was that Churchill, as usual, wanted everything: he wanted victory in Italy, he wanted 'Overlord', and he wanted an attack on 'Fortress Europe' from the south.

The invasion of Sicily marked a decisive stage in the internal political crisis in Italy which had long been smouldering. The Italians had suffered a series of shattering defeats in north Africa and had committed 227,000 ill-equipped and ill-trained troops to the eastern front where they were treated with undisguised contempt by the Germans. Italian strategy was inept. An enormous effort was invested in campaigns in Greece and the Soviet Union where the national interest was never at stake, whereas Malta and Gibraltar, essential to the command of the Mediterranean, were ignored. Although Mussolini was Commander-in-Chief as well as Minister for all three services, he had only a skeleton staff which failed to co-ordinate the efforts of the armed forces, and inter-service rivalry was intense. This resulted in Italy's cities being left open to air attack for lack of anti-aircraft defences, and the navy was destroyed from the air having refused to build the aircraft carriers without which enemy bases could not be attacked from the air. The army was poorly trained and its Officer Corps top-heavy: in 1939 there were 600 generals. War industry failed to provide the tanks, trucks and guns which the army desperately needed to fight a modern war. Italy's army was much the same as in the First World War. It was an infantry army of poor peasants, mainly from the south, even worse fed and worse clothed than in the previous war and using obsolete rifles and guns. The air force lacked long-range bombers and its fighters were too few and too slow. The navy lacked modern equipment such as radar, and was desperately short of fuel.

The lack of raw materials, always a major problem for the Italian economy, reached crisis proportions during the war. Oil imports dropped to half the peacetime aggregate. The Italians failed to realize that there was oil in Libya, and were supplied from Romania with heavy loss in transit across the Mediterranean. The Germans had little coal to spare for the Italians, so that steel production dropped and firms such as Fiat were producing almost half the number of vehicles in 1941 that they had built in 1938. An increase in armaments production in 1942 was cut short by Allied bombing raids on the industrial centres. A number of major factories were seriously affected by bombing, and civilians hastily evacuated the cities. By the end of 1942 the population of Milan was reduced by 500,000. Workers who remained took part in a number of strikes, many of them organized by the communists for political effect, although discontent over such material issues as allowances for evacuees was the ostensible reason.

There were ample grounds for such discontent. The food ration was pitifully low. By 1943 it was a mere one thousand calories per day, with only 400 grams of meat per month. Heating fuel was scarce and petrol no longer available for private consumption. In such an atmosphere a thriving black market soon sprang up. Hunger, bombing and a series of defeats led to a complete collapse in morale, an identification of fascism with starvation and chaos, and a marked increase in communist sympathies. This last was particularly alarming to the bourgeoisie, who were also becoming increasingly alienated from the regime.

A major problem was that Mussolini, although an expert propagandist, found it increasingly difficult to find a convincing reason why Italy was fighting a war at all. Few Italians could work up much enthusiasm for conquests in Greece or Tunisia, and most felt that they were being asked to die for Hitler. Mockery of the 'Anglo-Saxons' went down quite well, and some extremists supported the idea of an anti-bolshevik crusade, but many Italians had relatives who were happily settled in the United States which seemed to them like the promised land, and 'Mustachio' (Stalin) was widely seen as a rather more sympathetic and avuncular type than Mussolini. The Fascist Party was rapidly losing credibility under the leadership, since December 1941, of Aldo Vidussoni, a twenty-eight-year-old veteran of the Spanish Civil war who, in spite of his youth and his war wounds, was a ridiculous figure. He was replaced in early 1943 by a brutal *squadistra*, Carlo Scorza, but it was too late for him to lick the party into shape.

The Fascist Party was increasingly powerless. The Grand Council had not met since December 1939 and the party was rapidly becoming little more than a corrupt association of place-seekers and exhibitionists, which served to lower the country's morale still further. As authority collapsed at the centre, regionalism became more pronounced. The Sicilians sought to free themselves from the 'continentals' and Mussolini's decision to force all Sicilian-born civil servants to leave their native island served merely to strengthen the determination of the separatists. South Tyrol had virtually become a German province. Many Germans opted for German citizenship while remaining in Italy, and German speakers who did not were persecuted as anti-Nazis. Some 72,000 Germans from South Tyrol went 'home to the Reich', a decision which many lived to regret. Italian occupation policies in Yugoslavia triggered off an armed revolt by the Yugoslavs in Venezia Giulia, ably led by the communists.

By 1942 native anti-fascism was experiencing a revival, the exiles being hopelessly out of touch with the situation in Italy. Communists and socialists began clandestine operations and started an underground press. Republicans, radicals and liberals joined together to form the Party of Action. A new Christian Democratic Party (DC) was formed with the support of the Vatican. Vatican Radio and the *Osservatore Romano* provided a more objective account of world events than was available in the official Italian press. In his Christmas message for 1942 Pius XII condemned both 'state worship' and racialism, much to the fury of the fascists who condemned the Church for its defeatist attitude. None of this amounted to very much. The Church was painfully cautious, the political parties were still weak and posed little threat to the regime. Even the Communist Party was pitifully small: of the 21,000 workers at Fiat in 1943, only 80 were party members.

The man who held the key to the situation was, curiously enough, the King. Victor Emmanuel although clever was weak and indecisive, but he enjoyed the loyal support of the army which had never been seriously tempted by fascist rigmarole. Both the King and the army favoured a military Government to replace Mussolini, but they contemplated a civilian regime under a Giolittian liberal such as Bonomi of Orlando. The alternatives to the discredited Mussolini were not attractive. The Germans might impose an ultra fascist like the dreadful Farinacci on the unfortunate country. The communists and socialists might possibly seize power. The Americans might insist on a Government under their favourite, Carlo Sforza, who although impeccably blue-blooded was also distressingly republican and anti-clerical. On 29 May the American Government reassured the Apostolic Delegate that they would accept a military Government.

Meanwhile a group of prominent fascists, including Mussolini's son-in-law and Foreign Minister, Ciano, along with de Bono, de Vecchi, Grandi and Bottai, decided that the time had come to get rid of the Duce and negotiate a peace. On 5 February Mussolini sacked the lot of them, but now that they were free from the burdens of office they could devote all their time to their conspiracy. On 13 May the Axis troops in north Africa surrendered. When the Allies landed in Sicily the Chief of the General Staff recommended surrender. Mussolini came back empty-handed from what proved to be his last meeting with Hitler at Feltre on 19 July when he tried to persuade the Führer to send German troops from the eastern front to Italy. The Duce saw no way of avoiding Farinacci's call to convene the Grand Council, a move that was supported even by party moderates.

On 17 July Roosevelt and Churchill promised that Italy would have an honourable place in the European family of nations if the fascists were deposed. If not, Rome would be bombed. Two days later Rome was indeed bombed, resulting in 1500 deaths, among them General Hazon, the royalist head of the *Carabinieri*. On 24 July the Grand Council met and debated a masterly motion proposed by Grandi which was couched in deliberately obscure language and which, by asking the King to assume his constitutional role in the decision-making process, invited the monarch to oust Mussolini. After a lengthy debate the motion was passed by a comfortable majority. Mussolini visited the King the following day and was not only dismissed but placed under arrest, as were many other leading fascists. Marshal Badoglio, a former Chief of Staff who had been dismissed after the failure of the campaign in Greece in 1941 and who had devoted the intervening time to Roman social life, was appointed Prime Minister. He promptly proclaimed a state of emergency, banning all political parties, including the fascists, until the end of the war. Mussolini was bundled into an ambulance and packed off to a hotel on the Gran Sasso in the Abruzzi. Fascism was toppled in a bloodless coup and most Italians tried to forget that it had ever been.

Badoglio announced that the war would continue, although his intention was to stop it as soon as possible. Just as he hoped, the people did not believe him. He had no other choice but to make this statement, for had he been honest the Germans would have promptly occupied the country and established a Quisling Government. Hitler was not taken in by this move, however, and promptly sent reinforcements to northern Italy and prepared a contingency plan to seize the Italian fleet at Genoa and La Spezia and to disarm the Italian occupation forces in southern France should Badoglio's Government decide to change sides.

Badoglio began armistice negotiations on 4 August via the Italian embassy in Lisbon, but the Allies were stuck with their unconditional surrender formula which they had no idea how to implement. Badoglio could not surrender until he was certain that the Allies would get to Rome before the Germans. After much haggling, an agreement was reached on 3 September. Eisenhower reluctantly agreed to send paratroops to occupy Rome and went ahead with plans for a landing at Salerno. The Germans got wind of what was up and seized the airfields around Rome so that the Allied attack had to be cancelled. The Germans occupied Rome and the Badoglio Government offered no resistance. They then bombed the Italian fleet as it sailed to Malta, sinking the flagship *Roma*.

On 9 September the Americans landed at Salerno in what General Mark Clark imagined was a surprise move. It soon proved to be one of the worst-kept secrets in the war. Kesselring was convinced that the Allies would not attempt a landing beyond the reach of full air cover. The German 10th Army under von Vietinghoff was desperately short of fuel and the Americans knew all about their movements from 'Ultra' decrypts, but they launched a powerful counter-attack and disaster was averted only by the massive use of air power and the accuracy of naval gunnery. Montgomery was characteristically slow in coming to the assistance of the Salerno beach-head and did not arrive until 19 September. Members of the Allied press corps arrived twenty-seven hours ahead of the 8th Army reconnaissance units. On the east coast on 25 September the 8th Army took Foggia and thus had an important air base from which they could bomb the industrial areas of eastern Germany and the Romanian oilfields. The Americans reached Naples on 1 October. Vietinghoff withdrew to the 'Gustav Line', a strong defensive position which Kesselring had prepared across the Italian boot from Gaeta to Ortona.

While the Americans were struggling to establish a beach-head at Salerno SS Hauptsturmführer Skorzeny rescued Mussolini from the Gran Sasso and installed him in the Villa Feltinelli in Gargnano. Although Mussolini told Hitler that he did not want to be another Quisling, that was precisely what he became. The new state, known as the Republic of Salò to the amusement of those with a rudimentary knowledge of French, was named after the small town on Lake Garda where the Propaganda Ministry was housed. This was most appropriate, since propaganda was all that the new state was able to produce once Mussolini had ordered the execution of Ciano, in spite of the pleadings of his favourite daughter, and those of his accomplices who had voted for Grandi's motion and had not been prudent enough to flee. Mussolini announced that fascism was now radical, 'social' and republican. Boasts that industry would be nationalized alarmed the bourgeoisie and annoyed the Germans without impressing the workers. None of this was much cause for alarm, since the Republic of Salò had no power and was totally dependent on the good will of the Germans.

On 9 September the King and Badoglio fled from Rome and went to Brindisi. This further compromised the monarchy, which was regarded by fascists as treacherous and by democrats as a hindrance to reform. By abandoning the capital the King lost the good will of his subjects which he had regained on 25 July. This was perhaps a little unfair. How was he to know whether or not the Germans would have obliged Mussolini and had him shot?

Sicily and most of southern Italy were now under the Allied Military Government (AMGOT). The Badoglio administration was allowed to run Sardinia and four provinces in the south-east under the supervision of the Allied Control Commission. On 13 October the Badoglio Government declared war on Germany and was recognized as a co-belligerent, although not as an ally. It was not at all clear what this all meant, but it was hardly important since the Italians did not have much of an army left.

The Germans found themselves in a far better position in Italy than they had imagined. Rommel had already prepared a defensive position north of Rome across the Appenines from Civitavecchia to San Benedetto, and Kesselring conducted a brilliant defensive campaign to the south against an unimaginative and orthodox attack which soon ground to a standstill. The Allies rapidly got bogged down in a frustrating campaign in Italy which did little to take the pressure off the eastern front and which looked as if it might lead to a further postponement of the cross-Channel invasion. The Germans were actually able to withdraw troops from Italy and send them east, and it was an embarrassing fact that Tito's partisans were more successful at holding down Germans than were the Allied armies in Italy. Far from winning the war in Italy, as Churchill had hoped, it looked as if they were simply prolonging it.

In November and December the Allies made a series of attempts to break through the Gustav Line. In spite of overwhelming air superiority and the use of heavy artillery barrages, they met with only limited success. Clearly the only way to get some movement in the Italian campaign was to outflank the Gustav Line by landing somewhere further up the coast. The Americans felt that 'Overlord' was the first priority and therefore wanted to move the landing craft from Italy to England before the bad weather began. Churchill blamed the poor performance of the troops in Italy in part on the demoralizing effect of moving troops and landing craft to England in preparation for the cross-Channel invasion. He insisted that 'We must not regard "Overlord" on a fixed date as the pivot of our whole strategy on which all else turns', and pressed for an advance north of Rome to the Pisa–Rimini line. He also argued that the Allies should persuade Turkey to join the war, step up assistance for Tito's partisans and set the Balkans ablaze.

The Americans were less than enthusiastic about the implications of these proposals. At the Cairo meetings prior to the Teheran conference, Eisenhower professed to be opposed to breaking off the campaign in Italy, but he warned that lack of landing craft would make an amphibious turning movement impossible. At the back of their minds the Americans were suspicious that the British were trying once again to wriggle out of their commitment to 'Overlord'. The Soviets were equally suspicious, and at Teheran Stalin asked Churchill outright whether he believed in 'Overlord'. Churchill replied that he did provided that there was a reduction in German fighter strength in north-west Europe, that the Germans did not have more than twelve full-strength mobile divisions in France and the Low Countries, and that the Germans were not in a position to transfer more than fifteen top-line divisions to France in the first sixty days after the landing. After much debate it was agreed that 'Overlord' could be postponed, though for not more than a month, that the Allies should advance to the Pisa–Rimini line, and that troops should then be sent in support of an Allied landing in southern France, operation 'Anvil', designed to support 'Overlord'.

It has often been suggested that the Soviet insistence on a clear commitment to 'Overlord' and its enthusiastic endorsement of 'Anvil' were due to a determination to steer the Allies away from the Balkans and keep them fighting as far west as possible. There is doubtless some truth in this suggestion, but the overwhelming reason was that the Soviets believed, quite correctly, that the campaign in Italy was peripheral and that the best way to defeat the

Germans was in a major land battle directed at the heart of Germany, which was precisely what the Americans proposed. Churchill was prepared to give up his Balkan strategy and thus abandon south-eastern Europe to the Soviet Union, but in return he had won over the Americans to support a continued offensive in Italy. He did so for the chauvinistic reason that Italy was a British show, whereas 'Overlord' was run by the Americans. General Brooke complained that the Prime Minister 'put up strategic proposals which in his heart he knew were unsound, purely to spite the Americans', and pointed out that his enthusiasm for the Italian campaign was dictated by the desire 'to form a purely British theatre when the laurels would be all ours'.

On 22 January the Allies caught the Germans by surprise by launching 'Operation Shingle', a landing at Anzio to the south of Rome. It was an appallingly incompetent operation. The landing was virtually unopposed but Major-General John P. Lucas, who commanded the operation, lost a golden opportunity to strike the 10th Army in the rear and spent his time strengthening the beach-head and waiting for the counter-attack which 'Ultra' decrypts indicated was soon to be expected. Churchill complained that he had hoped 'we would be hurling a wildcat ashore, but all we got was a stranded whale'. The Germans were determined to teach the Allies a lesson on what to expect should they attempt another amphibious landing. General von Mackensen's 14th Army was amply provided with Panzers, assault guns and artillery and swept down from the Alban hills to drive the Americans back into the sea. The attempt failed. Once again overwhelming Allied fire-power from land, sea and air was decisive in beating back the hastily improvised 14th Army with its inexperienced troops. But the Americans were still stuck in their beach-head in a vulnerable salient and had not been able to establish contact with the forces to the south of the Gustav Line.

On the right wing of the main front the Allies were unable to breach the Gustav Line near Cassino. The Americans were unable to storm the heights around the great Benedictine monastery of Monte Cassino and had to be replaced by New Zealanders from the 8th Army. Although there were no German soldiers in the abbey the Allies assumed that it was being used as an observation post, which would account for the deadly accuracy of their fire against the attacking troops. On 15 February 450 tons of bombs were dropped on the monastery, thus reducing one of the great cultural monuments of Europe to rubble. Fortunately the Germans had already removed the abbey's art treasures to the Vatican and safety. The ruins of the monastery provided the 1st Airborne Division with an excellent defensive position, but the Allies were to repeat this mistake time and time again in the course of the Italian campaign. They flattened towns and villages where Germans were suspected of hiding, and thus provided them with almost perfect cover behind the rubble. Further attempts to take the monastery failed and it was not until 18 May that it was finally in Allied hands, thanks largely to the skill of the French, particularly the Moroccan mountain troops, and the courage of the Poles. The Gustav Line was now finally breached, and on 25 May troops from the southern front finally joined up with the Americans from the beach head and the German position in the Liri valley was hopeless. They withdrew to the Gothic Line from La Spezia to Rimini and waited while the Allies slowly slogged their way north.

Having broken through the Gustav Line, General Mark Clark, commanding the American 5th Army, was determined to head for Rome. Had he moved east he could have cut off the Germans as they retreated towards the Gothic Line. The Supreme Commander, General Alexander, failed to correct this serious error even though he had express orders to the contrary. Rome was of no strategic importance and its capture simply allowed Kesselring to extricate his troops from a very dangerous position. Although Rome had been declared an open city and therefore afforded the Allies an empty victory, its capture was deemed a great propaganda triumph. Churchill, imagining that the German troops in Italy had been 'mauled', found the news of the capture of Rome 'thrilling'.

The Anzio landings had been designed to punch a hole through the Gustav Line and enable the troops to the south to advance, but instead the southern forces spent weeks trying to break through the line to relieve the troops in their beach-head salient. These delays meant that 'Operation Anvil' had to be delayed until after D-Day. This made nonsense of the entire strategy, since 'Anvil' could no longer draw troops away from northern France and make life a little easier for the landing forces, nor was there an anvil against which 'Overlord' could hammer. Changing the name of the operation to 'Dragoon' hardly disguised this obvious fact.

The British were inclined to drop the idea of landing in the south of France and to concentrate on the campaign in Italy. General 'Jumbo' Wilson, the Allied Commander-in-Chief in the Mediterranean, imagined that the Allies would reach the line from Venice to Verona by the end of August. At General Alexander's headquarters there was much heady talk of sweeping through the Ljubljana Gap and heading for Vienna. It was an attractive vision which greatly appealed to Churchill, who seems to have overlooked the fact that the Ljubljana Gap was 2000 feet high and only 30 miles wide, and that once that easily defended obstacle had been overcome the Karawanken mountain range had still to be crossed before reaching the plains and Vienna. As if this were not difficult enough, it was proposed to carry out the operation in the winter in territory controlled by Yugoslav partisans who viewed the Allies with the deepest suspicion. The fiasco was averted by American insistence on sticking to the strategy that had been agreed upon at Teheran. The green light was given to 'Dragoon'; the idea of pushing on into the Balkans was dropped. 'Dragoon' achieved very little except that it kept the Americans happy, but it did so at the cost of weakening the Allied forces in Italy. The suggestion made after the war that a fatal mistake was made by going for the south of France rather than the Balkans is absurd. It had taken the Allies six months to go from Naples to Rome and it was three times the distance to Vienna. If the Allies had ever got to Vienna via the Balkans, they would have arrived months after the Soviets. At this stage of the war few were seriously worried about Soviet intentions towards eastern Europe and Stalin was still seen as an ally and friend, however awkward and inscrutable.

The Allies squabbled almost as much over the political future of Italy as they did over the strategic consequences of the Italian campaign. Churchill and Eden had little but contempt for the Italians and could be sure of a good laugh when making caustic references to them in their speeches. Many in Britain could not forget the Spanish Civil War, the invasion of Ethiopia, and the way that Italy had declared war on the Commonwealth at the time of greatest danger. Roosevelt, however, had six million Italian Americans to consider and there was an election in November. For most Americans Italy was too remote to be much of a villain; it was a holiday resort and museum rather than a great power. The Americans wanted a broader-based Government and saw the aristocratic, anti-clerical, liberal intellectual Sforza, who had been in exile since 1927 and who was badly out of touch with the realities of Italian politics, as the man best suited to lead Italy towards democracy. The British felt that Sforza would be seen in Italy as a tool of the Allies and wanted to broaden the Badoglio Government rather than overthrow it as Sforza intended. Sforza visited London in October and Churchill found him a 'useless gaga conceited politician' and an 'old fool' (he was in fact only one year older than the Prime Minister). The Soviets complained about the 'Anglo-American Gauleiter in the AMGOTs', but the British replied that a competent fascist was better than an incompetent anti-fascist. The determination to find anti-fascists was particularly disastrous in Sicily, since most of the competent opponents of Mussolini's regime were members of the Mafia which thus quickly regained control over the island. The Soviets then changed their tactics and recognized the Badoglio Government in March 1944. Whereas Sforza and the ageing philosopher Benedetto Croce refused Cabinet posts in Badoglio's Government, the Italian Communists (PCI) performed the '*svolta* of Salerno' and Togliatti announced that he was prepared to join the Government. Sforza and Croce were now faced with the choice of continuing to demand the resignation of Badoglio and the abdication of the King, thus allowing an enormous increase in communist influence, or swallowing their pride and joining the Government.

The broadened Badoglio Government did not last long. Immediately after the fall of Rome the King transferred power to his son, Umberto, who was made Lieutenant of the Realm. Badoglio was now without support and resigned. A new Government was formed under Bonomi, made up of the six parties of the Committee of National Liberation (CLN). Churchill was furious that the Italians had carried out this bloodless coup, establishing their own Government without consulting the Allies and without a popular mandate. For him Badoglio was 'the only competent Italian', and 'this wretched old Bonomi' was no adequate substitute. But gradually the British became reconciled to the Bonomi Government. They found him reasonably co-operative and comfortingly conservative. Even though his Government expressed a distressing willingness to purge fascists, they reassuringly did not do much about it, much to the distress of the Socialists and Actionists who left the Government in protest at the feebleness of the purge. The British accepted the Government, provided that the loathesome Sforza was not included, as the best guarantee against the communists who were becoming increasingly powerful, especially in the north.

Mussolini's 'Italian Social Republic' was run as a virtual colony by the German ambassador, Rudolf von Rahm, and by the SS boss Karl Wolff. Italians were interned in Germany and used as cheap labour. Industrial machinery was seized and taken to the Reich. Some 7500 Italian Jews were rounded up and the vast majority of them killed. Mussolini's army was small and unreliable, as was the newly formed police force, the Republican National Guard (GNR), which showed a singular lack of enthusiasm for tracking down anti-fascists and left the rural areas in the hands of the partisans. Prominent fascists had their own police forces made up of murderous thugs who terrorized the citizenry and fought among themselves. The Minister of the Interior, Buffarini Guidi, had the 'Koch band' run by a repulsive cocaine addict, Pietro Koch. Farinacci sponsored the 'Muti', who hunted down partisans when not otherwise engaged in kidnapping, blackmail and bank robbery. Mussolini presided over this anarchic parody of fascism, mouthing empty slogans at his bemused subjects. He was sick, abandoned by his favourite daughter whose husband he had executed, and surrounded by his tiresome and vexatious family; a pathetic puppet in the hands of the Germans.

The partisans were a mixed bunch. Many were simply brigands, others politically motivated. They gained large numbers of recruits from draft dodgers and workers who wished to avoid deportation to Germany. The partisans were primitive rebels against the state and against the cities as much as they were anti-fascists. They conducted a regular civil war of great brutality involving sabotage, political assassinations and vendettas in which whole villages were slaughtered. Most of the bands were associated with political parties. The Communists had their 'Garibaldi brigades', the Socialists the 'Matteotti bands', the Actionists the 'GL', the Christian Democrats their 'Green Flame'. Most joined the local group regardless of political affiliation, or because they followed a particular leader. The best organized were the Communists. Although the party had only about 5000 members in September 1943, they soon had about 50,000 partisans, roughly 60 per cent of the total number. Their urban guerillas, the *Gruppi di Azione Patriottica* (GAP), conducted political assassinations which provoked harsh reprisals from the Germans, which in turn won the Communists fresh sympathizers.

Many Communists hoped that the partisans would first destroy the fascists and then bring about the revolution, but Togliatti would have none of this. He knew that the Americans and the British had the real power in Italy, not the proletariat, however militant. Furthermore, he had clear instructions from the Soviets not to stir up trouble with the Allies. Stalin had no desire to see Togliatti become too powerful and independent. Communist political ambitions could be encouraged only in countries where the Soviets were in complete control, and even there they were still moving with a degree of caution.

The Actionists were far more radical in their demands than the Communists. They were led by intellectuals, a heterogeneous collection of professors, students and journalists bent on a righteous purge of the political system and the establishment of a virtuous and immaculately anti-fascist and democratic republic. It was too idealistic a vision ever to be realized, and the party disintegrated after the war. The Socialists had similar views and were sharply critical of the Communists for supporting Badoglio and abandoning the struggle for fundamental social change.

The Christian Democratic 'Green Flames' emerged from Catholic Action, particularly the youth sections. The clergy was sympathetic, although some had reservations about forming a specifically Catholic political party. Many priests fought with the partisans, and the Cardinal Archbishop of Turin administered the sacrament to the guerillas. The participation of the Church in the struggle against fascism underlined the fact that it was a popular struggle, not a revolutionary socialist or communist movement.

Throughout Italy the various political parties, even the more exotic breeds such as Anarchists and Trotskyites, co-operated in the Committees of National Liberation (CLNs) which the Actionists and Socialists hoped would form the basis of a new form of democratic organization after the war. They organized the fifteen partisan republics and had their own tribunals. One such body condemned the managing director of Fiat to death, but he was saved by the Allies at the last moment. In January 1944 the Committee of National Liberation for Upper Italy (CLNAI) was formed in Milan to co-ordinate the efforts of the CLNs and the partisans. The CLNAI was virtually a provisional Government and the Allies felt obliged to recognize it as the official representative body of the resistance although they were constantly worried that the resistance might become too independent as in Yugoslavia. The Italian General Cardona was therefore parachuted into Milan to keep the partisan units in line and to make sure that they were disarmed as soon as their area of operations was liberated. Since the Soviets instructed the Communists to co-operate fully with the Allies and to abandon all thought of a social revolution, the CLNAI worked closely with the Allies, providing temporary administration for the liberated areas, purging fascists from local Government and the police and handing over Milan with a workable administration.

The offensive against the Gothic Line began in the autumn. To the east it was a case of 'one more river to cross' and the offensive soon got stuck between the Uso (the classical Rubicon) and the Po. The Allies were therefore obliged to wait for the spring to resume the offensive, even though they were 50 miles from their main objective, the Po, and had failed to capture Bologna.

Vietinghoff, the new German commander in Italy, was hamstrung by Hitler's orders not to withdraw. He was desperately short of fuel and munitions as his supply lines over the Brenner were constantly under attack by Allied aircraft. He knew that in such a situation an Allied breakthrough would have disastrous consequences. SS Obergruppenführer Karl Wolff therefore began talks in Switzerland with the head of the American Office of Strategic Services, Allen Dulles, to sound out the possibility of a separate surrender of the German forces in northern Italy.

Wolff went to Zurich on 8 March and began talks with Allen Dulles. On 12 March the Soviets were informed of these talks and were invited to Caserta to take part in negotiations for an armistice. Molotov demanded the right to send a delegation to the preliminary discussions in Switzerland, but this the Americans and British refused on the grounds that the Germans would break off negotiations if the Soviets became involved. Molotov then demanded that the talks should be ended immediately, but the Combined Chiefs of Staff insisted that it was a purely military matter and thus the sole concern of the local Commander-in-Chief. On 19 March Kesselring handed over command of his army group to Vietinghoff, who decided that although the time was not yet ripe for a partial surrender, the talks should continue. On 23 March Molotov protested that the Allies were negotiating with the enemy behind the back of the Soviet Union, and on 3 April Stalin sent a telegram to Roosevelt claiming that the Allies were offering the Germans easy peace terms so as to enable them to advance eastwards, leaving the Soviet Union to do all the fighting. Roosevelt rejected these accusations as 'vile misrepresentations' and Churchill felt that they were 'insulting to the honour of the United States and also of Great Britain'. He concluded from this episode that the Allies would be prudent to push forward as far east as possible and try to get to Berlin.

On 18 April the Allies broke through the Argenta Gap and headed for Ferrara. In the centre they reached Bologna on 21 April. The Germans were now forced to retreat behind the Po with heavy losses of trucks and artillery. On 23 April Vietinghoff sent Wolff back to Switzerland to begin serious armistice negotiations. On 27 April partisans captured Mussolini and his mistress Clara Petracci at Dongo on Lake Como. The next day they were shot in the back and hung upside down in the piazzale Loreto in Milan, the object of macabre public derision. Other leading fascists were also captured and executed, among them Farinacci and Starace. On 29 April Army Group South-West signed an armistice at Caserta,and on 2 May the fighting in Italy ceased. 'Operation Sunrise', the negotiations between Allen Dulles and Karl Wolff, was thus successfully completed five days before the final capitulation of Germany.

The Italian partisans made an important contribution to the defeat of the German army in Italy and provided an example for an anti-fascist national consensus. The political parties from the Communists to the Christian Democrats were active participants in the partisan movement and it was they, not the Allies, who liberated the major cities of the north. In spite of all this the Italian partisans did not form a people's army, nor did they liberate the entire country on their own as did the Yugoslavs.

The partisan movement in Yugoslavia began immediately after the occupation of the country by the Germans. Under the leadership of a general staff officer, Draza Mihailovic, the 'Chetniks' (from the word *ceta* meaning band) made contact with the British, and when the German occupation troops were greatly reduced after the attack on the Soviet Union they began to attack their lines of communication. At the same time a new partisan group run by the Croatian leader of the Yugoslav communists, Josip Broz 'Tito', began operations. Savage German reprisals against the partisans led to a great increase in their numbers as many males fled from the towns and villages and headed for the partisan camps in the mountains.

Tito welcomed the German reprisals and was determined to keep up the pressure. Mihailovic wanted to avoid unnecessary bloodshed and wait for the decisive moment to launch a campaign of national liberation. By November 1941 the Chetniks and Tito's 'Proletarian Brigades' were fighting one another, and the Chetniks even signed a pact with the Italians by which they were provided with supplies to fight the communists while accepting Italian supremacy in the provinces under their occupation.

In the winter of 1941–42 Tito's forces were almost wiped out, and he made a narrow escape from his headquarters at Uzice. His new headquarters were at Foca, some thirty miles south of Sarajevo in the Italian occupied zone. By February Tito had lost 8000 men and the Germans had shot 20,000 hostages. In April he was encircled by German, Italian and Croatian troops and by collaborationist Chetniks, but managed to break out and head north-west. Along the 200-mile route to his new headquarters at Bihac he established local national liberation committees, and on 26 November 1942 he founded the Anti-fascist Council for the National Liberation of Yugoslavia (AVNOJ). This was a provisional Government for the whole of Yugoslavia on a federal basis which, by guaranteeing the rights of the national minorities, had great appeal to many Yugoslavs.

In order to secure the Balkans in anticipation of an Allied landing the Germans mounted 'Operation White'. The Italians were required to disarm the Chetniks but they refused, arguing that they were needed to destroy Tito's partisans. Tito was forced to abandon his position in the north, so he headed south and established his new base in the bare mountains of Montenegro where his men suffered terribly from hunger and disease. At this point Tito offered the Germans a truce if they would concentrate on destroying the Chetniks. This offer was ignored and General Lüters went ahead with 'Operation Black', the rounding-up of the Chetniks. Although the Italians allowed many of the Chetniks to escape, the operation was largely successful and Tito was now completely surrounded by the Germans. Against all expectations he managed to escape, and once again headed north.

The British eventually decided to back Tito rather than Mihailovic. The Chetniks were fighting alongside the Italians, whereas the communists were, in Churchill's words, killing more Huns. By the summer of 1943 SOE was providing the partisans with an average of 500 tons of supplies per month. In November the Anti-fascist Council met once again at Tito's headquarters at Jajce. Tito was appointed head of an alternative Government to that in exile and promoted to the rank of marshal. In February the following year the Soviets sent a military mission to Tito. The Germans planned a parachute attack on his headquarters at Drvar in Bosnia, but once again he narrowly escaped and established a new headquarters under British protection on the island of Vis. Under British pressure the Government-in-exile dismissed Mihailovic and recognized Tito's partisans as the official Yugoslav army. At Yalta the Big Three recommended that Tito's Anti-fascist Council should be broadened to include members of the pre-war Government. This did not take place. The Coalition Government between Tito and Subasic, which had been agreed upon on 1 November 1944, was dominated by the communists. On 11 April 1945 Tito's Government signed a pact with the Soviet Union in the hope of gaining support for his territorial demands against Austria and Italy. This resulted in Trieste being under both Yugoslav and British occupation, and there was constant friction between the two partners which threatened to break out into open conflict. The Soviet Union did not respect the spirit of the agreement made with Churchill in October 1944 that they should have an equal influence in Yugoslavia, and they protested strongly that General Alexander had planted his foot firmly in the door in Trieste. For the British Government the future of Trieste and Istria had to be decided at the peace table, and it was deemed prudent for British troops to move as far into Yugoslavia as possible. The problem had its positive aspects. It was hoped that Italian communists would be outraged at Tito's attempts to seize Istria and Venezia Giulia, and that the Soviets would be faced with dissention between their followers.

Albania followed the Yugoslav pattern. The communist National Liberation Movement (FNC), led by the stalinist Enver Hoxha, had a direct rival in the republican National Union (Balli-Kombetar). Hoxha fought both the Germans and the republicans. As soon as the Germans evacuated Albania he entered Tirana and established a provisional Government on the Yugoslav model, which he was soon to convert into a ferocious and long-lasting dictatorship. Churchill had hoped that the hapless King Zog would be able to return to his kingdom, but Eden pointed out that nobody wanted him and there was little hope of wresting Albania from Soviet control. Stalin liked to refer to Albania as the perfect and risible example of the small and insignificant state. The western Allies hardly troubled themselves about Albania, although a British diplomat reporting on the situation warned that Mr Hoxha with his 'wasp-waisted lounge suits and smelling heavily of scent did not inspire confidence'.

In Greece the political parties formed the National Liberation Front (EAM) on 27 September 1941 in which the communists held the key positions. A National Liberation Army (ELAS) was founded in April the following year. It, too, was under communist leadership. Its rival band, the National Republican Association (EDES), comprised a mere one thousand men and was of little significance. British agents parachuted into Greece organized a joint raid by EDES and ELAS against the railway from Saloniki to Athens which was guarded by the Italians and which was an important supply route for the Afrika Korps. But ELAS and EDES were soon fighting one another, the British supporting EDES. ELAS realized that without supplies from the British they would be unable to continue the struggle and therefore agreed to bury the hatchet with EDES, reaching an agreement with the rival partisan group in July 1943. Under this pact all guerilla organizations in Greece were to be treated as independent but were placed under the overall command of the British military authorities in Cairo, who undertook to keep them supplied.

In the summer of 1943 ELAS and EDES undertook a series of

major operations designed to provide cover for the preparations for the invasion of Sicily. These resulted in the serious disruption of German and Italian lines of communication, and the partisans were now in command of large areas where they established local Governments and even ran the postal and telegraph services. The Germans answered with draconian reprisals, as in Yugoslavia. In Kalitva in the Peloponnese 700 hostages were executed and twenty-four villages, along with a number of monasteries, were destroyed.

Operations against Rhodes, Kos, Leros and Samos, strongly urged by Churchill, were a failure since the Joint Chiefs were reluctant to allow the campaign in Italy and the preparation for 'Overlord' to be compromised by the diversion of men and landing craft to the eastern Mediterranean. ELAS was now convinced that the Allies were about to attempt a landing in Greece, and therefore decided to settle accounts with EDES before they arrived. The Allies responded by cutting off supplies to ELAS and the Allied military mission under Colonel Montague Woodhouse and the American Major Wines was able to negotiate a truce between the two factions. EDES had been reformed and renamed the 'National Bands' (EKKA) after a purge of collaborationists. ELAS was running short of supplies, many Greeks were disenchanted with their sectarian politics, and their guerilla activities did little damage to the Germans and provoked horrendous reprisals. In July the Soviets sent a military mission to ELAS which acted as a restraining influence. In September 1944 ELAS and EKKA negotiated an agreement at the Allied headquarters at Caserta whereby they agreed to submit to the authority of a Government of national unity which in turn placed them under the orders of the British commander, General Scobie.

The liberation of Greece had little to do with the partisans. With the collapse of Romania and Bulgaria the Germans were forced to evacuate Greece, Yugoslavia and Albania to save their troops from being trapped in the Balkans by the Red Army. ELAS did not honour the Caserta agreement. As soon as the Germans withdrew from the western Peloponnese they returned to their bad habits and massacred several hundred political opponents. General Zervas and his EKKA were rather more concerned with chasing Germans than settling political scores. When British troops entered Athens in October 1944 they were greeted not only as liberators from the horrors of the German occupation, but also as guarantors against ELAS terror. The major problem was that the Papandreou Government had virtually no authority outside Athens; in the rest of Greece ELAS was in control and took orders only from the communists. Papandreou therefore decided to form a national guard and to disarm all partisans. EAM and ELAS refused to disband and began the occupation of Athens, seizing a number of police stations. General Scobie was ordered to drive ELAS out of Athens. Serious fighting ensued between the small British garrison and ELAS troops, some of whom wore British uniforms to infiltrate the barracks of 23rd Armoured Brigade.

The sight of British troops firing on Greek patriots was greeted with horror in much of the western press. Roosevelt regarded it as a typical example of British imperialism and an unwarranted interference in the internal affairs of another country to the advantage of reactionary elements. Only the Soviets remained silent. Not a word of criticism of British policy in Greece was printed in the Soviet press. The British in return turned a blind eye to the Soviet-sponsored coup in Romania. The most that the British were able to do was to negotiate a tenuous political truce and to provide a modicum of security in a divided land. They were much criticized by both the left and the right, but at least they saved Greece from Soviet communism and prepared the way for elections in which the Greeks themselves could decide their future. It is ironical that the Government of the United States, which was so sharply critical of British policy in Greece in 1944 and 1945, was to intervene in the Greek civil war in February 1947 and as a result enunciated the 'Truman Doctrine', thus taking one of the most significant steps towards the Cold War.

CHAPTER TWELVE

The Soviet Advance (August 1943–April 1945)

From the outset of the war the Soviet Union made it clear that its minimum war aim was the restoration of all the lands it had seized in collusion with Hitler. This constantly reiterated demand created considerable difficulties for the Americans and the British since it was irreconcilable with the principles of the Atlantic Charter which was published on 14 August. The Soviets endorsed the Charter with the proviso that 'the circumstances, needs and historic peculiarities of particular countries' should be respected – in other words that the Soviet Union could ignore 'the sovereign rights of peoples' and the 'independence and territorial integrity' of the border states.

Whereas the United States Government initially refused to make any commitments before the peace conference the British, prompted by the ambassador in Moscow, Stafford Cripps, felt that some concessions were desirable in order to improve relations with the Soviet Union. Demands against Finland and Romania could be accepted since the Soviets had managed to force the British to declare war on these two countries. The Baltic states hardly counted for much and as there were no significant British interests involved they could be sold down the river in the interests of Allied harmony. The remaining and constant problem was Poland. The Polish Government-in-exile was established in London. It was violently anti-Soviet, insistent on its rights and had many influential sympathizers.

The Anglo-Soviet treaty of May 1942 made no mention of future frontiers and was a purely military agreement. The Soviets felt that this major concession would result in a more positive response by the western Allies to their persistent demands for a second front. On 30 May 1942 Molotov managed to get the President to promise 'the formation of a second front this year'. Since the Americans were planning the 'Torch' landings in north Africa this was a most unfortunate and disingenuous promise which was reaffirmed in the joint communiqué which stated that 'full understanding was reached with regard to the urgent task of creating a second front in Europe in 1942'. There can be little doubt that Molotov knew that there was no substance in Roosevelt's promise, and a few days later he was told by Churchill that a second front in 1942 was a virtual impossibility; but it suited the Soviets to pretend that they had been misled in order to win concessions over the future frontiers.

Stalin made it abundantly plain from the outset that he intended to annex the Baltic states. They had been Russian provinces under the Tsars and they were so violently anti-Soviet that there could be no question of negotiating a treaty with them which met the security needs of the Soviet Union. The Soviets had learnt to have a healthy respect for the Finns during the Winter War and had relatively modest territorial demands to make of them. They detested the Romanians who, unlike the Finns, had a formal alliance with the Germans, and they had never accepted the Romanian claim to Bessarabia. Bulgaria had prudently declared war only on the western powers, not on the Soviet Union, and there was still a Soviet legation in Sofia. The Soviets claimed that they would be content with military bases in Bulgaria after the war. Hungary declared war on the Soviet Union after Soviet planes bombed Kosice, probably by mistake. The Soviet pilots may very well have imagined that they were attacking a town in Slovakia, the country having unwisely joined in Hitler's anti-bolshevik crusade.

Stalin made it clear that he would settle for nothing less than the frontier with Poland of October 1939. In December 1941, when the German armies were at the gates of Moscow, he told the Polish Prime Minister, Sikorski, that he might consider allowing the Poles to keep Lvov, but he soon withdrew the offer when the military situation improved. The Poles sought to strengthen their position by proposing a confederation with Czechoslovakia which would be allied to a bloc including Norway, Holland and Belgium. The British Government was enthusiastic about such efforts towards regional integration, endorsing a similar plan between Yugoslavia and Greece. The Soviets at first made sympathetic noises but again, when the military situation improved, they scornfully pointed out that the Poles would have to choose between Luxembourg and the Soviet Union. The Americans gave the Poles no encouragement, since they were anxious not to give the Russians any cause for annoyance and wished to leave the discussion of all such schemes until after the war.

When Molotov began discussions with the Yugoslavs for a mutual assistance pact, Eden objected that this would establish an unfortunate precedent whereby small states would solicit the support of the great powers leading to the formation of power blocs. He therefore suggested a 'self-denying ordinance' for the duration of the war. Molotov broke off negotiations with the Yugoslavs and Eden imagined that he had secured a gentleman's agreement that all such treaties required prior consultation between the powers.

The Czech President, Benes, was the key figure in the evolution of Soviet policy towards central Europe. He was a vain and meddlesome man who enjoyed an undeserved reputation as a great statesman. He imagined that Czechoslovakia's interests would best be served by close friendship with Moscow, so that his country could become the vital link between east and west. Churchill was much taken by the man he chose to call 'Beans', and so was Roosevelt. Professional diplomatists were less impressed. The Foreign Office gradually came round to the conviction that he was hopelessly naïve and was being led by the nose by the Soviets. The State Department felt that the Czechs were little more than Soviet agents. The Soviets used their influence with the Czechs to sink the project of a confederation with Poland. Sikorski, who was keenly aware of the thrust of Soviet policy, vainly urged Roosevelt to open the second front as soon as possible so as to stop the Russians from overrunning central Europe. Even Benes began to become concerned that the Soviets were deliberately causing discord between the smaller states.

The Communist International took some time to adjust to the fact that they were no longer required to say nice things about Nazis. Two days after the German invasion of the Soviet Union the exiled German communists were still talking about the 'indestructible alliance' between the Soviet Union and Germany and for the next few days the German communist leader, Walter Ulbricht, was still referring to the Soviets' new allies as 'plutocrats', a favourite Nazi appellation. Gradually this gave way to equally primitive denunciations of Hitler as a capitalist stooge and offers of fraternal help to the exploited proletarian masses he held in his thrall. Along with shrill denunciations of capitalism in all its forms, the Comintern proposed an anti-fascist front which was to include the bourgeois parties. Such inconsistency created further confusion as to the Soviet Union's intentions and was probably the result of hopelessly muddled thinking in Moscow.

Although the Soviets founded communist parties in Poland and Albania, they also restrained the more active parties. The Yugoslavs were told that the future Government of their country would be decided after the defeat of the Axis powers and that they were not to make any mention of revolution. Similar instructions were sent to the Czech communists. Stalin was deeply suspicious of guerilla movements for they were likely to become too independent and be led by nationalists away from the narrow path of doctrinal orthodoxy. The Soviets preferred to drop Comintern agents into the occupied or enemy countries, but they were so poorly trained that they were almost all instantly arrested. In the spring of 1942 when the military situation in the Soviet Union again began to look desperate, the Comintern called for the 'shattering of the fascist's European rear' by guerilla activities and nationalist uprisings. Those who had been denounced as irresponsible adventurers of dubious trustworthiness were now the heroes of the hour. But the Soviets were still deeply suspicious of the communist guerilla leaders. They supported Mihailovic rather than Tito even longer than did the British, and when they decided that Tito was the more effective guerilla leader they gave him virtually no assistance. The Gestapo proved most efficient at destroying the communist undergrounds throughout Europe, and some of the organizations whose efforts Moscow praised were the purely imaginary concoctions of Comintern propagandists, among them the Bulgarian Fatherland Front, the Austrian Freedom Front and the German Peace Front. Awaiting the day that the Red Army would march west, the Soviets trained cadres of emigrés at the Comintern school near Ufa in the Urals who were to be placed in key positions in the liberated countries. They were felt to be far more reliable than the partisans or adventurers in the underground and spy networks, and were to play key roles in the puppet Governments set up after the war.

Soviet peace talks in Stockholm as Stalingrad was encircled, Stalin's Order of the Day of 23 February 1943 which implied that the war was something which concerned only the Russians and the Germans, his dissociation from the Casablanca declaration of unconditional surrender and his deliberate fabrication of the 'peace movement' in Germany all served as an indication that the 'Grand Alliance' was falling apart at the seams. The British did not believe that the Soviet Union was about to negotiate a separate peace, but the Americans were less certain. If it was simply a bluff then it could only be to hasten the second front, and this in turn placed an added strain on Anglo-American relations. The situation was made even worse by the announcement on 12 April 1943 of the unearthing of mass graves at Katyn near Smolensk. It was obvious from the evidence that the Soviets were responsible for the murder of some 13,000 Polish officers, offering Goebbels the chance for a propagandistic field day. The Soviets first claimed that the Germans had stumbled across an archaeological site, then suggested, contrary to all the evidence, that the Nazis were responsible for the massacre. Getting nowhere with this tactic, they abruptly broke off diplomatic relations with the Polish Government-in-exile in London.

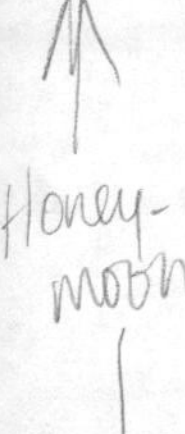

The British and Americans, although perfectly well aware who was responsible for the Katyn massacre, loudly denounced the Germans for the crime and Stalin replied in his May Day address by calling for German surrender and later by singing the praises of the Allies in north Africa, a campaign which he had previously dismissed as of trivial importance. This honeymoon period did not last for long. On 4 June Roosevelt and Churchill told Stalin that the second front would have to be delayed still further. Stalin was furious and recalled his ambassadors in Washington and London, replacing them by men deemed to be of no significance. Gromyko was sent to Washington, prompting a rash comment from Isaiah Berlin at the British embassy that he was not 'built of diplomatic timber' and was a man without a future. The formation of the National Committee for a Free Germany in Moscow, made up of sundry hopeful idealists, dupes and fellow travellers, along with hints that the Soviet Union favoured a mild peace settlement with Germany and rumours of renewed peace feelers in Stockholm, marked an end to this brief period of co-operation with the west.

While the Nazi leadership again began to sound out the possibility of a peace with the Soviet Union, which Hitler told Goebbels he preferred to a settlement with the western powers, the Soviets heard through Sándor Radó's incredible intelligence network that a group of German officers were plotting to overthrow Hitler. It may be that the Soviets formed the National Committee in preparation for such an event. Certainly the creation of the League of German Officers, made up of co-operative prisoners-of-war, was a direct response to this information.

On 22 May 1943 the Comintern was formally dissolved. No one was certain what this meant. Was it further evidence that the Soviet Union was no longer revolutionary and that its professed support for broad democratic coalitions was genuine? Was it mere deception, with the Comintern continuing under another guise? Was it a settling of accounts with unwelcome elements within the Comintern? In the west most diplomatists welcomed the move as further evidence that the Soviet Union was becoming reassuringly normal and bourgeois, but it did not result in any improvement in relations between the two sides of the alliance. Western diplomatists had never taken the Comintern very seriously and it had never been an obstacle to an understanding with the Soviet Government. There was considerable alarm and consternation within the Comintern at its dissolution, for it was obvious that Stalin was displeased with its failures and suspicious of its successes. It had failed miserably to make an effective contribution to the resistance movement, and in some countries such as Czechoslovakia was riddled with informers and spies. In as much as it was successful as a supra-national body Stalin was fearful that it might object to his imperialist ambitions, which were given a new lease of life with the victory at Kursk. Stalin now preferred to deal directly and 'fraternally' with the national communist parties, which were to be controlled by his stooges and which in turn were prepared for the time being to co-operate with the bourgeois parties.

The model relationship was deemed to be that between the Soviet Union and Czechoslovakia. Benes claimed that he had shown to all the world that the smaller states had nothing to fear from the Soviet Union and that the western powers had seriously misunderstood Soviet policy and intentions. Benes travelled to the United States in May and was successful in making the Americans even more starry-eyed and enthusiastic for the Soviet Union. On his return to London he announced that he was off to Moscow to sign a treaty. Eden was at first appalled. This was a serious breach by the Soviets of the 'self-denying ordinance', and he also feared that the Poles would react very unfavourably to the news. He warned Benes that such a treaty would make it seem that Czechoslovakia was in Stalin's pocket. The Soviets let the British Government know that they regarded what Eden was pleased to call a 'gentleman's agreement' as merely an expression of opinion and not as a binding obligation, and told the Czechs that they had better sign the treaty now before they changed their minds. Benes had now manoeuvred himself into the position of being caught between the Soviet Union and Britain. Although the Soviets altered the text of the treaty to make sure that the Czechs had all the obligations without the Russians making any definite commitments, Benes decided to go ahead at the risk of alienating the

British and Americans. Thanks to British intervention the Russians further modified the text and opened the way for Poland to become a co-signatory. Eden now dropped his objections, much to the alarm of the Foreign Office who felt that another diplomatic triumph for Benes would make him even more vain and self-important.

Benes was at his most loquacious and foolish during his visit to Moscow in December. Stalin and Molotov grew increasingly impatient with his seemingly endless monologues and when Stalin asked him what he should do about Poland, Benes replied that the Red Army would settle the Polish question and that the Polish Government in London would have to be dropped. This was after he had given every assurance in London that he would press the Russians to resume diplomatic relations with the London Poles. Stalin was amazed to hear his guest demand the expropriation of Hungarian, Polish and Czech capitalists and the exclusion of the Americans and British from eastern Europe since they were unlikely to support such measures. Benes told the Czech communists in Moscow that they would be the strongest party in post-war Czechoslovakia and that he would appoint a communist premier. He returned from Moscow convinced that he could 'swallow and digest' the communists and that he had nothing to fear from his friends in the Kremlin. They in turn had nothing but contempt for this puffed-up 'bourgeois radical', although they were delighted that he had willingly brought his country into the Soviet orbit. Stalin promptly suggested similar treaties with Poland, France and Italy, but none of these countries was so easily duped. Eden and the Foreign Office were pleased with the Soviet–Czech treaty and saw it as a model for treaties with other states. A few diplomatists, among them a rising star, Frank Roberts, warned that the treaty was an extremely dangerous precedent, but they were ignored.

Meanwhile, the Soviet autumn offensive began along the Sea of Azov. As the Red Army approached the Dnieper, the remaining German forces in the Crimea were trapped. Further north Koniev's 2nd Ukrainian front advanced towards Krivoi Rog and closed off the Dnieper salient, and Vatutin's 1st Ukrainian front pushed forward from its bridgeheads north of Kiev, liberated the Ukrainian capital and advanced some 90 miles to Zhitomir. This movement threatened the Germans' lines of communication and pushed Manstein's Army Group South towards the Romanian border. As the southern wing of Army Group Centre retreated, a gap opened up between the two army groups, offering Vatutin the possibility of driving towards Lublin. Hitler was obsessed with the relief of the Crimea and the defence of the ore deposits of the lower Dnieper, but Manstein, after lengthy and hefty arguments, was granted permission to counter-attack. By recapturing Zhitomir a very dangerous situation was avoided. Kluge's Army Group Centre was pushed back across the Dnieper after withstanding a series of punishing attacks in which Sokolovsky's 3rd Ukrainian front suffered heavy losses. Yeremenko was unable to exploit the gap between Army Groups Centre and North in spite of breaking through to Nevel.

The Soviets began a new offensive on Christmas Eve. Vatutin recaptured Zhitomir and pushed forward across the pre-war Polish frontier, reaching Lutsk at the beginning of February. The Soviet offensive swung south towards the river Bug, thus threatening once again to trap Manstein's forces in their massive salient which extended as far as Zaporozhye. Hitler would not listen to Manstein's plea for withdrawal, for he was still concerned about the loss of the ore fields and argued that should the Germans retreat, the Bulgarians and Romanians would sue for peace and the Turks would join the Allies. Manstein was able to stabilize the situation somewhat by beating back the Soviet offensive at Uman, but he could only fight for time. In February the Soviets liberated Nikopol and Krivoi Rog. Further north the Red Army pushed a wedge between Army Groups South and Centre, creating a situation which could be saved only by a drastic shortening of the front, which Hitler flatly refused.

Küchler of Army Group North had been obliged to send seventeen divisions to help out the other two army groups and was left without a single Panzer division to face an offensive by three Soviet fronts. In January the siege of Leningrad was lifted after 890 terrible days of siege. Little was gained strategically from this effort, although Finland felt obliged to begin a long and protracted series of peace negotiations. Küchler was forced back and obliged to take up a defensive position on either side of Lake Peipus. Leningrad was now finally free from danger and the Germans driven back to the frontiers of the Baltic states.

On 1 April Zhukov took over command of the 1st Ukrainian front, Vatutin having been shot by anti-Soviet partisans. At the beginning of March he renewed the southerly offensive. Although Zhukov was beaten back, Malinovsky and Koniev were more successful and the Germans were again in serious danger of being cut off along the Black Sea coast. Manstein and Kleist travelled to the Obersalzberg on 19 March to persuade Hitler to pull back the front, but the Führer ordered a stand on the Bug and the defence of Odessa, which he deemed an essential port since the Romanian railway system was proving inadequate to the demands of the German armies in the south. Lest there should be any doubt about his determination to hold on, and as a warning to the Romanians, Hitler ordered the occupation of Hungary on the same day.

Zhukov was soon on the move again and Koniev crossed the Dniester. The Germans were pushed back to the Carpathians, and Hungary was threatened. Manstein and Kleist went to see Hitler again on 25 March and were accused of thinking of nothing but withdrawal. On 30 March Hitler dismissed both Field Marshals. In their place he appointed Model and Schörner, two men known for their ruthlessness and their willingness to obey his orders without question.

In April Hitler had to agree finally to the evacuation of the Crimea, a move that had been left far too late and resulted in the loss of 60,000 men. Odessa was also lost on 10 April. The only compensation was that Model's Army Group North Ukraine was once again able to establish contact with Army Group Centre, but they were now 300 miles west of the point where they had been driven apart. In May the heavy mud brought operations to a halt and the Germans were able to strengthen their position, but they were faced with a drastic shortage of men and equipment and a gigantic Soviet bulge which placed the defenders in a strategically disadvantageous position.

When the Foreign Ministers met in Moscow in October 1943 the Soviets had only one item for the agenda: the opening of a second front in Europe. They had won many victories and were still advancing, but they had suffered terrible losses and still believed that the western Allies were fighting to the last drop of Soviet blood. In spite of apprehensions that the conference would get bogged down in denunciations of western inaction over the second front or endless wrangles over future Soviet frontiers, the conference was something of a success. The Soviets professed to be satisfied with the explanations given for the delay in the invasion of France, and they did not press the frontier question. Eden, much to Molotov's surprise, agreed to the text of the Soviet–Czech treaty and accepted that an exception could be made to the 'self-denying ordinance'. Molotov immediately took this as meaning that both the British and the Russians could 'conclude agreements on post-war questions with bordering Allied states, without making that action dependent on consultations and agreements between them'. Since only the Soviet Union had bordering states and one of those was Poland, Molotov had won a major victory. The British struggled to undo the mischief done by agreeing to the Soviet Czech treaty by calling for a committee to discuss the problem. The committee never met. Eden was pleased to get agreement for his proposal for a European Advisory Commission (EAC) designed to co-ordinate the efforts of the three powers in the liberated countries and in Germany. Neither the Americans nor the Soviets were particularly enthusiastic, but they eventually agreed to establish the Commission in London although it was to have very limited powers. In addition, an Allied Advisory Council for Italy was created which gave the Soviets some say in Italian affairs, but which also meant that Italy was to be the only country liberated by the western Allies in which the Soviets claimed a share of supervisory duties.

At the end of the conference an overblown and empty statement was issued on general security and the sovereign equality of peace-loving states. Cordell Hull, who had left all the negotiations to Molotov and Eden, felt that this was the dawning of a new age in which there would be no spheres of influence or alliances but universal harmony and understanding. Some shrewder American commentators pointed out that many awkward issues had been avoided and that the Soviets had won tacit acceptance of their claim to hegemony in eastern Europe. Eden was also beginning to have some second thoughts about the implications of the Soviet–Czech treaty, especially after talks with the Polish Premier, Mikolajczyk. The Soviets had every reason to be delighted with the conference. Molotov had played a relatively weak hand with considerable skill and had placed his country in an excellent position for the forthcoming meeting of the Big Three at Teheran.

Churchill arrived at Teheran at the end of November tired and frustrated with the slow progress of the campaign in Italy and with the unsatisfactory 'Sextant' conference with the Americans at Cairo. He was ill prepared and heading for a serious illness. Roosevelt seemed unwilling to come to grips with the real issues and imagined that the best way to win over 'Uncle Joe' was to stress the differences between him and Churchill over a wide range of issues. Teheran was a totally unsuitable place to hold such a conference. Stalin warned his visitors that the place was swarming with Nazi assassins, and placed the American delegation in the Soviet embassy where their conversations could be easily monitored. There was no agenda and Cadogan summed up the Foreign Office's feelings by complaining to his wife that: 'Winston and Joe and the President have bibulous parties, which I dare say will result in something concrete and useful, but at the present it's a pretty woolly conference – all over the place.'

Stalin got a commitment that the invasion of France would take place in May or June of 1944. There was tacit agreement that the Curzon Line should form the approximate frontier between the Soviet Union and Poland, and Churchill told Stalin that it would not break his heart if the Soviets took Lvov. Churchill's handling of the Polish question was so off-hand that Stalin must have gained the impression that it was not a matter of great importance to the British. Roosevelt announced that he 'could not participate in any decision' over Poland for fear of the effect it might have on Polish–American voters. Discussions over the future of Germany were hopelessly vague, though they were indicative of Stalin's fear of a revival of German power within twenty years of the end of the war. The Big Three agreed that Germany should be dismembered, but they could not agree how it should be done. A fortnight after the end of the conference Bohlen wrote that, as a result of the decisions made at Teheran, 'the Soviet Union would be the only important military political force on the continent of Europe'. It was a bleak but not unreasonable assessment. The central European and Balkan states would not be allowed to form any federations. The western powers had agreed that the Soviets had a right to demand 'friendly Governments' in the bordering states. Germany was to be dismembered, France stripped of its colonies and neither Poland nor Italy was to be allowed substantial military establishments.

With the D-Day landings the Soviet position began to harden. The Soviets were now assured of victory in central Europe and could afford to take their time in deciding how best to control the region. On 21 July they sponsored the Polish Committee of National Liberation, later to be known as the Lublin Committee, under the relatively obscure left-wing socialist Edward Osóbka-Morawski. Two days later Stalin told Churchill that he intended to use the Committee to administer liberated Poland. At the beginning of August, when the Warsaw uprising had already begun, Stalin demanded of Mikolajczyk that he include members of the Lublin Committee in his Government which was to be purged of undesirable reactionary elements.

The Soviet summer offensive began during the night of 20 June with large-scale partisan activities. Some 10,000 explosions along the railways supplying Army Group Centre effectively disrupted supplies. The main offensive began two days later and Hitler's orders that there should be no withdrawals and that certain designated 'strong points' should be defended to the last man resulted in the Red Army cutting off part of the 3rd Panzer Army in Vitebsk and encircling the 9th Army at Bobruysk. Even though von Tippelskirch ignored the order to stand fast and withdrew his 4th Army across the Dnieper and the Berezina to avoid being outflanked, he was trapped at Minsk. Field Marshal Busch, who commanded Army Group Centre, had asked Hitler for permission to withdraw in order to shorten his front, but had been treated to a long tirade about generals who could only look over their shoulders. Cowed by this harangue, Busch was determined to show his loyalty to the Führer by refusing to allow any retreat, and thus gave the Soviets the opportunity they were seeking completely to destroy Army Group Centre.

Field Marshal Model was given command of Army Group Centre in an attempt to stop the rot. He moved troops from his Army Group North Ukraine in a desperate attempt to save the situation, but it was too late. The Germans had lost 350,000 men in the most serious defeat they had suffered to date. It was not until August that Model was able to hold a line running along the Vistula just east of Warsaw to Kovno, but he was unable to plug the gap between Army Group Centre and Army Group North. General Bagramyan's 1st Baltic front exploited this situation and pushed towards Riga, trapping Schörner's Army Group North in the Baltic states. Hitler refused permission to withdraw from Estonia and Latvia so that Schörner was soon trapped in the area around the Gulf of Riga. In late August the Germans were able to fight their way through to relieve Army Group North, but Hitler refused permission for them to withdraw to Lithuania. On 10 October Bagramyan's 1st Baltic front reached the coast north of Memel, thus cutting off Schöner's Army Group. Hitler turned down Guderian's suggestion that they should break out, so that twenty-six divisions were trapped in Courland. Ten were evacuated by sea in early 1945; the remaining sixteen fought on with great courage until the end of the war.

The offensive against Army Group North Ukraine, now commanded by General Harpe, did not begin until 13 July. Koniev's 1st Ukrainian front advanced across the San and established a bridgehead across the Vistula near Baranow. His left wing trapped eight German divisions east of Lvov and then pushed on to the Carpathians alongside Petrov's 4th Ukrainian front. Further north, Rokossovsky's 1st Belorussian front reached Lublin on 23 July and then headed north-west for Warsaw. He was stopped at the gates of Warsaw by Model's counter-attack on 3 August in which he lost an entire tank corps. Although Rokossovsky was just able to establish two bridgeheads across the Vistula, the nearest some 30 miles south of Warsaw, his offensive had lost its momentum. Model's successful defence of Warsaw was a death sentence to the insurgents, which admirably suited Stalin's purposes.

The Finns had assumed that the Soviets would leave them alone until the defeat of Germany, and were therefore caught by surprise when the Red Army launched an offensive in the second week of June which resulted in the loss of the Karelian isthmus. A second offensive between Lake Ladoga and Lake Onega advanced 100 miles to the Finnish defences along the U Line. On 1 August President Ryti resigned and his place was taken by the seventy-seven-year-old Marshal Mannerheim who alone had the authority necessary to negotiate a peace. Hitler immediately sent Schörner to Helsinki to assure Mannerheim that the Germans would hang on to the Baltic, but Mannerheim was too good a soldier to be fooled by such wishful thinking. The award of the Knight's Cross with oak leaves did nothing to change his mind, and at the end of August, two days after the armistice with Romania was signed, Mannerheim sent out peace feelers to the Soviets via Stockholm. On 4 September shooting stopped on the Finnish front, and two weeks later the armistice was signed. Finland was granted the frontiers of 1940, but lost the ore fields of Petsamo and was required to pay $300 million in reparation within six years. The Germans hung on to northern Finland and when they began demolishing Finnish installations fighting broke out between the erstwhile allies. By mid October the Soviets had taken Petsamo and advanced to the Norwegian border, where they halted. The northern fronts of the Red Army were now free to devote all their energies to operations against Army Group North.

By the middle of August Army Group Centre, now commanded by General Reinhardt, managed to establish a defensive position near the East Prussian border, but on 16 October Chernyakhovsky's 3rd Belorussian front mounted an offensive in the direction of Königsberg. Attacks on the flanks of the Soviet thrust resulted in Chernyakhovsky being forced to retreat. German troops discovered that the Red Army had heaped a bestial revenge on the civilian population, which had been refused permission to evacuate by Erich Koch, the former Reichs Commissar for the Ukraine who, having lost his satrapy, was in charge of the Königsberg Home Guard (*Volkssturm*). This was a terrible warning of what was to come and strengthened the Germans' determination to stand up to the Soviets' winter offensive.

The Red Army did not begin its assault against Friessner's Army Group South Ukraine in Romania until 20 August. The German 6th Army was trapped between Malinovsky's 2nd Ukrainian front and

Tolbukhin's 3rd Ukrainian front near Kishnev, about 60 miles to the east of Jassy where 150,000 men were taken prisoner. The way was now open for a Soviet advance to Bucharest, and on 23 August King Michael dismissed Antonescu's Government. Antonescu had been discussing the possibility of a separate peace with the western Allies since the autumn of 1943, but these talks had broken down due to the the west's insistence that Romania had also to surrender unconditionally to the Soviet Union. Negotiations with the Soviets in Stockholm in the summer of 1944 were also inconclusive.

The new Government of General Sanatescu ordered the German troops to leave Romania and broke off diplomatic relations with Berlin. Hitler immediately ordered the King's arrest, but the attempt failed and Romania was provided with an excellent excuse to declare war on Germany on 25 August. Under the terms of the armistice Romania was required to provide twelve divisions to fight the Germans and, like Finland, to pay an indemnity of $300 million. The Germans had no choice but to abandon Romania as quickly as possible and thus lost the Ploesti oilfields, which left them desperately short of fuel.

The Soviets were now ready to push on into Bulgaria, even though the country had declared war only on the western powers. The Soviet Union declared war on Bulgaria on 5 September. The Bulgarians replied by instantly calling for an armistice and when this was refused they declared war on Germany. On 9 September the Patriotic Front, in which the communists played a leading role, seized power and it was they who declared war on Germany. Bulgarians, traditionally pro-Russian, gave the Red Army a moderately enthusiastic welcome and Bulgaria became the first communist-controlled state outside the Soviet Union. Some 30–40,000 who were not quite as keen on the new regime were killed without trial, in what the British Foreign Office described as an 'unpleasant procedure' about which they regretted they could do nothing.

Hitler was not particularly upset by the course of events. He told his generals that the Soviets would now head for the straits and would then clash with the western Allies. The fighting between ELAS and the British was merely the first round in this ideological struggle which would save the Third Reich. The Soviets, however, turned north-west towards Hungary, thus cutting off Löhr's Army Group E in Greece. Belgrade was taken by Soviet troops and Yugoslav partisans on 20 October, thus forcing Löhr to retreat further west through Sarajevo. Joining Army Group F under

Weichs, Army Group E helped form a defensive line running east of Sarajevo north to Croatia.

At the beginning of October the Red Army advanced across the Hungarian plains towards Budapest, but they were stopped on the Tisza. The Germans also mounted a successful armoured counter-attack near Debrecen which spoilt the Soviets' chances of outflanking Friessner's Army Group, which was now suitably renamed Army Group South. Clearly the Germans had only gained a breathing space, and Horthy had already begun negotiations for an armistice. An envoy was sent to Moscow on 1 October and Horthy accepted the Allied conditions on 11 October. SS Obergruppenführer von dem Bach-Zelewski, who had gained the admiration of his superiors for his forceful handling of the Warsaw uprising, had already prepared a coup against the Hungarian Government in co-operation with Ferencz Szálasi, the leader of the Hungarian fascist movement 'Arrow Cross', and Skorzeny who had carried out the daring action to free Mussolini. When Horthy informed the German envoy of the armistice agreement on 15 October, the Germans acted. Horthy was arrested and Szálasi named 'Leader of the Nation'. General Miklós-Dalnóki, who commanded the Hungarian 1st Army, formed an alternative Government at Debrecen which negotiated a separate armistice with the Allies in January. Along with the statutory $300 million in reparation, he agreed to send eight divisions against the Germans and to abandon the territorial gains made in 1938 and 1940.

The Soviets made slow progress across the Tisza, but eventually Tolbukhin broke out towards Lake Balaton and Malinovsky reached Budapest on Christmas Eve. The German defences in the 'Margarethe Line' were too weak to stop the advance, and a counter-attack at Székesfehérvar ('Operation *Spätlese*') was compromised by the removal of Panzers to meet the threat to the capital. Hitler refused to allow the German and Hungarian troops to break out of Budapest, and against the advice of Guderian moved troops from Poland to save the city and defend western Hungary. A further attempt to relieve Budapest was made in the middle of January, but the offensive was stopped on the Danube south of the city. On 11 February the Germans in Budapest surrendered. Shortly afterwards Hitler sent Sepp Dietrich's 6th SS Panzer Army, which had been resting after the Battle of the Bulge, to Hungary in a desperate attempt to push the Soviets back across the Danube. It was a pointless move since the Soviets were now only 50 miles from Berlin.

Germany's position in January 1945 was hopeless. Although there were 7.5 million men in arms and 260 divisions, only 75 divisions were on the critical front from the Carpathians to the Baltic. Here the Soviets had an overwhelming superiority of eleven to one in infantry, seven to one in tanks and twenty to one in artillery. The Chief of General Staff, Guderian, tried to convince Hitler of the need for a mobile reserve, but the Führer was still obsessed with such secondary objectives as the Ardennes offensive and a counter-attack in Hungary and would not listen. He dismissed General Gehlen's assessments of Soviet strength as 'the greatest bluff since Ghengis Khan' and imagined that an new offensive in the west would bring the British and Americans to the negotiating table. Guderian realistically insisted that the eastern front was a house of cards that could collapse at any moment.

The offensive began on 12 January when Koniev's 1st Ukrainian front broke out of the bridgehead across the Vistula and headed for Cracow, Katowice and Czestochowa. On his right, Zhukov broke out to the south of Warsaw. OKH misread the situation, imagined that Zhukov was heading for Warsaw and ordered the evacuation of the capital. Hitler declared Warsaw a fortress that was to be defended at all costs, but it was too late. A number of general staff officers were arrested and Guderian was cross-examined by the head of the Gestapo, Müller, and by Kaltenbrunner of the RSHA. Hitler dismissed General Harpe, whom he held responsible for the disaster on the Vistula, and replaced him with his current favourite, General Schörner. In order to stop any further retreat he demanded that henceforth all orders down to divisional level had to be sanctioned by his headquarters in the Berlin bunker.

Army Group Centre under General Reinhardt was soon reeling from the blows of Chernyakhovsky's offensive in East Prussia, and Rokossovsky threatened to cut off his line of retreat by crossing the Narew and heading north towards Elbing and Danzig. Reinhardt was determined to keep his lines of communication with Germany open, particularly since hundreds of thousands of refugees were heading west to avoid the revenge of the Red Army, but Hitler ordered the defence of East Prussia on all sides. This proved fatal, for on 26 January Rokossovsky's troops reached the Frische Haff and Army Group Centre was encircled. As soon as Hitler heard that Reinhardt was attempting to fight his way out he was dismissed and replaced by General Rendulic, an officer who shared many of his Führer's fantasies. But there was little he could do except try to hang on to Königsberg and the port of Pillau as long as possible and await the end. It came in the second week of April and was terrible.

Members of the *Volkssturm* were shot as partisans and the Red Army ran amok in an orgy of rape, plunder and murder. Tanks were run over wounded soldiers and others were burned alive.

Further south the Germans desperately tried to patch together a defensive position on the Oder using local police and *Volkssturm* units. Koniev's armies crossed the Oder at Steinau, drove along the western bank of the Oder and headed for Berlin. By the end of the month the Soviets captured the industrial region of Upper Silesia, and Speer promptly informed Hitler that the German economy would collapse within a matter of weeks. Hitler ignored this warning, which he attributed to faint-heartedness and lack of true National Socialist zeal.

A new front was hastily formed out of any available manpower to plug the gap between East Prussia and Silesia. This rag-tag force was given the impressive title Army Group Vistula and was commanded by none other than Heinrich Himmler. The valetudinarian Reichsführer SS commanded his troops from a bed in a clinic run by a Nazi quack, Dr Karl Gebhardt, who had conducted some very nasty experiments with Polish girls at Ravensbrück concentration camp. He pumped him full of strychnine, belladonna and a patent hormone tonic, and Himmler's spirits were further revived when he heard that the ice had melted on the Oder, a dramatic change in the weather which he attributed to divine providence. This did nothing to halt the Soviet advance and at the beginning of February Zhukov had crossed the Oder at Küstrin and was only 50 miles from Berlin.

Guderian now felt that the only possible course of action was to withdraw all the remaining troops from Italy, Norway, Holland and the Baltic and launch a counter-attack against the Soviet thrust towards Berlin from the north and south. At least this would give the Germans a breathing space in which to begin negotiations with the western Allies. On 25 January Guderian shared these ideas with Ribbentrop and suggested that they should go together to Hitler to convince him to begin armistice negotiations. Ribbentrop would not dare face the Führer with such a suggestion, and when Hitler heard of Guderian's views he accused him of high treason.

Rather than heading for Berlin, the Soviets decided to secure their flanks by pushing forward over the eastern Neisse to the Sudetenland. Breslau held out under the fanatical leadership of Gauleiter Hanke, who stayed in the city until 4 May when he left in a Fieseler Storch to take over Himmler's job as Reichsführer SS. He disappeared, probably shot by Czech partisans. Soviet troops did not enter Breslau until 7 March, the day of Germany's surrender at

Rheims. General Niehoff, the commanding general spent the next ten years in solitary confinement in the Gulag, another of his generals was hanged and the civilian population terrorized in the approved manner.

Hitler would not release the troops that Guderian needed for a counter-attack, and the most he could manage was an attack with six feeble divisions near Arnswalde which had to be broken off after four days. The Red Army now cleared Pomerania and invested Kolberg on 7 March. Goebbels did all he could to conjure up the spirit of Gneisenau, who had heroically defended Kolberg against Napoleon's forces, but to no avail. The commandant and his garrison wisely left on 18 March having made sure that the wounded and those wishing to leave the city had safely put to sea. The Soviets were now in full possession of the Oder–Neisse Line, with the exception of a few isolated pockets such as Breslau, Danzig and Königsberg, and were ready for the final assault on Berlin. The German navy was able to evacuate half a million soldiers and one and a half million refugees from the eastern provinces. The millions who tried to make their way by land in the harsh winter suffered appalling hardships and number among the countless tragic victims of Hitler's war.

Whereas in January 1945 the Soviets were ready for their final drive to Berlin the Allies had been held up by the Ardennes offensive and had yet to cross the Rhine. Stalin began to wonder whether Hitler's claim that the western Allies would be unable to resume their advance might not be an empty boast. This placed him in an awkward predicament. The very fact that Berlin was directly threatened by the Red Army strengthened the hands of those who were arguing for an arrangement between Nazi Germany and the western Allies. Although this notion was never entertained for a moment by anyone in a position of real authority either in Britain or the United States, Stalin remained deeply suspicious. On the other hand, if he pressed on with his offensive he would give the western Allies the relief they needed to continue their advance.

On the day that the Yalta conference opened, 4 February 1945, Marshal Zhukov ordered his front to halt, consolidate and prepare for the final assault on Berlin. There was sound military reasoning behind this decision. Ammunition was running low, supply lines were dangerously exposed and the Soviet advance had been so rapid as to become seriously disorganized. If the Germans had been able to assemble the troops, they could have delivered a devastating counter-attack. The decision to halt also placed Stalin in the best possible strategic position for his meeting with Churchill, and it is no wonder that he was at the peak of his form at Yalta. Cadogan wrote to his wife of Stalin: 'He *is* a great man and shows up very impressively against the background of two ageing statesmen.' Roosevelt he described as 'very woolly and wobbly' and Churchill as 'a silly old man'.

The decisions made at the 'Argonaut' conference were essentially the confirmation by the Big Three of decisions that had previously been made by subordinate organizations and officials. Thus an agreement was reached on the final occupation zones in Germany along the lines suggested by the European Advisory Commission, which was also empowered to draw up the final details. An important change was that at Churchill's insistence Stalin agreed to allow the French a share in the occupation of Germany. Stalin was encouraged by Churchill's remark that France was as essential for England's security as Poland was for Russia's to believe that by giving way over France he would gain a freer hand in Poland. He was also concerned by Roosevelt's statement that the Americans would leave Europe within two years. This was not a prospect which pleased Stalin since he was still concerned about a renewed threat from Germany. Nor did he see France as a threat, since the country was hopelessly weak after five years of division and occupation, and there was a powerful French communist party at his beck and call. No agreement could be reached on the question of the division of Germany or on reparations.

Roosevelt's main concern at Yalta was to reach an agreement on voting procedures for the United Nations Security Council, a problem which had not been resolved at the preparatory conference at Dumbarton Oaks. Stalin eventually accepted the American proposals, which included the right to veto, but in return Roosevelt had to agree to at least two Soviet republics becoming full members of the United Nations. It was further agreed that the founding conference of the United Nations should take place on 25 April 1945 in San Francisco.

By far the most difficult problem at the conference was that of Poland. Churchill announced that he 'could never be content with any settlement which did not leave Poland a free and independent state'. Poland must be 'mistress in her own house and captain of her soul'. The country had to have a genuinely representative provisional government, and its future would have to be decided by free elections. Stalin replied that for the Soviet Union the Polish question was one of national security. He denounced the London Poles for stirring up anti-Soviet sentiment in Poland and proposed a token enlargement of the Lublin Government so that it would be 'more broadly based'. He agreed to the Curzon Line as the eastern frontier, but demanded that the border should be drawn west of Lvov. In the west he proposed the line of the Oder and western Neisse. Churchill objected to the Western Neisse, saying 'it would be a great pity to stuff the Polish goose so full of German food that it died of indigestion'. Stalin replied that this was no problem, since the Germans had all run away. Stalin suggested that elections could be held within a month, but neither Churchill nor Roosevelt pinned him down to a precise date.

The British were delighted with the outcome of the Yalta conference. They had gone to the Crimea fearing the worst and had found Stalin genial and willing to compromise. On Poland they had got as much as they had hoped. The Americans were positively ecstatic. Hopkins said: 'We really believed in our hearts that this was the dawn of the new day we had all been praying for. The Russians had proved that they could be reasonable and far-seeing and there wasn't any doubt in the minds of the President or any of us that we could live with them and get along with them peacefully for as far into the future as any of us could imagine.' Not everyone was quite so thrilled. The London Poles correctly pointed out that the Russians could now do whatever they liked in Poland. The Lublin committee was now fully in control and the Soviet insistence on permitting only 'democratic' and 'anti-fascist' parties meant that the elections would be rigged. Leahy pointed out to Roosevelt that the agreement on Poland was 'so elastic that the Russians can stretch it all the way from Yalta to Washington without ever technically breaking it'. The President replied that it was the best he could do.

Yalta was one of the least important of the wartime conferences and it certainly does not deserve to be treated as Stalin's greatest victory over the gullible western leaders. Stalin got what he wanted in Poland, but it is difficult to see what more Roosevelt and Churchill could have done for the Poles. As Churchill told his cronies in the bar of the House of Commons: 'Not only are the Russians very powerful but they are on the spot; even the massed majesty of the British Army would not avail to turn them off the spot.' Stalin also made concessions at Yalta. He felt obliged to promise to declare war on Japan two or three months after the surrender of Germany. He also accepted the proposal to sign a treaty of friendship with Chiang Kai-shek's tottering nationalist Government and thus frustrated Mao's efforts to hasten the revolution. He had further agreed to allow France a seat on the Allied Control Council for Germany. Frustration over the outcome of the conference which soon set in, in both London and Washington, was fundamentally a response to the ugly fact that the balance of world power had shifted drastically in favour of the Soviet Union which was now incomparably the greatest power in Europe and whose grim dictatorship was determined to exploit this situation to the full. Yalta was certainly not a triumph of western statesmanship. But even the most skilful diplomacy could not have fundamentally ameliorated the position of the western powers.

The Soviet halt before Berlin strengthened Hitler's resolve to launch the long-awaited counter-attack by Wöhler's Army Group South in Hungary. The operation, optimistically codenamed 'Spring Awakening', was designed to drive Tolbukhin's 3rd Ukrainian front back across the Danube. Sepp Dietrich's 6th SS Panzer Army was to break out north of Lake Balaton near Székesfehérvár then fan out north to Budapest and south towards Baja; the 2nd Panzer Army was to drive due east from south of the lake; and a force from Weichs's Army Group E in Yugoslavia was to head for Mohács. The offensive began on 6 March and Sepp Dietrich's men were able to advance almost to the Danube then turned south, but the offensive soon ran out of steam as the Panzers got bogged down in the soft ground. Tolbuhkin's counter-attack was aimed at Sepp Dietrich's lines of communication, which forced 6th SS Panzer to beat a hasty retreat to avoid encirclement. Hitler was furious at the failure of his plan to save the Balaton oilfields and to win a prestige victory. He stripped all the SS Divisions which had retreated of their insignia. Even the crack *Leibstandarte Adolf Hitler* was not spared his anger. On 4 April the Red Army reached Bratislava and two days later Vienna. On 13 April Vienna surrendered and the Soviets continued their advance westwards until they were again halted on the Danube near Krems.

Guderian now threw all his reserves, including pensioners, children, the wounded and a curious assortment of Albanian and Slovene units, into a desperate attempt to make a stand on the Oder. He was also able to persuade Himmler to relinquish command of Army Group Vistula so that the Reichsführer could now devote more of his time to pondering the mystical drivel of Dr Wulf, who served as his personal Merlin, and to attempts to negotiate with the Allies. General Heinrici, who had successfully conducted a number of defensive battles on the eastern front, was given command of this rag-tag army and was ordered by Hitler to break out of his bridgehead on the eastern bank of the Oder, relieve Küstrin and attack the Soviet bridgehead in the rear. The plan was doomed from the start, and when it failed Hitler sent Guderian on sick leave and General Krebs took over as head of the general staff. SS Gruppenführer Reinefarth, who had ordered his garrison at Küstrin to break out of the encirclement, was court-martialed. Hitler then sent some of Heinrici's reserves to prop up Army Group Centre and Army Group South in Czechoslovakia and Austria, thus further weakening the defences on the Oder.

The German counter-attack at Küstrin having failed, the Soviets under Zhukov broke out of their bridgehead on 16 April, and further south Koniev also advanced. Although Zhukov made poor use of his armour and Heinrici's defences were skilfully placed, the two Soviet fronts now threatened to encircle Busse's 9th Army positioned to the south-east of Berlin. Heinrici realized that the 9th Army was doomed and since it would be impossible to build a new front to the east of Berlin, he proposed that they should withdraw to join the 3rd Panzer Army near Stettin, where Rokossovsky had yet to begin his advance. Hitler refused to allow Busse to withdraw, and thus lost most of the 9th Army. Heinrici now tried to patch up a new front between the Oder and the Havel which he placed under the command of SS Obergruppenführer Steiner. This 'Army Group Steiner' was in the process of formation when Rokossovsky's 2nd Belorussian front began its offensive.

The news that Army Group Steiner had been formed was the only comfort that could be offered to Hitler on his fifty-sixth birthday on 20 April. Otherwise it was a dreadfully gloomy affair. Himmler left the festivities to continue plotting a separate peace with Count Bernadotte of Sweden. Speer went off to devote his energies to sabotaging Hitler's scorched-earth policy. Göring disappeared to plan an escape route, to take a final look at his plundered art treasures and to attempt to overthrow Hitler and end the war. Bormann, Goebbels and Ribbentrop decided to stay in Berlin. Hitler still hoped that it might be possible to establish an 'Alpine Fortress' in Bavaria and Tyrol from which he could continue the war, but two days later he realized the futility of this plan and announced that he would stay in Berlin and die at his post.

CHAPTER THIRTEEN

From Normandy to The Elbe (June 1944–May 1945)

Churchill began to think about an invasion of northern France at the time of Dunkirk. He appointed a Combined Operations Staff under Admiral Sir Roger Keyes, who had led the raid on Zeebrugge in 1918, to investigate all the problems of large-scale amphibious warfare. Keyes was soon to fall out with the Prime Minister and with the inflexible bureaucracy of Whitehall. In October 1941 Captain Lord Louis Mountbatten, whose swashbuckling and opinionated style was more to Churchill's taste, replaced Keyes and was ordered, in characteristically exaggerated terms, to turn the whole of southern England into a springboard for the invasion of the Continent. Mountbatten was a very junior officer whose undoubted talents were more suited to diplomacy and politics than to complex military operations. He was largely ignored by the Chiefs of Staff, to whose committee he was appointed in spite of his modest rank, and Churchill came to believe that Germany could be crushed in an anaconda strategy – blockaded by the Royal Navy, flattened by Bomber Command and riven by internal dissent – that would obviate the need for invasion.

It was the Americans who now insisted on the priority of a cross-Channel invasion. At the 'Arcadia' conference in Washington in January 1942 General Marshall argued for an early invasion, 'Operation Sledgehammer', a small-scale operation to secure a bridgehead in France in 1942 and to ease the pressure on the Russian front, but Churchill urged caution and delay. Plans for an invasion were drawn up by a relatively unknown officer, Brigadier General Dwight D. Eisenhower, but with the 'Torch' landings in north Africa these had to be shelved. Mountbatten's appalling mishandling of the Dieppe raid on 19 August 1942, which was perhaps deliberately designed to silence critics of 'Torch' and proponents of 'Sledgehammer', further dampened enthusiasm for a cross-Channel invasion. At Casablanca in January 1943 the British proposals for 'Operation Husky', the invasion of Sicily, were accepted, thus leading to a further postponement of invasion. Planning for 'Roundup', a full-scale invasion of France with thirty American and eighteen British divisions following 'Bolero', the build-up in England, continued under the new codename 'Overlord'.

In March 1943 a British General, Frederick Morgan, was appointed Chief of Staff to the Supreme Allied Commander (Designate), or COSSAC, and was asked by Ismay to suggest an outline invasion plan. There seemed to be no pressing urgency. Ismay bade him farewell with the assurance, 'No hurry, old boy, tomorrow will do!' COSSAC's proposals were ready in three months and suggested a landing by three divisions in Normandy with an airborne attack on Caen. The invasion force would then secure the Cotentin peninsula and open the port of Cherbourg.

It was a hopelessly flawed plan. The landing force was far too weak and would be vulnerable to a devastating counter-attack as it slogged its way through enemy-occupied territory all the way to Cherbourg. But COSSAC had no choice in the matter, for he was told to make do with the resources available and three divisions was the most that he could scrape together. The proposed landing force was smaller than that used in the invasion of Sicily or in the Salerno landings. It was hardly a serious plan, and provides clear evidence of the grave reservations the British had about 'Overlord'. Churchill nevertheless accepted COSSAC's plan and presented it at the Quebec conference, where it was endorsed by the President. It was now assumed that Marshall would be the Supreme Allied Commander for 'Overlord'. Churchill had wanted a British Supreme Commander and told Brooke that he should have the job, but at Quebec he had to give way to the Americans. Roosevelt then decided to keep his Chief of Staff in Washington, thus leaving Eisenhower as the best candidate for the appointment. It was a most fortunate choice. He had the experience, the expertise and the sensitivity for the task and he was greatly admired by Churchill and the British, although many British officers in their overbearing arrogance felt that Eisenhower, like all American soldiers, was inexperienced and frequently inept.

Eisenhower's appointment was made known on 6 December 1943. Major General Omar N. Bradley was given the command of the American ground forces for the invasion. Churchill favoured the appointment of Alexander as commander of the British troops, but

Brooke preferred Montgomery who he felt had more drive and vision. The War Cabinet also favoured Montgomery, thinking that Eisenhower might need his battlefield experience and would benefit from Monty's proddings. On 22 December Churchill gave way and ordered the appointment of Montgomery. It was not an appointment which pleased Eisenhower. He said of Montgomery: 'Monty is a good man to serve under; a difficult man to serve with; and an impossible man to serve over.' Montgomery said of Eisenhower: 'When it comes to war, Ike doesn't know the difference between Christmas and Easter.' Montgomery was probably the better choice from a purely professional point of view, but Eisenhower's extraordinary patience was tried to the limit by this impossible human being.

Eisenhower knew that a three-division attack was too weak, and his Chief of Staff, Bedell Smith, described the proposal as a 'puny little attack'. Montgomery agreed with Eisenhower and Bedell Smith and was thus not alone in spotting the weaknesses in the plan, as he subsequently claimed. Montgomery returned to England from north Africa and set up headquarters in London at his old school, St Paul's. The first thing he did was to purge the staff of 21st Army Group, the designation of the British invasion force, replacing it with the staff of the 8th Army headed by the capable and likeable General Francis de Guingand.

Eisenhower appointed Montgomery temporary Commander-in-Chief and he immediately set about the drastic revision of Morgan's plan. He called for a large-scale landing with five divisions on a wider front to avoid congestion. An airborne division was to be dropped in the Cotentin peninsula to secure the capture of Cherbourg. In the course of subsequent modifications two additional airborne divisions were added, one in the Cotentin and the other on the left flank to secure the Orne canal and the high ground to the east of Caen.

The increase in the size of the proposed invasion force delivered another blow to 'Operation Anvil', the landings in the south of France, and led to a protracted and acrimonious exchange of notes between Roosevelt and Churchill. For the Americans and the Russians, 'Anvil' was evidence of a full commitment to the campaign in France and a downgrading of the Italian front, and for this reason, as much as its strategic importance, it was a vital part of 'Overlord'. A number of planners feared that Montgomery's plan spread the forces too thinly and compromised the chances of taking Caen by simultaneously going for the Cotentin peninsula and Cherbourg, the latter a port of strictly limited capacity and therefore not worth the cost. Montgomery was of course violently opposed to the alternative plan for four divisions to attack in the Caen sector, and there is no evidence that it was even shown to Eisenhower. On 1 February 1944 the Combined Chiefs approved Montgomery's plan for 'Neptune', a landing between Caen and Cotentin.

The key to the success of Montgomery's plan was that Caen should be taken on the first day in an armoured thrust, and the left flank along the Orne held against an inevitable counter-attack. Foremost in men's minds, particularly in Churchill's, was the fear that 'Neptune' would prove to be another Anzio, but Montgomery gave constant assurance of his offensive intent and determination not to get bogged down in his bridgehead.

The Germans were faced with two major problems: to decide where the Allies were most likely to attack, and to determine how best to meet the invasion. Von Rundstedt, the Supreme Commander West, assumed that the Allies would take the shortest route across the Channel, and consequently strengthened the Calais–Boulogne sector and concentrated on the area between the Somme and the Scheldt. This assessment seemed to be confirmed when the intelligence service picked up phoney messages pointing to a massive build-up of American forces in south-eastern England. The success of this deception, 'Operation Fortitude South', was confirmed when 'Ultra' decrypts indicated that the Germans had swallowed the bait. Rommel, however, felt that the Allies were more likely to land somewhat further west, around the Seine Bight. Heavy bombing raids on the roads and railways leading to Normandy strengthened him in this belief.

Rundstedt and Rommel also disagreed on the best means of countering the invasion. Rundstedt favoured a 'crust, cushion, hammer' concept: the invaders would be weakened by the coastal defences, absorbed by the infantry to the rear, and then smashed by the armour. Geyr von Schweppenburg, who commanded the Armoured Forces West, even wanted to lure the invaders inland and crush them with his armour between the Loire and the Seine. Rommel could not accept these ideas. He knew from his experience in north Africa the devastating effect of air power against the Panzers. He also knew that the Allies now had greatly improved tanks and anti-tank weapons. Above all, he was convinced that once the Allies established a bridgehead it would not be possible to dislodge them from the Continent, and that the Germans would then be forced to fight on three fronts. Rommel had, in fact, reached the point where he believed that the war would be decided on the beaches. His plan called for a belt about three miles deep made up of infantry and well-protected artillery, with the armour placed directly behind it so that the tanks would immediately be able to shell the beaches. Such a defensive system clearly lacked depth, but Rommel hoped to make up for this by beginning an extensive programme of placing underwater obstacles to destroy or impede landing craft. This ambitious scheme was far from complete by June 1944, but it still caused considerable damage. Rommel started his work on the defences too late and was hampered by severe shortages of artillery, concrete and armour plating.

Hitler and his entourage were not seriously concerned about an invasion. The Luftwaffe continued to bomb London rather than the embarcation ports and Hitler refused to allow the V1 rockets to be aimed at enemy troop concentrations in the south of England. He was comforted by the memory of the fiascos at Dakar and Dieppe. 'Torch' had met with little opposition. The landings in Italy had not been very impressive. Hitler was convinced that the Allies would be driven back into the sea without much difficulty and would then be destroyed by the V-weapons, the new jet aircraft and improved U-boats. Himmler summed up this attitude in the characteristic language of the Nazi hierarchy: 'I pray that the inflated plutocrats of the west will be foolish enough to invade the Continent.'

Eisenhower decided at 21.45 hours on 4 June that 'Overlord' should proceed on Tuesday 6 June. He reaffirmed this historic decision early the following morning when his Chief Meteorological Officer, Group Captain J.M. Stagg, told him that the weather would not change for the worse. During the night of 5–6 June the three Allied airborne divisions were dropped. The British 6th Airborne seized the Orne bridges, disrupted the enemy communications and took a number of strong points which menaced 'Sword' beach to the west of Ouistreham. On the Cotentin peninsula the airborne landings were a shambles, but this proved to be a blessing in disguise. The Germans were equally bemused by what was going on and since the Americans were widely dispersed, they imagined that they had landed in far greater numbers than was the case.

Rundstedt and Rommel's headquarters believed that these airborne landings were simply diversionary operations, and Rommel had left for Germany convinced that the weather was so bad that the Allies would not risk an invasion. H-hour was at 06.30 when the Americans landed at 'Utah' and 'Omaha' beaches. The worst fighting was on 'Omaha' beach, a formidable obstacle with cliffs as high as 200 feet and which never should have been attacked by direct assault even under optimum conditions. Unknown to Allied intelligence the veteran 352nd Infantry Division had been moved into this sector and was in the middle of defensive exercises. Heavy cloud cover meant that bombs had failed to hit the coastal defences and had merely killed a number of French cows. At 07.00 hours Bucknall's 30th Corps and Crocker's 1st Corps landed on 'Gold', 'Juno' and 'Sword' beaches.

The Germans still believed that the main attack would come in the Pas de Calais, and for the next few weeks Rommel's Army Group B was denied the reserves it requested. All German units north of the Seine were ordered to prepare for the expected invasion and were not allowed to move to Normandy. Rommel's Panzer reserves were under the direct operational control of OKW, and were not released until the afternoon of D-Day and did not arrive on the battleground until the next day.

The British 3rd Division's advance towards Caen was painfully slow. The Suffolk Regiment were unpleasantly surprised by the extent of the German defensive position 'Hillman' and had great difficulty in overrunning it. The 2nd Battalion, the King's Shropshire Light Infantry (KSLI), advanced rapidly to the outskirts of Caen but were beaten back by 21st Panzer Division with heavy losses. The Panzers pushed forward, driving a wedge between the British and Canadian bridgeheads, and reached the beaches, but their attack on the British flank was beaten back. Crocker ordered 9th Brigade to abandon the advance to Caen and go to the support of the sorely pressed airborne troops at Pegasus bridge, the only crossing across the Orne and Orne canal to the north of Caen and therefore a vital position. German defences were far too strong and the landing of armoured units too slow for there to be a chance of capturing Caen on D-Day. Had the Germans reacted faster and more decisively, the situation for the Allies could well have been disastrous. Particularly fateful was the delay in moving the fanatical SS General Kurt Meyer's 12th SS Panzer to Caen. The young thugs in his *Hitler Jugend* Division were to provide the Canadians and British with some singularly unpleasant surprises in the days to come.

Having failed to take Caen, Montgomery decided to modify his plans and proposed to encircle the town in a double envelopment in which the 1st Airborne Division was to play an important role in blocking the German retreat. Leigh-Mallory, commanding the Allied

Expeditionary Air Force, refused to give Montgomery the aircraft to drop 1st Airborne, insisting that the operation was too risky. Montgomery promptly denounced Leigh-Mallory as a 'gutless bugger'. Leigh-Mallory had every reason to be cautious, since the two pincers had been repulsed. General 'Boy' Browning was better known for his elegance than his competence and his airborne troops would have been hopelessly isolated. The attack by 7th Armoured Division on Villers-Bocage was badly handled by the corps commander, Bucknall, who lacked the drive to exploit a favourable opportunity. Rommel had been preparing a counter-attack, but on 11 June Geyr von Schweppenburg's Panzer Group West was mauled by the RAF who knew of the whereabouts of his headquarters from 'Ultra' decrypts from Bletchley Park. A large number of his senior officers were killed and Schweppenburg himself was wounded. Having recovered from his wounds he was soon to be dismissed for suggesting to Hitler that the logistic elements should be withdrawn from Caen. Command of his Panzer group was given to General Eberbach, who was to fight a very skilful defensive campaign but who was overshadowed by SS Oberstgruppenführer Sepp Dietrich, a man more remarkable for his loyalty to the Führer than for his abilities as a commander, who commanded 1st SS Panzer Corps.

Unable either to take Caen by direct assault or to encircle it, Montgomery now changed his plan, deciding to use it to bear the brunt of the German counter-attack and as a hinge for an American break-out. The historical record does not support Montgomery's absurd contention that this was what he wanted all along. One of his most striking characteristics as a commander was his ability to improvise, as he had shown at El Alamein, but he liked to claim, with sublime disregard for the truth, that everything went according to his master plans.

Montgomery now decided to have another crack at working his way around Caen. Feeling that the enemy was too strongly posted on his left flank he decided to send 8th Corps, commanded by O'Connor who had fought so brilliantly in north Africa and who had escaped from an Italian prisoner-of-war camp, across the Odon west of Caen to seize Hill 112 and the high ground which dominated the west bank of the Orne to the south of Caen. The new offensive was given the codename 'Epsom'. It was a tough assignment as Panzer Lehr, 12th SS Panzer Division, *Hitler Jugend* and 21st Panzers were lying in wait.

On 17 June Hitler went to France for the first time since 1940 to discuss the situation with Rundstedt and Rommel at Soissons.

Rommel requested permission to withdraw troops from the Cotentin peninsula and to bring in reserves from the Pas de Calais to counter the Allied break-out. Hitler refused to consider any withdrawals, confidently assured his audience that the new wonder weapons, particularly the V rockets, would destroy England, and suddenly departed for Berchtesgaden. The great storm, which began on 19 June, gave the Germans a breathing space. The artificial harbour 'Mulberry' on Omaha beach was totally destroyed, another 'Mulberry' at Arromanches was badly damaged, and more vessels were destroyed by the storm than by the Germans in the entire campaign. Virtually no men or supplies could be landed for three days.

As was expected of him, O'Connor led a spirited attack across the Odon. Rommel and Rundstedt were ordered to Berchtesgaden and were admitted to the presence on 29 June, having been kept waiting all day. They were then treated to another diatribe about miracle weapons and unjustified pessimism. Rundstedt was sacked and his place taken by von Kluge, a cheerful and aggressive commander who soon realized that Rundstedt's assessment of the situation was absolutely correct. The commander of the German 7th Army, Dollmann, was beginning to crack under the strain of the Americans taking Cherbourg and the British crossing the Odon, and committed suicide. The counter-attack against the British on Hill 112 was beaten back, but the over-cautious Dempsey ordered 8th Corps to draw back in anticipation of a further counter-attack which never materialized. The Germans were thus able to recapture Hill 112 and there followed a grim slogging match for this position in which 8th Corps suffered unacceptable casualties. Losses in the crack 15th (Scottish) Division were over 58 per cent. On 30 June Montgomery called off 'Epsom'.

Montgomery now decided to send in Bomber Command to flatten Caen and open the way for 1st Corps to enter the city. 'Operation Charnwood' began on 7 July but the bombing resulted merely in the pointless destruction of a beautiful ancient city. Miraculously William the Conqueror's Abbaye-aux-Hommes and the Hôpital du Bon Sauveur survived, but the rubble provided excellent cover for the German defenders and seriously impeded the Allied advance. Although the bombing was extremely accurate, no worthwhile military targets were hit. Allied losses in the attack on Caen were terribly high, averaging 25 per cent in infantry battalions. The capture of Caen, although trumpeted in the Allied press as a tremendous feat of arms, was a largely empty victory. The Germans still held the Orne and the high ground around Caen, thus blocking Montgomery's advance south-east to Falaise. Omar Bradley wrote:

> By July 10, we faced a real danger of a World War I type stalemate in Normandy. Montgomery's forces had taken the northern outskirts of Caen, but the city was not by any means in his control. The airfield sites still lay beyond his grasp. My own breakout had failed. Despite enormous casualties and loss of equipment, the Germans were slavishly following Hitler's orders to hold every yard of ground.

On the Cotentin peninsula the Americans sealed off the northern tip and German resistance ceased by the end of June, but they had had a terrible time fighting in the hedgerows of the Bocage and had got as badly stuck as the British at Caen. In 'Operation Cobra' Bradley planned a breakthrough to more favourable terrain for the 1st and 3rd Armies by softening up the German positions with a massive air strike and then sending in Collins's 7th Corps on a narrow front to punch a hole through the German lines. While the infantry held the shoulders of the bulge, two armoured divisions would drive through to Avranches.

While Bradley was planning 'Cobra' Dempsey was working on 'Goodwood', an armoured strike designed to achieve a breakthrough into the excellent tank country of the Caen–Falaise plain. After saturation bombing of the German positions three armoured divisions, supported on the flanks by infantry from the British 1st and 12th Corps, were to push south from the bridgehead east of the Orne held by 6th Airborne Division and head for Bourguébus, south-east of Caen. The newly arrived Canadian 2nd Corps were to drive the Germans out of the southern districts of Caen. West of Caen, 12th Corps was to launch a diversionary attack from which some gains were expected.

The Germans had excellent observation posts, particularly the towers of the steelworks at Colombelles, and were expecting an offensive. General Eberbach of Panzer Group West was lying in wait with brilliantly prepared defences. Rommel was severely wounded on 17 July, ironically near the village of St Foy de Montgomery, and was invalided back to Germany, never to fight another battle. Two days before this injury Rommel had advised Hitler that the situation in Normandy was hopeless and that the Allies were bound to break out within three weeks. Yet in spite of the weakness of the German forces they had plenty of fight left in them. 'Ultra' had revealed little of the German defences, which were to give the British a most unpleasant surprise. Eberbach had prepared four lines of defence about 10 miles deep behind which he had strong reserves. The

British squeezed their way across the Orne and through their own minefields and were halted long before 'Goodwood' had achieved its objectives. But the operation brought some gains. Montgomery now had a sizeable bridgehead over the Orne, he had taken all of Caen and had crossed the Odon. The Germans were at the end of their tether and even von Kluge began to wonder how long they could hang on.

Eisenhower was furious with Montgomery over the failure of 'Goodwood'. Montgomery had sold the operation to SHAEF as a breakthrough, for otherwise he would not have been given the massive air support he needed to soften up the German defences. Eisenhower bitterly complained that 7000 tons of bombs had been dropped and only 7 miles gained. Tedder felt that Montgomery should be replaced. Eisenhower told Churchill that Monty had sold him a bill of goods. Brooke thought Eisenhower unfair to Montgomery, who in turn was infuriated by the Supreme Commander's criticisms. In his memoirs Montgomery denounced Eisenhower for failing to understand the situation, but Eisenhower in his subsequent account of the campaign generously and tactfully made no mention of 'Goodwood'.

'Operation Cobra' was delayed by bad weather and began badly with the air force bombing short, thus causing numerous casualties and killing the Commander of Army Ground Forces, General McNair. But soon the Americans broke through the German defences for the first time in Normandy and unleashed General Patton's 3rd Army. Von Kluge described the situation succinctly as a *Riesensauerei* and requested permission from Hitler to retire behind the Seine. Hitler ordered an immediate counter-attack at Avranches and designated the Brittany ports as fortresses to be defended to the last man.

Patton was ordered west to capture the Brittany ports, a particular obsession of Montgomery's, even though he was virtually unopposed in the east. This would have been a serious mistake, but Patton saw the chance to drive towards the Orleans gap and managed to convince Bradley. Montgomery, to his lasting credit, agreed, thus dropping the 'Overlord' plan. Only the US 8th Corps was sent to Brittany, and Brest did not fall until 19 September. The Germans managed to hang on to some of the Brittany ports until the end of the war. Von Kluge patched up a Panzer corps from sundry SS units and threw it into a counter-attack in the direction of Avranches, but they were halted by a spirited defence, particularly at Hill 317 and destroyed by Quesada's IX Tactical Airforce.

On 7 August Montgomery launched 'Operation Totalize' in which the 1st Canadian Army was ordered to take Falaise. The British 2nd Army was to support the Canadian right flank, then both armies would wheel left and head for the Seine. To complete the process of long envelopment the US 1st and 3rd Armies were to dash across southern Normandy, join up with the British and Canadians and trap the Germans along the Seine. But on 8 August Bradley suggested to Eisenhower a short left hook at Argentan which would trap the Germans in the Falaise pocket.

The Canadians faced stiff opposition and made slow progress, partly because they stopped to take out strong points rather than by-pass them. Dempsey had little difficulty advancing through the Bocage, and Montgomery made a serious mistake in not reinforcing the Canadian right flank with units from the 2nd Army. Hitler obliged by refusing to halt the counter-offensive at Mortain aimed at Avranches, and Bradley made rapid progress to complete the entrapment of the German forces in Normandy. On 12 August Patton ordered his 15th Corps to head north on reaching Argentan and join up with the Canadians, who were still slogging away north of Falaise. Bradley was terrified that this would lead to a collision with the Canadians and ordered Patton to halt, as if any gap could be closed without two forces meeting. Patton said to Bradley, half in jest, 'Shall we continue and drive the British into the sea for another Dunkirk?' This celebrated if somewhat tasteless remark did not go down too well when reported to the British and did nothing to improve Anglo-American relations, which were already severely strained.

The Canadians reached Falaise on 16 August, but the Falaise gap from Falaise to Argentan was wide open. The Germans seized the opportunity and poured through the gap, which was not closed until 19 August when the Polish 1st Armoured, supported by the Canadians, joined up with US 90th Division. The Germans who escaped through the gap had to run the gauntlet all the way to the Seine, many losing their lives, most their equipment. Although badly bungled, it was still an impressive victory. The Germans suffered 10,000 casualties and 50,000 were taken prisoner. Army Group B was destroyed and stragglers dashed for the protection of the Seine. Kluge was relieved of his command on 17 August and committed suicide, leaving a note asking Hitler to save his people from further suffering and end the 'hopeless struggle'. A fanatical Nazi, Model, took over his command. By 25 August, D-Day + 80, the four Allied armies reached the Seine and the campaign in Normandy was over.

It had never been part of the invasion plan to capture Paris, and Eisenhower was concerned lest a struggle for its possession would lead to its destruction. Hitler issued instructions to the commandant of Paris to reduce the French capital to a 'heap of rubble' which was to be defended to the last man; but General von Choltitz, an honourable, sensible and brave man, ignored these orders and negotiated what amounted to a cease-fire with the resistance groups in the city. Curiously enough it was the Parisian police who first went into action against the German occupying forces, soon to be followed by the communist-led FFI (French Forces of the Interior). De Gaulle was appalled by the prospect of Paris being liberated by communists and insisted that the French Division, commanded by the impeccably aristocratic Jacques-Philippe de Hautecloque (better known by his assumed name of Leclerc), should be sent to Paris. Eisenhower, feeling that he had to choose between de Gaulle and the communists, opted for the former. De Gaulle put on a splendidly theatrical performance in Paris, refusing to proclaim the restoration of the Republic, insisting that it had never ceased to exist and that he was its President. Paris was thrilled. It had give Pétain an enthusiastic welcome in March; now it gave de Gaulle an even greater welcome in August. In fact, the communist threat was a phantom. Stalin had ordered his French minions to behave themselves, and Maurice Thorez, the communist leader, gave de Gaulle his full support. De Gaulle was now the uncrowned king of an independent France, an astonishing feat by an extraordinary man.

Meanwhile, Allied troops landed in southern France between Fréjus and Hyères on 15 August in 'Operation Dragoon'. Its new codename emphasized the fact that strategically it had little value since it could no longer serve as an 'Anvil' against which the hammer of 'Overlord' was swung, and 'Dragoon' strongly suggested that the British had been forced into an operation for which they had little enthusiasm. It was of questionable strategic value and was the cause of bitter controversy between the British and the Americans. Eisenhower insisted that it go ahead, largely for political reasons, although he insisted that he needed to open Marseille to supply the armies in France. 'Dragoon' not only emphasized that operations in France took precedence over the campaign in Italy, it also implied British subordination to the Americans. It was perhaps this, as much as strategic concerns, which made it so objectionable to Churchill.

Hitler ordered Army Group G to retreat and join up with the remains of Army Group B to form a defensive line along the Marne and the Saône up to the Swiss border. Toulon and Marseille were to be left as fortresses to be defended to the last. 'Ultra' decrypts revealed the details of this plan so that the Americans were able to trap the bulk of Army Group G near Montélimar as it retreated in the direction of Grenoble. The Allies bagged 50,000 prisoners in 'Dragoon', but the operation had the unfortunate effect of forcing the Germans back to the defence of the Reich, thus increasing the strength of the forces opposing Eisenhower's main advance.

On 1 September Eisenhower assumed command of the land forces and Montgomery was promoted to Field Marshal in a vain attempt to keep him quiet. With the collapse of the German armies in France, Montgomery argued for a full-blooded thrust by two army groups of forty divisions on a narrow front aimed at the Ruhr. Bradley and Patton wanted to strike further south past the Saar to Frankfurt. Eisenhower attempted to find a politically acceptable compromise whereby neither a British nor an American general would win the war on his own. The result was the broad front strategy, justified by concerns over logistical problems caused by the need to repair the French railway system and to seize Antwerp. The inadequate port of Cherbourg and the 'Mulberry' at Arromanches were under constant air attack, and the Britanny ports were still in German hands. Eisenhower also feared that what he unfairly termed a 'pencil-like thrust' would be terribly vulnerable to counter-attack. He therefore ordered an advance from Antwerp to the Saar but with priority given to Montgomery, at least until he had taken Antwerp. Patton, who announced that he would go through the Siegfried Line 'like shit through a goose', had his petrol allowance cut from 400,000 gallons a day to 32,000 and, in spite of ruthlessly cheating, he literally ran out of fuel at Metz where he got his first bloody nose. This he attributed to Montgomery's vainglorious behaviour. Montgomery for his part believed that the Americans were deliberately frustrating his drive into the Ruhr in order to appease Patton rather than for any valid strategic reason. The situation got so bad that Eisenhower was within an inch of demanding Montgomery's dismissal, and the ill-feeling between the two men was never overcome.

While Patton went cursing and grumbling in the direction of Metz and Nancy as fast as his fuel supplies allowed him, Hodges and the US 1st Army on his left trapped several of Model's Panzer divisions in a deep pocket from Compiègne to Mons. By 6 September

Hodges' army was in Liège and on 11 September it reached the German border near Trier where they were stopped by the German defences on the Mosel and the West Wall.

Montgomery's 21st Army Group reached Brussels on 3 September and on the next day they took Antwerp, and thanks to the splendid efforts of the Belgian resistance the port facilities were left virtually intact. Montgomery requested permission to advance into the Ruhr and to Berlin but Eisenhower refused, arguing that first the Scheldt estuary had to be cleared and the port of Antwerp opened. Supplies were indeed a problem. Valuable transport aircraft had been wasted in an aborted airborne attack on Tournai – aircraft which could have carried 1.5 million gallons of fuel. In supplies that were sent, too much emphasis was placed on ammunition, not enough on petrol. Some 1,400 British trucks had faulty pistons, which reduced the flow of supplies by 800 tons per day. Allied divisions were also extremely wasteful. They needed an average of 700 tons per day per division, while the Germans made do with about 200 tons

Major General Brian Horrocks argued that the war could have been over by September 1944. Most authorities agree. There were no proper German forces behind the Rhine and the front was wide open. By the end of August the British were in Antwerp, only 100 miles from the Rhine and the Ruhr, and there was a 100-mile gap in the German front. General Student was ordered by Hitler to plug this gap and to hold the Albert canal, but his First Parachute Army was made up of a few scrapings from the bottom of the barrel. On the entire western front the Germans had 100 tanks, the Allies 2000; the Luftwaffe had 570 aircraft against 14,000. Yet Student was able to hold up the British advance, the US 1st Army was halted at Aachen, and Patton's US 3rd Army was stopped at Metz. Montgomery's attempt to turn the German northern flank at Arnhem failed miserably, and the Canadians took until November to clear the estuary of the Scheldt so that the port of Antwerp could at last be opened. The Allies lost twice as many men after September as they had done in Normandy, where the casualties had been terribly high, and where the Germans were given valuable time to improve their defences.

Montgomery made a further serious mistake by allowing von Zangen's 15th Army to escape from the Channel coast and to establish themselves in Walcheren and South Beveland with a bridgehead across the Scheldt in the Breskens pocket. Montgomery also failed to secure the bridges across the Albert canal, which were duly destroyed by the Germans. In order to overcome these difficulties he proposed 'Operation Market Garden', the establishment of a bridgehead on the lower Rhine at Arnhem and Nijmegen which would outflank the West Wall and open the way for an offensive aimed at the Ruhr. Montgomery also hoped that the airborne troops dropped in 'Market Garden' would be able to destroy the V2 ramps, which were assumed to be somewhere between Amsterdam and Rotterdam. The success of the operation would convince Eisenhower, so Montgomery assumed, that his strategy of a swift blow at the Ruhr was preferable to that of the broad front.

'Market Garden' began in the afternoon of 17 September. The weather turned bad so that the isolated airborne forces at Arnhem could be given no air support and could not be properly supplied or reinforced. The British had ignored 'Ultra' information that Model's headquarters were located near Arnhem and that two SS Panzer divisions were lying in wait. British armour managed to fight their way through to the Arnhem bridgehead on 24 September, but two days later they were forced back across the Rhine. Of the 10,000 men dropped north of the Rhine, only 2000 escaped, the remainder were killed or taken prisoner.

The Germans tried desperately to destroy the Allied bridgehead between the Maas and the Rhine and concentrated on the bridges across the Waal at Nijmegen. They failed in this endeavour, but Montgomery was unable to push south-east into the Rhineland because of Hitler's counter-offensive in the Ardennes. The American offensive around Aachen also had to be called off because of this new threat. Further south, Patton had reached the Saar and the French had liberated Strasbourg and Belfort.

The Canadians suffered heavy losses taking South Beveland and Walcheren, and although they had thus driven the Germans away from the Scheldt estuary at the beginning of November, it was not until the end of the month that the first supplies were unloaded at Antwerp. The Germans bombarded Antwerp with V1 and V2 rockets and attempted to block the mouth of the Scheldt with U-boats and motor torpedo boats, but none of this stopped the flow of supplies through the port.

Ever since August Hitler had been planning a major counter-offensive and had cobbled together the 6th SS Panzer Army under Sepp Dietrich to do the job. The weak spot lay between the 1st and 3rd US Armies in the Ardennes between Echternach and Monschau. The offensive, 'Operation Autumn Mist', was planned for 25 November when it was hoped that bad weather would cancel out

Allied air supremacy. Sepp Dietrich's 6th SS Panzer Army, supported on the left by Manteuffel's 5th Panzer Army, was to break out and head for the Meuse between Liège and Namur. The 6th SS Panzer Army would then head for Antwerp, protected on their left flank by the 5th Panzer Army whose objective was Brussels. This shortened sickle, similar to the plan for the campaign in 1940, was designed to cut off and destroy all the American and British forces to the north. In 'Operation Grab' a special 'Panzer Brigade 150', made up of English-speaking troops under the forceful leadership of SS Obersturmbannführer Skorzeny, renowned for his dramatic exploits on the Gran Sasso, were to be dressed in American uniforms and dropped behind the lines to seize the bridges across the Maas and to conduct sundry sabotage actions. Even Model realized that the entire plan was hopelessly over-ambitious and was out of all proportion to the means available. Hitler would not listen to such objections and denounced Model's suggestion that the offensive should not go beyond the Meuse as a 'half-solution'. Hitler called his generals together to his temporary headquarters at the 'Eagle's Nest' in Ziegenberg near Bad Nauheim and announced that the offensive would cause the Allied front to fall apart 'with a gigantic thunder-clap' and that the British and Americans would seek a separate peace. Hitler was clearly clutching at straws, for only a few weeks earlier he had denounced the efforts of the 20 July conspirators to play the Soviets off against the western Allies as 'simply naive'.

The Ardennes offensive was bound to have initial success, for twenty-eight divisions were thrown against four badly positioned American divisions. Some American units lost their nerve and fled in panic. In two days Dietrich was at Stavelot, but his advance in the direction of Liège was halted south of Spa where Hodges had his headquarters and where there was a huge fuel depot on which the Germans had a hungry eye. The 1st SS Panzer Division, *Leibstandarte Adolf Hitler*, trapped some of the Americans who were moving from Aachen to defend the important traffic junction at St Vith, and murdered eighty-six American prisoners. When it was obvious that Sepp Dietrich would not reach the Meuse, Skorzeny's dramatic plans had to be dropped.

The Americans defended St Vith tenaciously, but it fell on 21 December. On the same day another important transport centre, Bastogne, was surrounded by Manteuffel's 5th Panzer Army. When called upon to surrender, the American commander General McAuliffe gave the famous reply of 'Nuts!' even though most of his troops had given up hope of getting out alive. Unfortunately the effect of the gallant General's remark was somewhat lessened by having to translate it into 'Go to hell!' for the benefit of the white flag party. The Panzers pushed on towards Dinant and Namur, but they were running critically short of fuel and their progress was impeded by appalling weather. Patton now moved up from the south to relieve Bastogne and the weather improved so the Allies could make full use of their overwhelming air power. The Germans could now move only by night and their lines of communication and airfields were under constant attack. On 26 December Patton managed to open up a corridor to the troops at Bastogne and on the following day Manteuffel was obliged to order the advance to halt. The offensive had now obviously failed, and Model asked Hitler's permission to withdraw and prepare for the Allied counter-attack. Hitler ordered his men to take Bastogne and to remain in the Ardennes salient. Model braced himself for the 'Battle of the Bulge'.

On 20 December Eisenhower put Montgomery in command of all the forces to the north of the bulge and, as one of his officers remarked, 'he strode into Hodges's HQ like Christ come to cleanse the temple'. His subsequent claim that he had saved the Americans from collapsing did little to improve inter-Allied cordiality. On 3 January 1945 the pincer movement began, with Montgomery pressing cautiously from the north, Patton vigorously from the south. Progress was slow owing to the snow and the Germans were able to escape, although shortages of fuel forced them to abandon a large amount of equipment including a number of Panzers. Montgomery began withdrawing his troops too soon to complete the destruction of the enemy still in the bulge. Hitler ordered a diversionary offensive, 'Operation North Wind', to relieve the pressure on the southern flank of the bulge. General von Obstfelder had an initial success, pushing the Americans back to the Vosges and Strasbourg. Hitler, strongly supported by Himmler who was given command of the Army Group Upper Rhine at the beginning of December, now imagined that he could regain Alsace. Eisenhower correctly judged that the German offensive was too weak to necessitate sending troops from the Ardennes to strengthen the defences in Alsace. De Gaulle was furious, fearing that Strasbourg would again fall to the Germans. His concerns were unfounded, and the German offensive soon ran out of steam.

The Ardennes offensive held up the Allied advance for a few weeks, but at a cost that Hitler could not afford. He lost 120,000 men and a great deal of valuable equipment. His new divisions had been wasted and he had no reserves with which to meet the Soviet offensive on the Vistula. The Big Three, far from falling apart, were soon to meet at Yalta in an unusually friendly atmosphere.

The British and American Chiefs of Staff had an acrimonious meeting in Malta on the eve of the Yalta conference to discuss future strategy. There were some unpleasant exchanges between Brooke and Marshall over responsibility for the Ardennes, and whether the next thrust should be entrusted primarily to the Americans or the British, or whether there should be two thrusts of roughly equal strength. Brooke attacked Eisenhower as a weak man who relied too much on Bradley and who could not control his generals. Marshall complained about Montgomery for being over-cautious, publicity-hungry, ill-mannered and contemptuous of the Americans. Bedell Smith proposed a two-pronged attack with Montgomery's 21st Army group aiming for Düsseldorf and the Ruhr and Bradley's 12th Army Group heading for Frankfurt. Bradley was disgusted that the Americans, who 'were doing all the fighting and dying in Europe with sixty-one divisions in the field next to fifteen under-strength British divisions', were always having to give way. Eisenhower skilfully overcame the crisis by convincing Bradley that Montgomery's offensive 'Veritable Grenade' to clear out the German pockets east of the Maas made military sense and should be supported by American forces, but he also warned Montgomery that one word denigrating Bradley or the Americans would result in him finding himself in a supporting role under Bradley's overall command.

Montgomery's offensive again bogged down. The Canadians came up against the strong resistance of experienced paratroopers and their advance was further hampered by spring flooding of the Rhine and Maas. The US 9th Army on the right flank was held up when the Germans flooded the Roer. Montgomery's Army Group did not reach the Rhine near Düsseldorf until 2 March. Hitler ordered the bridgehead across the Rhine from Wesel to Krefeld to be held at all costs in order to keep the Dortmund-Ems canal, which was vital for the transportation of coal and steel, open as far as Duisberg. By 10 March the Germans had to abandon the west bank of the Rhine.

Further south the US 1st Army reached Cologne on 5 March and drove the Germans back across the Rhine. On 7 March one of Hodges's armoured divisions found the Ludendorff railway bridge at Remagen still intact and stormed the bridge before the pioneers were able to destroy it. The Americans quickly established a bridgehead across the Rhine. Bradley was delighted and exclaimed: 'Hot dog, this will bust him wide open!', but he was restrained by Eisenhower who ordered him to wait until Montgomery was across the Rhine. His offensive was not due to begin until 24 March. The Germans tried desperately to destroy the bridge and actually succeeded in bombing it, but by that time the Americans had built alternative bridges. Hitler had to content himself with ordering the execution of all those responsible for failing to destroy the bridge.

Patton's 3rd Army crashed through the Eifel and forced the Germans over the Rhine and south over the Mosel. Patton was enraged at having to wait for Montgomery and went off in a huff chasing Germans down the west bank of the Rhine, crossing the river near Oppenheim between Mainz and Mannheim on 23 March. Eisenhower's main concern now was to drive the Germans from the Saar and the Palatinate back across the Rhine. This task was allotted to the US 6th Army Group under Devers. Once Patton was over the Mosel and the German flank was threatened, this could be only a matter of time. Field Marshal von Rundstedt urged Hitler to pull the troops back across the Rhine, but the Führer insisted that the industrial region of the Saar had to be defended at all costs. He promptly dismissed von Rundstedt and on 10 March appointed Field Marshal Kesselring, who had defended Italy so brilliantly, as Commander-in-Chief West. With Patton over the Rhine the situation was hopeless, and on 25 March the Germans abandoned their last bridgehead across the Rhine. Hitler's determination to defend the left bank of the Rhine played directly into Eisenhower's hands, for he was determined to destroy the German forces before having to cross the river. Between the beginning of February and the end of March the Germans suffered 60,000 casualties and 293,000 were taken prisoner. Fear of draconian reprisals was all that kept the Wehrmacht fighting on the western front. Most soldiers prudently preferred to be taken prisoner rather than follow Hitler's instructions to fight to the death.

Montgomery began to cross the Rhine between Rees and Rheinberg on the night of 23–24 March. It was a typically cautious operation. First he flattened the area with a series of bomber strikes which destroyed the enemy lines of communication, then he unleashed a massive barrage with 3000 guns. He refused to move until he had built twelve bridges across the river and had assembled twenty divisions with 1500 tanks in his bridgehead. Progress out of the bridgehead was painfully slow, in part because the barrage had left the ground virtually impassable.

Hitler issued his 'Nero order' on 19 March in which he instructed that everything in the path of the invader should be destroyed. He reasoned that all the good Germans had been killed and that only the inferior remained, so that whether or not they survived was a matter of indifference. The future belonged to the people of the east (*Ostvolk*), who had proved to be the stronger. This scorched-earth policy was deliberately sabotaged by Speer who was supported in his efforts even by soldiers as fanatical as Model, who realized that all was lost and the best that could be done was to try to save the German people from further needless destruction and suffering and to leave something behind to form the basis for post-war reconstruction.

Eisenhower's strategy was to surround the fiercely defended Ruhr and send Bradley's 12th Army Group straight across Germany in the direction of Leipzig and Dresden to meet the Red Army on the Elbe, thus cutting Germany in two. Montgomery would then push towards Hamburg and Lübeck, so isolating the German forces in Denmark and Norway. Devers and his US 6th Army Group would advance towards Linz and crush the German forces in the south against the Alps. Eisenhower informed Stalin of this plan before telling the British who were angered by this lack of consultation. Churchill minuted the Chiefs of Staff on 31 March: 'The idea of neglecting Berlin and leaving it to the Russians to take at a later stage does not appear to me correct. . . . The fall of Berlin might cause nearly all Germans to despair.' To Eisenhower he wrote: 'I do not consider myself that Berlin has yet lost its military and certainly not its political significance. . . . The idea that the capture of Dresden and junction with the Russians there would be a superior gain does not commend itself to me.' Churchill was concerned to meet the Russians as far east as possible and was also worried about the political implications of allowing the Russians to get to Berlin first. Equally distressing to him was the fact that Eisenhower's plan gave the British a distinctly subordinate role. He charged Eisenhower with relegating 'His Majesty's forces to an unexpectedly restricted sphere'. Eisenhower, however, was concerned about the possibility of the Germans forming an alpine redoubt and felt that a quick dash across Germany would make it impossible for them to move forces south. For him Berlin was a political rather than a strategic objective. He was not prepared to risk a serious clash with the Soviets in order to give Montgomery the satisfaction of entering the capital of the Reich in triumph.

In the Ruhr 250,000 troops and 100,000 anti-aircraft personnel were surrounded. They were running desperately short of food and ammunition and were subjected to endless aerial bombardment. Model's attempt to break out of the envelopment and open up supply lines to the east failed. Allied attacks from the north and south split the Ruhr in two, and on 16 April 80,000 men in the eastern sector surrendered. Two days later the western cauldron surrendered and the Americans took thirty generals and 325,000 men prisoner. On 21 April Model shot himself.

Meanwhile the Americans crossed the Elbe at Magdeburg on 12 April and were only 80 miles from Berlin with no natural obstacles in their way at a time when the Soviets were still stuck on the Oder. The Americans were, however, slowed down by the fanatical resistance of SS and Hitler Youth units in a well-defended pocket in the Harz mountains, and by the determination of the 12th Army under General Wenck to stop the Americans crossing the Elbe at other points between Wittenberge and Dessau. On 16 April Wenck threw everything he had at the Americans and drove them out of their bridgehead across the Elbe at Magdeburg. The Soviets were by now across the Oder and Eisenhower informed them that his troops would stay on the Elbe and the Mulde. On 23 April Keitel visited Wenck's headquarters and ordered him to head east to defend Berlin. On 25 April the US 69th Infantry Division met the Soviet 58th Guards Division at 16.40 hours, and Germany was now cut in two.

Montgomery met with some tough opposition from the 1st Parachute Army as he fought his way through the Teutoburg Forest and the Lüneburg Heath until he crossed the Elbe at Harburg and joined Bradley's forces at Wittenberge on 24 April. The British had not attacked 'Fortress Holland' for fear that the Germans would destroy the dykes on the Zuider Zee and ruin Dutch agriculture for years to come. But the Dutch were suffering a terrible famine and Eisenhower was able to negotiate what amounted to a separate armistice with the Reich Commissar for the Occupied Netherlands, Seyss-Inquart, on 30 April. The Allies undertook not to attack the German forces in Holland and to provide food for the Dutch. The Germans agreed not to destroy the dykes and to distribute the food. This came too late to save many thousands of Dutch from death by starvation.

In the south, Patch's US 7th Army reached Nuremberg on 16 April. Hitler ordered that the home of the Reich party rallies should be defended to the last man, but it was able to hang on for only four days. Eisenhower ordered Patton to halt near the Czechoslovakian border and he headed south through the Bohemian Forest, liberating Karlsbad and Pilsen and reaching Linz on 5 May.

On 4 May Eisenhower suggested that Patton should take Prague, where Czech patriots had begun their uprising, and advance to the Elbe, but this suggestion met with such vigorous protests from the Soviets that he remained behind the demarcation line.

Much has been made of Eisenhower's decision not to go to Prague when the way was open, with Schörner's forces some hundred miles to the east of the city, but there were powerful reasons for not taking the risk of antagonizing the Soviets. They were already in possession of Vienna and could easily move into western Austria. They were also in a position to move towards Denmark from Stettin, and there were even reports that Soviet parachutists had landed in Copenhagen. Most important of all, Czechoslovakia had a Government which was recognized by all three major powers, and its future seemed guaranteed by the Czecho-Soviet treaty.

On 4 May Churchill sent a telegram to Eden in San Francisco in which he said:

> I fear terrible things have happened during the Russian advance through Germany to the Elbe. The proposed withdrawal of the United States Army to the occupational lines which were arranged with the Russians and the Americans in Quebec, and which were marked in yellow on the maps we studied there, would mean the tide of Russian domination sweeping forward 120 miles on a front of 300 or 400 miles. This would be an event which, if it occurred, would be one of the most melancholy in history.

Later in the day he phoned Eisenhower and urged him to get to Prague. Ten minutes later Montgomery called with the news that Admiral von Friedeburg had signed an instrument of surrender. On 7 May Churchill telegraphed Eisenhower suggesting that he should advance to Prague, but with no sense of urgency. Celebrations of victory were now uppermost in people's minds.

Meanwhile, in the bunker deep below the Reich's Chancellery on 20 April, Hitler issued a series of totally unrealistic operational orders to the Army Group Steiner to establish a defensive line along the Spree and the Oder. Steiner's army could not break out of the encirclement and the 9th Army to the south-east of Berlin was also unable to fight its way through to relieve the capital. By 22 April the Red Army arrived in the suburbs of Berlin, and the city was soon surrounded. Hitler denounced his armed forces for their cowardice and incompetence and at the same time clung to the belief that what Goebbels called the 'perverse coalition between plutocracy and bolshevism' would fall apart. He took the death of Roosevelt on

12 April as a sign that Frederick the Great's salvation when the Tsarina died during the Seven Years War was about to be repeated. He was encouraged in this belief when the Americans advanced well beyond the demarcation lines of the occupation zones, details of which had been captured during the Ardennes offensive.

There were more signs of dissension within the Nazi ranks than there were within those of the Allies. On 23 April Goering sent a telegram from the Obersalzberg in which he stated that if he did not hear from Hitler by 22.00 hours he would assume the leadership of the Reich and begin negotiations with Eisenhower. Bormann managed to work Hitler up into a towering rage over his paladin's disloyalty. He denounced Goering as a corrupt morphine addict and stripped him of all his offices and responsibilities and ordered his arrest. But he soon relapsed into his customary depression, remarking that since the war was lost it did not matter who negotiated the armistice. General Ritter von Greim flew into Berlin in a small plane with the famous aviatrix Hanna Reitsch to be personally appointed Commander-in-Chief of the Luftwaffe in place of Goering. The pair were treated to long diatribes about treason and cowardice and Hitler handed 'dear Hanna' a vial of poison, telling her that all depended on whether General Wenck's army could fight its way through to Berlin.

On 28 April Hitler heard the astonishing news that Himmler was negotiating an armistice through the intermediary of Count Bernadotte of Sweden. He ordered von Greim to leave Berlin, arrest Himmler and assume overall responsibility for the relief of Berlin. Himmler had approached the Swedish consulate in Lübeck on 24 April and had proposed a separate peace with the western Allies. Churchill's response was that the Germans would have to surrender to all three Allies simultaneously, and Truman agreed. When Hitler heard of the failure of this attempt to split the Grand Alliance, he decided to make an honest woman of his long-time mistress, Eva Braun, in a hastily improvised ceremony with Goebbels and Bormann as witnesses. Shortly afterwards he dictated his political testament, a pathetic and sordid document. On the following day, 30 April, he received a telegram from Keitel informing him that there was no hope of relieving Berlin. At 15.30 hours the newly-weds swallowed cyanide and Hitler made doubly sure by shooting himself with a 7.65 millimetre Walther. The bodies were soaked in petrol and burnt.

Bormann informed Admiral Dönitz that Hitler had appointed him his successor, but he was not told that Hitler was dead. Goebbels sent a telegram to Stalin announcing that the Führer was dead and suggesting a cease-fire between Germany and the Soviet Union. General Krebs emerged from the rubble of Berlin with a white flag and approached General Chuikov. With staggering gall he said in his faltering Russian, which he had learnt while serving as military attaché in Moscow: 'Today is the first of May, a great holiday for our two nations.' Chuikov, with admirable self control, gave the unforgettable reply: 'We have a great holiday today. How things are with you over there is less easy to say.' Chuikov rejected this attempt to reach a separate armistice and Goebbels, having failed to split the alliance, followed his Führer's admirable example by committing suicide along with his wife, having first murdered their six children. On 2 May General Weidling surrendered Berlin to the Soviets.

While the Soviets took Berlin, Montgomery crossed the Elbe and on 2 May reached Schwerin and Wismar, thus threatening the rear of Army Group Vistula. German troops, justifiably concerned not to fall into the hands of the Russians, surrendered en masse to the Americans and British. With the British army in Lübeck, Dönitz ordered the surrender of Hamburg. On 3 May Montgomery halted, waiting for the end.

Meanwhile, Dönitz appointed the conservative Minister of Finance, Count Schwerin von Krosigk, as his political advisor and informed Himmler that he had no further use of his services. At first Dönitz thought that Hitler was still alive and as a faithful Nazi he announced that the war would continue to the last man. When he heard of Hitler's death his main concern was to end the war as quickly and as advantageously as possible. In a radio address Dönitz announced that the war was still being fought to 'save the German people from annihilation by the advancing bolshevik enemy' and that hostilities would continue against the western Allies only if they attempted to frustrate this aim.

On 2 May the German forces in Italy capitulated. On the following day the delegation under Admiral von Friedeburg began armistice negotiations with Montgomery. On 4 May Montgomery accepted the capitulation of the German forces in north-west Germany, Holland and Denmark and the surrender of the German fleet stationed in this area. Dönitz promptly ordered the end of the U-boat war. On 5 May Hausser's Army Group G in southern Germany surrendered to the American 6th Army Group in Munich.

Dönitz's main concern was now to avoid surrendering to the Soviets, who in turn were beginning to suspect that the western

Allies were up to some more dirty tricks. Montgomery had refused to accept the surrender of the three German armies withdrawing from the east, and Friedeburg bitterly complained that the Germans could hardly be expected to surrender to the Russians since they were savages. Montgomery replied that they should have thought of that in June 1941. Attempts were made to get Eisenhower to agree to a partial surrender in the west, but he refused to discuss anything without a Soviet representative at his headquarters in Rheims, and would not alter his demand for a complete and unconditional surrender. Finally, at Berlin-Karlshorst on 9 May 1945, at 00.16 hours, Keitel, General Stumpff (acting on behalf of von Greim) and von Friedeburg signed the surrender documents which were witnessed by Tedder, Spaatz and Chuikov. At midnight the fighting ceased in Europe. As a result of Dönitz's delaying tactics more than half of the troops on the eastern front, some 1,850,000 men, were able to move west and thus avoid being taken prisoner by the Russians.

Churchill was inclined to treat with the Dönitz Government, but the Soviets demanded the dissolution of the 'militaristic-fascistic Dönitz clique'. On 23 May the entire Government, along with the OKW, were arrested and on 5 June the four Allied commanders signed the official document prepared by the European Advisory Commission by which the victorious powers accepted the unconditional surrender of the armed forces and the state and took over full responsibility for the governance of the prostrate country.

CHAPTER FOURTEEN

The End of the War in Asia (October 1944–September 1945)

As the war in Europe drew to a close the British became increasingly concerned about the future of the 'Grand Alliance', and particularly about the role of the Soviet Union. When the Americans began to withdraw troops from Europe to finish off the Pacific war it was obvious that the Soviet Union would be overwhelmingly powerful on the Continent. Both Roosevelt and Truman refused to consider delaying the shipment of these troops and felt that British warnings were part of a sinister attempt to play the Russians off against the Americans in order to strengthen their position in Europe. With Britain facing a severe financial crisis and clearly relegated to the status of a second-rate power, there was precious little that could be done but to give way to the Americans. This did nothing to lessen the fury in Whitehall at having to listen to American denunciations of British imperialism and power politics, so frequently delivered with equal measures of platitude and hypocrisy.

The Japanese entrusted the land defence of the Philippines to General Yamashita, the victor of Malaya, but they staked everything on a battle at sea. Yamashita was to pin down the landing forces while the navy lured the American fleet to the north where it would be destroyed in a pincer movement. The Americans landed first at Leyte, a small island in the central Philippines, in order to divide the Japanese forces. The ensuing naval battle in Leyte Gulf was the largest naval engagement of all time. There were in fact four separate battles in which classic tactics of 'crossing the T' by Admiral Oldendorf's battleships were combined with the modern technique of sinking ships from aircraft carriers. The Japanese used their kamikaze pilots for the first time, but not to much effect. In the course of the battle, an unusually confused and confusing encounter, the Japanese lost the *Musashi*, which was by far the largest battleship in the world, along with four aircraft carriers without whose support the battleships were terribly vulnerable. The Imperial Navy was effectively destroyed at Leyte Gulf and could no longer guard the sea approaches to Japan.

MacArthur landed at Leyte Gulf amid the full glare of publicity, for which he had a unique flare, on 20 October 1944. On 27 December he announced a victory, although mopping-up operations were to take four tough and costly months. In January the Americans pushed on to the main island of Luzon. Yamashita ordered that Manila should be considered an open city, but General Iwabuchi refused to obey these instructions and defended the city house by house. The result was the senseless loss of thousands of civilian lives and the destruction of large parts of the city. By 4 March Manila was in American hands, and the Japanese retired to the mountains to carry out rearguard actions which some fanatics continued for the next thirty years. Yamashita prudently surrendered at the war's end.

To the north, Admiral Spruance landed his marines on Iwo Jima, a small volcanic island only 4 miles long but defended by 20,000 well-entrenched Japanese. It took more than five weeks of heavy fighting to conquer the island. Only 216 Japanese soldiers were taken alive.

On Easter Sunday, 1 April 1945, the Americans reached Okinawa. The Japanese decided not to fight on the beaches, where they would be pulverized by naval bombardments, but defended the island in depth, taking skilful advantage of the rugged terrain. Yet another bloody slogging match ensued in which the Japanese were gradually forced back by overwhelming firepower. On 31 May General Buckner announced that the battle for Okinawa was over but for the cleaning up of a few pockets of resistance. But it was not until 17 June that General Ushijima and his staff admitted defeat by committing ritual suicide. This time 7400 Japanese soldiers surrendered, sensibly refusing to follow their intrepid commander's path to immortality. The Japanese suffered 10,000 casualties in Okinawa, the Americans 49,000 and lost 34 naval vessels. A further 368 American ships were damaged, many of them by kamikaze planes. It was the most costly battle in the Pacific war and a terrible foretaste of what might be expected if the Americans were to attempt a landing on the Japanese mainland.

On 18 June President Truman and the Joint Chiefs endorsed plans for operations 'Olympic', a landing on Kyushu, and 'Coronet', a landing on Honshu near Tokyo, to be commanded by MacArthur. The British were excluded from this planning, and although the Australians were still fighting under MacArthur and the Royal Navy helped to destroy the remainder of the Imperial Navy in the battle of the East China Sea, the war with Japan was, as Admiral Leahy put it, 'pretty much an American show'.

Meanwhile in Burma, Slim crossed the Irrawaddy and managed to give the impression that his main objective was Mandalay. The brunt of his offensive was, however, Meiktila, the nodal point of the Japanese communications system and the key to the route to Rangoon. Having taken Meiktila and Mandalay he pushed on rapidly to Rangoon, in spite of fanatical resistance. Here he joined up with the seaborne landing, 'Operation Dracula', launched on 5 May. The campaign in Burma was now virtually over and the Japanese withdrew most of their remaining troops to meet the American advance in the Pacific.

The campaign in Burma was the most skilful operation by the British army in the war. Slim was an outstanding soldier who had a clear grasp of strategic priorities, an unmatched understanding of the use of air power, and a tactical mastery of armoured support for the infantry. He was very much a soldier's general, telling the truth however unpleasant in the men's own language whether English, Urdu or Gurkhali. He inspired in them the justifiable confidence needed to fight a very difficult campaign against a tough, clever and ruthless enemy.

In the final stages of the war in Asia, Britain was pushed aside and condemned as an imperialist power while the Soviet Union was guaranteed the Kuriles, South Sakhalin and the nearby islands along with a lease of Port Arthur as a naval base. Soviet demands in Darien and in South Manchuria were also met and Outer Mongolia was recognized as being under Soviet domination. The future of Asia was to be decided largely by the United States and the Soviet Union, and Britain's role as a dominant power in the Pacific had ended.

By the summer of 1945 many American officials hoped that the war would be over before the Russians intervened and that it might be possible to ignore the assurances made to them at Yalta. But a quick peace was possible only if the Americans would drop their demand for unconditional surrender, as the British were urging them to do. The British were also beginning to wonder whether Mao Tse Tung was the Tito of China. Much depended on whether he could be seen as an agrarian reformer or as a true communist, and if the latter there was the further problem of what flavour of communism he preferred. As one official put it: 'The Moderator of the Church of Scotland tends to have rather less influence over the Catholic clergy than His Holiness the Pope.' The Americans were equally confused about what to do in China. Was it desirable to build up China as an important military force which could play a decisive role in the defeat of Japan? Was it necessary to have a strong China? Was it essential to prop up Chiang Kai-shek? What would be the consequences of a victory by Mao's communists?

Both the British and the Americans were divided in their answers to these fundamental questions. If China was still to play an important role in the struggle against Japan, then it would be better to back Mao, for he was a military leader of incomparably greater calibre than Chiang. Would a strong China necessarily be democratic and pro-western, or would it emulate Japan as seemed to be suggested by some of Sun Yat Sen's writings, echoed by Chiang Kai-shek? Both insisted on China's need for territorial expansion, so the Allies began to wonder whether by defeating one Asiatic imperialist power they might not be clearing the way for another. Some officials began to ask whether the territorial guarantees made to the Soviet Union at the expense of China would finally drive the Chinese into the Japanese camp. Lastly, there was the nagging question of whether Chiang was really the star to which the west should hitch its wagon, or was he as corrupt, autocratic and incompetent as the growing number of his critics suggested? Many Americans, from Roosevelt down, believed that most of these difficulties could be overcome if only Chungking and Yenan could get together, and they managed to convince themselves that this was indeed possible. The British had fewer such illusions and pointed out that even if Chiang were to talk with Mao there were still the questions of who would be the senior partner and what would be the attitude of the Soviet Union. The British decided that they should hang on to Hong Kong but stay out of China, leaving it to the Americans to sort things out as best they could. That the Americans fell flat on their faces came as no great surprise and was greeted in Whitehall with a degree of smug satisfaction.

The Americans imagined that there were a number of homogeneous peoples in Asia longing for freedom and the right to emulate the United States. They overlooked the vexed problem of ethnic minorities and underestimated the strength and ideological fanaticism of local communist movements. The Europeans were soon to begin their long-overdue withdrawal from Asia, in spite of Churchill's reactionary imperialism and the efforts by the French and Dutch to hang on to their possessions by force. The Americans tried to impose their will but failed to do anything but cause endless misery to the hapless folk whom they had championed during the war against the wicked British and French imperialists. It was a bitterly ironic twist of fate brought about by years of naive insouciance and self-deception.

The Japanese dictatorship which crushed the last vestiges of democracy and which controlled all aspects of public life was a quite distinct form of rule from that of the fascist Governments of Germany and Italy. Whereas fascism and national socialism were enthusiastically supported by mass movements, the Japanese dictatorship was imposed upon the country by the military, the senior bureaucrats and a relatively small rightist clique. The attempt to form a mass political party in support of the Government was not particularly successful, and the major achievement of the Imperial Rule Assistance Association was to force Japanese women out of their delightful kimonos and into hideous baggy trousers, and their menfolk into drab uniforms.

As in Germany and Italy there were arbitrary arrests, torture and false confessions, but Japan was spared the full horror of Nazi concentration camps and mass executions. It would seem that only one Japanese man, Ozaki Hotsumi, was executed for treason for the part he played in Richard Sorge's Soviet spy ring. In spite of an exaggerated fear of communism, only Hotsumi and Sorge were actually executed, all the other members of the ring being imprisoned. On the other hand, such ultimate forms of terror were hardly necessary since police spies and informants were so ubiquitous and the population was reduced to a state of abject docility. By the end of the war there were only about 2500 political prisoners, known as 'thought criminals', still in jail. The police never became a law unto itself as did the Gestapo. The Special Higher Police (*tokko*) was under the strict control of the Ministry of the Interior, and the Military Police (*kempei*), which made anything remotely connected with the war effort its concern, was subordinate to the army ministry. Even the Government and the military became prisoners of their own systems. They were starved of accurate information and stumbled in the dark, blissfully unaware of the precarious position of the country and the hollowness of many of the much-trumpeted victories.

The Japanese military, while busy planning an aggressive war, were determined to crush the democratic forces within the country and to pursue their policies without regard to the popular will. In

January 1934 the Army Minister recommended stringent control over freedom of speech, rigorous censorship of the press, the suppression of all opposition groups and, perhaps most ominous of all, a programme of 'purification of thoughts'. The nation was to be mobilized behind the war effort by encouraging such patriotic organizations as the Boy Scouts and sundry religious organizations. By December 1940 press censorship and propaganda were centralized in the powerful Cabinet Information Bureau which placed the media under the direct control of the military. The National Defence Security Law of 1941 provided for harsh punishments for anyone found guilty of spreading 'false reports or rumours' or 'information that confuses public sentiment', and greatly increased the scope of information designated as 'state secrets'. Political activists and critics of the regime were subject to arbitrary arrest and detention without trial.

By the summer of 1937, by which time the war in China had become a major conflict, the press was reduced to mouthing empty Government slogans, and this took on quite grotesque proportions after Pearl Harbor. The initial triumphs of the Japanese military were grossly exaggerated and their subsequent defeats disguised by innocuous euphemisms. Guadalcanal was described as a 'transfer of forces', the atomic bomb was simply a 'new type of bomb'. Journalists who bravely tried to expose the atrocities of the Japanese military were prosecuted and convicted *pour encourager les autres*. Academic books were rigorously censored; literature, painting and music were purged of noxious western influence. In April 1944 steel guitars, banjos and ukuleles were banned in a determined effort to purify the musical life of the nation, a harsh measure which no doubt caused a profound sense of deprivation in a country curiously addicted to the products of Nashville, Tennessee.

The educational system was obliged to emphasize emperor worship and militarism. Liberal teachers were purged and patriotic textbooks were provided by the Government. The official history textbook used in all schools described the descent of the august imperial grandchild (*Ninigino-mikoto*) from the plains of heaven as a literal fact. The final examination of one middle school typically contained the following loaded questions:

1 Why are loyalty and filial piety united in our country?
2 Discuss the necessity for overseas expansion.
3 Why is Japan's constitution superior to those of other nations?

4 What kind of spirit is required to overcome the present difficulties facing the nation?

Liberal and socialist ideas, which had been prevalent in the late 1920s, were completely eradicated from the educational system and Japanese children were made into mindless nationalistic robots, their individualism crushed, their sole purpose unquestioningly to serve the three-thousand-year Empire.

The ruling elite was resentful of laissez faire capitalism and of the large business concerns (*zaibatsu*) and wanted stringent Government control of the economy so as to mobilize the resources of the nation for war. In 1939 compulsory cartels were established under Government supervision to set production quotas and to allocate resources. The control associations (*toseikai*), which were not unlike the Italian fascist corporations, were headed by prominent businessmen, with the result that the power of the *zaibatsu* was not diminished. There was no central Government authority to direct the efforts of the various cartels, which might have been used to restrain the *zaibatsu* and co-ordinate the efforts of war industries. But probably the main reasons why Japanese industrial output rose by only one-quarter between 1940 and 1944 (in the United States the figure was two-thirds) and why war production was surprisingly low were the chronic shortage of raw materials and inadequate shipping facilities.

For all the anti-capitalist rhetoric and the extolling of traditional values, the large manufacturing and trading combines doubled their share of corporate and partnership capital between 1941 and 1945. They gobbled up smaller companies and achieved such a commanding position in the Japanese economy that, in spite of American efforts to restrain them during the occupation, they are now among the world's largest and most powerful corporations.

Industrial growth during the war resulted in a serious labour shortage which could be overcome only by bringing women into the workforce. Women were coerced into war industries if they were single, or driven to work through economic necessity if they were married. This was a trend, observable in all belligerent nations, which was accelerated rather than caused by the war and it worked against the Government's efforts to strengthen traditional family ties and to establish a conservative and essentially pre-capitalist social order. Yet in spite of these strong pressures on the family, traditional forms were remarkably resilient, certainly much more so than in the

United States or Britain. The state tried desperately to increase the birth rate but was unable to maintain it at its pre-war level. Mrs Tojo told Japanese women that 'having babies is fun', but with desperate food shortages and terror bombing most of her fellow countrywomen remained sceptical. Rampant inflation, shortages of food and clothing, the racketeering of black-marketeers, a dreary austerity campaign, mindless censorship and numbing propaganda made wartime Japan a miserable place. Even the greatest triumphs of Japanese arms brought little benefit to the people at home, only calls for greater effort and more heroic sacrifices.

The most unattractive aspect of Japanese militarism was undoubtedly the complete contempt shown for human life. This applied not only to the enemy but also to the imperial forces. Wounded soldiers were expected to commit suicide or be shot so as not to be a burden to their comrades. The Japanese soldier's instruction manual warned: 'Bear in mind the fact that to be captured means not only that you disgrace yourself, but your parents and family will never be able to hold up their heads again. Always save the last bullet for yourself.' A Japanese soldier who was taken prisoner ceased to exist and his name was struck from the register of his town or village.

The most extreme and best-known manifestation of the Japanese military spirit was the Divine Wind (*Kamikaze*) Special Attack Unit of the Imperial Navy, named after the winds which had scattered the fleets of the Mongol invaders in the 13th century. The unfortunate pilots were subjected to such intensive psychological pressure that they were unable to resist and the vast majority of the 'volunteers' were, in the best traditions of the military, assigned to the task. The results of all this effort were disappointingly meagre. Only 3 per cent of the kamikaze planes actually hit their targets. Suicide submarines and small boats or soldiers wrapped in explosives who flung themselves at tanks were no more successful. Nor were civilians spared this suicidal madness. As the Americans advanced, the hapless Japanese peasants were encouraged to commit suicide or ordered to hand over their food supplies to the army and thus be left to starve.

With such an attitude towards their own people it is hardly surprising that the Japanese military were capable of the most frightful barbarities against their enemies. Terrible atrocities were committed against the Chinese during the China War, culminating in the 'Rape of Nanking' when tens of thousands, possibly a quarter of a million, were slaughtered. The 731 Unit in Manchuria conducted experiments in bacteriological warfare in which thousands of human guinea-pigs died horrible deaths. Their commanding officer,

Lieutenant General Ishii Shiro, passed on the information gained in these inhuman experiments to the US military after the war, and in recompense for these services was permitted to live in comfortable retirement. Similar experiments were carried out on captured US airmen at Kyushu Imperial University.

A Japanese soldier who allowed himself to be taken prisoner was regarded as a man without honour and therefore no longer human. It is thus perhaps not entirely surprising that the treatment of Allied prisoners-of-war and of civilian captives was brutal in the extreme, showing utter contempt for the conventions of war, to say nothing of elementary human decency. Prisoners were regarded as sub-humans, worthy of no consideration and fit only to be treated as abject slaves. The Japanese Diet never ratified the 1929 Geneva Convention governing the treatment of prisoners-of-war. The wretched inmates of the 300 prisoner-of-war camps were starved, beaten and denied medical treatment. Prisoners slaved in the coal and sulphur mines of Manchuria or on the roads and railways that were built through malaria-infested jungles. Stragglers on the 65 miles of the 'Bataan Death March' were clubbed to death, left to die of malnutrition and disease, and sometimes even buried alive. The 250 miles of the Burma railway were built at a cost of 400 lives per mile. On the day of the cessation of hostilities, Japanese officers gave vent to their frustration and humiliation by hacking sixteen American airmen to death with their swords in a final act of barbarity.

The Japanese not only inflicted a great deal of misery and pain; they also suffered themselves, although not on the same scale as the Germans. The Doolittle raid on Tokyo on 18 April 1942 was little more than a propaganda stunt and the saturation bombing of Japan did not begin until the summer of 1944. Then industrial and residential targets were bombed indiscriminately day and night until the whole country was disrupted. The Tokyo raid on 10 March 1945 resulted in 80,000 deaths and the city was burnt to the ground. Soon afterwards Hiroshima and Nagasaki were to become symbolic of the horrors of atomic power and of the inhumanity of modern warfare.

For all the repression, violence and militarism, wartime Japan never became a full-scale military dictatorship. The military leaders determined Government policy, but the army and the navy remained independent and jealous of each other. Both general staff chiefs had equal right of access to the Emperor, as did the Army and Navy Ministers. At the outbreak of war with China an Imperial Headquarters and Cabinet Liaison Committee was formed, consisting of the Prime Minister, the Foreign Minister, the two service

Ministers, the two Chiefs of Staff and sundry other personalities. When important decisions were made it met in the imperial palace in the presence of the Emperor, but its decisions had to be approved by its two constituent parts, the Imperial Headquarters and the Cabinet, before they could be put into effect. Each service had a collective leadership whose personnel was frequently changed. Imperial Headquarters, which was supposed to co-ordinate the military effort, consisted of the general staffs of the two services and was thus a forum for debate rather than a truly unified command. The principle of the independence of the High Command, enshrined in the Meiji constitution, secured the independence of the military from civilian control.

Within this curious system no commanding figure ever emerged with the stature of a Hitler, a Churchill or a Roosevelt. Even Tojo was unable completely to control the navy, the bureaucracy or the imperial court, and this led to his downfall. He was by far the most powerful Prime Minister in Japan in the twentieth century, but even he was a first among equals with less real power than Churchill. Although communists and 'pacifists' were flung into jail, many of Tojo's critics remained free to plot his overthrow and his opponents were not executed or assassinated in the approved fascist manner of Germany or Italy. In the general elections of 1942 no less than eighty-five independent candidates were elected to the Diet. The courts of justice were never totally subservient to the Government and occasionally had the temerity to rule against its wishes. In spite of the censorship, critical comments occasionally crept into the newspapers. Thus within a rigorously authoritarian regime there were still some pockets of freedom remaining which provided a modest guarantee against completely arbitrary rule.

The regime had no ideological system to support it comparable to that of communism or fascism. The Japanese were immensely proud of the achievements of the military, and even the left was delighted to see the arrogant white man expelled from his Pacific colonies. Many artists and intellectuals managed to delude themselves that the 'Great East Asia Co-prosperity Sphere' was the dawning of a new age in which eastern 'spirit' would triumph over western 'matter' and the traditional values of Japan would prevail over the decadent materialism of the west. All this was a complete illusion. Western influences were deeply ingrained in Japanese culture and could not be eradicated by decree. The Japanese crusade had to be fought with western technology. Even the English language could not be dispensed with, either in everyday speech or as a means of communication within the Co-prosperity Sphere. The Japanese continued to be fascinated by western culture and were even more enthusiastic than ever to emulate the western model of industrial society after the war.

The Great East Asia Co-prosperity Sphere was seldom seen by those unfortunate enough to be co-opted into it as anything more than naked old-style imperialism. The idea had first been suggested by Prince Konoye in 1938 when he claimed that the Japanese army in China was not there to conquer the country but to build a new Asia which would be based on high ethical principles and be placed under the benevolent tutelage of Japan. This new order in Asia would provide the necessary guarantees against western materialism, individualism and communism. Many Japanese honestly believed that they were fighting an unselfish and idealistic crusade against western imperialism and that fellow Asians who thought otherwise were perverse and deluded.

The vast majority of Asians who suffered under Japanese occupation were not taken in by this claptrap. Most found the harsh rule of the Japanese army even more unpleasant than that of the European imperialist powers, and the ideology of the new order was dismissed as transparent hypocrisy. The Japanese had no clear idea what they intended to do with their Empire and did not trouble to work out a programme or ideology for the Greater East Asia Co-prosperity Sphere. They were content to grab raw materials and to follow the dictates of their strategy, but had nothing positive to offer. With their overbearing conviction of their racial superiority there could be no question of co-operation with the lesser breeds, any more than the Germans could offer anything to the European subhumans with their New Order.

The people of India, Burma, Indo-China and Indonesia were all anxious to get rid of their European oppressors, but the Japanese proved incapable of exploiting this situation and simply substituted one form of imperialism for another. Some Asian nationalists imagined that they stood to gain by a victory of Germany and Japan over the British and French, and proposed active collaboration with the anti-Comintern powers. The most remarkable of these misguided men was the Bengali extremist Subhas Chandra Bose. He travelled to Berlin via Moscow early in 1941 where he told Ribbentrop that he wished to organize an armed revolt in India against British rule and that he would co-operate with the Japanese, the Moslem peoples and the Axis powers. The Germans were not particularly impressed. Hitler felt that British rule in India was the perfect example of how a handful of racially superior people could control a vast mass of subhumans and wanted to emulate, not destroy, the Raj and use it as a model for his empire in the east. Although he regarded Bose as a 'brown monkey', he felt that he had a certain nuisance value. Bose was thus given propaganda facilities, was allowed to organize an Indian Legion out of Indian prisoners-of-war, and was permitted to collaborate with the anti-British Faquir of Ipi in Afghanistan. None of this amounted to much. His propaganda campaign had some effect, although the Congress Party's policy of support for the Allied war effort as the wisest course towards eventual independence was never seriously challenged. The Indian Legion of some 35,000 men sensibly mutinied rather than fight on the eastern front and ended up in France, where they devoted most of their desultory energy to raping and pillaging and very little to fighting the invaders or combating the resistance.

Such was Hitler's admiration for the British Empire that he regretted the Japanese conquest of Singapore, and he had no desire to see his Asian Allies include India in their New Order. In February 1943 the Germans sent Bose to Asia and in October he proclaimed his provisional Government of a free India (*Azad Hind*) in Singapore. The Japanese did not recognize this Government and found Bose distinctly tiresome. His Indian National Army disgraced itself in battle and was treated with contempt by the Japanese. In spite of his forceful personality, Bose never had much following in India outside his native Bengal, where he was known as 'Nitaji', an approximate translation of 'Führer', and his fortunes were inextricably linked to those of his Japanese patrons. When these began to fade he decided to escape, but he was killed in a plane crash on his way to Moscow. It is doubtful whether the Soviet authorities would have allowed him to live much longer had he survived the journey.

In the countries which they occupied, the Japanese established Governments which they deemed appropriate to the level of political development. In the Philippines it was an Executive Commission comprising seven prominent local politicians. In Malaya they ruled through the sultanates. Indo-China became a protectorate and a launching-pad for further conquest. The Dutch East Indies were deemed too important economically to be allowed even the smallest degree of independence and were ruled directly by the military. In Burma Ba Maw, who had once been Prime Minister under the British, was appointed by the Japanese to head a puppet administration. In all these countries there was a direct conflict between the nationalist aspirations of the individual nations and the military exigencies of the Japanese Empire. The Asian peoples bitterly resented the racial arrogance of the Japanese, the hypocrisy of their protestations of brotherhood and the brutal insensitivity of the military.

None of the attempts to paper over the cracks was successful. The most publicized was the Tokyo conference in late 1943, attended by representatives of the Governments of Burma, the Philippines, Thailand and Manchukuo as well as by dissident Chinese politicians and by Subhas Chandra Bose. There was much talk of the common purpose and a joint declaration of Asian freedom, but nothing much came of the conference, not even an outline of a common economic policy. The Japanese were uncertain what to do. The Foreign Office tended to be concerned not to create the impression in south-east Asia that Japan was simply pursuing its own selfish interests and saw the Asian independence movement as an admirable opportunity to embarrass the Allies. The Americans were deeply, if hypocritically, suspicious of British imperial pretensions, and the Japanese were determined to feed these suspicions by championing their fellow Asians against the British. The military had no patience for such arguments, and many civilians shared their impatience. Thus when Tojo established a Greater East Asian Ministry in 1942 the Foreign Minister resigned in protest against what he felt might be thought a somewhat provocative move.

Some army officers showed a certain respect for other civilizations. Some politicians and businessmen shared the Foreign Office's concern to temper the harshness of military rule and to win the confidence of the subject peoples. All this was to no avail. By late 1943, by which time the army was on the defensive, some concessions were made, particularly in the Philippines, but it was too late. Throughout Asia the Japanese were detested as callous oppressors and their defeat and downfall enthusiastically welcomed.

The American landing in Okinawa precipitated a major political crisis in Japan. For some time an opposition group, the *Jushin*, had been attempting to establish contacts with the enemy to discuss peace terms with them. They were determined to save Japan from total destruction and to preserve the imperial dynasty. They were able to persuade the Emperor to appoint the ancient Admiral Suzuki as Prime Minister. He was supported by the Foreign Minister, Togo, and the Naval Minister, Yonai, in his efforts to end the war. The military party, headed by the Minister of War, General Anami, and the Chiefs of Staff of the army and navy, General Umezu and Admiral Toyoda, felt that the best chances for a favourable peace would be after the successful repulse of an attempt to invade Japan, and thus opposed any premature negotiations.

Togo, like Hitler, counted on the Allies falling out and therefore concentrated on negotiations with the Soviet Union on the assumption that the Soviets had no desire to see Japan dominated by the Americans. He had no idea that Molotov's assurance on 5 April 1945 that the Soviets would respect their neutrality pact with Japan until April 1946 was a lie, and that Stalin had agreed at Yalta to enter the war against Japan. The Soviets rejected all Japanese peace feelers, so that on 18 June the Japanese Supreme Council agreed to inform the Soviet Union that they desired a peace as long as the monarchy was preserved. The Soviets replied that they needed concrete proposals before answering and used the Japanese démarche as a warning to Truman to respect the agreements made at Yalta on the Far East. The United States, Britain and China reacted to this move by issuing the 'Potsdam Declaration' on 26 July in which they warned the Japanese that now that the war in Europe was over they were doomed. Either they surrendered unconditionally or the alternative was 'prompt and utter destruction'.

Togo was in favour of accepting the terms of the Potsdam Declaration and the Emperor saw no viable alternative, but the three military members of the Supreme Council argued that it should be rejected. Togo therefore decided to wait and see whether the Soviets responded to his initiative, and made the unfortunate announcement that the Potsdam Declaration contained nothing new. This was taken as an outright rejection, and on 2 August Truman gave the order to drop the atomic bomb on Japan.

There was almost universal support for the decision to drop the bomb. American lives were saved and the war was brought to a swift conclusion. No moral distinction could be made between large-scale terror bombing with conventional weapons, as was practised against Germany and Japan, and the achievement of a similar effect with a single bomb. There were a few protests, mainly from pacifists, clergymen and black leaders. But Truman never had a second thought about a decision which marked the beginning of a new and terrible chapter in the history of armed conflict.

By the outbreak of the war the international scientific community was fascinated by the possible effects of bombarding uranium atoms with neutrons to the point that they would split. In late 1939 a group of scientists told President Roosevelt that this process could be used to create an incredibly powerful bomb, and they warned that the Germans might be the first to develop such a frightful weapon. It was not until October 1941 that Roosevelt ordered an all-out effort to build such a bomb, the project to be headed by Dr Vannevar Bush, director of the Office of Scientific Research and Development (0SRD). In June 1942 the programme was greatly expanded and placed under General Leslie Groves of the War Department. The 'Manhattan Engineering District Project' was highly secret and few members of Roosevelt's cabinet knew of its existence.

Vannevar Bush and his deputy, James B. Conant, were well aware that the bomb would greatly enhance America's diplomatic and political influence, and partly for this reason did not want to share atomic secrets with the British whose contributions to atomic research, codenamed 'Tube Alloys', were modest. At first Roosevelt also wished to exclude the British, largely because he feared that they would pass on atomic secrets to the Soviet Union. The President was assured by the British that they had no desire to share any of their technical secrets with the Soviet Union, and at the 'Trident' conference in Washington in May 1943 the way was opened for the joint production of the atomic bomb. The United States and Britain were now partners, though obviously very unequal.

The agreement was reaffirmed at the Quebec meeting in August 1943, when the two powers pledged a 'full and effective interchange of information and ideas', undertook 'never to use this agency against each other' and not to use it against third parties 'without each other's consent'.

On 19 September 1944 at their meeting at Hyde Park during the 'Octagon' conference, Roosevelt and Churchill again discussed the atomic bomb. It was assumed that a 20 to 30 kiloton bomb would be ready by August 1945 and if the war with Japan still continued it would be used against them until they surrendered. Some scientists argued that the explosive effect of the atom bomb would be even greater, but even at the most conservative estimate it was an awesome weapon. About 270 bomber sorties were needed to deliver the equivalent of one kiloton, or one thousand tons of TNT, with conventional bombs. It was agreed that the bomb should still be kept absolutely secret until it was dropped on Japan and all information relating to the development of the bomb should be withheld from the Soviets.

On 4 May 1945 Stimson, the US Secretary for War, having discussed the bomb with President Truman, appointed a select committee 'for recommending action to the executive and legislative branches of our Government when secrecy is no longer in full effect [and also] actions to be taken by the War Department prior to that time in anticipation of the postwar problems.' Stimson chaired this committee, with George Harrison, the president of New York Life, as vice-chairman. It was an immensely distinguished committee whose members included Vannevar Bush; James B. Conant, the president of Harvard; Karl T. Compton, president of MIT; Ralph Bar, Under-Secretary of the Navy; William Clayton, Assistant Secretary of State; three Nobel laureates – Enrico Fermi, Ernest O. Lawrence and Arthur H. Compton; and lastly, a brilliant young theoretical physicist, J. Robert Oppenheimer, the director of the Los Alamos laboratory. After what later critics have described as a somewhat perfunctory debate, the committee agreed that the bomb should be dropped on Japan as soon as possible, that it should be used against military installations and civilian housing, and that it should be dropped without any prior warning.

Some scientists at the Chicago laboratory were concerned about the effects on relations with the Soviet Union of using the bomb against Japan. They proposed a demonstration use of the bomb, preferably on some Pacific island, to threaten the Japanese and raised the possibility of international control of the bomb. Fear was also expressed that the bomb might lead to a costly and dangerous arms race once the war was over. Stimson's committee discussed the Chicago report and proposed that Britain, the Soviet Union, France and China should be consulted 'as to how we can co-operate in making this development contribute to improved international relations', but insisted that the bomb should be dropped on Japan without warning. At a further meeting of the committee it was agreed that Truman should tell Stalin at Potsdam that the United States had the bomb and intended to use it against Japan.

Truman arrived at Potsdam on 15 July and on the following day he was informed that the Alamogordo test was successful. On 21 July he was given full details of the test. On 24 July the President casually mentioned to Stalin that the United States had a 'new weapon', and the Soviet leader mumbled that he hoped they would make good use of it. On 26 July the United States, Britain and China issued the Potsdam Declaration calling for Japan to surrender. The declaration contained no guarantees of the position of the Emperor, as Stimson and Grew, the Under-Secretary of State, had wished. Nor was there any mention of the bomb. The Soviets were not invited to sign the declaration. The Americans knew from decoded messages that the Japanese were negotiating with the Russians to act as intermediaries for a peace short of unconditional surrender, and were uncertain how the Soviets would respond. When Stalin heard of what he called the 'Anglo-American ultimatum to Japan' he told the plenary meeting of the conference that the Soviet Government had been approached by the Japanese and had responded with 'an unhesitating negative'.

The American military were anxious to avoid the invasion of Japan, which they knew would be a costly and bloody campaign. 'Operation Olympic', a landing with thirteen divisions on Kyushu was planned for 1 November 1945 and was to be followed on 1 March 1946 by 'Operation Coronet', a landing near Tokyo. Two million Japanese troops with adequate supplies of ammunition were waiting for the invaders, and in June the Japanese Parliament had passed a law in preparation for a *levée en masse*. Okinawa gave an unpleasant foretaste of what might be expected in the hilly landscape of Japan which offered such excellent cover to the defence. With widely dispersed industry and a highly concentrated civilian population, Japan seemed an ideal target for area bombing. The atom bomb was the ideal terror weapon. Not only was it highly destructive, it was also spectacularly frightful. Oppenheimer pointed out that 'the visual effect of an atomic bombing would be tremendous. It would be accompanied by a brilliant luminescence which would rise to a height of 10,000 to 20,000 feet.' General Marshall and Stimson both argued that the shock value of the bomb was such that the Japanese would be bound to surrender. Since this shock value was the key to its success, a demonstration explosion was out of the question. Marshall argued: 'It's no good warning them. If you warn them there's no surprise. And the only way to produce shock is surprise.'

None of the key policy-makers questioned the use of the bomb against Japan. Eisenhower was the only leading military commander who objected, although he subsequently stated that it was a spontaneous reaction before he had studied the matter. On 24 July General Spaatz was ordered to prepare twenty USAAF aeroplanes to drop the bomb on Hiroshima, Kokura, Nagasaki or Niigata at any suitable time after 3 August. At 09.15 hours on 6 August the 'Enola Gay' dropped a 14-kiloton uranium bomb on Hiroshima. Of the 320,000 inhabitants, 78,000 were killed, 14,000 lost and 19,000 wounded. Of the survivors, 171,000 were left homeless.

On the following day the Emperor begged Togo to end the war regardless of the conditions, but the army would not surrender and tried to suppress all information about the effects of this new weapon. On 8 August the Soviet Union announced that they would go to war with Japan on the following day. The Red Army promptly crossed into Manchuria and Inner Mongolia, anxious to control as much territory as possible before Japan surrendered. Within a few days General Yamada's Kwantung Army was overrun so that the Red Army controlled all of northern China and Korea. Under the terms of the Sino-Soviet Friendship Treaty, signed on 14 August, the Soviets agreed to hand over the administration of Manchuria to the nationalists, having refused to support Mao's communists in their struggle against Chiang Kai-shek.

News of the Soviet invasion of Manchuria prompted the Emperor again to urge Suzuki and Togo to accept the Potsdam Declaration. The Supreme Council met to discuss the situation and agreed, provided that the position of the Emperor remained unchanged. But the War Minister and the Chiefs of Staff insisted that a cease-fire was acceptable only if the Allies agreed not to occupy Japan, that the armed forces should be allowed to return home and the Japanese Government must supervise the demobilization, and lastly that any suspected war criminals should be tried by Japanese courts.

While the Supreme Council was in session a 20-kiloton plutonium bomb was dropped on Nagasaki, resulting in 40,000 deaths and about the same number of wounded. Truman announced that the United States would continue to drop atomic bombs on Japan until the country surrendered. Suzuki was still unable to convince the military that their conditions were totally unrealistic and therefore took the constitutionally questionable step of asking the Emperor for his decision. He promptly replied that the Allied conditions should be accepted provided that the rights of the Imperial House were respected. On 11 August Secretary of State Byrnes replied through the intermediary of the Swiss Government that the Emperor and Government of Japan would be subject to the Supreme Commander of the Allied Powers until the ultimate form of the Government of Japan was decided by 'the freely expressed will of the Japanese people'. Suzuki, Togo and Yonai felt that since the Japanese people would never reject the Emperor this formula was acceptable, but there was still a strong feeling in the army that capitulation was dishonourable and that the plebiscite suggested by the Americans was a trick to destroy the monarchy. The Emperor announced that it was his will that the war be ended, and he was supported by his entire family so that there was no hope of a palace revolt supported by a member of the imperial family. Officers in the War Ministry and the general staff overwhelmed the imperial guards and attempted to isolate the palace and seize the recording of the peace appeal. The revolt was put down by the energetic intervention of the district commander, and similar efforts by fanatical officers, including a plot to murder Suzuki, were stymied. The leaders of the revolt, among them the War Minister, Anami, committed suicide in the approved Japanese manner. On 15 August the Emperor's message urging acceptance of the terms of the Potsdam Declaration was broadcast to the nation.

The Suzuki Government resigned and a new administration was formed under an uncle of the Empress, Prince Higashikuni who, as a serving general, combined the offices of Prime Minister and War Minister. Imperial princes were dispatched to Singapore, Manchuria and China to ensure that the armistice was respected. The kamikaze corps was persuaded to drop its plans to attack the American fleet bringing the Supreme Commander, General MacArthur, to Japan. On 2 September the formal instrument of surrender was signed aboard the American warship *Missouri*.

The war was hardly over when the debate over the use of the atomic bomb began. Although there was virtual unanimity that the bomb should be dropped, the decision has become one of the most vigorously debated issues in recent history. An almost endless series of questions has been raised. Why did the United States not invite the Soviet Union to sign the Potsdam Declaration? Did the Americans want to avoid Soviet involvement in the war in Asia? Why did Truman not give Stalin fuller details of the bomb instead of merely casually mentioning it at Potsdam? Why did the Americans not delay the dropping of the bomb until they had more precise details of the Japanese peace feelers? If victory by conventional means was so close, why was it necessary to drop the bomb? Why were the moral and political implications of the bomb not discussed in greater detail? Was the bomb used to impress the Soviets and to win concessions from them at Potsdam? Did the dropping of the atomic bomb mark the true beginning of the Cold War?

The answer given by Truman and most of his senior associates is simple: the bomb shortened the war and saved thousands of American lives. This explanation was clear and convincing. After all, the bomb worked. Japan surrendered and the world was at last at peace. But the question was soon raised whether the use of the bomb was not morally equivalent to murdering a man on his deathbed. Hanson Baldwin, the military analyst of the *New York Times*, wrote in 1950 that America was 'branded with the mark of the beast' by its use of a bomb which won the war but which was used in a manner which lost them the peace. This argument was taken up by other writers who agreed that, since the bomb was not necessary for victory, its use was immoral, and that the post-war political consequences of the use of the bomb were so disastrous that it was also politically foolish.

Other writers of what was to become known as the 'revisionist school' went much further. They agreed that the use of the bomb was unnecessary, immoral and unwise, but they further argued that it was aimed primarily against the Soviet Union rather than against Japan. The United States used the bomb as soon as possible in order to impress the Soviets, delayed the Potsdam conference so that the Alamogordo test would have the maximum deterrent effect, and were thus primarily responsible for the onset of the Cold War. *Atomic Diplomacy* (the title of Gar Alperovitz's influential book) was used to intimidate the Soviets and marks a radical break with Roosevelt's policy of accommodation with the Russians.

There is some evidence to support at least part of this contention. It is clear that American leaders realized that the bomb gave them a considerable advantage in negotiations with the Soviets, and this may have contributed to a hardening of the American position at Potsdam. But this did not mean that the primary reason for dropping the bomb was to scare the Soviets, nor did the Americans use explicit atomic threats against them. With virtually no bombs and no sure way of delivering them, they were in no position to threaten the Soviets even if they had wished to do so. When Churchill heard of the successful test of the bomb he immediately and gleefully announced that now the western Allies had a club with which to beat the Russians. His military advisors concluded that he had taken leave of his senses. There can be no doubt that the primary reason for dropping the bomb was to secure the speedy and unconditional surrender of Japan. If a secondary effect was to stiffen Truman's attitude towards the Soviet Union, it should also be noted that the Soviets took little notice and that the British, who did not yet have a bomb, were far tougher negotiators with the Soviets than were the Americans.

It is unlikely that there will ever be agreement over the central issues of why the bomb was dropped, or whether atomic weapons are more morally reprehensible than more conventional means of mass destruction. On one issue, however, there can be no doubt: 'Little Boy' and 'Fat Man' changed the face of war and brought about a fearfully dangerous peace. The weapon that is said to have won the war against Japan can never again be used to win a war, and the fear of its further use has done much to preserve a semblance of peace.

CHAPTER FIFTEEN

Conclusion

The Allies had every reason to rejoice at the news of the German Supreme Command's surrender at Rheims on 7 May and the Japanese capitulation on 14 August. They had fought a successful war for a good cause. Horrifying newsreels of the liberation of the concentration camps revealed that the reality of Nazi rule was infinitely worse than anything that the most lurid propagandist could possibly invent. Few questioned that Hitler and his cronies were wicked men bent on world conquest and that the pursuit of his downfall was the cause of all good men. Similarly, most people agreed that Japan was a brutally aggressive power which had to be stopped and the murderous occupation policies in China, the perfidy of Pearl Harbor and the humiliation of Singapore revenged. Germany and Japan were destroyed, their cities levelled, their economies shattered and their sovereignty destroyed. Their surrender was unconditional, the victory of the Allies total.

It soon became apparent, however, that this glorious victory for the Allied cause created at least as many problems as it solved. For Britain, six years of war had resulted in a catastrophic level of external disinvestment and industry was run down and desperately short of investment capital. On 21 August President Truman suddenly cut off Lend-Lease and Britain faced what Keynes called a 'financial Dunkirk'. The Americans gave Britain a loan, but the terms were harsh. The British Government was obliged to ratify the Bretton Woods Agreement and thus had to accept the convertibility of sterling into dollars, a liberalization of the sterling area and the lifting of restrictions on American exports to Britain. The much-vaunted 'special relationship' with the United States appeared to be in ruins; Britain lost much of its financial sovereignty and was reduced to the humiliating status of an American pensioner.

Although the British faced austerity, a reduction in the rations for clothing and fats and, for the first time, bread rationing, the country still faced worldwide obligations which it was hardly in a position to meet. The Labour Party, which had been returned to power in the general election in May, had no coherent foreign policy but the new Foreign Secretary, Ernest Bevin, was an exceptionally capable statesman determined to defend and strengthen British interests wherever possible. This led to further problems with the Americans, with their high-minded objections to British imperialism coupled with a curiously contradictory reluctance to subsidize socialists, of however moderate a hue, and their dismissal of the British as 'cry-babies'. Britain was no longer a great power, but was determined to continue playing the role. It could do so only with the active support of the United States, which in turn had serious reservations about its closest ally. This offered an opportunity to the Soviets which they were quick to exploit.

The Soviet Union suffered heavier losses than any other country in the war. They did most of the fighting and most of the dying for the Allied cause. The industrial centres in the western regions had been destroyed and agriculture laid waste. But the Soviet Union's two greatest potential rivals, Germany and Japan, had been devastated and it was now unquestionably the greatest military power in Europe. In the course of defeating Nazi Germany the Soviet Union had emerged as a world power second only to the United States, had occupied most of central Europe and was now seen by the British and Americans as a serious menace to European security.

In the course of the war most British officials had come to the conclusion that the best way to deal with the Soviet Union was to reach an agreement over spheres of influence. Roosevelt did not share the concerns of men such as William Bullitt, Averil Harriman and George Kennan about Soviet preponderance in eastern Europe and believed that he could charm Stalin into submission. Stalin was quick to exploit these differences between the Americans and the British, thus further weakening an already tenuous alliance.

Stalin remained obsessed with the Soviet need for future security, and with his deep suspicions of the west was determined to isolate his country from the rest of the world and build a *cordon sanitaire* against a western bloc which was in the process of formation. The intransigent and unbending attitude of Molotov at the post-war conferences was to do much to bring the British and the Americans together again, and the Americans found themselves forced to become closely involved in European affairs to compensate for British weakness. The British were no longer able to control the situation in Turkey and Greece and the Americans felt obliged to step in, for fear of a further increase in Soviet influence. Gradually the United States began to take over Britain's old imperial role, of which they had been so high-mindedly critical throughout the war.

The war thus confirmed the United States' role as by far the strongest of the great powers. It alone had fought a full-scale war in the Pacific and Europe. The mobilization of its wartime economy had resulted in a spectacular growth of industrial output. The country had never been so prosperous nor in so confident a mood, but it was reluctant to shoulder the burdens of responsibility that are the necessary concomitant of great power. It took time for the American Government to realize that Bretton Woods and the United Nations were not sufficient to meet their security needs as they reluctantly accepted the role which Britain was no longer able to play, and as they grew increasingly frustrated with the Soviets.

The 'Grand Alliance' had always been largely a fiction. Relations between the British and the Americans had been highly strained throughout the war, although the deadly seriousness of the common cause meant that fundamental differences over strategy and politics never led to a serious breach. The Soviets fought a separate war and made no effort to co-ordinate their strategy with the western Allies, who in turn were reluctant to share any of their military secrets with an ally about whom they still harboured serious reservations.

The Axis powers were party to an even weaker alliance. Hitler told the Japanese ambassador in Berlin on 3 January 1943 that this was the first time in history that two great powers had fought a major war together from opposite sides of the globe, and stressed the importance of working out a common strategy. With his 'Barbarossa' strategy in ruins, Hitler confided that he was confident they would be able to defeat Britain but that he was uncertain how the United States could be conquered. He also told Oshima that he did not trust their Italian Allies, though he still had confidence in Mussolini. In spite of this insistence on the need for co-operation, the Japanese and Germans never co-ordinated their war plans. The agreement signed in Berlin on 18 January 1942 merely established a demarcation line at 70 degrees longitude so that all of Asia to the east of the Indus was left to the Japanese. The question of whether the

Germans or the Japanese would control the valuable Siberian industrial region to the east of this line was never settled. The Germans agreed to send naval units to the Pacific should the British and Americans decide to concentrate their navies there, and the Japanese agreed to reciprocate should the Allies send the bulk of their navies to the Atlantic. A committee was established in Berlin to co-ordinate the efforts of Germany, Italy and Japan, but it achieved very little beyond the exchange of a few secrets.

Hitler was mainly concerned with the land war with the Soviet Union and ignored Raeder's pleas for a global concept. He regarded the Japanese as duplicitous liars and as racially inferior, in spite of their ludicrous status as 'honorary Aryans'. He greatly admired the British Empire and had no desire to see the Raj replaced by a Japanese occupation. In his wilder moments he argued that sooner or later Germany would have to destroy Japan to eliminate a dangerous rival to world power. He was never able to decide whether this should happen before or after the defeat of the United States. The Japanese, for their part, had little regard for their German Allies. They concentrated all their efforts on establishing their Empire in Asia and treated the Germans as racially suspect outsiders for whom there was no place in the Great East Asian Co-prosperity Sphere.

Hitler intended, at least initially, to fight a land war in Europe which would consist of a series of limited and swift campaigns. The Soviet counter-offensive at the gates of Moscow in December 1941 ruined this strategy and he was then faced with fighting a war which he had little chance of winning. The industrial power of the United States and the Soviet Union dwarfed the efforts of the Germans and Japanese. Augmented by the output of Britain and Canada, which in the course of the war became a major sea power and a leader among the smaller nations, the Allies had an overwhelming superiority in a war of attrition. Combined with the astonishing capacity of the Soviet Union for sustained sacrifice of human life on an unbelievable scale, in part the result of Stalinist terror, in part in response to the horrors of Nazi occupation, the Allies could hardly fail to win the war. In retrospect it is not surprising that the war was won, only that it took so long to achieve victory.

The Soviet Union, with a guarantee of Japanese neutrality, had the great advantage of fighting on only one front, but it was a very broad front which was defended at terrible cost. It was also the front on which the German army was defeated. The Germans lost some seven million men on the eastern front, under two million elsewhere.

The German army had better morale and a higher degree of unit cohesiveness than any of the Allied armies. Its officers were better trained and its men more skilled and resilient. The fearful and those who doubted a final victory were promptly executed. But none of this counted against the overwhelming might of Allied war industry and the sheer numbers of tough Soviet soldiers. Trapped between a ruthless enemy in front of them and NKVD killers behind them, the Red Army soldiers fought with an unmatched fanaticism born of desperation as much as ideological conviction or national sentiment. A lasting literary monument to their frightful ordeal can be found in Vasily Grossman's *Life and Fate*. Stalin and most of his generals showed a total contempt for human life, and that so many Soviet citizens died in the war was not solely due to the deadly efficiency of the Wehrmacht or the brutality of the Nazi occupation.

Initially it was generally assumed that the Soviet Union would take between five and ten years to recover from the war and that there would be a certain ideological relaxation as a reward for past sacrifices. With the Red Army occupying most of eastern and central Europe and bent on subjecting the entire area to its will, the Soviet Union gradually replaced Nazi Germany in the eyes of the western powers as the major menace to world peace and security. The Soviets sealed off their sphere of influence, clamped down on the unfortunates whom they had liberated, maintained a vast military establishment and were intransigent and abusive towards their erstwhile Allies. They thus confirmed the worst fears of those who had been warning of their sinister intentions.

At first President Truman was considerably tougher with the Soviets than Roosevelt had been, but he soon adopted a more conciliatory position, believing that the Security Council of the United Nations would be able to deal with any awkward issues that might lead to tension between the Soviets and the west. Truman certainly hoped that the possession of the atomic bomb would strengthen his hand, but Stalin appeared to be unimpressed and the President resisted any temptation to use 'atomic diplomacy'. It was Churchill who imagined that the bomb was the God-given answer to the Soviet menace, much to the horror of his military advisors who knew only too well that for the foreseeable future, and probably beyond, the bomb was a weapon which could not be used to bully the Soviets into submission.

The Labour Party had, by and large, always taken a harder line towards the Soviet Union than had the Conservatives, and Truman was positively alarmed at the truculent attitude taken by Bevin towards the Russians which was in marked contrast to Churchill's occasional outbursts of peevishness. The Soviets, faced with a weak negotiating partner in the new Secretary of State, James F. Byrnes, quickly drove a wedge between the British and the Americans and obtained a number of concessions from the Americans at Potsdam, including the acceptance of the western Neisse as the Polish frontier and increased reparations from Germany. Attlee and Bevin could do nothing but tag along with the Americans and complain about the feeble efforts of Secretary of State Byrnes.

Thus even before the fall of Japan the tensions which had existed within the wartime alliance had become exacerbated, but not to the point of Cold War. As the Americans took over many of Britain's commitments in Europe and the Middle East and as the British began their withdrawal from Asia, the United States and the Soviet Union found themselves face to face, twin super-powers stumbling towards confrontation. The Americans set about 'containing' the Soviet Union, first by economic and then by military means. The Soviets clamped down on their satellites and became increasingly threatening and unco-operative. Both sides began to justify their antagonistic stance by massive propaganda campaigns which were in part a continuation of wartime ideological mobilization. The image of the enemy was quickly transferred. Bevin was soon complaining of Molotov's 'Hitlerite philosophy', and the Soviets intoned endless denunciations of the west's 'Hitlerite tactics'. It was an exceedingly dangerous game which was the direct cause of the Korean war of 1950, a pointless ideological conflict in which some four million died.

The growing split between the Soviet Union and the western powers did much to frustrate the hopes of many Europeans that the post-war world would be one in which old-style capitalism would be replaced by some form of social-democratic planned economy. The Soviets denounced American capitalism and imperialism and established Stalinist dictatorships in their satellites. The Americans eventually responded by claiming that communist expansionism could be contained only by military alliances and by powerful doses of the American Way of Life. In the long run neither the Soviets nor the Americans succeeded. Western Europe never came totally under the American sway, and cracks soon began to appear in the Stalinist monolith. That the world could be built anew, even after such a catastrophic war, was soon shown to be an illusion. There was to be no 'Zero Hour', not even amid the ruins of Germany. History cannot be made to stop and start afresh. Amid the deprivations and hardships of the first years of peace this was deeply frustrating to many, but in the long run it was comforting to all but the most fervent apostles of brave new worlds.

Although the world was soon perilously divided, this was not an inevitable consequence of the war. In 1945 a cold war was predicted by some as an unlikely and certainly avoidable contingency. Not even the bleakest of these Cassandras felt that it was inevitable. The notion of the inevitability of this conflict is a result of the ensuing ideological struggle. It was held not only by Marxist–Leninists with their belief in imperialist aggression as the inevitable result of monopoly capitalism, but also by those who otherwise abhorred all theories of historical inevitability but still felt that Soviet expansionism was the inevitable result of the bolshevik revolution.

As in Europe, the power relationships in Asia were fundamentally altered by the war. The Soviet request to participate in the occupation of Japan was denied, so that the country was spared partition and could devote all its energies to economic recovery. The Japanese, like the Germans, were soon to achieve a level of prosperity which rendered totally absurd their earlier insistence on the vital necessity for the Great East Asia Co-prosperity Sphere or for *Grossraumwirtschaft*. China was economically, politically and militarily prostrate and the Kuomintang was in no position to resist Mao's communist guerillas with their compelling programme of drastic social and economic change. As long as China remained so weak Soviet predominance in east Asia was assured, and it was only when Mao established a powerful regime independent from Moscow that this hegemony was challenged. General MacArthur's 'General Order No. 1' established demarcation lines for the occupation zones along the 38th parallel in Korea and the 16th parallel in Indo-china. They were totally artificial boundaries which were to give rise to bloody conflicts that further tarnished the idealistic self-image of the United States.

The extension of the Cold War to Asia was no more an inevitable result of the war than was the division of Europe. There can be little doubt, however, that the war gave an enormous boost to the independence movements throughout Asia. They in turn were supported by the Soviet Union in order further to weaken the imperialist powers, and also initially by the Americans with their idealistic Wilsonian vision of a new world free from formal Empires and colonial dependence and enjoying the material benefits of free trade and disinterested dollar diplomacy, as foreseen in the Bretton Woods Agreement. This was soon seen to be sham, and it was in

Asia that the United States was to suffer its worst political, military and moral humiliations.

At the height of the Cold War there were some who asked whether the war had been fought in vain. Few regretted the passing of Nazi Germany or imperial Japan, but the question remained whether a world dominated by the Soviet Union and the United States was much better. Stalinist terror was obviously repulsive and the American Way of Life was not immediately attractive to traditional European or Asian susceptibilities. Some began to ask whether the enormous sacrifices that had been made during the war had not been for the greater glory of world communism or for the enrichment of American capitalists. Envious glances at the Federal Republic of Germany and at Japan, and within the Soviet bloc at the economic achievements of the German Democratic Republic, were accompanied by cynical questions about who had really won the war.

In 1945 all this was uncertain and far from inevitable. People were justified in celebrating VE and VJ Days in the belief that the wicked had been vanquished. That the world they inherited was divided, grimly austere, profoundly unjust and threatened by nuclear destruction does not mean that they were misguided. Europe had been saved from Nazi domination, Asia from Japanese imperialism. That new problems arising from new power constellations would arise was inevitable; the form that they took was not. That a way has to be found for their solution must surely be the most compelling contemporary lesson to be drawn from the horrors of the Second World War.

Select Bibliography

Addison, Paul, *The Road to 1945*, London 1975.
Allen, Louis, *The End of the War in Asia*, London 1976.
Alperovitz, Gar, *Atomic Diplomacy: Hiroshima and Potsdam: The Use of the Atomic Bomb and the American Confrontation with Soviet Power*, New York 1965.
Argyle, C.J., *Japan at War*, London 1976.
Armstrong, J.A. (ed.), *Soviet Partisans in World War II*, Wisconsin 1964.
Aronsen, Lawrence and Martin Kitchen, *The Origins of the Cold War in Comparative Perspective: American, British and Canadian Relations with the Soviet Union, 1941–48*, London 1988.
Barker, Elizabeth, *British Policy in South-east Europe in the Second World War*, London 1976.
Barker, Elizabeth, *Churchill and Eden at War*, London 1978.
Barnett, Correlli, *The Collapse of British Power*, London 1972.
Barnett, Correlli, *The Desert Generals*, London 1983.
Beaumont, Joan, *Comrades in Arms: British Aid to Russia 1941–1945*, London 1980.
Beitzell, Robert, *The Uneasy Alliance: America, Britain and Russia, 1941–1943*, New York 1972.
Bernstein, Barton J., 'The Peril and Politics of Surrender: Ending the War with Japan and Avoiding the Third Atomic Bomb', *Pacific Historical Review*, 46.1, February 1977.
Bialer, S. (ed.), *Stalin and his Generals*, London 1970.
Blum, John Morton, *From the Morgenthau Diaries: Years of War, 1941–1945*, Boston 1967.
Blum, John Morton, *V Was for Victory: Politics and American Culture during World War II*, New York 1976.
Boyle, J.H., *China and Japan at War*, Stanford 1972.
Bór-Komorowski, Tadeusz, *The Secret Army*, London 1953.

Bradley, Omar, *A General's Life*, New York 1983.
Bryant, Arthur, *The Turn of the Tide, 1939–1943*, London 1957.
Bryant, Arthur, *Triumph in the West*, London 1959.
Bullock, A., *Hitler: A Study in Tyranny*, New York 1964.
Butler, J.R.M., *Grand Strategy*, Vol. II, London 1957.
Calder, Angus, *The People's War: Britain 1939–45*, London 1969.
Calvocoressi, Peter and Guy Wint, *Total War*, London 1972.
Chandler, Alfred D et al, (eds), *The Papers of Dwight D. Eisenhower: The War Years*, 5 vols, Baltimore 1970.
Chiukov, Vasili, *The End of the Third Reich*, London 1975.
Churchill, Winston S., *The Second World War*, 6 vols, London 1948–1954.
Ciechanowski, Jan, *The Warsaw Rising of 1944*, Cambridge 1974.
Clemens, Diane Shaver, *Yalta*, New York 1970.
D'Este, Carlo, *Decision in Normandy*, London 1983.
D'Este, Carlo, *Bitter Victory: The Battle for Sicily July–August 1943*, London 1988.
Dallek, Robert, *Franklin D. Roosevelt and American Foreign Policy 1932–1945*, New York 1979.
Dallin, A., *German Rule in Russia 1941–45*, London 1981.
Davis, Lynn E., *The Cold War Begins*, Princeton 1974.
Dawidowicz, Lucy S., *The War Against the Jews, 1933–1945*, New York 1975.
Dawidowicz. Lucy S., *The Holocaust and the Historian*, Cambridge, Mass. 1981.
Deakin, F.W., *The Brutal Friendship: Mussolini, Hitler, and the Fall of Italian Fascism*, London 1962.
Dedijer, Vladimir, *Tito*, New York 1953.
Dilks, David (ed.), *The Diaries of Sir Alexander Cadogan, 1938–1945*, London 1971.
Djilas, Milovan, *Conversations with Stalin*, New York 1962.
Djilas, Milovan, *Wartime*, New York 1977.
Doenitz, K., *Memoirs*, London 1959.
Ehrman, John, *Grand Strategy*, Vol. V., *August 1943–September 1944*, London 1956.
Eisenhower, Dwight D., *The Reckoning*, New York 1948.
Erickson, John, *The Road to Berlin*, London 1983.
Erickson, John, *The Road to Stalingrad*, London 1975.
Fest, J.C., *Hitler*, Harmondsworth 1982.
Fest, J.C., *The Face of the Third Reich*, Harmondsworth 1979.
Foot, M.R.D., *Resistance*, London 1978.

Foot, M.R.D., *Resistance. European Resistance to Nazism 1940–45*, London 1976.

Gaddis, John Lewis, *The United States and the Origins of the Cold War, 1941–1947*, New York 1972.

Gaddis, John Lewis, *The United States and the Origins of the Cold War, 1941–1947*, Chicago 1970.

Gilbert, Martin, *Finest Hour: Winston S. Churchill 1939–1941*, London 1983.

Gilbert, Martin, *Road to Victory: Winston S. Churchill 1941–1945*, London 1986.

Gorodetsky, Gabriel, *Stafford Cripps' Mission to Moscow 1940–1942*, Cambridge 1984.

Gowing, Margaret, *Britain and Atomic Energy, 1939–1945*, London 1964.

Graml, H., *The German Resistance to Hitler*, London 1970.

Greenfield, Kent Roberts, *American Strategy in World War II*, Baltimore 1963.

Gross, Jan Tomasz, *Polish Society under German Occupation: The General Government, 1939–1944*, Princeton 1979.

Harriman, W. Averell, *Special Envoy to Churchill and Stalin, 1941–1946*, New York 1975.

Harris, Sir Arthur, *Bomber Offensive*, London 1947.

Harrisson, Tom, *Living Through the Blitz*, London 1978.

Harvey, John (ed.), *The Diplomatic Diaries of Oliver Harvey, 1937–1940*, London 1970.

Hastings, M., *Bomber Command*, London 1979.

Havens, Thomas, *Valley of Darkness: The Japanese People and World War Two*, New York 1978.

Heckmann, Wolf, *Rommel's War in Africa*, London 1981.

Hilberg, Raul, *The Destruction of the European Jews*, New York 1985.

Hildebrand, Klaus, *The Foreign Policy of the Third Reich*, Berkeley 1973.

Horne, Alistair, *To Lose a Battle: France 1940*, London 1969.

Howard, Michael, *Grand Strategy*, Vol. IV, *August 1942–September 1943*, London 1972.

Howard, Michael, *The Mediterranean Strategy in the Second World War*, Cambridge 1968.

Ienaga, Saburo, *The Pacific War: World War II and the Japanese, 1931–1945*, New York 1978.

Iriye, Akira, *Power and Culture: The Japanese–American War, 1941–1945*, Cambridge, Mass. 1981.

Iriye, Akira, *The Origins of the Second World War in Asia and the Pacific*, London 1987.
Jacobsen, H.-A., and Arthur L. Smith Jr, *World War II: Policy and Strategy*, Oxford 1979.
Jacobsen, H.-A. and J. Rohwer, *Decisive Battles of World War II*, London 1965.
Jain, R.K., *China and Japan*, London 1977.
Kimball, Warren E. (ed.), *Churchill and Roosevelt: The Complete Correspondence*, 3 vols., Princeton 1985.
Kitchen, Martin, *British Policy Towards the Soviet Union During the Second World War*, London 1986.
Kolko, Gabriel, *The Politics of War: The World and United States Foreign Policy, 1943–1945*, New York 1968.
Laqueur, Walter, *The Terrible Secret: Suppression of the Truth about Hitler's 'Final Solution'*, London 1980.
Lash, Joseph P., *Roosevelt and Churchill 1939–1941*, New York 1976.
Leach, A.B., *German Strategy against Russia*, 1939–41, London 1973.
Lewin, Ronald, *Churchill as Warlord*, London 1973.
Lewin, Ronald, *The Chief*, London 1980.
Lewin, Ronald, *Ultra Goes to War: The Secret Story*, London 1978.
Li, Lincoln, *The Japanese Army in North China, 1937–1941*, Oxford 1975.
Liddell Hart, B.H., *History of the Second World War*, London 1970.
Liddell Hart, B.H., *The Other Side of the Hill*, London 1948.
Longmate, Norman, *How We Lived Then*, London 1971.
Louis, W.R., *Imperialism at Bay: the United States and the Decolonialization of the British Empire, 1941–1945*, Oxford 1978.
Macmillan, Harold, *War Diaries: The Mediterranean 1943–1945*, London 1984.
Maisky, Ivan, *Memoirs of a Soviet Ambassador*, London 1967.
Mastny, Vojtech, *Russia's Road to the Cold War: Diplomacy, Warfare and the Politics of Communism, 1941–1945*, New York 1979.
Matloff, Maurice, and E.M. Snell, *Strategic Planning for Coalition Warfare, 1941–1942*, Washington 1953.
Milward, A.S., *The German Economy at War*, London 1965.
Moran, Lord, *Winston Churchill: The Struggle for Survival, 1940–1965*, London 1966.
Morison, Samuel Eliot, *The Two-Ocean War 1939–1945*, New York 1963.
Morton, Louis, *United States Army in World War II: The War in the*

Pacific: Strategy and Command: The First Two Years, Washington 1962.

Myers, R.H. and M.R. Peattie, (eds), *The Japanese Colonial Empire*, Princeton 1984.

Overy, R.J., *The Air War 1939–1945*, London 1980.

Paxton, Robert O., *Vichy France*, New York 1972.

Pogue, Forrest C., *George C. Marshall*, Vols 2 and 3, New York 1966–1973.

Polenberg, Richard, *War and Society: The United States, 1941–1945*, Philadelphia 1972.

Polonsky, Anthony, *The Great Powers and the Polish Question 1941–1945*, London 1976.

Prange, Gordon W., *At Dawn We Slept: The Untold Story of Pearl Harbor*, New York 1981.

Rich, Norman, *Hitler's War Aims*, Vol. 2, *The Establishment of the New Order*, New York 1974.

Roskill, Stephen W., *The War at Sea 1939–1945*, London 1954–1961.

Seaton, A., *The Russo-German War, 1941–45*, London 1971.

Slim, W.J., *Defeat into Victory*, London 1956.

Smith, Bradley and Elena Agarossi, *Operation Sunrise: The Secret Surrender*, New York 1979.

Smith, Bradley F., *The Shadow Warriors*, New York 1983.

Smith, Bradley F., *The War's Long Shadow*, New York 1986.

Spears, E., *Assignment to Catastrophe*, London 1954.

Speer, A., *Inside the Third Reich*, London 1979.

Stacey, C.P., *Arms, Men and Governments: The War Policies of Canada 1939–1945*, Ottawa 1970.

Stafford, David, *Britain and European Resistance, 1940–1945*, London 1980.

Stein, G.H., *The Waffen SS, 1939–45*, London 1977.

Stoler, Mark A., *The Politics of the Second Front: American Military Planning in Coalition Warfare, 1941–1943*, Westport, Conn. 1977.

Terraine, John, *A Time for Courage: The Royal Air Force in the European War, 1939–1945*, London 1985.

Thorne, Christopher G., *Allies of a Kind: The United States, Britain and the War against Japan, 1941–1945*, London 1978.

Trevor-Roper, H.R. (ed.), *Hitler's Table Talk, 1941–44*, London 1973.

Trevor-Roper, H.R. (ed.), *Hitler's War Directives 1939–1945*, London 1964.

Tuchman, Barbara W., *Stilwell and the American Experience in China 1911–1945*, New York 1971.

van Creveld, M., *Hitler's Strategy, 1940–41*, London 1973.
van Creveld, M., *Fighting Power, German and US Army Performance, 1939–1945*, Westport 1982.
Warlimont, Walter, *Inside Hitler's Headquarters*, London 1964.
Warner, Geoffrey, 'From Teheran to Yalta: Reflections on FDR's Foreign Policy', *International Affairs*, July 1976.
Webster, Sir Charles and Noble Frankland, *The Strategic Air Offensive against Germany, 1939–1945*, 3 vols, London 1961.
Wedemeyer, Albert C., *Wedemeyer Reports!*, New York 1958.
Weigley, Russell F., *Eisenhower's Lieutenants. The Campaign of France and Germany, 1944–1945*, Bloomington 1981.
Werth, Alexander, *Russia at War 1941–45*, London 1964.
Wilmot, Chester, *The Struggle for Europe*, London 1952.
Wilson, G.M., *Politics and Culture in Wartime Japan*, Oxford 1981.
Winterbotham, F.W., *The Ultra Secret*, New York 1974.
Wood, D. and D. Dempster, *The Narrow Margin*, London 1969.
Woodward, Llewellyn, *British Foreign Policy in the Second World War*, 5 vols, London 1970–76.
Wright, Gordon, *The Ordeal of Total War, 1939–45*, New York 1968.
Yergin, Daniel, *Shattered Peace: The Origins of the Cold War and the National Security State*, Boston 1977.
Zhukov, Georgi, *The Memoirs of Marshal Zhukov*, New York 1971.
Ziemke, E.F., *Stalingrad to Berlin*, Washington DC 1968.

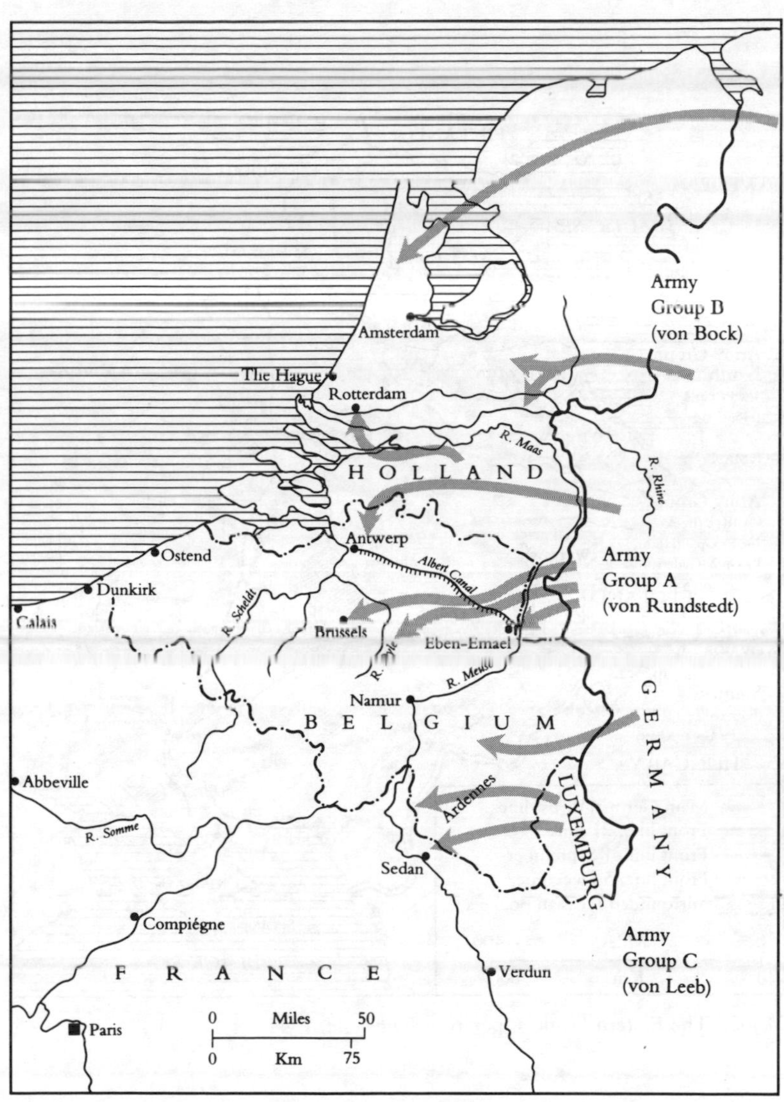

Map 1. Germany attacks in the West: May 1940

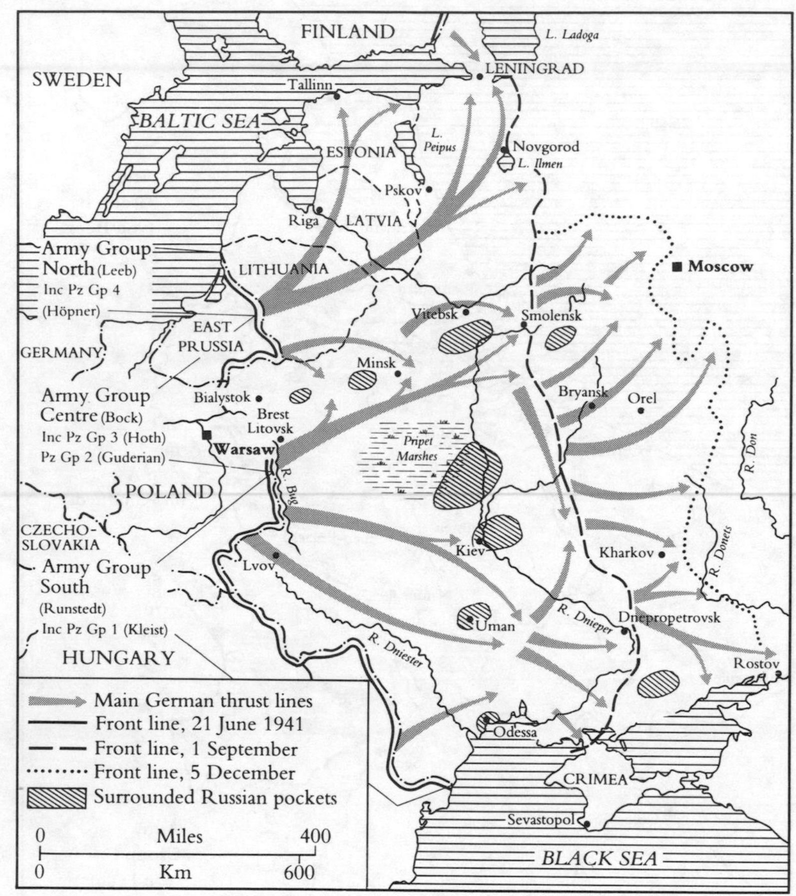

Map 2. The Eastern Front: Operation *Barbarossa,* 1941

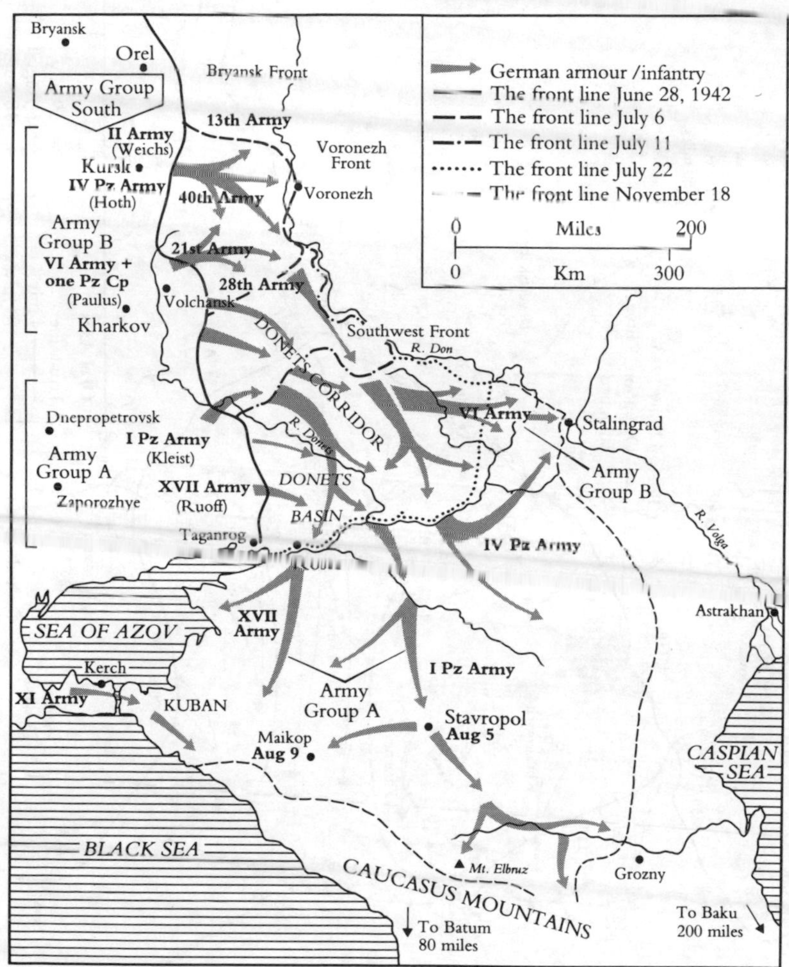

Map 3. The German Summer Offensive, 1942

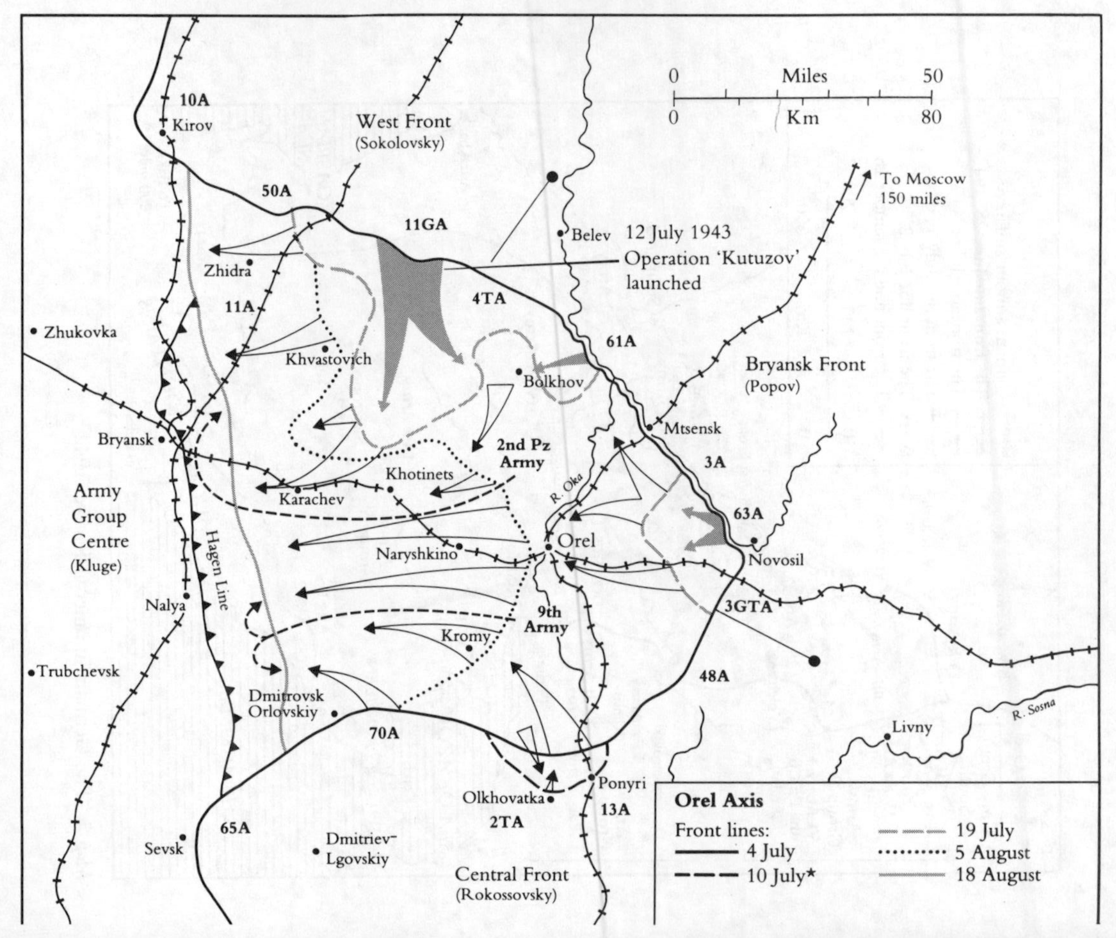
0
Miles
50
0
Km
80
West Front
(Sokolovsky)
To Moscow
150 miles
10A
Kirov
50A
11GA
Belev
12 July 1943
Operation 'Kutuzov'
launched
Zhidra
11A
4TA
Zhukovka
61A
Khvastovich
Bolkhov
Bryansk Front
(Popov)
Bryansk
2nd Pz
Army
Mtsensk
3A
Khotinets
Karachev
R. Oka
63A
Army
Group
Centre
(Kluge)
Orel
Naryshkino
Novosil
Hagen Line
Nalya
9th
Army
3GTA
Kromy
Trubchevsk
48A
Dmitrovsk
Orlovskiy
70A
Livny
R. Sosna
Ponyri
Olkhovatka
13A
2TA
65A
Sevsk
Dmitriev-
Lgovskiy
Central Front
(Rokossovsky)
Orel Axis
Front lines:
4 July
10 July*
19 July
5 August
18 August

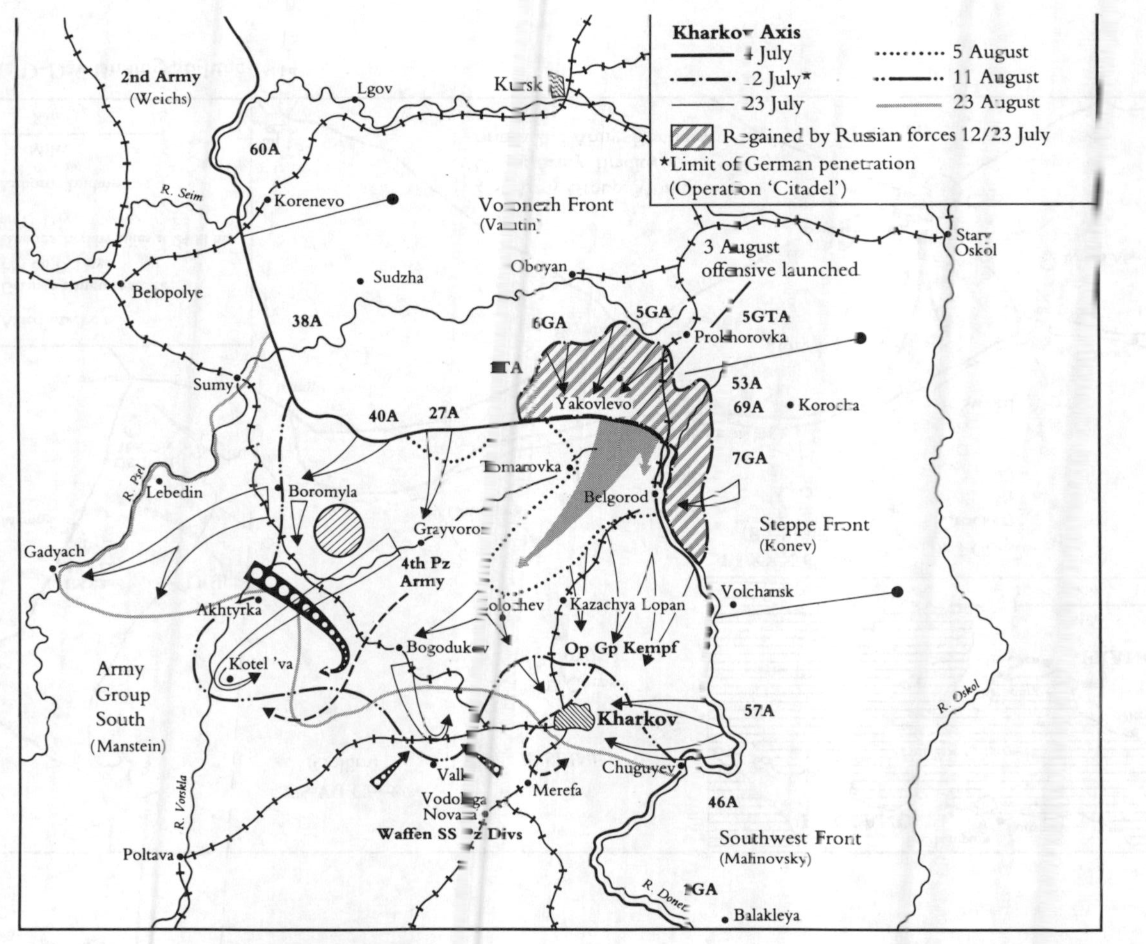

Map 4. The battle of Kursk, August 1943

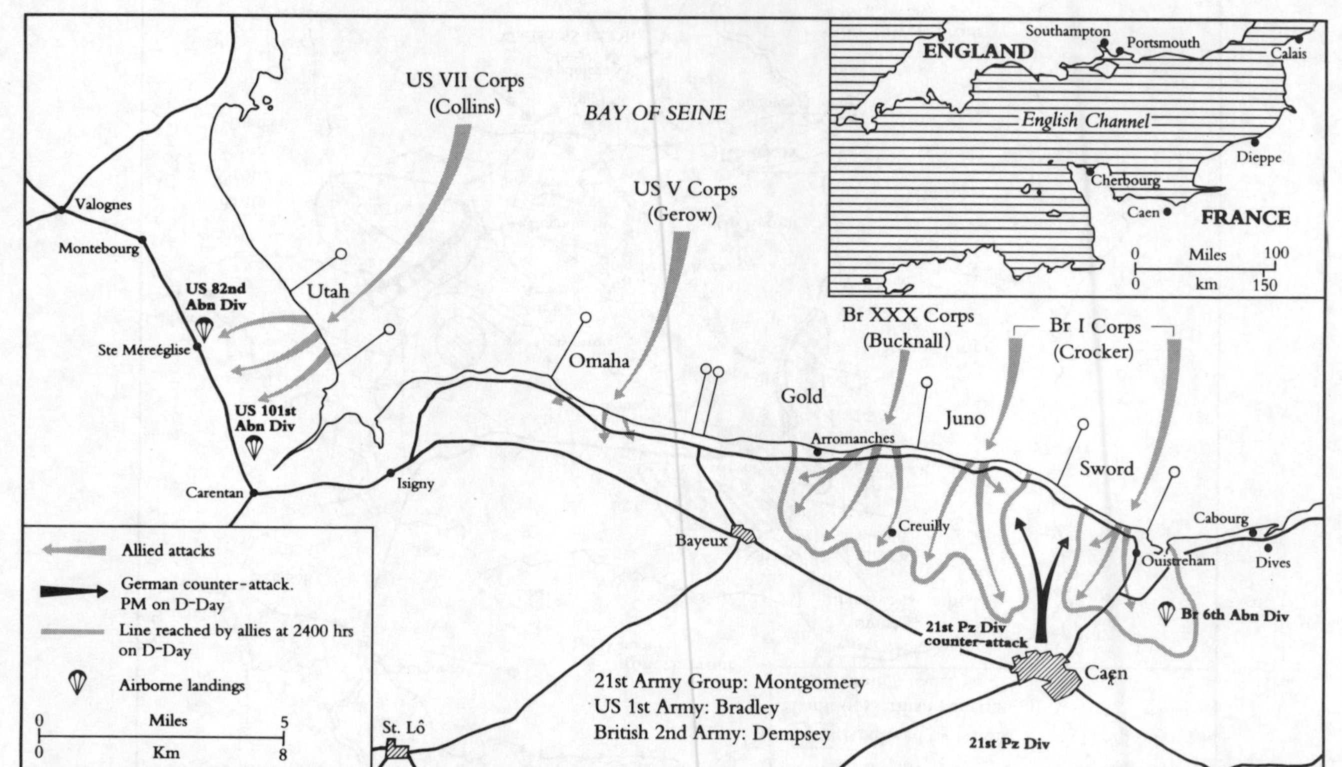

Map 5. The D-Day landings, 6 June 1944

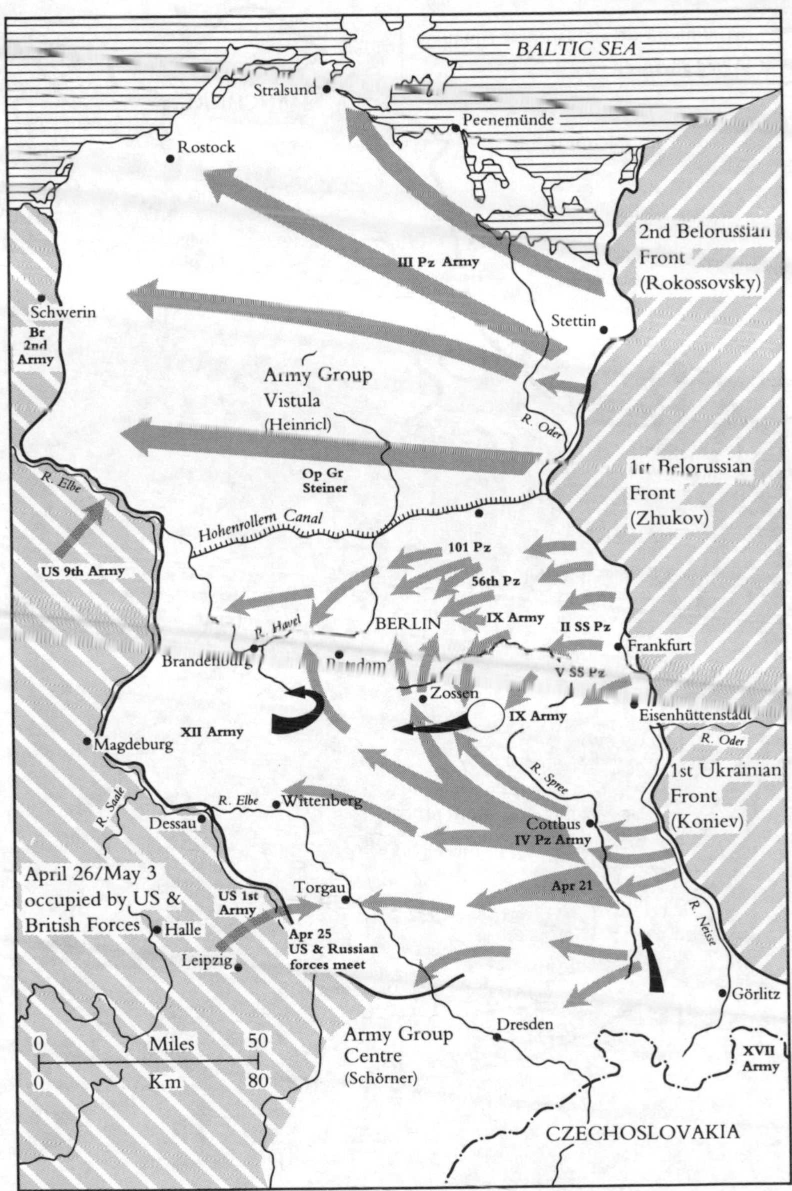

Map 6. The final stages in Europe, April and May 1945

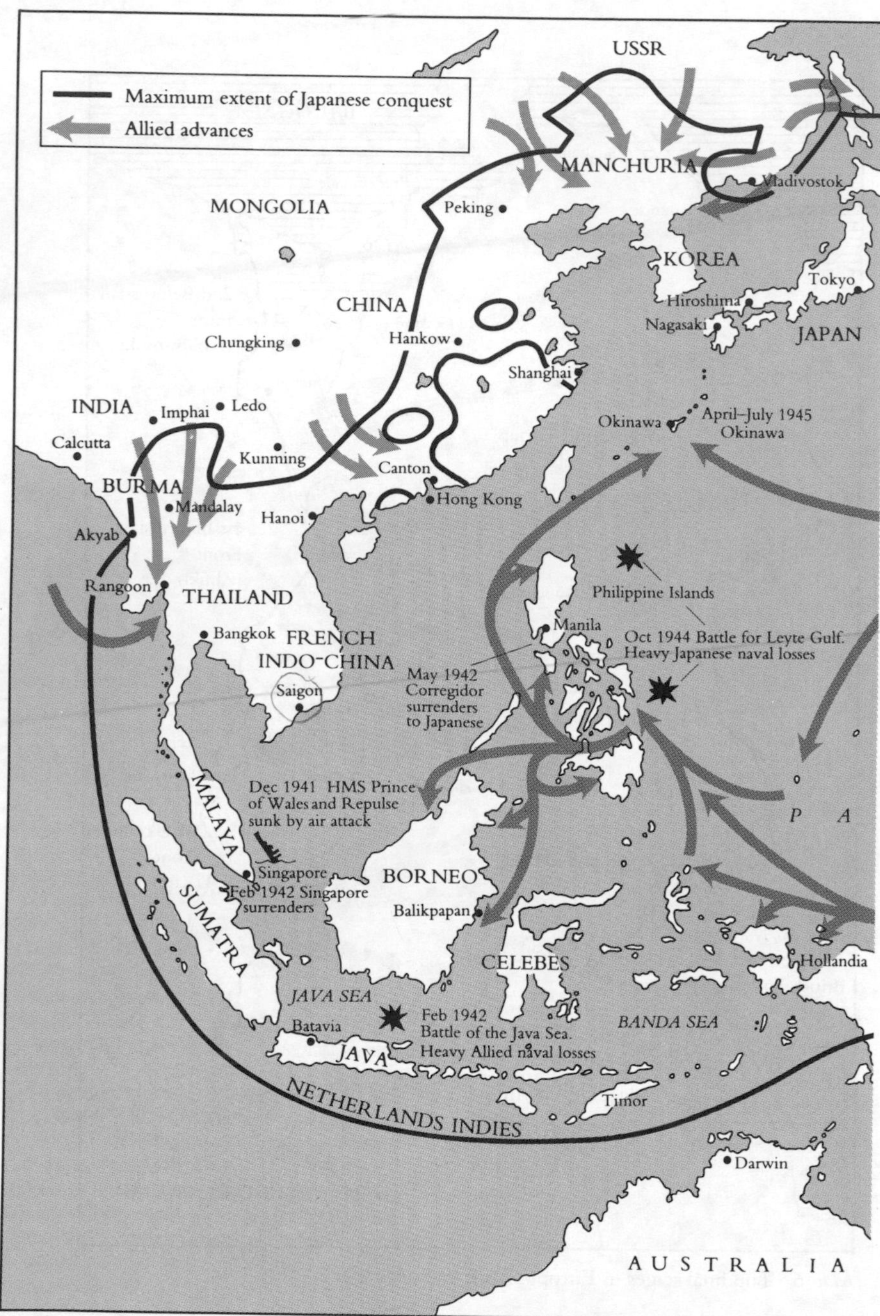

Map 7. The war in the Far East

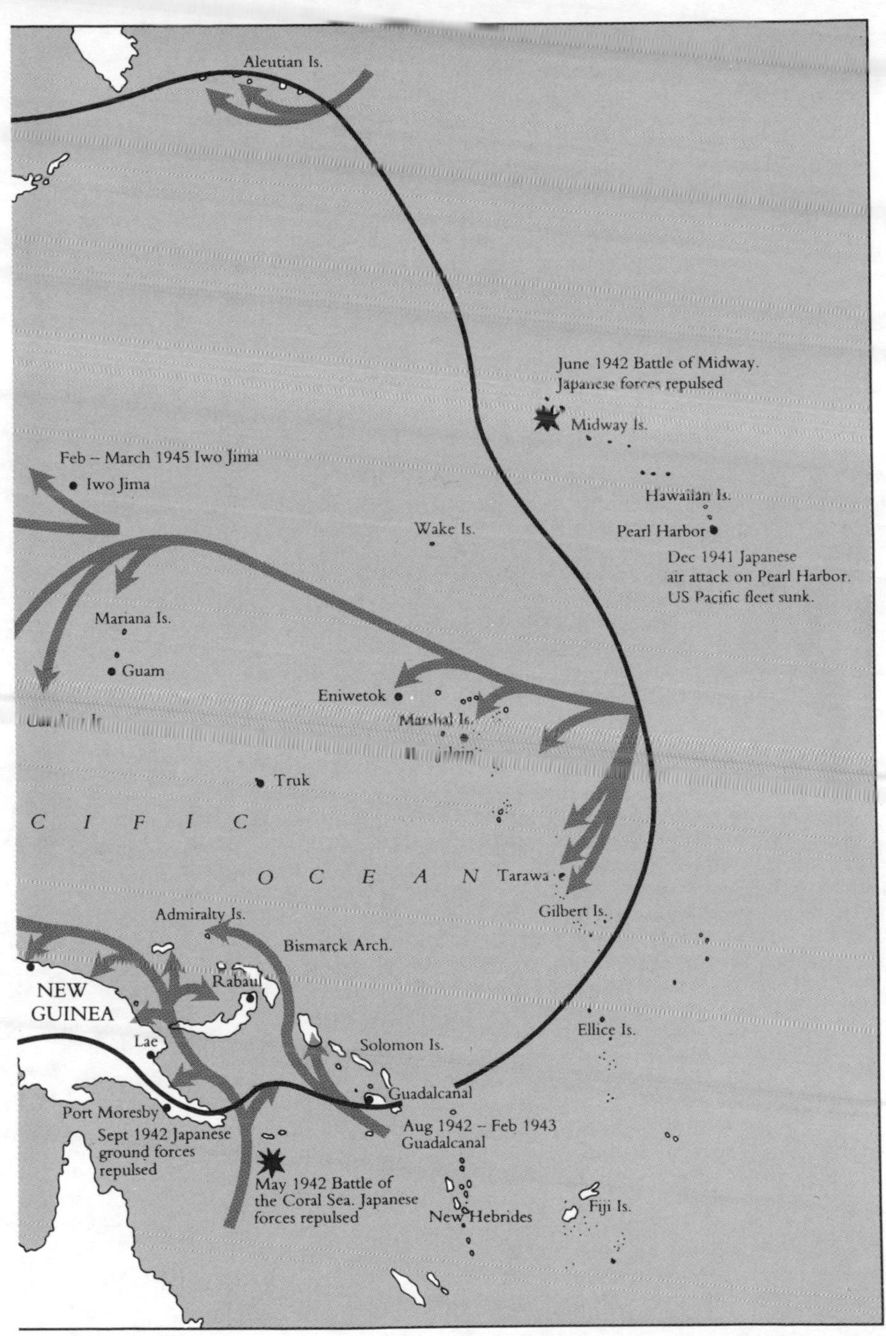
Aleutian Is.
June 1942 Battle of Midway. Japanese forces repulsed
Midway Is.
Feb – March 1945 Iwo Jima
Iwo Jima
Hawaiian Is.
Wake Is.
Pearl Harbor
Dec 1941 Japanese air attack on Pearl Harbor. US Pacific fleet sunk.
Mariana Is.
Guam
Eniwetok
Truk
C I F I C
O C E A N
Tarawa
Gilbert Is.
Admiralty Is.
Bismarck Arch.
Rabaul
NEW GUINEA
Lae
Solomon Is.
Ellice Is.
Guadalcanal
Port Moresby
Sept 1942 Japanese ground forces repulsed
Aug 1942 – Feb 1943 Guadalcanal
May 1942 Battle of the Coral Sea. Japanese forces repulsed
New Hebrides
Fiji Is.

Index